MW01634373

School Counseling Research

School Counseling Research

Advancing the Professional Evidence Base

Edited by

Brett Zyromski Ph.D. and Carey Dimmitt Ph.D.

OXFORD
UNIVERSITY PRESS

Oxford University Press is a department of the University of Oxford. It furthers
the University's objective of excellence in research, scholarship, and education
by publishing worldwide. Oxford is a registered trade mark of Oxford University
Press in the UK and certain other countries.

Published in the United States of America by Oxford University Press
198 Madison Avenue, New York, NY 10016, United States of America.

CIP data is on file at the Library of Congress

ISBN 978-0-19-765013-4

DOI: 10.1093/oso/9780197650134.001.0001

Printed by Integrated Books International, United States of America

Contents

Contributors

Jennifer Betters-Bubon, PhD
University of Wisconsin-Whitewater

John C. Carey, PhD
University of Massachusetts Amherst

Ellen Chance, PhD
Capella University

Blaire Cholewa, PhD
University of Virginia

Demetrius Cofield, PhD
Sam Houston State University

Amy L. Cook, PhD
University of Massachusetts Boston

Carey Dimmitt, PhD
University of Massachusetts Amherst

Ileana Gonzalez, PhD
Johns Hopkins University

Emily Goodman-Scott, PhD
Old Dominion University

Catherine Griffith, PhD
University of San Diego

Holly Kortemeier, MS
Oregon School District

Matthew E. Lemberger-Truelove, PhD
University of North Texas

Dodie Limberg, PhD
University of South Carolina

Melissa Mariani, PhD
Florida Atlantic University

Shekila Melchior, PhD
George Mason University

Jennifer Melfie, MEd
Fairfax County Public Schools

Taryne M. Mingo, PhD
University of North Carolina at Charlotte

Citlali E. Molina, PhD
University of Texas at Tyler

Patrick R. Mullen, PhD
William & Mary

Timothy A. Poynton, EdD
University of Massachusetts Boston

Dee C. Ray, PhD
University of North Texas

Mandy Savitz-Romer, PhD
Harvard University

Sam Steen, PhD
George Mason University

Tori Stone, PhD
George Mason University

Michael S. Trevisan, PhD
Washington State University

Chia Vang, MS
Milwaukee Public Schools

Elizabeth Villares, PhD
Florida Atlantic University

Anita Young, PhD
Johns Hopkins University

Brett Zyromski, PhD
The Ohio State University

1

A Framework for Conducting School Counseling Research in the Current Educational Environment

Carey Dimmitt and Brett Zyromski

A Framework for Conducting School Counseling Research in the Current Educational Environment

Research is a complex aspect of school counseling. On the one hand, there is general consensus that it is useful, is necessary, and can inform best practices (ASCA National Model, 2019; CACREP, 2016 [standards]; Villares & Dimmitt, 2017). On the other hand, there is also agreement that it can be reductionistic and often by necessity ends up oversimplifying the multiplicity of variables that impact the students we serve and that influence educational outcomes (Hart Research Associates, 2012; Ratts & Pederson, 2014). We hold the stance that school counselors can simultaneously acknowledge that people and schools and counseling are all more complicated and unknowable than the research indicates, without diminishing value for the power and importance of good scholarship for the profession.

Exploring the Parameters of Research

In this book's discussion of research in school counseling, it makes sense to start with some agreement about what we mean by research. To start, research is context specific, in that it is (by definition) a reflection of the predominant cultural paradigms, and as such it is constantly changing as our ideas and societies shift. This can be seen as problematic or, preferably, seen as exciting! Our understanding of learning, of human change, of what it means to be educated, of equity in education, and so on, have all been transforming over time—sometimes rapidly so—to reflect what is happening in the world.

Carey Dimmitt and Brett Zyromski, *A Framework for Conducting School Counseling Research in the Current Educational Environment* In: *School Counseling Research*. Edited by: Brett Zyromski and Carey Dimmitt, Oxford University Press. © Oxford University Press 2023. DOI: 10.1093/oso/9780197650134.003.0001

Even in just the 2 years since we started this book, we have seen rapid shifts in awareness of systemic and institutional racism, in knowledge of the possibilities and challenges of remote instruction and learning, and in understanding how political ideologies shape economics and access to healthcare and other resources.

Research is also ultimately about the generation of knowledge, whether it is a deeper understanding of something already explored, an innovative way of thinking, or new ways of understanding. Sometimes that knowledge is very general, and sometimes it is very specific and minute. The purpose of research is to learn something new, and in education and counseling, there is often a goal of improving practice, situations, or student/client outcomes (Rossman & Rallis, 2016). Originally many professions—including natural sciences, social sciences, and even history and philosophy—argued for objectivity and neutrality as goals of the work. This has been roundly critiqued in postmodern scholarship (see Bernstein, 2011, for discussion), especially by feminist and antiracist scholars (Crenshaw, 2017; Dei, 2005; Harding, 1998, 2016). We hold that all research (all action, really) is located in contexts and thus inherently value laden and necessarily subjective (Harding, 2016; Teo, 2017).

One ongoing tension in school counseling research—that also emerges in other mental health fields and in education as well—is between the more empiricist and quantitative approach to research (see Chapters 7 and 10) and the more constructivist and qualitative approach to research (see Chapters 8 and 9). Our research paradigms and practices are reflections of our ontology—beliefs about the nature of reality, how knowable that reality is, and what is knowable (Guba & Lincoln, 1994). Empiricism assumes that there is an approximation of truth in research—maybe we cannot completely know it, but we can get closer to it through replication and revision of hypotheses over time (Johnson & Christensen, 2020). It follows the scientific method and prioritizes numerical data and related statistics. Medical and natural sciences research is often empirical, relying heavily on randomized control trials (RCTs) and quasi-experimental designs to indicate causality, or at least the suggestion of causality. If we know that a specific drug works better than a placebo in a blind RCT, that is valuable information, and we rely on research like this to make decisions about not just what medicine to take, but which vaccine to get, which safety measures to engage in, what foods to eat to improve our health, and so on. And yet, *science is an imperfect science!*

Constructivism assumes that truth is highly relative, that we all approach the material world through our own cognitive lenses that are the result of prior experiences and understanding, and that those lenses are constrained by the limitations of the human sense organs and brain (Rossman & Rallis,

2016). In this way of thinking, there is no full understanding of anything, only variations of perspective and awareness. We construct knowledge, rather than finding or discovering it, and truth can change. In the constructivist paradigm, who we are and how we think about things completely shape our way of being in the world, our way of approaching problems—our ideas about what is even possible. Social constructivism acknowledges that there are social agreements generated by people who share contexts but posits that there still cannot be fully shared knowing or universal truths (Davis & Sumara, 2002; Palincsar, 1998).

Qualitative research from this paradigm then, is very concerned with awareness of those unique individual ways of approaching the situation, with related efforts to articulate the researcher viewpoint and perspective and how those might be impacting the work (Corbin & Strauss, 2014; Hays & Singh, 2012). Data may be numerical but are also likely to include interviews, field notes, observations, and more narrative-based collection strategies. Qualitative researchers tend to prioritize alternative options and ideas, to try to be open to multiple ways of explaining or understanding their data (Corbin & Strauss, 2014).

There are critiques of both quantitative and qualitative methods. Some theorists have challenged that much of empirical science as historically practiced is a reflection of, and can be a perpetuation of, a dominant culture that doesn't always include the voices of all people (e.g., who is and is not in the sample, or who decides what questions matter; Martinez et al. [2017]; Patton [2015]). Much early medical research, for instance, was done only with white men (O'Hara et al., 2021). As for constructivism, if all truths are held to be equally valuable, does that mean any belief someone holds is viable? We wonder whether this "all versions of truths are equally valid" perspective contributes to recent social events such as removing evolutionary science from schools, vaccine refusal, and election result denial—where people hold their beliefs to be true, to be based on their understanding, and to be as equally valid as the more scientifically based position.

Increasingly, the *both/and* stance on research is held (Creswell, 2014; Wester & McKibben, 2019). In this way of thinking, both types of research provide unique information, both have value, they each contribute to knowledge generation in a field, both are exploratory and confirmatory, and each has limits. The mixed methods approach allows researchers to address multiple research objectives in the same study and to collect multiple types of data to inform the research better (Johnson & Christensen, 2020). In this book, you will see that multiple research paradigms (qualitative, quantitative, and mixed methods) are referred to and used to describe the work the authors are doing in school counseling research. Depending on a researcher's goals and research questions, each way of conducting research has value and utility. As an analogy, quantitative research can tell us that a drug improved symptoms better than a placebo (or did not do so), and qualitative research can explore why people were taking the drug—what they hoped would happen, their beliefs in the possibility of medicine to ameliorate symptoms, and so on. We know that placebos have a powerful impact (Howe et al., 2017), so we need to consider how beliefs and attitudes might influence the people in a study taking both the drug and the placebo. We also know that there are some surprising differences in cultural beliefs that impact how drug taking and related outcomes are understood (Maier et al., 2018). Additionally, it has been found that the ideas and beliefs of the researcher may impact the ways that questions are asked and data are interpreted (Open Science Collaboration, 2015). All of these more subtle aspects of our hypothetical drug study's outcomes could be explored through qualitative methods such as interviews, journaling, and focus groups.

Why Do We Need Research in School Counseling?

If we can agree that a central purpose of research is the generation of new and increased knowledge and understanding—both subjective and somewhat objective—then research in professions is critically needed to confirm (or equally useful, disconfirm) existing practices, and to identify promising new ways of working. Specifically in school counseling, there is a vast amount of information we don't yet have about how to best do the work, about how to support student development and positive outcomes most effectively, about how to improve training for people going into the profession, and ad infinitum.

In addition to new and increased knowledge, research in a profession helps to define the parameters of the field. What is unique about the work of school counseling, and how is it similar to and different from related professions such as social work, teaching, and psychology? Research-based answers can promote professional legitimacy and identity. There are challenges and opportunities when working with youth in schools versus in clinical settings or in research laboratories. In schools, the work is impacted by multiple contextual factors. It is more complicated to identify student outcomes that are the result of a school counseling intervention or program component when there are integrated school-wide efforts working toward similar goals. School counseling research provides useful information about the specific work (counseling youth in schools) in these contexts (K–12 schools) in support of particular outcomes for students (academic, social, emotional, college and career competencies, and positive development). Additional factors such as family and community contexts, students' social identities, and the multitude of cultural contexts that impact students' lives—all of which may serve to support or impede their success—are also of interest for the research done in the profession. Human experience is multi-determined, and our work and research must reflect that understanding.

In addition to clarifying the outcomes of school counseling interventions and programs in K–12 schools, research in school counseling can provide clarity for counselor education programs in higher education. What should these programs be teaching their students to know, understand, and be able to do? When we have more research information about the practices that are relevant and impactful, then making these types of instructional decisions is more likely to result in informed and effective practitioners.

When a profession has research that is specific to its values and aims, it is strengthened and legitimated. While we always support the use of research done by related professions such as social work, psychology, child psychiatry, and education, school counselors' distinctive intersectional focus on academic, social and emotional, and college and career outcomes should have its own body of scholarly work. School counseling has a broad range of research that examines multiple aspects of the profession. For example, Matthew Lemberger-Truelove developed a theoretical approach specific to school counseling (Lemberger, 2010; Lemberger & Hutchinson, 2014) and has researched its application (Bowers et al., 2020). Cheryl Holcomb-McCoy (2007) articulated a social justice approach to school counseling that has had a profound impact on the profession. Ian Levy has developed a recent school counseling intervention using hip-hop (Levy, 2019). Linda Webb, Chari Campbell, and Greg Brigman are former school counselors who became counselor educators, who then developed and researched the highly impactful and widely used school counseling curriculum *Student Success Skills* (Brigman & Campbell, 2003; Brigman, & Webb, 2003; Campbell & Brigman, 2005). Aida Midgett, Diana Doumas, and others at Boise State University have spent years researching and showing evidence of the impact of a brief, bystander bullying intervention (Midgett et al., 2018, 2020; Moran et al., 2020). Gerta Bardhoshi, along with her coauthors, looked at an app-based classroom counseling intervention for students in kindergarten that improved their social skills (Bardhoshi et al., 2020). These are only a few examples of the impactful school-based research that is shaping and informing the school counseling profession.

A big caveat here. Professions are supported and legitimated when the research is good research, not just any research for research's sake. We will unpack in a few pages what *good research* or *useful research* might mean, but for now, let's just say that arguably the most important and useful research for a profession is thoughtfully and carefully done, and it focuses on knowledge or information that has real relevance and value to the people and contexts that are the focus of the research, as well as to the researcher(s) and related profession.

Antiracist and Social Justice Research

Parker Palmer famously said we teach who we are (2017), and we would modify that to say that we also research who we are. What questions we ask, what ideas we find interesting, what research projects we have the excitement and drive to spend the amount of time needed on—these reflect our values, our experiences, and our passions. What and who we choose to study, how we write about what we've found—these are reflections of our internal logic (Adler, 2006); our social identities (Gay, 2018; Ratts et al., 2007); our experiences, our beliefs, and our level of awareness (Ratts & Greenleaf, 2017; Ratts & Pedersen, 2014).

Most research also inherently and legitimately reflects not just our personal, but also our professional and historical, contexts. It is designed to build on prior knowledge—even the opening page of Google Scholar says, "stand on the shoulders of giants." At the same time, those prior contexts need to be challenged for the ways that they have left out certain voices (students with disabilities, students of color, youth voices in general, etc.) or perpetuated systemic inequities, prejudices, and oppression. It is ethical practice as counselors and as educators to be aware of the myriad ways our own social contexts and prior experiences impact the ways we are in relationships with our clients and students. We work to become ever-more intentional and thoughtful about enacting antiracist and social justice counseling and pedagogical practices, interrupting stereotypes, and preventing microaggressions (Francis & Mason, 2022; Mason et al., 2021). In our work as researchers, we need to find that balance between valuing and building on prior scholarship in the field, while also creating new ways of thinking about and conducting research that addresses the wide-ranging inequities and prejudices in our culture and in our schools. We also need to make sure that we are not inadvertently perpetuating the systemic and institutional ways that racism, sexism, classism, ableism, and other oppressions have manifested in our profession and in our scholarship (Goodman & Gorski, 2015; Holcomb-McCoy, 2022; Polk et al., 2022).

Figuring out how to do actively antiracist social justice research—not neutral or race-blind research—is another complex challenge. Several studies point out that race-neutral approaches to addressing school inequities can instead lead to increased school segregation (Gullen, 2012; McDermott et al., 2015). What does antiracist and social justice research look like? To start, it means making sure that our research participant groups represent (as accurately as possible) current student demographics (Carter et al., 2017) both nationally and for the schools we are working in. When we are in a more segregated district, it means making sure to work in several schools to access the full experience of students in that district. As several authors in this text write about, it means engaging in relationships with our school partners in ways that honor and respect their work and their time, that our research benefits students and our school partners as well as the profession, that we are making sure we include the voices of multiple stakeholders in the process of developing our research agendas, and so forth. It means being aware of the potential for our social roles as scholars and academics to give us unwarranted power and privilege in schools, and to empower and engage our practitioner partners as well as students in the research process actively (Polk, et al, 2022).

This work requires thought about the social justice and antiracist implications of all aspects of our research work, with consideration given to what is studied, who is studied, who is served by the study, the language we use, the named limitations, and what might be left out. It involves naming and challenging power dynamics and privileges that have become part of the status quo as well as avoiding deficit narratives that diminish the full experience of students. It means defining our constructs—what do we mean by "urban schools" or "low-income," for instance? And how are we using and engaging with the constructs of race, ethnicity, gender, family, and so on in our work?

Such efforts go beyond just naming the situation and identifying existing inequalities and inequities, however (O'Hara et al., 2021). They also seek ways to create more equity and more equal opportunities—of correcting and addressing what has happened in the past, of acknowledging the damage still being done, and of generating new ways of working. Critical race theory provides a useful theoretical frame for this work (Delgado & Stefancic, 2017; Taylor et al., 2009) as does recent work on social justice frameworks for the counseling profession (Ratts & Greenleaf, 2017; Singh et al., 2020) and antiracist school counseling (Holcomb-McCoy, 2022).

The topic of the possibilities and importance of antiracist and social justice research in school counseling deserves its own book, and we hope that one will soon be forthcoming. In the meantime, we recommend the recently published *Antiracist Counseling in Schools and Communities* (2022) edited by Cheryl Holcomb-McCoy and the additional resources about antiracist and social justice research provided in Table 1.1.

Table 1.1. Antiracist and Social Justice Research Resources

Citation or Website URL	Summary
https://www.bu.edu/antiracism-center/	Antiracist research primer from the Center for Antiracist Research at Boston University, founded by Ibram X. Kendi
https://libguides.umn.edu/antiracismlens	How to conduct research using an antiracist lens from the University of Minnesota
https://www.american.edu/centers/antiracism/	Antiracist Research and Policy Center at American University
https://researchguides.uoregon.edu/antiracism	Definitions, books, and other resources from the library at the University of Oregon related to antiracism and antiracist research
https://nmaahc.si.edu/learn/talking-about-race/topics/being-antiracis	The National Museum of African American History and Culture's guide to antiracist resources and actions
https://cehd.gmu.edu/faculty-and-research/anti-racist-research-methods/anti-racism-resources	Media, readings, and resources on antiracist research from George Mason University
https://www.umass.edu/diversity/antiracism-resources	Antiracism, diversity, and inclusion resources including books, podcasts, videos, children's books, etc., from the University of Massachusetts
Buchanan, N. T., & Wiklund, L. O. (2020). Why clinical science must change or die: Integrating intersectionality and social justice. Women & Therapy, 43(3–4), 309–329.	Applies social justice critiques to clinical practice and research.
Dei, G. J. S. (2005). Chapter One: Critical Issues in Antiracist Research Methodologies: An Introduction. Counterpoints, 252, 1–27. http://www.jstor.org/stable/42978742	A foundational text on antiracist research methodologies
Sensoy, O., & DiAngelo, R. (2017). Is everyone really equal?: An introduction to key concepts in social justice education. Teachers College Press.	Critical social justice education and research, integrating critical thinking, critical theory, intersectionality, and social change models
Welton, A., Owens, D., & Zamani-Gallaher, E. (2018). Anti-racist change: A conceptual framework for educational institutions to take systemic action. Teachers College Record, 120(14), 1–22.	Identifies systemic antiracist change models, based on research on organizational change.

What Is Good Research?

Research is inherently value laden, reflecting not just the values of the researcher and the related profession, but larger cultural contexts as well. Thus, defining what constitutes *good research* is a moving target, and can (and should) be ongoingly challenged. Is it research that provides useful knowledge that impacts how a profession is practiced (for example, the body of research on Student Success Skills)? Is it research that is relevant to practitioners (as with current multi-tiered systems of support [MTSSs] and ASCA National Model research)? Is it research that is methodologically sound and well conducted (as with Sue Whiston's work on outcome research)? Is it research that actively pursues social justice and antiracist outcomes (see Polk et al., 2022, and Holcomb-McCoy et al., 2022, for discussions)? In addition—who decides? Academics? Practitioners? Journal editors?

In applied professions like school counseling, where much of the research is related to the work of the field, the utility and relevance of scholarship is often paramount. For many of us, reading and doing research that helps us to provide better college/career/academic/social-emotional/mental health counseling, or that supports our ability to deliver better classroom and small-group interventions, or that gives us ideas for effective program infrastructure, are why we read and do research! When a good study is published that demonstrates relevant and practical outcomes—for example, that an intervention decreases social anxiety (Masia Warner et al., 2016) or improves student academic self-efficacy (Lemberger et al., 2012)—we can know with greater certainty that using these interventions will make a difference. Ensuring that our research is then used in school counseling practice is a critical (and sometimes forgotten) aspect of scholarship explored more fully in Chapter 14.

Good research also explores factors beyond students' control that directly impact their ability to be successful. For example, it is vital for research to advance school counselors' work that addresses the social determinants of health that negatively impact students'—and disproportionately Black and Brown students'—life experience (Johnson & Brookover, 2021). Good research is thus not just focused on individual student factors, but also on the systemic factors that shape experience (Holcomb-McCoy, 2018), including education, health, child welfare, criminal justice, and economic policies. Research is never atheoretical. The philosophical aspects of our jobs matter a great deal (Dollarhide & Lemberger, 2019) and, for many of us, inform the work we do that reflects our passion for making a difference for our students.

Good research places the needs, rights, and interests of our students at the center of the process. It goes beyond "do no harm" and moves to "do the best possible we can for those we serve." This is both a professional imperative and an ethical one. It requires paying attention to the processes used as well as the outcomes (Gambrill, 2018). Part of this is being deeply thoughtful about who our subjects/clients/students are, making sure to include their voices in the decisions about how and what to study (Caraballo et al., 2017). It asks the hard questions on behalf of and with these youth—even when doing so challenges the status quo or makes people uncomfortable (Dimmitt, 2003; Lemberger-Truelove & Bowers, 2019).

For those of us doing studies in schools, good research involves collaborating in a deep and meaningful way with partners in those settings so that the research benefits not just the students but our school colleagues, as well as the profession more broadly (see Chapters 2 and 5). A truly synergistic and collaborative research relationship can be impactful at multiple levels, with both immediate and long-term benefits for all involved.

Good research uses a diverse and representative sample. For too long, studies used mostly or even all white or male or middle-class students. The generalizability of those findings is then suspect—once we challenge the idea that white male middle-class students are the norm, and that what's true for that group is true for all, it becomes clear that a broader representation of students and student social contexts is necessary for research to be truly of value. Collaboration can be essential for creating a more diverse sample in a study—if a researcher doesn't have easy geographical access to school partners with diverse populations, collaborating across contexts can exponentially increase the opportunities to work with diverse populations.

Good research uses methodologies that are a match for the question(s) being asked, the contexts being explored, and so on. Each way of working has both strengths and weaknesses, and these are identified in specific chapters (see Chapters 7, 8, 9, and 10 for more on effective research methodologies and when each can be most useful). This is one reason why the limitations of conversation in a research article are so important.

Good research is humble. It has a clear description of all the limitations and caveats to the findings—there is a real sense that the results are tentative, need replicating, and are only theoretically generalizable. There is awareness of the ways that there may be bias—both explicit and implicit—and that the results may be shaped by the values and perspectives of the researchers (and by parameters placed on the work by the school personnel involved), by weaknesses or bias in the measurements, by challenges to implementation fidelity (see Chapter 12), and by myriad other factors. Good research acknowledges all the ways that change is constant, and that while the findings certainly might reflect real changes due to the variable under consideration, they might also have been impacted by developmental shifts in the subjects (particularly possible with children), by unforeseen contextual factors (a change in principals, a parental death), or by cultural conditions (such as the recent Covid-19 pandemic or increased social awareness of race-related violence).

Good research is inherently ethical, in that it requires "a willingness to critically appraise beliefs and claims no matter who promotes them, to ferret out our blind spots, to view knowledge as tentative, and to view theories as tools rather than dogma to be guarded" (Gambrill, 2018, p. 286). Perhaps tautologically, good research questions even itself—the inherent biases, assumptions, methods, and ways of working that with time or reflection may come to be seen as less effective or even problematic. We see this as a strength of research! It is not a closed door; it is a meandering path through the dark woods of the unknown, with new vistas available around each turn as new ideas and understandings light the way to the next view into what is possible.

Another ethical aspect of good research is the independence of ideas, which is what creates trust that a research finding is legitimate (Chapter 3 addresses ethics in research). When a study is sponsored or funded by an organization that serves to benefit from outcomes of that research, there is an inherent risk of bias, and potential conflicts of interest. This is why the disclosures about funding of journal articles are so important. For instance, even though the developers of an intervention usually are the ones to do the initial outcome studies demonstrating its efficacy, replication of those results by someone who is an independent investigator adds a critical level of validation to the findings. While ethical scholars obviously work to prevent bias regardless of the sponsor, the investment in the outcomes going a certain way may unintentionally shape what questions get asked or don't get asked, how data are interpreted, and how the study is written up.

In addition to these philosophical and "big-picture" aspects of good research, we also want to acknowledge that there are many details that also matter a great deal. What assessment instruments we use to gather data (Chapter 6) and how we do the data analysis for a study (Chapter 13) inform and impact the research findings and can also provide legitimacy and rigor to research regardless of the methodology. Having a research partnership or team where different people have unique strengths related to vision, data gathering and analysis, project management, and organization (to name only a few skills) can be helpful with this aspect of the work.

Research in School Settings: Challenges and Opportunities

Collaborative Research Teams

Conducting research in schools can be challenging! Multiple authors in this book explore the challenges and benefits of conducting research in school settings. And when scholars feel pressured to conduct research to gain tenure or promotion, additional problems may arise. For example, due to the pressure to publish, scholars may approach the task with a "just get it done" approach, without full consideration of the needs of the schools and students participating in the research, or the future users of the research. The authors of Chapter 2 argue for a transformative research approach (National Science Foundation, n.d.) that grounds school-based research projects in the voices and vision of those doing the work in schools, resulting in mutually beneficial outcomes to all parties involved in the work.

Building such collaborative partnerships can be both difficult and rewarding. After transitioning from being school counselors to school counselor educators, emerging scholars can often enhance existing relationships with schools they recently worked in to conduct school-based research. Building partnerships in this way can help scholars address school-specific complexities such as navigating the politics of school stakeholders, creating buy-in with school personnel, and overcoming previous negative experiences staff may have had with other researchers (see Chapter 5). Creating ethical partnerships (see Chapters 2 and 3 for additional details) is foundational to ensuring that school partners work together to define the research project parameters, that no harm is done to stakeholders in the school, and that all partners directly benefit from school-based scholarship (Mason et al., 2016).

Collaborative research work in schools may require years of foundation building, such as providing free professional development for the district, partnering to write a grant for external funding, and establishing ongoing practicum and internship placements in the district. These investments in partnerships take time and effort—both are commodities that feel scarce for school counseling scholars on the tenure clock. It is beneficial to create a wide variety of research projects with multiple districts that can create a collaborative network of possibilities for both schools and researchers, so if one location falls through (a common occurrence), then others remain viable.

School counseling scholars at research-intensive universities can also create fruitful partnerships with colleagues at teaching-intensive universities.

In my own experience (Brett), the time allotted for relational investment in the community was greater at a teaching-intensive university with a regional service mission where I worked than at a research-intensive university with a scholarship- and external-funding focus. Building research teams with people from a variety of environments, including faculty at research-intensive universities and teaching-intensive universities, doctoral students, school counselors, and district leaders, can result in external funding and scholarship production that benefits all involved and that is built on the strengths of each of the team members. Research teams also provide space and time for research mentorship to occur. Such collaborative approaches also build from the natural interpersonal giftedness possessed by many in the school counseling field.

Inclusive Innovation Tenets in School-Based Research

Lemberger-Truelove and Molina's suggestion (see Chapter 4) that scholars pursue their passion areas to drive the work and maintain motivation resonates for us. When we use our passion and belief about the value of school counseling to invest in children and adolescents and to deconstruct inequitable systems, we can focus on the importance of the work rather than external pressures to accumulate a certain type or number of publications. However, at the same time, it is important to analyze the lens through which we conceive of and conduct our work, as issues of class, gender, race, age, and professional stature (among others) all inform how we view the world in which we conduct research (see Chapter 2). As written about previously in this chapter, good research is social justice research. How our passion areas drive our work is central to staying focused and motivated but must also be informed by self-awareness about how our cultural identities, training, and upbringing in a white-centric educational system inform our views. It is useful to apply inclusive innovation tenets that require scholars to answer the question of *who benefits* from our research (McMahon & Patel, 2019).

This approach also suggests asking ourselves why some schools are participating in research partnerships while others are not, and how the schools with populations with the greatest needs could benefit from our research (McMahon & Patel, 2019). Approaching school collaboration with an inclusive innovation lens can lead to intentional partnerships with schools in communities that have historically been denied access to resources and opportunities (George et al., 2012). As a result, school-based scholars can thoughtfully and humbly consider the multiple contexts that impede or enhance student success and ensure that our partnerships with schools serve our students and their communities more than they serve our pathways to tenure.

Overview of Research in the Profession Now

Excitingly, in the past 10 years school counseling research has continued to improve and expand. Our access to evidence-based interventions has been supported by national resource databases such as the Federal Department of Education's *What Works Clearinghouse* (https://ies.ed.gov/ncee/wwc/), the Collaborative for Academic and Social Emotional Learning's *Program Guides to Effective Social and Emotional Learning Programs* (https://casel.org/guide/), and the Substance Abuse and Mental Health Services Administration's *Evidence-Based Practices Resource Center* (https://www.samhsa.gov/resou rce-search/ebp). All three of these resource centers provide valuable information about individual, group, and classroom interventions that have research evidence of efficacy. They also provide suggestions for effective implementation and systemic supports needed to be successful in these efforts.

Our national professional organizations (the American School Counselor Association [ASCA] at https://www.schoolcounselor.org/ and American Counseling Association (ACA) at https://www.counseling.org/) have created online databases of resources and related research to inform practices. Relevant university-based research centers that have developed research and practice resources for school counseling practitioners and scholars include the Fredrickson Center for School Counseling Outcome Research and Evaluation (at https://www.cscoreumass.org/), the Center for Postsecondary Readiness and Success (at https://www.american.edu/centers/cprs/), and the Center for Equity and Postsecondary Attainment (at https://education.sdsu. edu/cepa).

There is exciting new scholarship related to school-based research in school counseling. The following are only a few selected examples of recent school counseling research topics:

- College and career readiness knowledge and skills (Lapan & Poynton, 2020; Villares & Brigman, 2019)
- Free Application for Federal Student Aid (FAFSA) completion support (Owen & Westlund, 2016)
- Increasing fifth-grade girls' relational skills and social connectedness (Schietz & Villares, 2017)

- Social-emotional learning and mindfulness (Lemberger-Truelove et al., 2021)
- Bullying interventions (Midgett et al., 2018, 2020)
- Goal-setting curriculum (Zyromski et al., 2019)
- Hip-hop spoken-word therapy (Levy, 2019)
- Increasing student college-going knowledge (Poynton et al., 2021)
- Ameliorating social anxiety (Masia Warner et al., 2016)
- Social-emotional skill development with elementary-aged students (Bardhoshi et al., 2020; Bowers et al., 2020)

There has been new work on programmatic aspects of school counseling:

- The Advocating Student-Within-Environment theory and related models of practice (Bowers et al., 2020; Lemberger-Truelove & Bowers, 2019)
- Rethinking school counselor roles and functions (Savitz-Romer, 2020)
- School counselor roles in multi-tiered systems of support (MTSS; Goodman-Scott et al., 2019; Hatch et al., 2019)
- Clarifying the power of the school counseling title rather than guidance counseling (Baker et al., 2021)
- The impact of school-counselor-to-student ratios on outcomes (Goodman-Scott et al., 2018)

There is new scholarship on theoretical, philosophical, and political aspects of school counseling:

- Antiracist and social justice school counseling (Atkins & Oglesby, 2018; Griffin & Steen, 2011; Holcomb-McCoy, 2022; Mason et al., 2021; Mayes, 2021; Ratts & Greenleaf, 2017).
- The balance of school counselor roles as both educators and counselors (Lambie et al., 2019; Levy & Lemberger-Truelove, 2021)
- School counseling theories (Dollarhide & Lemberger-Truelove, 2019)

There is still much that we need to know, and the potential research needs are theoretically endless. A recent Delphi study identifying research goals for the profession (Villares & Dimmitt, 2017) found that the expert panel's highest rated questions were: (1) What are the impacts of using the ASCA National Model or not using the ASCA National Model? (2) What are the best practices related to the use of evidence-based interventions and practices? (3) What are the best practices for school counseling interventions that improve social justice, equity, advocacy and close student achievement gaps? (4) What are the impacts of using evidence-based practices (EBPs)? (5) And, what are the best practices related to program evaluation? As we consider our next steps, knowing what has been done and what still needs doing, and intentionally mentoring the next generation of school counseling research scholars—there is much to keep in mind!

Implications: What Is Next for School Counseling Research?

We fervently hope that this entire book will serve as a *what's next* for our profession, paving the way for more school counseling–focused research that provides relevant information about which interventions and program components provide the greatest impact for our students, what the most effective and efficient ways to do school counseling work are, and how we can continue to evolve the profession so that we are providing the best supports and resources that improve children's lives. An underlying commitment to and value for what research provides for our profession are obviously a key part of this, as is creating socially just and equitable educational contexts for all students. And a corollary is that we also need research that identifies the optimal methods for training school counseling practitioners to do this critical work.

Part of deciding what professional research is needed now has to do with understanding what has been done already in the field, and then identifying where the gaps are. Chapter 4, on developing a research question, does an excellent job of articulating this process. It is a strength for school counseling that—since we are working with our graduate students in schools—many of us also have ongoing relationships with practitioners, and we can work with our school partners to identify needed research and to collaborate on that work.

Antiracist School Counseling

A clear future focus for the profession is models for and research about the impact of antiracist school counseling (Mayes, 2021). Recent scholars have rightfully called for the school counseling and education professions to go further than addressing barriers and opportunity gaps and to consider deconstructing racist and patriarchal systems that create the problems in the first place (Atkins & Oglesby, 2018; Ladson-Billings, 2021; Washington, Byrd,

& Williams, 2022). School counselors can also use an antiracist lens to provide K–12 students with the social justice awareness and understanding that is so essential for their success in our increasingly global contexts. And we can do much more—we can shed light on the practices and policies that are perpetuating inequities, we can use our interpersonal skills to question historical ways of educating and counseling that may be unintentionally (or intentionally) maintaining an unjust status quo, we can use disaggregated data to name inequities incontrovertibly, and we can advocate for our students who are marginalized or invisible in the system for any reason (Atkins & Oglesby, 2018; Love, 2019).

Systemic change is challenging, is time consuming, and may require not just good research but effective policies and strong relationships. The barriers are not insurmountable, though—there are both models for how to do this work in school counseling (Bowers et al., 2018; Gruman et al., 2013; McMahon et al., 2014; Shields et al., 2017) and multiple narratives about school counseling programs and even individual school counselors who have managed (often through using good research and evidence of efficacy) to create real school-wide shifts in school counseling practices and related school outcomes (Geiger & Oehrtman, 2020; Goodman-Scott et al., 2018; Griffen, 2019; Harper & Singh, 2013). In future school counseling research, a focus on systemic change—in service to social justice and antiracist efforts in particular—seems paramount.

Level of Focus

In our efforts to identify what is effective, one ongoing question in school counseling research is the extent to which our scholarship should prioritize specific aspects of the work done by school counselors or research that supports the comprehensive structure of the ASCA's National Model for comprehensive school counseling programs (ASCA NM) (ASCA, 2019). It is beneficial for practitioners to have research on specific aspects of a program such as advocacy efforts or interventions, or on specific student outcomes such as career knowledge or social and emotional skills, as that helps with decision-making and time use (Carey & Dimmitt, 2012). A targeted research project can be (usually) less complicated to conduct. Martin and Carey (2014) created a logic model for the ASCA NM that helpfully lays out the theoretical outcomes of its various components—very helpful when considering how any examination of outcomes is related to the broader program implementation.

Research that has looked at comprehensive school counseling more broadly suggests that components of the ASCA NM have evidence of impact (Carey, Harrington, Martin, & Hoffman, 2012; Carey, Harrington, Martin, & Stevenson, 2012), and that schools using a comprehensive model have improved student outcomes (Lapan et al., 2001; Sink & Stroh, 2003). Research using Recognized ASCA NM Program (RAMP) status as an indicator of full model implementation has found impact for some student outcomes more than others (Akos et al., 2019; Wilkerson et al., 2013), with inconsistent findings across studies. In a summary of six statewide studies on comprehensive school counseling program implementation, the authors wrote, "These findings clearly indicate that certain school counseling activities create specific and measurable results and that all school counseling activities are not equally impactful for students and for critical school-wide outcomes such as attendance and discipline" (Carey & Dimmitt, 2012, p. 148).

Challenges of investigating comprehensive school counseling, and the ASCA NM more specifically, include the difficulty of studying an integrated program that—when done well—becomes an intrinsic part of the school, with broad impacts for student experiences. It's common parlance in the field to suggest that school counselors doing the ASCA NM are part of every student outcome, but because the work is so deeply collaborative, they are almost never solely responsible for any one outcome. School counselors are working to improve student academic outcomes, social/emotional skills, and postsecondary readiness—but so is almost every other professional adult in the building. Teasing out the specifics of school counselor impact then is challenging!

Bridging the Research-to-Practice Gap

Bridging the research-to-practice gap is an ongoing process, and a perpetual area of growth for many fields—not just school counseling (National Research Council, 1999; Tabak et al., 2012). The good news is that this historical area of concern has improved because of technology, web-based dissemination processes, and open access resources such as ScholarWorks (https://scholarworks.umass.edu) and Google Scholar. The publishing technology has also speeded up considerably, so that the time it takes for a manuscript to go from submission to publication is usually faster than it has been historically. And still this remains a priority and an area of growth because the field progresses the most when the research done in higher education is accessible to and utilized by professional practitioners. Chapter 14 of this book effectively addresses this topic in depth.

Mentoring

Research mentoring is clearly a priority for the future of the school counseling profession. The dispositions and skills that make us good school counselors (compassion, creativity, flexibility, interpersonal awareness, focus on equity, etc.) don't always overlap with the dispositions and skills that support good research (organization, fidelity of treatment, stringent standards related to protocols and procedures, data management, etc.)—though there are certainly people who are good at both (many authors in this book, for instance!). This is why mentoring and research teams can be useful. Working together, we can seek to have a balance of strengths that would be hard for any one person to have on their own.

Early mentoring can also help to fill gaps in research knowledge that exist for those coming out of even strong counselor education programs. Council for Accreditation of Counseling and Related Educational Programs (CACREP) standards prioritize (and, we think, rightly so) all of the clinical competencies required of doctoral-level practitioners and counselor educators—supervision, counseling skills, content knowledge specific to counseling, and so on. While research is included in this list, it may not be the priority, since counselor educators work in multiple contexts, some of which don't have research expectations. But what this means is that graduates of rigorous counseling programs may not get the years of research training that disciplines like psychology and natural sciences require for doctorates. A quick glance at Ph.D. counseling psychology program requirements finds that they typically require a minimum of six to eight research methodology and statistics courses. I (Carey) did this degree and have always appreciated how much I learned about research. In comparison, at The Ohio State University (an R1 institution) the requirement for the Ph.D. in Counselor Education includes two program-specific research identity courses with three additional required methodology and statistical methods research courses, with the option to take three more as a cognate if desired. We don't necessarily think the answer is longer doctoral programs, nor extra research courses that are not needed by all counselor educators. But we do need structured mechanisms in our field to support better research skill development for those who are interested or who need to fulfill scholarship requirements as faculty members.

Conclusion

It is exciting and rewarding to see how the research in school counseling is continuously evolving, as we push ourselves to be more rigorous and more inclusive, to be more social justice oriented and more relevant in our efforts to ensure the success of all students. A foundation clearly has been established upon which to build future research, and we have many skilled scholars in the profession who are dedicated to doing this work with integrity and passion. We are curious to see what is next and hope that this book will prove useful.

References

Adler, A. (2006). Education for prevention: Individual psychology in the schools; The education of children (G. L. Liebenau, Trans.). In H. T. Stein (Ed.), *The collected clinical works of Alfred Adler* (Vol. 11, pp. 1–260). The Classical Adlerian Translation Project. [ISBN: 0-9770186-1]

Akos, P., Bastian, K. C., Domina, T., & de Luna, L. M. M. (2019). Recognized ASCA model program (RAMP) and student outcomes in elementary and middle schools. *Professional School Counseling, 22*(1), 1–9. https://doi.org/10.1177/2156759X19869933

American School Counselor Association. (2019). *The ASCA National Model: A framework for school counseling programs* (4th ed).

Atkins, R., & Oglesby, A. (2018). *Interrupting racism: Equity and social justice in school counseling.* Routledge.

Baker, E., Zyromski, B., Granello, D. H. (2021). School or guidance counselor: How the title influences public perception. *Professional School Counseling, 25*(1), 1–8. https://www.doi.org/10.1177/2156759X20981034

Bardhoshi, G., Swanston, J., & Kivlighan, D. M. (2020). Social–behavioral stories in the kindergarten classroom: An app-based counseling intervention for increasing social skills. *Professional School Counseling, 23*, 1–14. https://doi.org/10.1177/2156759X20919374

Bernstein, R. J. (2011). *Beyond objectivism and relativism.* University of Pennsylvania Press.

Bowers, H., Lemberger-Truelove, M. E., & Brigman, G. (2018). A social-emotional leadership framework for school counselors. *Professional School Counseling, 21*(1b), 1–10. https://doi.org/10.1177/2156759X18773004

Bowers, H., Lemberger-Truelove, M. E., & Whitford, D. K. (2020). Kindergartners are ready to learn: Applying Student-Within-Environment theory to a school counseling intervention. *Journal of Humanistic Counseling, 59*, 3–19. https://doi.org/10.1002/johc.12126

Brigman, G., & Campbell, C. (2003). Helping students improve academic achievement and school success behavior. *Professional School Counseling, 7*, 91–98.

Brigman, G. A., & Webb, L. D. (2003). Ready to learn: Teaching kindergarten students school success skills. *Journal of Educational Research, 96*(5), 286–292.

Campbell, C., & Brigman, G. (2005). Closing the achievement gap: A structured approach to group counseling. *Association for Specialists in Group Work, 30*(1), 67–82. https://doi.org/10.1080/01933920590908705

Caraballo, L., Lozenski, B. D., Lyiscott, J. J., & Morrell, E. (2017). YPAR and critical epistemologies: Rethinking education research. *Review of Research in Education, 41*(1), 311–336. https://doi.org/10.3102/0091732X16686948

Carey, J., & Dimmitt, C. (2012). School counseling and student outcomes: Summary of six statewide studies. *Professional School Counseling, 16*(2), 146–153. https://doi.org/10.1177/2156759X0001600204

Carey, J., Harrington, K., Martin, I., & Hoffman, D. (2012). A statewide evaluation of the outcomes of the implementation of ASCA National Model school counseling programs in rural and suburban Nebraska high schools. *Professional School Counseling, 16*(2), 100–107. https://doi.org/10.1177/2156759X0001600202

Carey, J., Harrington, K., Martin, I., & Stevenson, D. (2012). A statewide evaluation of the outcomes of the implementation national model school counseling programs in Utah high schools. *Professional School Counseling, 16*(2), 89–99. https://doi.org/10.1177/2156759X0001600203

Carter, P. L., Skiba, R., Arredondo, M. I., & Pollock, M. (2017). You can't fix what you don't look at: Acknowledging race in addressing racial discipline disparities. *Urban Education, 52*(2), 207–235.

Corbin, J., & Strauss, A. (2014). *Basics of qualitative research: Techniques and procedures for developing grounded theory.* Sage Publications.

Council for Accreditation of Counseling and Related Educational Programs. (2016). *2016 CACREP standards.* http://www.cacrep.org/

Crenshaw, K. W. (2017). *On intersectionality: Essential writings.* The New Press.

Creswell, J. W. (2014). *Research design: Qualitative, quantitative, and mixed methods approaches* (4th ed.). SAGE Publications

Davis, B., & Sumara, D. (2002). Constructivist discourses and the field of education: Problems and possibilities. *Educational theory, 52*(4), 409–428.

Dei, G. J. S. (2005). Chapter one: Critical issues in anti-racist research methodologies: An introduction. *Counterpoints, 252,* 1–27.

Delgado, R., & Stefancic, J. (2017). *Critical race theory: An introduction* (Vol. 20). New York University Press.

Dimmitt, C. (2003). Transforming school counseling practice through collaboration and the use of data: A study of academic failure in high school. *Professional School Counseling, 6*(5), 340–349.

Dollarhide, C. T., & Lemberger-Truelove, M. E. (Eds.). (2019). *Theories of school counseling for the 21st Century.* Oxford University Press.

Francis, D., & Mason, E. (2022). Proactively addressing racial incidents in schools: Two perspectives. In C. Holcomb-McCoy (Ed.), *Antiracist counseling in schools and communities* (pp. 57–80). American Counseling Association.

Gambrill, E. (2018). *Critical thinking and the process of evidence-based practice.* Oxford University Press.

Gay, G. (2018). *Culturally responsive teaching: Theory, research, and practice.* Teachers College Press.

Geiger, S. N., & Oehrtman, J. P. (2020). School counselors and the school leadership team. *Professional School Counseling, 23*(1, part 3), 1–9. https://doi.org/10.1177/2156759X20903566

George, G., McGahan, A. M., & Prabhu, J. (2012). Innovation for inclusive growth: Towards a theoretical framework and a research agenda. *Journal of Management Studies, 49*(4), 661–683. https://doi.org/10.1111/j.1467-6486.2012.01048.x

Goodman, R. D., & Gorski, P. C. (Eds.). (2015). *Decolonizing "multicultural" counseling through social justice.* Springer. https://doi.org/10.1007/978-1-4939-1283-4

Goodman-Scott, E., Betters-Bubon, J., & Donohue, P. (Eds.). (2019). *The school counselor's guide to multi-tiered systems of support.* Routledge.

Goodman-Scott, E., Hays, D. G., & Cholewa, B. E. (2018). "It takes a village": A case study of positive behavioral interventions and supports implementation in an exemplary urban middle school. *The Urban Review, 50*(1), 97–122. https://doi.org/10.1007/s11256-017-0431-z

Goodman-Scott, E., Sink, C. A., Cholewa, B. E., & Burgess, M. (2018). An ecological view of school counselor ratios and student academic outcomes: A national investigation. *Journal of Counseling & Development, 96*(4), 388–398. ttps://doi.org/10.1002/jcad.12221

Griffen, J. (2019). Families and counselors taking action to transform culture: An action-inquiry case study of an urban high school. *Education and Urban Society, 51*(4), 501–525. https://doi.org/10.1177/0013124517728101

Griffin, D., & Steen, S. (2011). A social justice approach to school counseling. *Journal for Social Action in Counseling & Psychology, 3*(1), 74–85.

Gruman, D. H., Marston, T., & Koon, H. (2013). Bringing mental health needs into focus through school counseling program transformation. *Professional School Counseling, 16*(5), 333–341.

Guba, E. G., & Lincoln, Y. S. (1994). Competing paradigms in qualitative research. In N. K. Denzin & Y. S. Lincoln (Eds.), *Handbook of qualitative research* (p. 105–117). Sage Publications.

Gullen, J. (2012). Colorblind education reform: How race-neutral policies perpetuate segregation and why voluntary integration should be put back on the reform agenda. *Journal of Law and Social Change, 15*, 251–283.

Harding, S. G. (1998). *Is science multicultural?: Postcolonialisms, feminisms, and epistemologies.* Indiana University Press.

Harding, S. (2016). *Whose science? Whose knowledge?* Cornell University Press.

Harper, A., & Singh, A. A. (2013). Counselor agency and action in developing safe schools: Six directions for systemic change. *Journal of LGBT Issues in Counseling, 7*(4), 405–415

Hart Research Associates. (2012). *The College Board 2012 national survey of school counselors and administrators. Report on survey findings: Barriers and supports to school counselor success.* The College Board. Retrieved from https://secure-media.collegeboard.org/digitalServices/pdf/nosca/Barriers-Supports_TechReport_Final.pdf

Hatch, T., Kruger, A., Pablo, N., & Triplett, W. (2019). *Hatching tier two and three interventions in your elementary school counseling program.* Corwin.

Hays, D. G., & Singh, A. A. (2012). *Qualitative inquiry in clinical and educational settings.* The Guilford Press.

Holcomb-McCoy, C. (2007). *School counseling to close the achievement gap: A social justice framework for success.* Corwin Press.

Holcomb-McCoy, C. (2018). Conducting socially just and relevant research. In C.C. Lee (Ed.; 3rd ed.) *Counseling for Social Justice* (pp. 221–238). John Wiley & Sons.

Holcomb-McCoy, C. (Ed.). (2022). *Antiracist counseling in schools and communities.* American Counseling Association.

Holcomb-McCoy, C. Schuschke, J., & Henfield, M. S. (2022). Sustaining antiracism in the counseling profession. In C. Holcomb-McCoy (Ed.), *Antiracist counseling in schools and communities* (pp. 219–225). American Counseling Association.

Howe, L. C., Goyer, J. P., & Crum, A. J. (2017). Harnessing the placebo effect: Exploring the influence of physician characteristics on placebo response. *Health Psychology, 36*(11), 1074. https://doi.org/10.1037/hea0000499

Johnson, K. F., & Brookover, D. L. (2021). School counselors' knowledge, actions, and recommendations for addressing social determinants of health with students, families, and in communities. *Professional School Counseling, 25*, 1–12. https://www.doi.org/10.1177/2156759X20985847

Johnson, R. B., & Christensen, L. B. (2020). *Educational research: Quantitative, qualitative, and mixed approaches* (7th ed.). Sage.

Ladson-Billings, G. (2021). I'm here for the hard re-set: post pandemic pedagogy to preserve our culture. *Equity & Excellence in Education, 54*(1), 68–78. https://www.doi.org/10.1080/10665684.2020.1863883.

Lambie, G. W., Haugen, J. S., Borland, J. R., & Campbell, L. O. (2019). Who took "counseling" out of the role of professional school counselors in the United States? *Journal of School-Based Counseling Policy and Evaluation, 1*(3), 51–61. https://www.doi.org/10.25774/7kjb-bt85

Lapan, R. T., Gysbers, N. C., & Petroski, G. F. (2001). Helping seventh graders be safe and successful: A statewide study of the impact of comprehensive guidance and counseling programs. *Journal of Counseling and Development, 79*, 320–330

Lapan, R. T., & Poynton, T. A. (2020). Surviving toward college graduation. *Journal of Counseling & Development, 98*(4), 412–422. https://doi.org/10.1002/jcad.12343

Lemberger, M. E. (2010). Advocating student-within-environment: A humanistic theory for school counseling. *The Journal of Humanistic Counseling, Education and Development, 49*(2), 131–146. https://doi.org/10.1002/j.2161-1939.2010.tb00093.x

Lemberger, M. E., Brigman, G., Webb, L., & Moore, M. M. (2012). Student Success Skills: An evidence-based cognitive and social change theory for student achievement. *Journal of Education, 192*(2–3), 89–99.

Lemberger, M. E., & Hutchison, B. (2014). Advocating Student-Within-Environment: A humanistic approach for therapists to animate social justice in the schools. *Journal of humanistic psychology, 54*(1), 28–44. https://doi.org/10.1177/0022167812469831

Lemberger-Truelove, M., & Bowers, H. (2019). An Advocating Student-Within-Environment approach to school counseling. In C. Dollarhide & M. Lemberger-Truelove (Eds.), *Theories of School Counseling for the 21st Century* (266–294). Oxford Press.

Lemberger-Truelove, M. E., Ceballos, P. L., Molina, C. E., & Carbonneau, K. J. (2021). Growth in middle school students' curiosity, executive functioning, and academic achievement: Results from a theory-informed SEL and MBI school counseling intervention. *Professional School Counseling, 24*(1, part3), 1–8. https://doi.org/10.1177/2156759X211007654

Levy, I. P. (2019). Hip-hop and spoken word therapy in urban school counseling. *Professional School Counseling, 22*(1b), 1–11. https://doi.org/10.1177/2156759X19834436

Levy, I. P., & Lemberger-Truelove, M. E. (2021). Educator-counselor: A nondual identity for school counselors. *Professional School Counseling, 24*(1b), 1–7. https://www.doi.org/10.1177/2156759X211007630

Love, B. L. (2019). *We want to do more than survive: Abolitionist teaching and the pursuit of educational freedom.* Beacon Press.

Maier, L. J., Ferris, J. A., & Winstock, A. R. (2018). Pharmacological cognitive enhancement among non-ADHD individuals—A cross-sectional study in 15 countries. *International Journal of Drug Policy, 58*, 104–112. https://www.doi.org/10.1016/j.drugpo.2018.05.009

Martin, I., & Carey, J. (2014). Development of a logic model to guide evaluations of the ASCA National Model for school counseling programs. *Professional Counselor, 4*(5), 455–466. https://www.doi.org/10.15241/im.4.5.455

Martinez, R. R., Dye, L., & Gonzalez, L. M. (2017). A social constructivist approach to preparing school counselors to work effectively in urban schools. *The Urban Review, 49*(4), 511–528. https://www.doi.org/10.1007/s11256-017-0406-0

Masia Warner, C., Colognori, D., Brice, C., Herzig, K., Mufson, L., Lynch, C., . . . & Klein, R. G. (2016). Can school counselors deliver cognitive-behavioral treatment for social anxiety effectively? A randomized controlled trial. *Journal of Child Psychology and Psychiatry, 57*(11), 1229–1238. https://www.doi.org/10.1111/jcpp.12550

Mason, E. C., Land, C., Brodie, I., Collins, K., Pennington, C., Sands, K., & Sierra, M. (2016). Data and research that matter: Mentoring school counselors to publish action research. *Professional School Counseling, 20*(1), 1096–2409.

Mason, E., Robertson, A., Gay, J., Clarke, N., & Holcomb-McCoy, C. (2021). Antiracist school counselor preparation: Expanding on the five tenets of the transforming school counseling initiative. *Teaching and Supervision in Counseling, 3*(2), Article 2.

Mayes, R. (2021, March). *Using data to drive antiracist school counseling practice [Conference keynote speech]*. 2021 Evidence-based School Counseling Conference, held virtually.

McDermott, K., Furstenberg, E., & Diem, S. (2015). The "'post-racial" politics of race: Changing student assignment policy in three school districts. *Educational Policy, 29*, 504–554.

McMahon, H. G., Mason, E. C., Daluga-Guenther, N., & Ruiz, A. (2014). An ecological model of professional school counseling. *Journal of Counseling & Development, 92*(4), 459–471. https://www.doi.org/10.1002/j.1556-6676.2014.00172.x

McMahon, H. G., & Patel, S. (2019). Who benefits? Adding inclusive innovation into the evidence-based school counseling research agenda. *Professional School Counseling, 22*(1b), 7–13. https://www.doi.org/10.1177/2156759X19834439

Midgett, A., Doumas, D. M., & Johnston, A. (2018). Establishing school counselors as leaders in bullying curriculum delivery: Evaluation of a brief, school-wide bystander intervention. *Professional School Counseling, 21*, 1–9. https://doi.org/10.1177/2156759X18778781

Midgett, A., Doumas, D. M., Peralta, C., Bond, L., & Flay, B. (2020). Impact of a brief, bystander bullying prevention program on depressive symptoms and passive suicidal ideation: A program evaluation model for school personnel. *Journal of Prevention and Health Promotion, 1*(1), 80–103. https://doi.org/10.1177/2632077020942959

Moran, M., Midgett, A., Doumas, D. M., Porchia, S., & Moody, S. (2020). A mixed method evaluation of a culturally adapted, brief, bullying bystander intervention for middle school students. *Journal of Child and Adolescent Counseling, 5*, 221–238. https://doi.org/10.1080/23727810.2019.1669372

National Research Council. (1999). *How people learn: Bridging research and practice*. National Academies Press.

National Science Foundation. (n.d.). *Definition of transformative research*. National Science Foundation. https://www.nsf.gov/about/transformative_research/definition.jsp

O'Hara, C., Chang, C. Y., & Giordano, A. L. (2021). Multicultural competence in counseling research: The cornerstone of scholarship. *Journal of Counseling & Development, 99*(2), 200–209. https://doi.org/10.1002/jcad.12367

Open Science Collaboration. (2015). Estimating the reproducibility of psychological science. *Science, 349*(6251), Article aac4716. https://doi.org/10.1126/science.aac4716

Owen, L., & Westlund, E. (2016). Increasing college opportunity: School counselors and FAFSA completion. *Journal of College Access, 2*(1), Article 3. Retrieved from https://schol arworks.wmich.edu/jca/vol2/iss1/3

Palincsar, A. S. (1998). Social constructivist perspectives on teaching and learning. *Annual Review of Psychology, 49*(1), 345–375.

Palmer, P. J. (2017). *The courage to teach: Exploring the inner landscape of a teacher's life*. John Wiley & Sons.

Patton, M. Q. (2015). *Qualitative research & evaluation methods: Integrating theory and practice* (4th ed.). SAGE Publications.

Polk, W., Savitz-Romer, M., & Brion-Meisels, G. (2022). Dismantling white supremacy in school counselor training programs: Preparing counselors to enact antiracist practices. In C. Holcomb-McCoy (Ed.), *Antiracist counseling in schools and communities* (pp. 151–181). American Counseling Association.

Poynton, T. A., Lapan, R. T., & Schuyler, S. W. (2021). Reducing inequality in high school students' college knowledge: The role of school counselors. *Professional School Counseling, 24*(1, part 3), 1–9. https://doi.org/10.1177/2156759X211011894

Ratts, M. J., DeKruyf, L., & Chen-Hayes, S. F. (2007). The ACA advocacy competencies: A social justice advocacy framework for professional school counselors. *Professional School Counseling, 11*(2), 90–97.

Ratts, M. J., & Greenleaf, A. T. (2017). Multicultural and social justice counseling competencies: A leadership framework for professional school counselors. *Professional School Counseling, 21*(1b), 1–9. https://doi.org/10.1177/2156759X18773582

Ratts, M. J., & Pedersen, P. B. (2014). *Counseling for multiculturalism and social justice: Integration, theory, and application.* John Wiley & Sons.

Rossman, G. B., & Rallis, S. F. (2016). *An introduction to qualitative research: Learning in the field.* Sage Publications.

Savitz-Romer, M. (2020). *Fulfilling the promise: Reimagining school counseling to advance student success.* Harvard Education Press.

Sensoy, O., & DiAngelo, R. (2017). *Is everyone really equal?: An introduction to key concepts in social justice education.* Teachers College Press.

Shields, C. M., Dollarhide, C. T., & Young, A. A. (2017). Transformative leadership in school counseling: An emerging paradigm for equity and excellence. *Professional School Counseling, 21*(1b), 1–11. https://doi.org/10.1177/2156759X18773581

Schietz, R., & Villares, E. (2017). Effects of the girl squad curriculum on grade 5 females' transition to middle school. *Counseling Outcome Research and Evaluation, 8*(1), 2–14. https://doi.org/10.1080/21501378.2017.1327747

Singh, A. A., Nassar, S. C., Arredondo, P., & Toporek, R. (2020). The past guides the future: Implementing the multicultural and social justice counseling competencies. *Journal of Counseling & Development, 98*(3), 238–252. https://doi.org/10.1002/jcad.12319

Sink, C. A., & Stroh, H. R. (2003). Raising achievement test scores of early elementary school students through comprehensive school counseling programs. *Professional school counseling, 6*(5), 350–364.

Tabak, R. G., Khoong, E. C., Chambers, D. A., & Brownson, R. C. (2012). Bridging research and practice: Models for dissemination and implementation research. *American Journal of Preventive Medicine, 43*(3), 337–350. https://doi.org/10.1016/j.amepre.2012.05.024

Taylor, E., Gillborn, D., & Ladson-Billings, G. (2009). *Foundations for critical race theory in education.* Routledge. doi:10.1177/0741713610389784

Teo, T. (2017). From psychological science to the psychological humanities: Building a general theory of subjectivity. *Review of General Psychology, 21*(4), 281–291.

Villares, E., & Brigman, G. (2019). College/career success skills: Helping students experience postsecondary success. *Professional School Counseling, 22*(1b), 1–8. https://doi.org/10.1177/2156759X19834444

Villares, E., & Dimmitt, C. (2017). Updating the school counseling research agenda: A Delphi study. *Counselor Education and Supervision, 56*(3), 177–192. ttps://doi.org/10.1002/ceas.12071

Washington, A. R., Byrd, J. A., & Williams, J. M. (2022). Decolonizing the counseling canon. In In C. Holcomb-McCoy (Ed.), *Antiracist counseling in schools and communities* (pp. 17–32). American Counseling Association.

Welton, A., Owens, D., & Zamani-Gallaher, E. (2018). Anti-racist change: A conceptual framework for educational institutions to take systemic action. Teachers College Record, 120(14), 1–22.

Wester, K. L., & McKibben, B. (2019). Integrating mixed methods approaches in counseling outcome research. *Counseling Outcome Research and Evaluation, 10*(1), 1–11. https://doi.org/10.1080/21501378.2018.1531239

Wilkerson, K., Pérusse, R., & Hughes, A. (2013). Comprehensive school counseling programs and student achievement outcomes: A comparative analysis of RAMP versus non-RAMP schools. *Professional School Counseling, 16*(3), 172–184. https://doi.org/10.1177/2156759X1701600302

Zyromski, B., Martin, I., & Mariani, M. (2019). Evaluation of the true goals school counseling curriculum: A pilot study. *The Journal for Specialists in Group Work, 44*(3), 170–183. https://doi.org/10.1080/01933922.2019.1634781

2

Access to Schools

Relationships With Stakeholders and Systems

Sam Steen, Shekila Melchior, Tori Stone, and Jennifer Melfie

Access to Schools: Relationships With Stakeholders and Systems

The purpose of this chapter is to provide the reader with mutually beneficial specific steps to gain access to schools in order to conduct research that is of value for everyone involved. We firmly believe that a collaborative approach to research means that as often as possible students, families, teachers, staff, school administrators, and other relevant stakeholders must be included in the planning and implementation of the research partnership. Schools are complex systems that vary in size, location, resources, climate, leadership, student demographics, teacher education, and curriculum. No matter the complexity of the system, one fact remains: the mission of a school is to educate children and to prepare them for a successful life ahead. Educating students in the 21st century is a complicated notion considering the many ecological systems involved; however, maintaining a focus on students and their families is essential. Likewise, teachers and staff are the first responders involved in the daily effort to educate children despite a myriad of barriers to learning. To be effective, educational researchers must view students, families, teachers, and staff at the core of their work. In this chapter we aim to model this approach through a collaborative sharing of scholarly research approaches as well as our own experiences and expertise.

Our Process: The Impact of Reciprocal Relationships on Partnerships

We are culturally diverse (e.g., race, ethnicity, and gender) practitioners, researchers, and faculty members, who were determined to enact a

Sam Steen, Shekila Melchior, Tori Stone, and Jennifer Melfie, *Access to Schools* In: *School Counseling Research.* Edited by: Brett Zyromski and Carey Dimmitt, Oxford University Press. © Oxford University Press 2023. DOI: 10.1093/oso/9780197650134.003.0002 collaborative writing process that mirrored the subject matter. This was important because of the value we believe our own identities and experiences bring to the content. In the following section, we provide many details of our professional identities and experiences to provide the reader with a clear picture of our emerging relationships, process, and approach to collaborative writing and research. We believe our experience provides a parallel to the process needed to build relationships with school stakeholders.

To begin, this intentional process was facilitated in a collaborative manner by Sam, the first author, who is a school counselor educator (SCE). After receiving the call for publication, Sam recruited Jennifer, who was currently serving as his graduate research assistant. Next, Sam solicited one senior and one junior faculty, Tori and Shekila, respectively, both of whom are SCEs. Sam expressed a desire for all of the team members to feel empowered, equal, valued, and able to build on their current expertise and skills, while also learning from one another and the overall collaborative writing process.

After the team was assembled, we met via a Zoom platform to identify the goals and objectives of the ensuing chapter. The scope of work was discussed, a flexible timeline was agreed upon that could be managed with competing obligations (e.g., family, work, etc.), and the meeting adjourned with the agreement that we would each think about what it would entail to commit to this project from a personal standpoint. Moving forward, Shekila set up the virtual meetings and platform.

At the second team meeting, the dialogue that emerged was engaging and highlighted areas of expertise and interest that each of the team members had based on their own personal and professional experiences engaging in school-based practice and research endeavors. For example, both Tori and Shekila have extensive practice and research experience within secondary schools, and Sam has experience working and conducting research within elementary and secondary school settings. Jennifer has been placed within an elementary and high school for a practicum and internships. All three faculty have worked at different institutions (e.g., universities and school districts), and so have navigated the myriad expectations for supervising school counseling interns and consultation with peers. During this meeting, Shekila took copious notes on the discussion and an outline emerged. It became clear that one of my (Sam) strengths was to process what was emerging in our discussions while Shekila kept us focused by writing down the numerous thoughts, ideas, and questions that continued to develop over time. Following this meeting, each author was assigned a section, and our next step was to find research that aligned with our topic as well as other interesting literature that was not necessarily research based but that could facilitate an opportunity for dialogue. In the meantime, Jennifer and Shekila created a Google Docs folder as a repository for the articles collected by the team.

At the third meeting, team members presented the research articles and other related literature and artifacts (e.g., American School Counselor Association [ASCA] ethical standards) they had found. The presentation of these findings fostered conversation and reflection on how the information could be conveyed in a meaningful and engaging manner. During these meetings it became clear that each team member placed significant value on their individual intersecting identities and the ways in which those identities would impact relationship building with stakeholders. Shekila, who identifies as a cis-gendered Black woman, engages in research that is transformative in nature. Sam, who identifies as a cis-gendered Black man, is experienced in research and the formation of relationships over the course of his career. He carries a unique lens as we experience a double pandemic of Covid-19 and the recent public killings of Black people in the United States. Both Sam and Shekila recognize the lens through which they are reflecting and writing this chapter as a means of education but most importantly as a concerted effort toward more social justice research in school settings. Tori, who identifies as a cis-gender white woman, actively engages in antiracist practices in her teaching, research, and service. She is vocal about providing spaces for other white people who may need more encouragement about how to begin engaging in this difficult work. Jennifer, who identifies as a cis-gendered biracial Asian and white woman, is a budding professional. She carries additional relevant intersecting identities as a counselor intern, graduate student, and research assistant who is actively engaged in social media and using technology to create user-friendly tools for other school counselors. Following this meeting, the authors set a deadline for their drafts to be finished. Below you will find a chapter that concisely captures hours and hours of dialogue, research, reflection, and critical discourse that others can build upon in their efforts to engage stakeholders in our nation's schools.

Rationale for Collaborative Research Partnerships With School Districts

Research partnerships between universities and school districts can be valuable endeavors. However, the research partnership is likely to be initiated by the researchers from the outside in, and from the top (senior school administrators, principals) down (e.g., teachers and staff, then families, then students; Dinella & Ladd, 2009). In some cases, research questions that are relevant to students and families are not always easy for teachers and staff to see value in pursuing. When these efforts are coming from the outside into the school community, they often create more work for the teachers and staff and may disrupt the work that they strive to accomplish. This is not to imply that teachers and staff are not consumers or facilitators of research, but that they may be less interested in this work, as it is often beyond the scope of their training or their professional practice (Huber & Savage, 2009).

The research framework that aligns with this chapter initially could have been summed up as a form of action research, defined as a systematic process of inquiry conducted by and for folks taking action to help educators improve their work (Lyon et al., 2018; Sagar, 2000) (also see Chapter 9 on action research). Typically, this type of research is facilitated by educators working in schools or districts being studied rather than by others from outside organizations, who are often impartial observers. However, after careful thought and critical discussions, we decided that *transformative research* (National Science Foundation, n.d.), with an infusion of collaboration as a significant component to the work, more clearly aligns with what we are describing. Essentially, we explore how to engage in research that is meaningful and mutually beneficial to all parties, not just the research teams (Lyon et al., 2018). The Figure 2.1 modified by Tori and Sam compares action and transformative collaborative research.

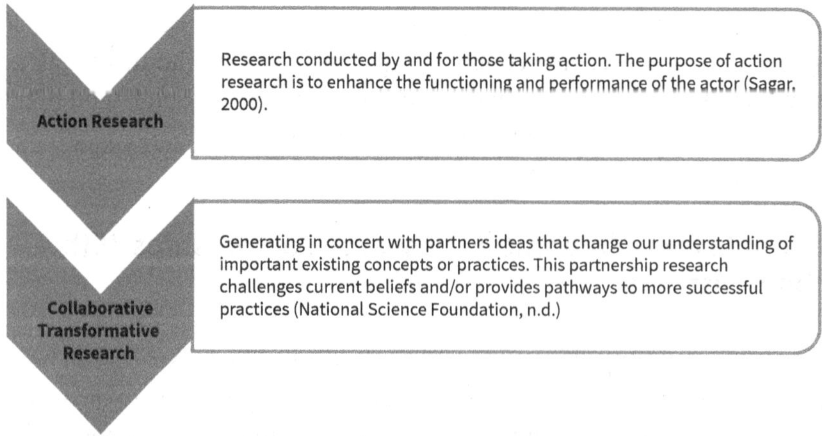

Figure 2.1. Collaborative Transformative Action Research

Research Guidelines for Mentorship Relationships

The Association for Counselor Education and Supervision (ACES) provides detailed guidelines for research mentorship relationships (Borders et al., 2012). While these guidelines are specific to mentors and mentees within the counseling profession, there are some general components that align well with the subject of this chapter. Researchers desiring school partnerships must embody the components of the ACES guidelines while being open to the needs of the school community, as well as the scope of their research project. The school partner can be invited by the research team to chronicle their needs as clearly as possible; in response, the researcher can demonstrate their openness to feedback and the reciprocal exchange of ideas. The remainder of this chapter includes discussions on ethical partnerships, facilitating relationships, identifying stakeholders, and research expectations. The chapter ends with a step-by-step guide, applicable case study, and emerging definition of collaborative transformative research.

Ethical Partnerships

Generating ethical research partnerships will look different for each individual depending on their researcher identity and contextual background as well as the school(s) and community(ies) involved. The process of cultivating relationships is multifaceted and should be tackled with multiple approaches, including cultivating relationships with faculty, contributing through service, and considering the unique resources your position holds that can provide benefit to the research relationship. In order to develop ethical partnerships, you must critically assess your researcher identity, which comprises your personal values, research goals, and existing relationships (also see Chapter 3 on ethical research).

For example, I (Jennifer) obtained a position with Sam as his graduate research assistant (GRA). My ties to the university as a master's student coupled with my past experiences as volunteer researcher and research lab member during undergrad facilitated the partnership formation. This research partnership has expanded my research opportunities, expanded my network of stakeholder relationships, and further developed my personal researcher identity/ agenda. To ensure ethical partnerships, I continually assess and address risks, personal biases, and barriers present. In addition, I consider the reciprocal nature of research partnerships, my unique position as a counselor intern, and the benefits of my position (e.g., ability to serve as a liaison between the university and public school).

If you are a researcher no longer actively practicing as a school counselor, consider how that impacts your lens and the relationships and connections you have in these schools. To ensure no harm is done to the stakeholders in a school, researchers must stay up to date on current practices and school data. We must continuously assess and address assumptions and personal biases. Additionally, the longer you are away from these schools, the more likely your personal connections change. We can fill gaps in our research team with school and community partners who have a variety of cultural, social, and professional roles. The longer you are away from these positions, the more you must work to create affirming and effective relationships as outsiders. Furthermore, you must consider who the research is for and how differing researcher/stakeholder identities can best serve the given population and research agenda (McMahon & Patel, 2019).

Cultivating meaningful research opportunities that benefit the countless stakeholders must be done without doing harm to students, the school, or the community (Mason et al., 2016). Ethical considerations specific to the schools often address accreditation and subsequent equitable access or barriers. The ethical considerations outlined by a district aim to provide the best services to the students, families, faculty, and staff. The ASCA as well as the American Counseling Association (ACA) have developed ethical standards for practicing counselors that research practitioners should also adhere to. In all cases, one must first consider the differing levels of access that researchers may hold within their school partnerships. Considering the context of each partnership will ensure that ethical relationships underpin the research work. For example, serving as an internship supervisor provides current and future opportunities to foster relationships related to research. Connecting ethics to ethical partnerships is difficult because there are multiple systems (e.g., university, school district, school) and numerous individuals involved (e.g., university faculty, site supervisors, PTA representative).

Nevertheless, key ethical issues surrounding counseling research stem from the power issues inherently present in counselor–client relationships. Client/students enter counseling services in a less powerful position because they are seeking help from the counselor (West & Byrne, 2009). Furthermore, researchers should consider the intersecting identities at play within their therapeutic and professional relationships. Issues of class, gender, race, age, and professional stature serve to support or hinder researchers' abilities to develop ethical partnerships. Ethical considerations that should inform formation of research relationships and research within schools are listed in

Table 2.1, and there is further discussion of ethical research in Chapter 3 of this book. This table is not an exhaustive outline, but an overview. Moreover, researchers should become familiar with both the ACA's and the ASCA's code of ethics and utilize consultation, supervision, and collaboration to serve their population and research agenda best.

Developing ethical relationships and adhering to our professional codes of ethics serve as the foundation for meaningful research opportunities that support student achievement. The table provided focuses on the ACA Code of Ethics; ASCA also provides a code of ethics that can be applied to counseling in

Table 2.1. Ethical Considerations

Component	Ethical Guidelines	ACA Code of Ethics
Communicating with stakeholders	– Use clear and understandable language. – Consider cultural implications. – Obtain informed consent and explain the voluntary nature of participation.	A.2.c.; G.2.a.
Forming relationships	– Do not engage in counseling relationships with friends/family where one cannot be objective. – Work to develop and strengthen relationships with stakeholders from other disciplines (social worker, university professors, district administration). – Develop clear agreements in advance regarding the tasks, duties, compensation, etc.	A.5.d.; D.1.b.; G.3.b.; G.3.a.; G.5.e.
Advocacy and social justice	– Advocate at individual, group, institutional, and societal levels to address barriers. – Maintain awareness and sensitivity regarding cultural meanings of confidentiality and privacy. – Assess and address your personal biases, privileges, and barriers to forming relationships.	A.7.a.; B.1.a.
Sharing information	– Ensure privacy and confidentiality are maintained by the research team (e.g., student counselor). – Inform stakeholders of the research team's existence, composition, and purpose. – Inform stakeholders of research procedures and outcomes.	B.3.a.; B.3.b.; G.2.h.
Technology	– Ensure that technologically administered assessments function properly. – When using technology in supervision, ensure counselor supervisors are competent in the modalities and protect confidentiality. – Acknowledge the limitations of confidentiality when using technology. – Consider the accessibility to persons with disabilities and other cultural barriers. – Consider the differences in online communication (verbal vs. nonverbal cues).	E.7.c.; F.2.c.; H.2.c.; H.5.d.; H.4.f.

the schools, forming and navigating partnerships, and conducting counseling research (ASCA, 2016a). School-specific considerations include abiding by the Family Educational Rights and Privacy Act (FERPA) by ensuring that the use of student data and records is ethically coordinated with the school administration. Furthermore, researchers should be knowledgeable about their target school districts' policies, confidentiality safeguards, and overall protocol concerning research in the schools. Assessing and addressing the unique chain of command, stakeholders, and accreditation of schools will also inform the research relationships.

Moreover, ASCA values the collaborative relationships held between the school counselor and school–family–community partnerships as a critical component of equitable, data-informed, school programs (ASCA, 2016b). Actively pursuing collaborative relationships with stakeholders inside the schools is especially critical for researchers who are not currently practicing. Navigating partnerships within the school as a researcher should be done to assess and address each setting's unique barriers and strengths in relation to the research goals. Examples of barriers that may arise in navigating school–family–community partnerships include mistrust and miscommunication between parties, resistance to the concept and practice of doing research, transportation and childcare issues, and accessible meeting times (ASCA, 2016b). To mitigate these potential concerns, the authors offer ways for the researcher to facilitate, identify, and grow relationships with various stakeholders.

Pop-Out 2.1. Challenges and Opportunities

Take a moment and reflect on the following:

1. What are some barriers to developing partnerships? Identify each challenge and consider strategies to overcome these.
2. Language is often overlooked as a challenge. When language is addressed, it is usually to offer translation services for Spanish speakers. How do we more intentionally address opportunities to expand services beyond English and Spanish speakers?
3. How can both the research partners and the school district partners be held accountable for cultural sensitivity for every aspect of the partnership?
4. Sustaining a program that is ethically sound can be difficult when there is a lot of turnover. How can one mitigate the fallout from staff turnover?

Facilitating, Identifying, and Building Relationships With Stakeholders

When conducting school-based research, counselor educators and researchers should consider the following:

- the goals of the research project
- the needs of the school community, district, state, etc.
- the broader areas of need for research, e.g., opportunity gaps, etc.
- the benefits of the research for both the school and the researcher or research team

Once these considerations have been addressed, researchers should think about existing reciprocal relationships that can be built upon. For example, counselor educators might consider relationships with schools and districts hosting practicum and internship students. When conducting site visits, counselor educators can talk with the site supervisors regarding student and/or schoolwide concerns that might benefit from research partnerships. They can ask the school counselor to facilitate partnerships by serving as an envoy to connect researchers with decision-making stakeholders at the school and district level (Savitz-Romer et al., 2018; Young et al., 2014).

Similarly, opportunities for research partnerships might arise when practicum or internship students share experiences from their school sites during group supervision meetings. Often, site supervisors will ask practicum and internship students to bring an issue or question to the professor or internship group for brainstorming and problem-solving. At times, the interns themselves will identify areas of need at their placement site; when this occurs, the counselor educator can encourage the intern to design a targeted intervention to address the concern and can also reach out to the supervisor to offer additional assistance or a partnership. The following vignette provides an example of this scenario.

One of my (Tori) interns was placed in an alternative middle school in a large, suburban school division. The school was housed in a modular unit behind another middle school; students from all of the middle schools in the division cycled in and out of the alternative school based upon disciplinary infractions at their base schools. Due to size or oversight, the alternative school had no library. My intern rightly saw this as unjust. As a part of her targeted intervention project for the internship course, she was working with students who had academic difficulties and low test scores in reading. Procuring reading materials for these students in a school without a library was proving to be a challenge. Another student in my internship section had been placed at a large, affluent, traditional middle school in the same school division. Students at that school had access to a large, current library, as well as numerous books of their own. My interns decided to partner to address the library issue at the alternative school. The student who was placed at the traditional school organized a book drive to create a library at the alternative school. The intern at the alternative school worked with her supervisor and the school administration to create a space to house the library. Through community outreach the intern obtained shelves, beanbags, tables, rugs, and other decor for the library. The book drive at the traditional school was a tremendous success, and more than 1,200 books were donated to the alternative school library.

I visited the alternative school to tour the library and meet with the site supervisor, a former student in our program who had also been my intern. After a series of conversations with her and her principal, it was clear that there were other school-wide issues that could be addressed through collaborative partnerships. Data were collected from the faculty via a needs assessment, and the topic of understanding students with emotion regulation and behavior management concerns emerged as an area of interest and need for the faculty. I worked with the school counselor to develop interventions to provide support and psychoeducation for the staff and delivered in-person staff development for all school stakeholders. The success of this program led me to connect with stakeholders at other schools and provide variations of the training for teachers, parents, and students.

The vignette provides an example of a service partnership that subsequently morphed into a research partnership. Oftentimes, small partnerships can provide a profile of success that can be shared with decision-making stakeholders at the school and district level to gain access to a larger sample of participants. A partnership like the one described in the vignette could be expanded by conducting the same needs assessment that was used at the alternative school with all of the schools in the district. The data collected could be disaggregated by school to identify and develop targeted interventions to meet specific school needs. The researcher and school leaders could then measure the success of the targeted intervention after its implementation. In the authors' experience, research partnerships that are collaborative are more likely to be mutually beneficial.

When planning to partner with a school, it is important to consider the needs of stakeholders as well as the larger school community. Many educational researchers offer small incentives like gift cards or school supplies but miss the larger point that research partnerships resulting in effectively implemented programs that enhance student learning and behavior are rewards unto themselves (Martin et al., 2019). If educational researchers treat each project as an opportunity to develop partnerships with school stakeholders, those partnerships can benefit the researcher and school community for years to come. A great question to reflect upon prior to engaging in educational research is *"How can I provide support to this school community through my work?"* This service-minded focus will shape interactions with school stakeholders and cultivate a spirit of collaboration (McMahon & Patel, 2019).

Researchers should also consider the timing of the request for studies, as poor timing can come off as inconsiderate to school stakeholders. For example, statewide outcomes-based assessments in our home state of Virginia are given in May; if we were to ask to conduct a research project that involved removing students from class during test review and administration in May, we would be seen as out of touch with the school's priorities. This lack of understanding and connection between researchers and the realities of schools can impair relationships and diminish participation in research. If a researcher is unfamiliar with the policies and practices of a state, division, or school, it will behoove them to learn about school timelines, trends, and school culture prior to engaging in research projects. It is also helpful to research district policies and procedures to gain access to conduct school-based research.

In some school districts an established protocol exists to obtain permission to conduct educational research, and that process must be followed to gain access to schools. In large districts especially, there is typically a department that oversees educational research that will request information from the researcher such as the purpose, nature, and scope of the research, a copy of the university Institutional Review Board (IRB) approval, plans to protect the confidentiality of participants, etc. Depending on district policies, consent for educational research may be subject to approval from the superintendent of schools and/or the school board. In other districts, especially those using a site-based management model, the building principal can give permission for certain school-based research activities. In either of the above scenarios, researchers will benefit from existing relationships with school stakeholders who can provide an overview of division protocols or make an introduction to a principal or division director that could facilitate a partnership. The next chapter in this book (Chapter 3) explores this topic in more depth. Next, a summary of school culture and research benefits is presented.

School Culture, Research Benefits, and Application

Research in the field of education or counseling is often conducted to make discoveries and generate new knowledge (Zyromski et al., 2018). Individuals engaging in educational research need to consider the culture of the school, how the school benefits, and the ways in which the research is applicable to the setting. The researcher should consider the types of schools they are seeking to engage with in research partnerships and, when selecting a school or schools, should reflect on the following concepts and questions. *Goodness of fit*: Does the school meet the criteria outlined in the study? *Benefits*: Does the research study benefit the school overall? Does it support the vision and mission of the school? In the context of school counseling, how does the study aid the school counselor in improving their comprehensive school counseling plan? Does the research also support the school improvement plan? As we have said before, school-based research should not only contribute to the researcher's professional growth and scholarly contribution to the field; it should also shed light on the needs of the school community.

Pop-Out 2.2. Questions to Consider

In consideration of research benefits and application in schools, the researcher is encouraged to consider the following questions:

- What are the needs of the community?
- What aspects of the researcher's identity should be reflected on?
- Does the researcher have prior school counseling experience?
- Do they have an established rapport with stakeholders?
- How do we facilitate relationships to meet the needs of the school while remaining student centered?
- What cultural implications should be considered when conducting research?
- What do our code of ethics, our multicultural competencies, and the ACA Advocacy Framework say?
- How, if at all, could the researcher's study be perpetuating discriminatory practices in K–12 education?

By answering these questions, the researcher takes into consideration more than just their study. Research is enhanced by reflection on processes and outcomes, as well as the recognition that ethical research practices should address the needs outlined by the school.

Researcher Expectations, Considerations, and the Researcher Self

The researcher is encouraged to examine their own expectations, as these can be important considerations related to the proposed study and the role of the researcher when further forming relationships and conducting research within schools. School systems are layered and varied; the relationships the researcher has with various stakeholders will inform how the researcher will engage in their work. The following section will discuss the ways that researcher expectations, concerns, social roles, and identities can impact conducting research in schools.

Expectations

As a researcher, I (Shekila) wanted to explore the impact that two major issues (immigration and Black Lives Matter) have had on the culture of the school. My expectation was to interview faculty and staff as well as students. I conducted this research in the fall of 2020, prior to a presidential election. My aim was to shed light on the actions or lack thereof of school personnel and the ways in which they engaged in advocacy efforts in their school with individual students, in their programming, and also in how they may have reviewed their school policies related to these issues.

As the researcher begins to develop her study, she holds the following expectations: the timing of the study will allow for a richness of data, she will be more than likely to gain participants given the nature of the topic and the timing, and finally, she will contribute to the growing literature in her field. The researcher's current expectations neglect the following: Does the timing of the study benefit all parties involved, and could the study do harm as it relates to the psychological impact of the interviews being conducted? Is it a healthy time for the researcher, who identifies as a Black woman, to conduct this research? Has she reflected on her ability to conduct the research at this time?

Furthermore, who is the research for? When conducting research that can have direct implications on minoritized communities, there should be a point of reflection for the researcher. Will the study contribute simply to the field, or will the research have a greater reach into advocacy? Finally, the researcher should inquire about the need for the study and ways to conduct the study that are both fruitful and beneficial to various stakeholders who are still in the schools. The researcher who is no longer engaged in practitioner work will benefit from the lens of a current practitioner. Ultimately, the expectations held by the researcher and the aims of her study should align with expectations that best serve the school. The researcher must also address concerns related to the study.

Considerations

Conducting research in a school setting raises a number of concerns. While the researcher may follow protocol outlined by the IRB, there are issues to consider when engaging in research within a school. As a point of practicality, the researcher should consider how frequently they are conducting research in a school / school district. If the members of the school community experience research fatigue or find the increase in research to be disruptive, the researcher may face barriers to future school access as a result.

Researcher Selection. Upon selecting the school, the researcher ought to observe the specific setting and needs of the school. The researcher is encouraged to examine the question(s) they are looking to answer through the lens of the schools they are seeking to work with. Consider the schools' student, faculty, and staff makeup. Is the school in a rural, urban, or suburban environment? Is the community actively involved? Moreover, the researcher should host stakeholders' meetings to discuss the viability of the study, examine the community in which they intend to conduct the research, reflect on the concerns and needs presented in the study, and make adjustments accordingly. Research, like education, is not conducted in isolation. Stakeholder input can decrease the possible concerns attributed to the study and further regulate the expectations articulated at the start. Finally, the researcher should consider themselves in relation to the project.

Researcher Self

When engaging in research, researchers should contemplate their role as a researcher and the role of the members of the research team since most research is collaborative in nature. For researchers who are graduate students or individuals who are not familiar with the area in which they are researching, the formation of relationships prior to conducting a study is imperative.

The researcher self can directly impact the success of the study because the identity of the researcher and the *why* for conducting the research can have bearing on the outcomes of the study. Prior to conducting research, the researchers should ask themselves (McMahon & Patel, 2019):

- Who is this work for?
- Who will benefit from my study?
- Why am I conducting this research?

Individuals who actively engage in research or continue to engage in practitioner work are more inclined to receive strong participation due to the relationships and partnerships fostered in the community. Continued relationships provide both the researcher and the school with the opportunity to engage in collaborative work that utilizes the strengths of all involved. For those, however, who have not had the opportunity to form those relationships, the following recommendations are provided:

- *Engage in service*—offer a service to your local school district, join your state school counseling organization, and get involved.
- *University partnership*—serve as an internship supervisor to further foster relationships. Consider finding individuals in the department or college who can assist or mentor you in forming collaborative relationships or gaining access to local stakeholders. Additionally, be intentional at cultivating relationships with emerging scholars and students in the program, as they oftentimes become colleagues upon graduation.
- *Cultural brokers*—who in the community, school, and institution are cultural brokers that can provide expertise and experience as it relates to your topic?

I, (Shekila) am currently serving as a faculty advisor to a student who is conducting a research study here in Virginia. This is my first experience mentoring a student through research, and I wanted the experience to be a meaningful one of mentorship and learning. My student and I worked through the IRB process with him taking the lead on all aspects. Once we received IRB approval, he began data collection. I quickly knew that my assistance in providing names of school counselors in the state would be severely limited, as I have just returned to Virginia from another state. I do, however, work with two senior school counseling faculty who are both well known and established in the state. I recommended my student reach out to them for assistance. My relationship with these two faculty members allowed for an opportunity to quickly gain participants in a way I could not achieve alone. As an aside, I also recognize that many people do not have more than one school counseling faculty in a school program and do not take that privilege lightly. I must also add that our work as school counselors, and not necessarily as SCEs, served as the groundwork for the relationships we have today. Furthermore, my connections as a state counseling organization division president also afforded me the opportunity to make connections for his study. The value of relationships formed and maintained through the researcher's continued commitment to school counseling proved advantageous to my student's work. As a faculty member, I value relationships and aim to model that for my students.

I, (Sam), have a similar experience with my graduate assistant, the fourth author on this chapter. I was intentional in getting to know Jennifer as an individual first and as my graduate assistant second when we started working together last year; in doing so there was a sense of collegiality built, which ultimately strengthened our work together. Jennifer shared her thoughts, "Initially I felt the need to prove myself to Dr. Steen, that I respected him and was qualified to meet his expectations. Over time, the anxiety or imposter syndrome I felt diminished, and I was able to recognize the contributions I could make."

Faculty members should strive to cultivate a collegial relationship with doctoral student(s) and explore their goals and hopes for engaging in research. Consider how the student can have agency in their work and the role of faculty in facilitating this. Ultimately, the relationships researchers pay attention to should include their students, who will become significant stakeholders both in schools and as counselors. We offer the following suggestions to faculty researchers when working with students as research mentors:

- Be aware of the benefits we hold having extensive practitioner experience.
- Participate in state and national leadership.
- Recognize the value of having more than one SCE at the same institution.
- Be aware of the nature of our relationships with our colleagues.
- Consider the readiness of the student to engage in research.
- Consider how previous experience as a school counselor may impact the way we engage in research with a graduate student.
- Remember that research mentorship with a student begins in the classroom—for example, make mention of pursuing research when grading an assignment or using it as an exemplar for future classes.

One way that the authors of this chapter modeled these ideas is through an internal grant application to an innovation fund that we submitted to the university in response to a request for proposals. The grant we submitted was prior to the writing of this chapter, so the authors used this as an example of what they actually created.

Case Study

The case study is outlined and detailed below. The case encourages and acknowledges the necessity for school community partnerships. We first provide a simple step-by-step guide to implementing collaborative research practices, and then we apply that guide to our own case study using a recent internal funding proposal to illustrate the collaborative and relationship-focused research process.

Step-by-Step Guide to Collaborative Research Practices

Step 1:   Identify research goals and questions and establish methodology.

Step 2:   Identify schools that could participate in the study.

    Step 2a: Identify stakeholders at two to three schools.

    Step 2b: Learn about/ensure understanding of the culture and identity of the school.

Step 3:   Secure funding (if applicable).

Step 4:   Begin to form or further strengthen relationships with stakeholders.

Step 5:   Pursue an IRB.

Step 6:   Hold meetings for faculty and staff about the goals and procedures of the study.

    6a: Provide a presentation.

    6b: Discuss incentives.

    6c: Initial incentive—dinner, university swag, for example

    6d: Consider the culture of the group, group dynamics, and the politics of the school system

Step 7:   Collect data and maintain communication.

    7a: Divide your team to communicate with stakeholders consistently.

Step 8:   Data analysis

    8a: Continue to maintain communication with stakeholders.

    8b: Consider which stakeholders could be peer reviewers.

    8c: Provide incentives to stakeholders.

Step 9:   Findings

    9a: Publication and presentations

    9b: Presentations to any relevant stakeholder groups (students, parents, school board, etc.)

Step 10:   Be sure to thank the various stakeholders.

A Case Study

The authors submitted a proposal in the amount of $10K for a university-sponsored innovation fund that provided administrative support, opportunities for schoolwide collaborations, faculty compensation, and program evaluation resources that are necessary to ensure that adequate time and resources are leveraged for success. The outcomes of this program benefited the graduate students' professional school counselor partners and local school communities. Goals of the program were to highlight the outcomes of school counseling programs, enhance partnerships with local schools, and use lessons learned to engage in ongoing curricular development.

The researchers desired to implement an academic innovation program that

- created opportunities for students to engage in the application of theory in the 1st year of their graduate program as school counseling students,
- fostered a commitment to innovative and experiential learning that impacts local school communities,
- highlighted school counseling program outcomes as a recruitment tool for the counselor education program,
- serve as a model for other school counselor education programs, and
- strategically enhanced partnerships with local schools.

The research team established an advisory council that was deployed during the development and implementation of the study. The advisory council was composed of both a graduate and K–12 student, school counselor, teacher, administrator, and district-level school counselor administrator. The researchers felt that gaining insight prior to and during the course of the study would ensure that the best possible program was offered to the school community.

The proposed program was introduced and implemented in two graduate-level school counseling classes: Introduction to School Counseling, and Principles and Practices of School Counseling. During the introductory course, students developed a project focused on a population that is historically underserved in school and implemented their project in the principles course. Students were given the opportunity to gather and explore preliminary data while visiting partnering schools to collaborate on the development of their group projects, which taught the students the value of school community partnerships. During the principles course, students, in collaboration with partnering schools, implemented the projects they developed in the introductory class.

The program culminated with a mini conference whereby the participating graduate students presented and reflected on the findings from their projects and their related growth as collaborators and practitioners. Additionally, faculty presented and reflected on the program outcomes. The mini conference served as professional development and as an opportunity for networking and strengthening relationships for future collaborations. Ultimately the program benefits were many: (a) the school was supported in meeting the needs of a specific group, (b) the program students gained tangible experience early in their graduate studies and gave life to the theoretical knowledge they had gained, and (c) the faculty strengthened and gained relationships with various stakeholders. The following questions are meant to be a starting point of reflection on this case study.

In the case illustration provided in this chapter, the authors proposed generating ideas with partners that further develop our understanding of school counseling practices. The collaborative transformative research that we proposed aimed to improve school counseling practice and the local community.

Pop-Out 2.3. Thought to Application

When reviewing the case above, consider the following:

1. To what extent does this proposal demonstrate a commitment to the partners?
2. In order to sustain a program like this, how much money is needed moving forward? Who would be responsible for providing these resources: the university partners or the school district?
3. Should school employees be required to participate in a project like this? What if compensation is provided for their efforts?
4. If you were in an SCE role and desired to create a similar research project, where would you begin? Who is the first individual (e.g., person or role they hold) that you would invite to participate as you begin? What would you say to that person about the project?
5. If you were a school counseling practitioner, what do you think would be the most important aspect of a research project that would be used to convince you to participate?

Conclusion

We believe that research should be action oriented, transformative in nature, collaborative in approach, and grounded in relationships. Researchers are encouraged to foster relationships with the school and community where they hope to engage in research through meetings that address the strengths and challenges of the school. As a researcher, communicate your research intentions, as well as the contributions your project will make to the school, the community, and ultimately the children the school serves. Focus on fostering relationships with stakeholders and connecting with graduate students and faculty colleagues to establish a diverse team. Identify and cultivate relationships with individuals who can act as cultural brokers to address gaps in the research team. Finally, continuously assess and address personal biases/potential barriers as they pertain to your research goals, relationships, and the target population. Research is ultimately strengthened by the relationships we have and the ways in which it can strengthen the overall outcomes for all involved.

References

American Counseling Association. (2014). *Code of ethics.* https://www.counseling.org/resources/aca-code-of-ethics.pdf

American School Counselor Association. (2016a). *ASCA ethical standards for school counselors.* https://www.schoolcounselor.org/getmedia/44f30280-ffe8-4b41-9ad8-f15909c3d164/EthicalStandards.pdf

American School Counselor Association. (2016b). *The school counselor and school-family-community partnerships.* https://www.schoolcounselor.org/Standards-Positions/Position-Statements/ASCA-Position-Statements/The-School-Counselor-and-School-Family-Community-P

Borders, L. D., Wester, K. L., Granello, D. H., Chang, C. Y., Hays, D. G., Pepperell, J., & Spurgeon, S. L. (2012). Association for Counselor Education and Supervision guidelines for research mentorship: Development and implementation. *Counselor Education and Supervision, 51*(3), 162–175.

Dinella, L. M., & Ladd, G. (2009). Building and maintaining relationships with school stakeholders. In L. M. Dinella (Ed.), *Conducting science-based psychology research in schools* (pp. 9–31). American Psychological Association. https://doi.org/10.1037/11881-001

Huber, C. H., & Savage, T. A. (2009). Promoting research as a core value in master's-level counselor education. *Counselor Education and Supervision, 48*(3), 167–178.

Lyon, A. R., Whitaker, K., Locke, J., Cook, C. R., King, K. M., Duong, M., Chayna, D., Weist, M. D., Erhrhart, M. G., & Aarons, G. A. (2018). The impact of interorganizational alignment (IOA) on implementation outcomes: Evaluating unique and shared organizational influences in education sector mental health. *Implementation Science, 13*, 1–11. https://doi.org/10.1186/s13012-018-0721-1

Martin, I., Zyromski, B., & Gigliotti, E. W. (2019). Enhancing evidence-based practice through university–practitioner partnerships. *Professional School Counseling, 22*(1b), 1–7. https://doi.org/10.1177/2156759X19834437

Mason, E. C. M., Land, C., Brodie, I., Collins, K., Pennington, C., Sands, K., & Sierra, M. (2016). Data and research that matter: Mentoring school counselors to publish action research. *Professional School Counseling, 20*, 184–193. https://doi.org/10.5330/1096-2409-20.1.184

McMahon, H. G., & Patel, S. (2019). Who benefits? Adding inclusive innovation into the evidence-based school counseling research agenda. *Professional School Counseling, 22*(1b), 1–7. https://doi.org/10.1177/2156759X19834439

National Science Foundation (n.d.). *Definition of transformative research.* National Science Foundation. https://www.nsf.gov/about/transformative_research/definition.jsp

Sagar, R. (2000). *Guiding school improvement with action research.* Association for Supervision and Curriculum Development (ASCD).

Savitz-Romer, M. S., Nicola, T. P., Jensen, A., Hill, N. E., Liang, B., & Perella, J. (2018). Data-driven school counseling: The role of the research–practice partnership. *Professional School Counseling, 22*(1), 1–9. https://doi.org/10.1177/2156759X18824269

West, W., & Byrne, J. (2009). Some ethical concerns about counselling research. *Counselling Psychology Quarterly, 22*(3), 309–318. https://doi.org/10.1080/09515070903285668

Young, A., Gonzales, I., Owen, L., & Heltzer, J. V. (2014). The journey from counselor-in-training to practitioner researcher. *Professional School Counseling, 18*, 217–226. https://doi.org/10.1177/2156759X0001800120

Zyromski, B., Dimmitt, C., Mariani, M., & Griffith, C. (2018). Evidence-based school counseling: Models for integrated practice and school counselor education. *Professional School Counseling, 21*, 1–12. https://doi.org/10.1177/2156759X18801847

3

Ethical Research in Schools

Navigating the Institutional Review Board Process at the District and University Levels

Anita Young and Ileana Gonzalez

Ethical Research in Schools: Navigating the IRB Process at the District and University Levels

Conducting research is no longer an anomaly in schools; rather, it is a necessity to advance student achievement, close inequitable gaps, promote education reform, and develop district policies that lead to sustainable outcomes for K–12 students. Moreover, developing professional identity and defining the scope and practice of school counselor scholars who may encounter ethical dilemmas as practitioners requires a working understanding of how to conduct research through formulating research questions, collecting data, analyzing data, and implementing "closing the gap" interventions.

Day to day, school counselors interact with students, staff, and other stakeholders to address issues that could ultimately become meaningful school-based research studies. Yet, some school counselors may not correlate the impact of their interventions to research outcomes or even consider the potential impact of implications on the counseling profession. In contrast, school counselors must begin to understand the value of conducting school-based research as a counselor scholar in order to grasp the imperative of ethical research.

Exposing and training counselor scholars how to use **ethical decision-making leads to the practice of conducting ethical research.** However, **engaging in research without an ethical conscience is unethical.** Ethical behavior requires a philosophical belief that governs one's behavior and actions (Remley & Herlihy, 2014). The obvious path to ethical behavior is to gain a familiarity with **professional and research ethical standards and codes of ethics** and then engage in research decision-making using those standards (ASCA, 2022 [ethical standards]; ACA, 2014 [code of ethics]; Rubin & Bellamy, 2012).

Anita Young and Ileana Gonzalez, *Ethical Research in Schools* In: *School Counseling Research.* Edited by: Brett Zyromski and Carey Dimmitt, Oxford University Press. © Oxford University Press 2023. DOI: 10.1093/oso/9780197650134.003.0003

Ethical decision-making drives the professional discernment of school-based research that leads to policy changes, the funding of resources, and equitable transformative results.

Purpose of Chapter

In this chapter, we describe how to navigate the ethics of successful school-based research with steps and recommendations that can be useful when partnering with school districts. The purpose of this chapter is to **demystify the school-based research process by increasing the knowledge and skills required to engage in principled research that protects the rights** of all participants. We believe this chapter fills an essential gap and expands the literature with implications for the training of prospective counselor educators, school counseling practitioners, and other educational scholars. The chapter is divided into three overarching sections:

- "Research and Ethics in Schools"
- "Institutional Review Board Process"
- "Navigating the University and K–12 School-Based Research Process"

Throughout the chapter, the reader will have opportunities to complete activities through application of conceptual examples and self-reflection exercises. The reader will also have an opportunity to understand how to rectify any unconscious biases that hinder access to and equitable processes for conducting ethical school-based research. Most importantly, recommendations are provided for conducting ethical school-based research.

Research and Ethics in Schools

Ethics: Developing a professional identity includes understanding the history of one's profession, the parameters of the scope and practice for serving the constituents, and preparatory standards and credentials needed to be an effective counseling professional (Remley & Herlihy, 2014; Stone, 2017). Ethics undergird professional identity and ground the knowledge, skills, and attitudes needed to respond to day-to-day interactions with colleagues, students, parents/guardians, and other stakeholders. Ethics also need to be examined through an antiracist lens to understand the needs of different populations. In the context of school-based research, there are two helpful approaches that should guide the researcher in appropriate decision-making about studies. They are ***moral principle ethics*** and ***virtue ethics*** (Wilczenski & Cook, 2011). According to Remley and Herlihy (2014), virtue ethics asks, "**Who should I be?,**" and principle ethics addresses, "**What should I do?**" A virtuous researcher is concerned with integrity, discernment, acceptance of emotion, self-awareness, and interdependence with the community. Essentially, there must be a commitment to dismantling racist ideologies through multiple truths and realities that yield an antiracist stance. Our obligations as ethical researchers are to ensure that we are giving voice to marginalized individuals whose truth is not often heard. Antiracism also includes cultivating a commitment to engage actively in dismantling systems and structures of oppression (Kendi, 2019). The five moral principles of autonomy, beneficence, nonmaleficence, justice, and loyalty are most frequently referenced in educational research (Kitchener, 1984; Stone, 2017; Urofsky et al., 2009). Let's unpack the meanings of these terms with relatable school-based examples (Figure 3.1).

Virtue Ethics

Acceptance of Emotion—is the acknowledgment of our emotions that affect our decision-making. Acceptance means being in touch with our emotions. *An example is a school counseling scholar recognizing their personal grief over the loss of their parents in the past and not allowing those emotions to cloud research focused on effective interventions for students who have lost a parent.*

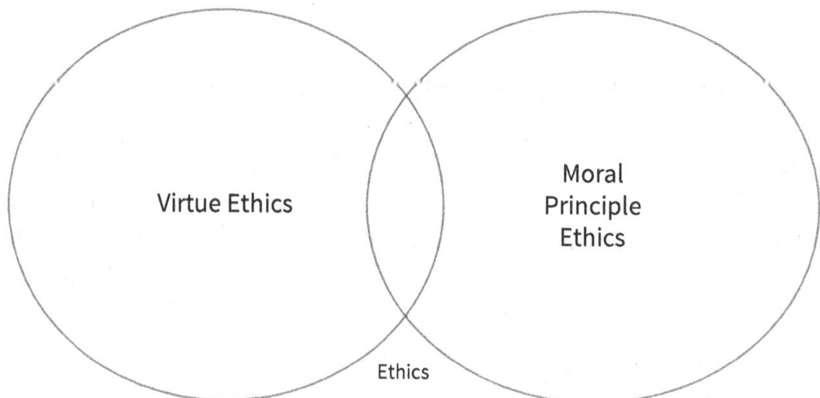

Figure 3.1. Connecting Ethics

Discernment—is the ability to remain nonjudgmental and objective about right and wrong. *An example is to explain thoroughly all the limitations of your research study.*

Interdependence with the community—endorses the value of stakeholder buy-in and the mutual commitment of all parties. *An example is giving power and voice to the community stakeholders during the research planning process.*

Integrity—is keeping promises. *An example is when school counseling scholars maintain the confidentiality of the study and participants.*

Self-awareness—is always being in tune with one's environment. *An example is understanding the moral imperative to collect and analyze data to close achievement gaps.*

Moral-Principle Ethics

Autonomy—refers to the researcher's commitment and ability to invoke self-determination on behalf of and for the participant while maintaining their human dignity. *An example is to ensure that booster club parents agree to participate freely in a school-based study without influence or fear of repercussions if they do not participate.*

Beneficence—refers to the researcher's expectations to maintain the best interest and welfare of the participants by promoting good for them and others. *An example is considering other methods to collect data from students that minimize their time outside of the classroom.*

Fidelity—refers to how the researcher is able to build trust prior, during, and after the research process. *An example is when the researcher establishes authentic relationships with school-based stakeholders through prolonged engagement and support of student interventions.*

Justice—refers to the researcher's commitment to equity and fairness, regardless of race, ethnicity, age, sexual orientation, disability, or socioeconomic status. *An example is ensuring that all 12th-grade students are afforded the opportunity to participate in a college access initiative.*

Nonmaleficence—is the commitment to do no harm and not place the participants in danger. *An example is ensuring the confidentiality of participant responses to sensitive questions such as immigration status or gender identity.*

School-Based Research. As achievement and opportunity gaps continue to widen due to various reasons (e.g., lack of educational resources, mental health stressors, global pandemics), so will economic disparities and the

---

Pop-Out 3.1. Reflective Activity 1

Consider how the moral principles and virtue ethics apply to shaping the professional identity of counselors-in-training.

1. What are the similarities and differences of each principle?
2. How should the principles be prioritized? In the context of schools, do they have equivalent values or are some more important than others?
3. At what point in your graduate training program should the principles be introduced?
4. Why is there a moral imperative for future practitioners to use ethics as the foundation for their professional identity?
5. How do you believe practitioners can use research to dismantle racism?
6. How do you believe antiracism shapes your professional identify as a counselor?

---

need for sustainable solutions to eliminate inequities. School counselors and other educators are held accountable and are expected to provide data that demonstrate measurable student outcomes that can dismantle systems that are oppressed to certain groups such as students of color (Rowell, 2006; Young & Kaffenberger, 2018). School counseling scholars may conduct school-based research grounded in (qualitative or quantitative) data collection to explore how school counselors are employing evidence-based practices (EBPs) as the catalyst to addressing educational disparities (Zyromski & Mariani, 2016). As we consider the various research questions that drive the work of school counseling scholars, it is important to consider that school-based research requires the same tenets, if not more intentionality around consideration of ethical practices, as research implemented in other contexts. School-based research also requires scientific components grounded in ethical standards that lead to evidence-based outcomes and best practices (ASCA, 2022 [ethical standards]; Gambrill, 2018). Theoretically, school-based research refers to **any method of collecting data** (e.g., interviews, focus groups, surveys, observations) or a **request to access secure records** about students or staff for the purpose of conducting a study (Rosenthal, 2008; Wilson, 2017). Two approaches, **basic and applied research**, have applicability in educational settings but serve different purposes. Basic research lends itself to exploring uncharted knowledge (Wu et al., 2016). For example, there may be an investigation of the impact of exposing counseling scholars to urban K–12 school settings. Applied research is more frequently conducted in educational institutions using quantitative,

---

Pop-Out 3.2. Reflective Activity 2: Where Do I Start?

---

1. What impact do you want your research to have?
2. Who is the targeted population?
3. What are some questions that you want to answer?
4. What ethical considerations might I need to consider when thinking about how to answer my questions?
5. How does your research aid in dismantling systems?

---

qualitative, and mixed methods designs to investigate questions posed by scholars and practitioners (Campbell & Groundwater, 2007). Action research (see Chapter 9 for additional insight into this approach) is a popular and user-friendly form of applied research that educators use to understand a plethora of issues plaguing students. In Chapter 4, you will learn how to create research questions and match them to specific designs such as quantitative ones in Chapter 7, and qualitative ones in Chapter 8.

Before we continue to dive into operationalizing the ethics of research, use the reflective questions in Activity 2 to begin grounding yourself in the research process.

Institutional Review Board Process

Ethics govern the standards for conducting all scientific research. This is important because ethics can serve as a gatekeeper for human dignity and fairness. All universities have a process for approving research projects so that human subjects, commonly known as participants, are protected legally and ethically.

What is an IRB? An important concept in ethical research is to understand the institutional review board (IRB) process. An IRB is governed by the U.S. Department of Health and Human Services (HHS) with an aim to provide objective oversight for ethical and scientific-based studies. The board ensures the protection of the safety, rights, and welfare of the human subjects and determines if the benefit of the research (to the individual or society) exceeds the risk to the participant. Committee members consist of individuals from diverse backgrounds (gender, race, sexual orientation, non-university affiliation) whose skills are explicit to render exceptional scientific, ethical, and objective review.

All human-subject research studies are required to be reviewed by the IRB prior to any level of data collection. The IRB determines the appropriateness of the study for the intended audience and the plans for how the results will be used and shared. *Human subjects*, the technical term for participants, are classified as living individuals who a researcher obtains information from through interventions or interaction (45 Code of Federal Regulations [CFR] 46.102§ [1]). While most higher education institutions have IRBs, many K–12 districts do not have a formal IRB (although some do), but that does not preclude or excuse the need to seek permission to collect data in K–12 schools. While there may be a research department available, collaboration and consultation with counselor educators is an effective strategy for gaining insight about ethical practices and the approval process. The IRB approval is a necessity for educational institutions, and the requirements are similar across universities and other educational institutions. As a researcher, you will need to obtain the relevant research protocols and processes for the district and also gain approval from the university and the district. If a school district does not have a formal IRB approval process, at minimum, the researcher should request a letter from the district with documented approval for the study.

Effective January 2019, studies that involve minimal risk or lack adverse impact on participants are exempt from specific regulations in Title 45, Part 46 of the Code of Federal Regulations, and any information collected must be documented by the primary investigator in such a way that the identity of the human subjects cannot be determined. Furthermore, any disclosure of the human subjects' responses outside the research should not reasonably place the subjects at risk for criminal or civil liability nor cause damage to the subjects' financial standing, employability, educational advancement, or reputation. The majority of research conducted in educational environments qualifies for exempt status because the interaction with students, in most cases, is minimal, and neither participants nor data are identifiable. Common examples of approved exempt reviews are the use of surveys, interview procedures, and other educational protocols. Research that evaluates the effectiveness of instructional strategies or classroom management are also examples of exempt reviews.

Without approval from the school district, you will be liable for the rights of the participants. Therefore, let's discuss the procedures for IRB district procurement. The first step is to explore the school district's website thoroughly to ascertain the process for approval *or* if they have a formalized approval. Remember, in the absence of an approval process, as a researcher you have an ethical obligation to seek approval from the appropriate authority who may be a school administrator, district superintendent, or school board. Let's assume there is a formal process for approval. Questions to ponder in this step are: *What is the timeline?* Unlike the university process, districts may have timelines for new data research submission applications that may range from monthly to quarterly. *Is there a fee application?* Some districts require a non-refundable fee for application submission. *Do you need a district sponsor?* In some instances, districts require a district liaison throughout the process. If so, delineate the responsibilities of the district liaison versus the researcher.

In Step 2, clearly understand what the application process requires. Before you apply, confirm the appropriateness of your research and how it aligns with the district's mission. Obviously, as a researcher, one believes there is the potential to contribute to the counseling profession. However, it is important that the proposed research has utility for the school district's advancement of student achievement and benefits all stakeholders. *Are there other practical considerations?*

Finally, complete the application. Clearly state the purpose of the study, without ambiguity. For example, describe the anticipated participants, any risks and benefits to the participants, and that participation is voluntary. Discuss the informed consent and all aspects of the study. *Is your informed consent user friendly?* Let's assume the application was approved and you are ready to collect data. Two days before the data collection is to begin, the principal requests revisions to your proposed research. As the researcher, you are obligated to meet with the principal, and it is your responsibility to provide documentation to the IRB committee of any procedural changes prior to collecting data. If, at the conclusion of the meeting with the principal, requests for modifications are not substantive, proceed with the data collection.

Now that you have an understanding of the IRB process, read the scenarios in Reflective Activity 3 and see if you can determine if they are exempt. After reviewing the scenarios, try creating a draft situational proposal that is applicable to your current line of research inquiry or setting.

Informed Consent

Now that you understand what an IRB is and that approval is the gateway to beginning a study, the next consideration is to comprehend the relevancy of consent from potential participants to conduct the research. Research should not be conducted without the permission of the participants, which is the premise of informed consent. The legal precedence of informed consent dates back as early as the 1900s when medical patients were granted the right to determine legal treatment. One of the most infamous cases frequently

---

Pop-Out 3.3. Reflective Activity 3: What Categorical Response Might an Institutional Review Board Render?

Scenario 1

Imagine that you want to conduct a study that measures the effectiveness of FAFSA initiatives in a high school where the majority of the population of students are first-generation college students. The interventions include a parent night that informs and assists participants in the completion of the Free Application for Federal Student Aid (FAFSA) application process. Additionally, school counselors will facilitate groups with students during the school day to assist in the FAFSA completion process. Data will be collected through focus groups and surveys from participants who attended the parent night and participated in the groups. Is this study exempt?

Scenario 2

A researcher wants to measure the relationship between student attendance and grade point average for all Black and Latinx students in middle schools in a specific district. The researcher downloads grade and attendance data from the district's data software system. Is this study exempt?

---

referenced that violates informed consent from patients is the Tuskegee Study that spanned over 40 years. Although designed to evaluate the progression of syphilis in African American males, participants agreed to examinations and treatment under the pretense that they were being treated for syphilis and anemia, which was commonly known as "bad blood." In reality, the researchers did not obtain consent, nor did the participants receive adequate treatment or notification of voluntary participation. This study became the landmark contributor for the passage of the **National Research Service Award Act of 1974**, which mandated that all research funded by the US Department of Health and Human Services must comply with IRB regulations.

Common Rule

The Belmont Report was the impetus for the 1991 Federal Policy for the Protection of Human Subjects known as the **Common Rule**. The policy requires that potential participants are provided a thorough explanation (verbal and nonverbal) of all aspects of the intended study. Federally funded clinical research governs the Common Rule, the foundational or baseline standard for ethics that upholds the rights of funding research. The Common Rule is also called *45 CFR 46, Code of Federal Regulations* and protects participants from risks in research studies that any federal agency or department conducts. The Common Rule defines the guidelines for IRB membership, the process for reviewing research, and how to obtain informed consent. Designing the informed consent form for a study is an opportunity for the researcher and practitioner to collaborate with one another. This process ensures that compliance with the Common Rule is adhered to and the rights of the participants are upheld. The informed consent should further clarify the methods by which confidentiality of all records and documents will be maintained, and if and how participants will be compensated. Contact information for research-related questions should be readily available to the participants and their parents, if minors. The informed consent process should also allow adequate time for potential participants to decide whether to participate and should not imply any level of coercion (University of Michigan, 2020).

The Belmont Report also laid the foundation for the ethical principles of respect for persons, beneficence, and justice, which are all included in Kitchener's (1984) moral principles. An example of respect for persons is considering the parents/guardians or siblings of children when collecting data through observation within their environment. Protecting the privacy of student participants from a detention center to ensure they are not singled out for research is an example of beneficence. When thinking about justice, consider if the recruitment for the study is inclusive.

Participants must be informed if the treatment may involve unforeseen risk, about any expenses that may be incurred, how to withdraw or terminate procedures, the process for informing them of new data that could affect their willingness to continue in the study, and finally, the approximate number of participants expected for the study. Figure 3.2 illustrates the parameters of the Common Rule as it relates to the Belmont Report.

The Common Rule was updated and substantially revised in 2017, amended twice, and became effective in 2019. One important revision was to simplify interpretation and the intent of the informed consent process. According to the latest revisions, informed consent forms must begin with the purpose of the research and the expected duration of the study. A description of the procedures should follow, along with the identification of any procedures that could be classified as experimental. The potential participants should also be informed of foreseeable risks, benefits, or alternative procedures that might be advantageous to them. How the confidentiality of data will be obtained, stored, and maintained should be explained. If the research is determined to involve more than minimal risk, an explanation of viable resources should be included if the potential of injury (physical or emotional) may be present. If

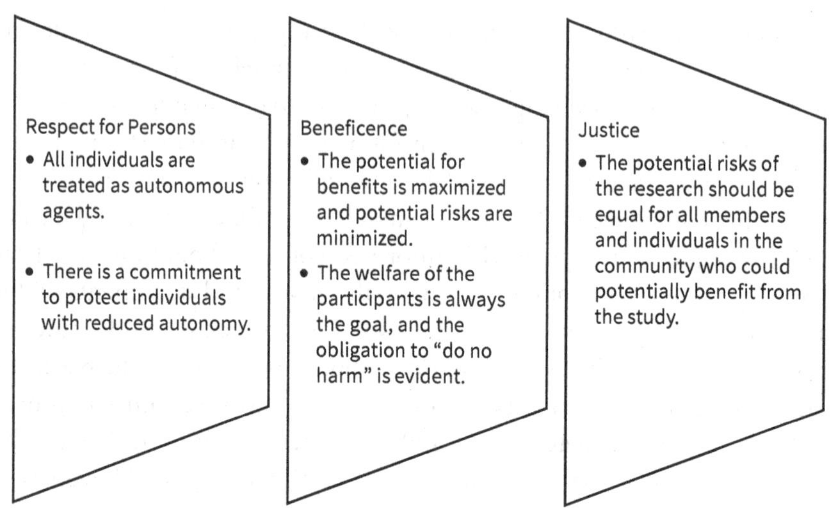

Figure 3.2. Belmont Report (Common Rule)

Pop-Out 3.4. Reflective Activity 4: Applying Common Rule Concepts

You are a researcher investigating the effects of a college-going intervention on first-generation college-going students. As part of your needs assessment, you want to collect demographic information including an item asking if students are currently undocumented so that you can tailor your intervention to encompass the needs of the students in that situation. How would you apply the concepts of respects for persons, beneficence, and justice to this scenario?

---

the participant has questions, there should be reference as to where and how to seek answers. Lastly, if at any point a participant wants to withdraw, they should be allowed to do so without identifiable associated data.

Although many institutions provide an IRB-informed consent template, the format is relatively easy as illustrated in Figure 3.3.

When conducting research with minors, parental or legal guardian consent must first be obtained. Active consent requires parents to sign and submit a consent form if they agree to having their child participate in a research study. Passive consent, also known as "opt-out consent," gives parents the opportunity to sign and submit a form by a certain date only if they do not consent to participation. Therefore, nonresponse assumes the parents agree that their

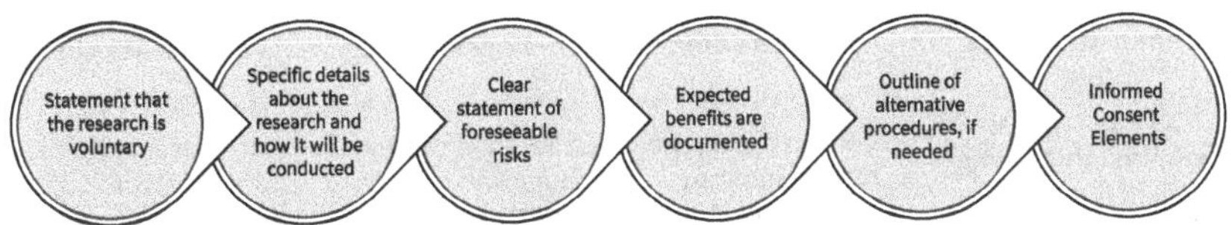

Figure 3.3. Process to Parental Consent

child may participate in the study. Researchers have pointed to the benefits of using passive consent in terms of saving time and resources (Ellickson & Hawes, 1989). Passive consent also yields higher participant rates—especially in school settings (Range et al., 2001). Some of the ethical risks of using passive consent are, first and foremost, a researcher has no guarantee that the consent form is obtained by parents or guardians; secondly, the passive consent form may not provide the time or information needed to understand the research study in order to refuse participation.

In making the decision of whether to use active or passive parental consent, a researcher needs to explore IRB and district regulations. Some school districts may require active parental consent regardless of IRB, so the researcher will need to ask the participating school district(s) prior to any development of a passive consent process. Ultimately, if the researcher uses passive consent, they must evaluate the risks to the subjects and must provide parents with sufficient information and time concerning the opt-out procedures. Regardless of the method chosen, it is a researcher's ethical responsibility to provide parents with the autonomy to make their own decisions and assert that they are not being coerced as they make the decision to whether or not to allow their child to participate.

In addition to parental consent, students need to assent to participating in the study. Child assent means a child provides some affirmation, whether written or verbal, to participate in the research study. Deciding how best to obtain the student's assent to participate in the study can be challenging depending on the age and developmental level of the child. Although children do not have the legal capacity to consent to participate in research studies, they can be part of the process if they are able to assent by having the purpose of the study explained to them. This can be done by either reading a simple script about the study to the child and requesting verbal assent, or by providing a written form, depending on the child's experience, developmental level, and level of understanding. A researcher may want to consult the child's parents or teacher to make this determination. See Figure 3.4 for general guidelines for obtaining child participant assent. Also see Chapter 5 in this volume on developmental considerations in research.

Infants to 5 years old	6–7 years old	7–12 years old	13–18 years old
In most cases, children this young will not be able to participate in the assent process, and only a consent form for the parents or legal guardians is needed.	In certain cases, the researcher may deem a child in this age range capable of being involved in the assent process. If so, give the child a simple verbal explanation of what will happen to them, and then document on the parental consent form or in the study records that you obtained verbal assent. **Child Verbal Assent Script: 1** am trying to learn more about (describe the study in the simplest terms). I would like your help by (describe what the child will do). Your parent(s)/guardian said it would be okay, but it is up to you to decide if you want to do it. It is okay for you to say no, and if we start and you want to stop, just tell me and we will stop. Would you like to (fill this form out, talk, draw etc.)?	Children in this age range will be able to participate in the assent process, using a simplified assent form. A separate, more detailed permission form will be needed for the parents or guardians. See Appendix A for a sample assent form for this age range.	In most cases, adolescents should be fully informed about a study and give assent to their own participation in the research. One form can be written for both parent or guardian consent and student assent. See Appendix B for a sample assent form for this age range.

Figure 3.4. General Guidelines for Obtaining Child Participant Assent by Age

Navigating the University and K–12 School-Based Research Process

Now that we have discussed the background components of ethical research, let's discuss the steps for actually conducting the research. The process for conducting ethical research involves building relationships and partnerships to identify collaborative, purposeful goals. For example, counselor educators who are practicum and internship instructors form natural alliances with school counselor practitioners, district leaders, and K–12 teachers and often

> ## Pop-Out 3.5. Reflective Activity 5: Informed Consent Scenario
>
> You are studying the effects of a social-emotional learning curriculum on discipline referral rates of third-grade classrooms at two elementary schools in an urban school district. You will randomize which school will receive the intervention and which school will be the control that will receive the intervention after the study is completed. You plan to collect data discipline rates at both sites throughout the intervention. Create a sample informed consent letter to parents and decide how you will obtain student assent.

have first-hand knowledge about the culture of the school environment and opportunities to learn stakeholder needs. Many school counselor educators maintain relationships in districts where they were practitioners and may also choose to collaborate intentionally with local districts or districts that are interested in engaging in research.

Understanding the District Process

The approval from the IRB board is a moral imperative and the gateway to conducting ethical research for systemic outcomes. Researchers and school practitioners should partner to identify a common research agenda that not only benefits both the school's needs and that of the researcher but also are mutually aligned with antiracist principles (Boser & McDaniels, 2018). This **mutually beneficial partnership** can narrow the gap between research and practice (see Chapter 2 for additional details on building strong partnerships with schools). Ideally, this collaboration would be more than just a one-time project; rather, this partnership can be an iterative process of implementing interventions and evaluation to improve both practice and the profession (Coburn et al., 2013). Typically, collaboration happens most intensively at the start of the study when process decisions need to be determined, and at the end of a study when researchers report findings and discuss implications of those findings. We argue that collaboration needs to happen at every stage. Turley and Stevens (2015) suggest that one representative from the university and one individual from the district take a leading role to ensure that both perspectives have **equal power** guiding the project. Coburn et al. (2013) detail partnerships that have governing boards composed of stakeholders that help set the research agenda.

Part of collaborating means being proactive by identifying potential conflicts such as anticipating the barriers in the research process and facilitating discussion around possible ethical conflicts. Potential challenges can include miscommunication around processes or miscalculation in terms of accomplishing tasks in the timeline. Priorities may also vary as part of the research process, so communicating what tasks take precedence at what stages of the research process is important to avoid conflict. For example, as timelines shift, there may be potential conflict over judging what is in the best interest of the subjects. Additionally, researchers have the ethical responsibility to maintain their integrity by keeping promise; however, there may be some situations that are out of the researcher's control. Individuals in the partnership must also identify areas of strength and learn to build on those strengths over the length of the partnership.

By the time the researchers enter the building to discuss with practitioners the nuts and bolts of the research project, they should have a number of documents ready to share and discuss as the project transitions to the implementation phase. These documents include: IRB and district approval documentation; procedures for obtaining parental consent and student assent, a research project timeline, resources needed, a calendar including potential meeting dates for collaboration, and plan of how results will be disseminated. This communication should be reciprocal and **transparency** is needed. When parties come to the table to discuss the partnership and the project, several specifics should be mapped out, including the research methodology, timeline, specific tasks, and the roles each party will take in completing those tasks.

When researchers and practitioners collaborate to co-design projects, this stretches the boundaries and roles for all involved. For the researcher, this may include additional interpersonal roles, including that of a facilitator, active listener, and negotiator (Coburn et al., 2013). A researcher needs to ensure that all voices are heard and to become fully aware of the organizational culture and climate of the system in which they are conducting research. This will be discussed in the next section.

For those within the school, being a member of a research partnership may add additional roles outside one's normal job responsibilities. School practitioners may take the lead in developing measures or collecting data. Coburn et al. (2013) argue that engaging practitioners in this way may foster a sense of ownership and nurture a greater respect and understanding of the research process. These new roles may take time to learn and apply to day-to-day duties, so researchers need to employ some patience and flexibility to ensure these tasks are performed well. Collaboration involves mutual agreement about how these new responsibilities will be integrated into the existing job roles and routines.

Organizational Cultures and Ethical Practices

Ethical practices are contextual in nature. What is considered ethical behavior such as applying the concepts of respect for persons, beneficence, and justice in one context may not be true for another. Therefore, understanding the organizational cultures of schools and school districts is beneficial in terms of anticipating potential ethical conflicts. Building and maintaining successful research partnerships can be challenging because researchers and practitioners come from different organizational cultural worlds.

Turley and Stevens (2015) outline six research partnership stakeholder categories: (a) school district leaders, (b) school district research staff, (c) external researchers, (d) school board members, (e) vendors and organizations that design or implement educational products, and (f) students and parents. It is imperative that researchers understand the interests represented within each of these groups and examine where there may be potential for ethical conflicts.

Researchers and practitioners have different **priorities and agendas** (Turley & Stevens, 2015). District superintendents or chief executive officers are school district leaders, and their priority is to improve academic outcome measures. School leaders have a greater sense of urgency when it comes to making decisions compared with researchers. School leaders are looking for interventions that meet the needs of their students right now. Researchers, on the other hand, conduct studies that have less of a sense of urgency. This conflict between the best approach and the most realistic approach can often place the mission of the research project at odds between the parties (Coburn et al., 2013), resulting in disagreement over what is in the best interests of the subjects as the partnership progresses.

School district research staff, where they exist, are tasked with district program evaluation conducted within the school district to improve school outcomes. Turley and Stevens (2015) argue that due to the multitude of research requests within the district, research staff may not have the time to do in-depth program evaluation that goes beyond descriptive statistics or simple correlations that are not informative in terms of making evidence-based decisions. They also face pressures and tight timelines from district leaders to provide these reports in order to justify decisions that are made. Researchers, on the other hand, do not face these pressures and typically use more complex methodologies and analyses. These differing priorities may create ethical conflict around what is the best methodological research design.

School board members are responsible for the policies in school districts. Because they are elected officials, they face political pressure to make decisions that often do not rely on evidence but, rather, on constituent desires and available resources within the district (Turley & Stevens, 2015). Therefore, a researcher may want to conduct research using a specific intervention or method based on evidence, whereas a school board member may make these decisions based on voter pressure. Outside retailers that create educational products are looking to sell through evidence that their product is effective. These stakeholders are looking to prove that their product will improve outcomes, so they may question unfavorable findings or conduct their own research to place their products in a positive light (Turley & Stevens, 2015). Therefore, researchers may face ethical conflicts involving what the "best practices" to conduct their research projects are. Lastly, parents and students are the stakeholders who are the most vulnerable in terms of research partnerships. They may have the least amount of power in terms of making research-based decisions. Since they stand to benefit the most from these partnerships, researchers have an ethical responsibility to inform them of the research projects in a manner they can comprehend by directly linking the research project to individual parent and student interests.

Organizational cultures also have differences in **power status**, so not all individuals have equal power in decisions. Practitioners can be silenced when sitting at the same table with principals or district leaders if they are not aware of the power of their voice, as they may feel they are not the definitive authority for the direction a research project takes when in fact they may possess the most knowledge (Coburn et al., 2013). Therefore, a researcher may assume that practitioners are satisfied with a decision since they do not vocalize concerns. From beginning to end, the university researcher has an ethical obligation to ensure that any partnering school practitioner is comfortable with decisions concerning the study and empower that practitioner to feel equally involved in the decision-making process no matter the organizational power structure.

Building Trusting Relationships

Although the partnership journey may have begun, collaborations between researchers and schools do not happen naturally but, rather, are built **strategically** through a foundation of trust between partners. For research partnerships to run effectively, a considerable amount of time and effort put into building trust, especially at the outset, is key to forming this foundation. Transparency about a researcher's values is imperative, and we should bring to the table our worldview about topics such as equity and antiracism. Ethical conflicts will arise, so it is important to have an understanding of the organizational culture built through trusting relationships. In the beginning stage, individuals from both parties are becoming aware of organizational cultures, norms, and expectations, as well as personal values and characteristics.

As collaboration continues, trust can play a critical role in helping institute norms in the partnership by setting up **routine processes and procedures**; this is especially important for sustainability, as many school districts tend to experience leadership changes (Turley & Stevens, 2015). This sustained presence of researchers is crucial in building relationships and learning about the community (Coburn et al., 2013). Their presence will also further inform the researcher of the context of the study.

Establishing trust minimizes **risk** to both the researcher and the school district. For example, as data are collected from school districts, researchers need to be mindful of the extent to which school districts are vulnerable and exposed. The impact of reporting research outcomes has the potential to create consequences for school districts, as they are held accountable for outcomes and can be portrayed negatively in the media (Coburn et al., 2013). Researchers need to honor their commitment to trust through full transparency in the research process. Coburn et al. (2013) describe a "no surprises" policy to ensure that district stakeholders have an opportunity to review reports about their district before releasing them for publication.

Following through on commitments and acting in a way that is aligned with the values of the school systems are ways to forge that trust (Coburn et al., 2013). First, both institutions must be invested in the larger mission of the partnership. This is done by ensuring both parties have input on the mission, priorities, and timelines of the project. There will be many moments throughout the partnership where mistakes will be made. It is important that both parties admit to those mistakes and use them as opportunities for learning by discussing them critically for school improvement (Turley & Stevens, 2015).

After solidifying district/university relationships, the next step of accountability is to have a complete understanding of the IRB or approval process within the district. Whether requesting current or collecting new data, most **districts prefer prior or concurrent approval from the IRB**. In some instances, any level of data request may first require a memo of understanding (MOU), proof of university approval, and a completed proposal or executive summary. To be fully prepared, we recommend completion of a checklist before meeting with the district. Ask yourself the following questions.

The District-Level Approval Process

Once the university and district relationships have been solidified, the journey has just begun. Securing permission to conduct research in school districts is a tricky process, as school districts are their own autonomous entities that have the right to accept or reject research being conducted in their institutions with their employees and the students and families they serve. Moreover, districts

<table>
<tr><td colspan="3">Pop-Out 3.6. Checklist</td></tr>
<tr><td>Tasks</td><td>Yes</td><td>No</td></tr>
<tr><td>Do you have a thorough understanding of the district application requirements?</td><td></td><td></td></tr>
<tr><td>Are stakeholder approvals needed?</td><td></td><td></td></tr>
<tr><td>Is the proposed study relevant to district needs?</td><td></td><td></td></tr>
<tr><td>Is an Memorandum of Understanding required?</td><td></td><td></td></tr>
<tr><td>Is a sponsor required?</td><td></td><td></td></tr>
<tr><td>Is there a clear timeline?</td><td></td><td></td></tr>
<tr><td>Does the proposal fulfill IRB requirements?</td><td></td><td></td></tr>
<tr><td>What will be the university responsibilities?</td><td></td><td></td></tr>
<tr><td>What will be the district responsibilities?</td><td></td><td></td></tr>
<tr><td>How are you transparent about your world views?</td><td></td><td></td></tr>
</table>

have their own definitions of what constitutes research and data collection. A researcher will need to become familiar with the intricacies of the approval process and the designated representatives at each district before creating any research timelines, as each district has its own application procedures.

Some districts have very streamlined processes where one individual reviewer approves research proposals, other districts have a formal online process that requires proof of university IRB approval before even considering an application, and some districts solely require principal approval (Alibali & Nathan, 2010). Additionally, each district has its own timeline, including deadlines for applications and review cycles. In some instances, the researcher may have to go back and forth between the district and university IRB as school districts may make changes to consent documents that require the university IRB to review these documents again for approval (Alibali & Nathan, 2010). Typically, districts require securing permission at a district level before contacting individual principals and schools. Researchers will need to be transparent in their communication with principals in terms of explaining the potential impact of the research process on teachers and classrooms and what effort, if any, will be required from teachers and school staff. Alibali and Nathan (2010) suggest sending a packet with all the information to principals ahead of a phone call or meeting to give them the opportunity to become familiar with the research study before meeting with the researcher.

After all parties agree and the application has been submitted, it is critical and ethically imperative to maintain communication and stay engaged with the district. Dinella (2009) emphasizes that there should be no assumptions about the approval of the research study until it is formally approved by all parties. Similarly, IRB approval does not imply the study's outcomes will yield the intended results. It simply means the study can be conducted.

Implementing the Study

Once the project gets underway, practitioners may decide to make changes to the research plan, or original plans may not be feasible in the realities of the school context. A researcher has the ethical responsibility to notify the IRB office of any modifications to the approved study before implementing any change. Essentially, the IRB office needs to review and approve any changes related to any added, revised, or removed segments of the sample and re-cruitment procedures, informed consent documents and procedures, data collection instruments, and interventions. The only exception to this rule in circumstances during the data collection stage is that a researcher can make changes needed to protect human subjects. In this case, the researcher can de-viate from the original study plan to reduce risk to study participants and then must notify the IRB immediately after.

Protection of Subjects

As a study gets underway and the researcher has obtained parental consent and student assent, a researcher's ethical obligation to protect subjects does not end. The researcher has the ethical responsibility to protect participants by securely storing any identifiable data, remain consistent with the approved IRB plan, and honor any commitments that were agreed upon as part of the research study. This includes any compensation promised to subjects for participating in the study.

Data storage includes retaining documentation of parental consent and student assent (if applicable) and any data collected throughout the study. This can be in the form of audio tapes, videos, or electronic documents. After the research study is complete, the HHS protection-of-human-subject regulations require investigators to maintain this documentation for at least 3 years after completion of the research.

Informing School Districts and Practitioners of Results

Sharing the results of the study completes the research cycle process and has the potential to bring about more questions and opportunities for collabora-tion rather than closure on a project. Researchers may not think to link ethical practices to this stage of the research process, but there is potential for eth-ical conflicts at this stage in thinking about what the results may mean and be used for. Researchers need to provide opportunities for dialogue with school districts about a dissemination plan before the research project is implemented and results are obtained. This is imperative so that before the results are disseminated, there is ample opportunity for discussion and feedback about who the results will be shared with, what the results mean, when the results will be disseminated, and how the results will be communicated with stakeholders. These conversations ought to be based on school stakeholder needs and preferences for information. Furthermore, dialogue around the impact of results of the study should be explored, as school districts may want to limit disclosure of the results in order to protect the reputation of the school or may use the results as evidence of a practitioner's success or failure. Therefore, explicit decisions around communication of all or parts of the results to general and specific audiences need to occur before the study gets underway.

Informing Participants of Results

Ethical principles of respect for persons extends to offering the opportunity to inform subject participants of the results of the study. This avoids exploiting subjects and treating participants as just a means to end. Additionally, informing participants of the results of the study may lead to greater beneficence in terms of quality of life and avoidance of risk or harm.

Respect for persons gives participants and their parents the right to decline to be given the results of the study if they so choose (Fernandez et al., 2003). Fernandez and colleagues (2003) suggest that the offer to share results should extend to all participants to include those who may benefit directly from learning the results (such as those who directly participated in the study by filling out a survey or participating in an intervention) and those who also indirectly benefit (such as those participants who were part of the control group or whose academic data were collected). The benefits to this group may be less visible, but respect for persons extends to include participant feelings of self-worth knowing that they participated and contributed to enriching knowledge in some way (Fernandez et al., 2003). Respect for persons also includes the manner in which results are communicated. A researcher is obligated to present the results in a clear manner that participants can comprehend, which may require developmental considerations with students. Researchers need to make sound ethical judgments regarding the impact of conveying research results to participants or their parents.

Conclusion

This chapter outlined ethical considerations for conducting school-based research. Schools now more than ever need evidence-based research that will close educational and opportunity gaps for students. We hope that this chapter enhanced your ethical knowledge related to applying ethical principles to conducting research. From research idea inception to dissemination of results, each step of the process requires the researcher to reflect carefully on who one is and what one does in the research process. Ethics serve as the gateway to human dignity and fairness. The institutional review board serves as the established body holding researchers to a standard of ethical practice requiring documentation to protect the rights of research participants. As school counseling scholars, we are groomed for the ethical research process as we build trust and establish collaborative relationships with school districts. It is our moral imperative to do what is best for the participants' welfare. Always know and live by these professional standards.

References

Alibali, M., & Nathan, M. (2010). Conducting research in schools: A practical guide. *Journal of Cognition & Development, 11*(4), 397–407.

American Counseling Association. (2014). *2014 ACA code of ethics.* https://www.counseling.org/docs/default-source/default-document-library/2014-code-of-ethics-finaladdress.pdf.

https://www.schoolcounselor.org/About-School-Counseling/Ethical-Legal-Responsibilities/ASCA-Ethical-Standards-for-School-Counselors-(1).

Boser, U., and McDaniels, A. (2018, June 20). *Addressing the gap between education research and practice.* https://www.americanprogress.org/issues/education-k-12/reports/2018/06/20/452225/addressing-gap-education-research-practice/

Campbell, A., & Groundwater, S. (Eds.). (2007). *An ethical approach to practitioner research: Dealing with issues and dilemmas in action research.* Routledge.

Coburn, E., Penuel, W., and Geil, K. (2013). *Research-practice partnerships: A strategy for leveraging research for educational improvement in school districts.* William T. Grant Foundation. http://wtgrantfoundation.org/library/uploads/2015/10/Research-Practice-Partnerships-at-the-District-Level.pdf

Dinella, L. (2009). *Conducting science-based psychology research in schools.* American Psychological Association.

Ellickson, P. L., & Hawes, J. A. (1989). An assessment of active versus passive methods for obtaining parental consent. Evaluation Review, *13*(1), 45–55. https://doi.org/10.1177/0193841X8901300104

Fernandez, C., Kodish, E., & Weijer, C. (2003). Informing study participants of research results: An ethical imperative. *IRB: Ethics & Human Research, 25*(3), 12–19. doi:10.2307/3564300

Gambrill, E. (2018). *Critical thinking and the process of evidence-based practice.* Oxford University Press.

Kendi, I. (2019). *How to be an anti-racist.* Bodley Head.

Kitchener, K. S. (1984). Intuition, critical evaluation and ethical principles. The foundation for Ethical decisions in counseling psychology. *The Counseling Psychologist, 12*(3), 43–55.

National Commission for the Protection of Human Subjects of Biomedical and Behavioral Research. US Department of Health and Human Services. *The Belmont Report.* (1979). www.hhs.gov/ohrp/regulations-and-policy/belmont-report/read-the-belmont-report/index.html

Range, L., Embry, T., & MacLeod, T. (2001). Active and passive consent: A comparison of actual research with children. *Ethical Human Sciences and Services: An International Journal of Critical Inquiry, 3*, 23–31.

Remley, T. P., & Herlihy, B. (2014). *Ethical, legal, and professional issues in counseling.* Pearson.

Rosenthal, R. (2008). Science and ethics in conducting, analyzing, and reporting psychological research. In D. N. Bersoff (Ed.), *Ethical conflicts in psychology* (pp. 390–397). American Psychological Association.

Rubin, A., & Bellamy, J. (2012). *Practitioner's guide to using research for evidence-based practice.* John Wiley & Sons.

Stone, C. (2017). *School counseling principles: Ethics and law.* American School Counselor Association.

Turley, R. N., & Stevens, C. (2015). Lessons from a school district–university research partnership: The Houston Education Research Consortium. *Educational Evaluation and Policy Analysis, 37*(1, suppl), 6S–15S. https://doi.org/10.3102/0162373715576074

United States Department of Health and Human Services. (n.d.). *Criteria for IRB approval of research.* 45 CFR §46.111. Pre-2018 requirements. Protection of human subjects. Retrieved July 12, 2020, from www.ecfr.gov/cgi-bin/retrieveECFR?gp=&SID=83cd09e1c0f5c6937cd9d751 3160fc3f&pitd=20180719&n=pt45.1.46&r=PART&ty=HTML #se45.1.46_1111

University of Michigan. (2020). Research ethics & compliance, informed consent guidelines & template. https://research-compliance.umich.edu/informed-consent-guidelines

Urofsky, R., Engels, D., & Engebretson, K. (2009). Kitchener's principle ethics: Implications for counseling practice and research. *Counseling and Values, 53*, 67–78.

Wilczenski, F., & Cook, A. (2011). Virtue ethics in school counseling: A framework for decision-making. *Journal of School Counseling, 1*, 1–15.

Wilson, E. (Ed.). (2017). School-based research: A guide for education students. Sage.

Wu, M., Tam, H. P., & Jen, T. H. (2016). *Educational measurement for applied researchers. Theory into practice.* Springer.

Young, Anita, & Kaffenberger, Carol. (2018). *Making DATA work.* American School Counselor Association.

Zyromski, B., & Mariani, M. (2016). *Facilitating evidence-based, data driven school counseling: A manual for practice.* Corwin Press.

Appendix A

Sample 7-to-12-Year-Old Child Assent Template

Hello. I want to introduce myself as (researcher name), a researcher who is doing a study I would love for you to be a part of. Research helps us learn new information about things. I want to learn more about how to make school better; that's why I want to learn more about (describe study here).

If you don't understand something, you can ask me at any time. If there are some words in this form you don't understand, you can circle or highlight them and ask me now or later.

You are being asked to be in this research study because (explain reasoning here).

For you to be in this study, both you and your parent (or guardian) must say it's okay. It is up to your parents/guardians to give the okay, but it's up to you if you want to do it. If you say no, you won't be in trouble or treated any differently. And you can stop at any time if you want to.

If your parent says yes and you say yes, then this is what will happen (detail procedure here).

I do not know for sure if you will be helped by being in this study, but we could learn something that will help other students like you someday.

Thank you.

Contact Information: (insert PI email and phone number)

I have read this or someone has read it to me.

Please check one box:

☐   **YES,** I want to be in this study and I know I can change my mind later.

☐   **NO,** I do not want to be in this study.

Child's name (print legal name): _______________________________________

Child's signature: ____

Date of signature: ________________ Birthdate ____________________

Appendix B

Sample 13-to-18-Year-Old Child Assent Template

We are asking you to be part of a research study that plans to investigate (study description here). We wanted you to take part in the study because (insert reasoning here).

Aside from your parent or guardian providing consent to participate, we want to ask you if you will consent to participate. Even if your parents say yes, you can still say no. If you say yes and change your mind, you can stop at any time.

If you agree to be part of this study, you will (describe participant procedure process). This should take about (insert time here). When we publish the results of the study, we will be sure not to include any information that directly identifies you. Your real name will not be used in the publication of the results of the study.

While you may not receive a direct benefit from participating, the information you provide could help other students like you.

If you feel uncomfortable answering any question at any time, you can stop.

If you have any questions about anything on this form, please contact us.

Contact information

(PI Phone number and email)

By signing this form, you are agreeing to be in the study. We will give you a copy of this form for you to have in case any questions come up. Thank you.

I agree to participate in this study.

___________________________________   ___________________________________

Signature   Date

4

Research Questions That Contribute to Sound Study Designs for School Counseling

Matthew E. Lemberger-Truelove and Citlali E. Molina

Research Questions That Contribute to Sound Study Designs for School Counseling

What Is a Research Question?

Research is a formal process that an investigator uses to describe and explain qualities about a phenomenon or predict how a phenomenon will manifest in the future (Babbie, 2016). For school counseling scholars, an example phenomenon that one might want to *describe* is how 504 duties are perceived by professional school counselors (e.g., Goodman-Scott & Boulden, 2020) whereas another school counseling researcher might want to *predict* how a particular therapeutic technology promotes students' social behaviors (e.g., Bardhoshi et al., 2020). Each of these research endeavors started and concluded with a research question. A research question is the conceptual frame that scholars use to (1) identify the qualities required to study a particular phenomenon, (2) inform the choices and methods a scholar uses to investigate the phenomenon, and (3) provide the scholar with a lens to interpret the results derived from the method used in the study. In short, a research question is a thread that holds the total research project together.

Although the research question establishes the basis for inquiry, there is still incredible variation in how a particular research question can affect a researcher's study design or the interpretation of the results. For example, Silberzahn and colleagues (2018) recruited 29 teams of research scientists and provided each team with the same research question and data. Across almost

Matthew E. Lemberger-Truelove and Citlali E. Molina, *Research Questions That Contribute to Sound Study Designs for School Counseling* In: *School Counseling Research*. Edited by: Brett Zyromski and Carey Dimmitt, Oxford University Press. © Oxford University Press 2023. DOI: 10.1093/oso/9780197650134.003.0004 all research teams, the analytic approaches varied greatly, resulting in incredibly different and often contradictory outcomes. Silberzahn and colleagues (2018) further found that neither the researchers' interests nor their expertise in the topic or statistical analyses explained the differing outcomes. These types of results can make one quite skeptical of the utility and veracity of research. If there is so much variation in how to study a phenomenon, how can consumers trust the experts who perform research activities? This skepticism is further confounded by the replication and generalization crises in contemporary research, where researchers have been unable to replicate some of the most seminal findings in the social and applied sciences (see Maxwell et al., 2015; Yarkoni, 2019).

One should not be completely disenchanted about research, whether you are a new researcher who is riddled with intimidation regarding empirical practices, or a more senior scholar who is skeptical that data-related results might not corroborate with reality or even influence change in individual students or entire school systems. As authors, we offer an alternative position where the utility of research is not to offer peer scholars or consumers with a final and definitive truth about a phenomenon or an unassailable means to challenge the incredible layers of bureaucracy in school systems; instead, we suggest that the true importance of a strong research question for school counseling scholars is to engage authentically with the object of inquiry, to think about it more deeply and deliberately, and to open oneself up to new vistas of thinking and behaving. In fact, the authors of this chapter encourage scholars to embrace the ambiguity implicit in research and persevere as scholars given the perspective that a strong research question should stoke conversations and future research endeavors, rather than anticipate final and stable truths about students, schools, or even counseling practices.

For school counseling scholars in particular, thinking of research questions as inconclusive and subjective should feel quite familiar. As school counseling practitioners, it is unhelpful to dictate students' experiences or aspirations; rather, an effective school counselor is interested in each student's unique perspective and the various influences that contributed to their worldview, behaviors, and goals. Furthermore, an effective school counselor does not suggest that a given intervention approach or concept can serve as a stand-alone panacea that works for all students or school stakeholders in the same way in perpetuity. As practitioners, instead, we are open to multiple interpretations, and we customarily adjust when new and inevitable complexities arise. School counseling research is no different. When we construct a study and witness a result, we understand that even the most aptly constructed study was limited in relevance to the population studied or the means used to collect the data. Nonetheless, research is still important. The preparation that one invested in asking a compelling research question and designing a coherent study made the investigator more attentive to the unique needs of the sample. The choices made to design should humble the researcher to consider the complexity inherent in each student and across the total school constellation. Effective school counseling research is not a quest for final ends or definitive answers, but an opportunity to create an ongoing dialogue between researcher, participant, stakeholders, and the various consumers of research knowledge (Bowers & Lemberger, 2016).

Purpose of the Chapter

There are many potentially helpful resources that school counseling scholars can use to strengthen their research questions, ranging from web pages to chapters found in research textbooks. Two of our favorites that were written with counselors in mind include Balkin and Kleist's (2016) *Counseling Research: A Practitioner-Scholar Approach* and Heppner and colleagues' (2016) *Research Design in Counseling*. While we encourage readers of the current chapter to consult these and other related resources, the scope of this chapter pertains specifically to how a school counseling scholar can formulate an effective research question that might contribute to useful research designs that are relevant to students in school environments. For the most part, many of the principles and step-by-step recommendations offered by research scholars outside of school counseling can be useful in the construction of an effective and relevant research question, but we contend that there are particular nuances about the school counseling context that must be considered in our unique form of scholarship.

To support school counseling scholars in particular, we posit that there are at least five qualities that must be present in an effective research question (i.e., specificity, innovativeness, practicality, relevance, and coherence). In addition to proffering the five qualities of an effective school counseling research question, we offer six flexible step-by-step activities involved in formulating a research question using examples from the current school counseling literature. Each of these qualities and steps is intended to inform the design of effective studies utilizing the various research traditions, practices, and recommendations discussed in the other chapters found in this book.

Authors' Note on Example Research Questions

To illustrate how a school counseling scholar might formulate a research question that contributes to effective study design and compelling results, throughout this chapter we will describe a number of empirical studies found in the school counseling literature. Some of the studies were identified because we believe that they effectively illustrate a principle or process necessary in formulating a high-quality research question. Additionally, we have embedded examples drawn from our own experiences as school counseling scholars in tables found throughout this chapter. We have used our own research experiences because we are intimately familiar with most of the considerations that contributed to the construction of the question and the related research design. We have not picked our own examples because they are necessarily the acme of empirical study. There are a great variety of ways to approach research, and each of the examples offered in this text is merely illustrative; therefore, we encourage the readers to consider how the authors of these research questions devised them, rather than being consumed by the specific details about a particular question or research design.

As authors of this chapter, we have both been school counselors, teachers of school counselor trainees, and school counseling scholars. As first author (Matthew), I am at the midpoint in my career, and I have completed many grant-funded projects and other empirical studies, in addition to serving as an editorial board member or editor-in-chief for a number of academic journals. The second author (Citlali) is at the front end of her academic career after many years in the field, and already she has participated in a number of empirical research projects in a variety of capacities. Our different positions as more senior and more junior scholars affected how we wrote this chapter, hoping that our differing statuses in the field would make the contents relevant across the developmental continuum of research professionals.

My (Matthew's) academic interests generally pertain to evidence-based school counseling interventions, especially culturally responsive approaches intended to support the social and emotional development of children and the adults in their lives. This work is grounded in a unique school counseling theory—namely, the Advocating Student-within-Environment (ASE) approach (see Lemberger, 2010; Lemberger-Truelove & Bowers, 2019; Lemberger & Hutchison, 2014). The theoretical and practical assumptions implicit to the ASE approach contribute to many of the features found in the research questions I have pursued. For example, the ASE approach to school counseling proceeds from the belief that an intervention should help both students and adult stakeholders activate inherent abilities in such a way that each individual might better coregulate experience, leading to more fully connected school environments. Inspired by this belief, I have performed a number of studies that aim to satisfy the following general research question: How does student or teacher participation in a certain school counseling intervention contribute to changes in students' executive functioning (i.e., self-monitoring; emotional control; task initiation, organizing, monitoring, shifting, and completion) and feelings of connectedness to the school environment (i.e., safety, contribution, and meaningfulness), and how do these perspectival changes contribute to changes in students' academic performance and other desirable school behaviors?

My (Citlali's) school counseling research interests mostly reflect my coauthor's (Matthew's) interests. This fact is not surprising given that he is my current doctoral advisor; in this way, this illustrates that research questions can either be inspired by or reinforced by the scholars whom you are in relationships with. An effective mentor or colleague will bring out the best in your scholarly goals without forcing or determining your goals or practices. In my case, Matthew introduced me to the ASE theoretical framework, and I found that it provided language and a perspective for practice that expressed what I already believed contributed to healthy school environments and student growth. With the language to formulate a grounding research question, even early in my research career, I have found a way to frame my interest in discovering evidence-based practices (EBPs) intended to support students from underserved communities and their teachers. In particular, I am interested in effective interventions for teachers that lead to positive impact on student–teacher relationships, including how a counselor can engender mutual feelings of connectedness in those relationships.

Our stories as researchers illustrate an important initial consideration for the development of an effective research question—what generates the question itself? There are a variety of sources for research questions, many of which we will describe in the following paragraphs. This said, we want to offer a couple of important caveats that we believe are important to consider throughout one's scholarly career. First, we encourage scholars to consider their passions for school counseling, for students, for school environments, for education, and all other contributing influences that motivate your work. In a similar way, our passions and beliefs about the relevant features of school counseling can serve as important inspiration for research questions, but, furthermore, these core features should protect us from the urge to pursue research for the sake of research or to accumulate a certain number or type of publications. Although at first blush this might appear trite or like a platitude, this warning can have incredible implications on how you spend your time as a scholar and the types of experiences you have in pursuing your work. For example, speaking for myself, I (Matthew) have exhausted a lot of time and energy working on research questions that were not closely aligned with my interests. One way to look at this is that working on diverse topics has provided me with insights into different perspectives related to my own interests, it has exposed me to new research practices, and it has informed me about knowledge in and beyond my own academic discipline. All of these culminate into a second caveat that one should look beyond one's own myopic biases. One should not pursue a research question to prove oneself or an idea correct; strong research should have the potential to surprise and challenge! This said, I (Matthew) have certainly compromised because I was not always fully invested or informed in a given research activity. In short, a research question should balance one's inquisitiveness to learn more about a topic with one's mastery. A third caveat, which can often come in conflict with the passion caveat, pertains to pragmatism and patience. For example, early in my career I wanted to complete a sophisticated intervention study but lacked the background, resources, and social capital to do so. I almost turned away from the project because the school district partner deviated from our original agreements and decided to not release students' academic achievement scores. Although disappointed, I soon realized that our research team had created the project with multiple research questions that were important and not completely tied to achievement outcomes alone. As a result, the final manuscript was my first publication in a flagship counseling journal (Lemberger & Clemens, 2012). It included important implications in support of school counseling interventions, and the learning that occurred as a result of the study activities contributed to later projects (e.g., Bowers et al., 2020; Lemberger et al., 2018). To synthesize these three caveats together, it is sensible for researchers to consider the importance of a given research question as it operates within a single study, but we also encourage the reader to consider how a research question can reflect and build across multiple studies or even across an entire research career.

The Centering Influence of a Research Question

The research question centers the entire research venture. There is a great diversity of ways that research is pursued, yet there is also a widely accepted structure in contemporary empirical study. For the most part, this structure is utilized because it provides the scholar with a systematic way to organize and disseminate information. In a similar way, the predictability of this structure affords consumers of scholarship a scheme by which to consume the information and critically reflect on its veracity and relevance. Stated plainly, the conventional way that research is designed, collected, and articulated is intended to aid with coherence between the scholar and the recipient of the scholarship.

Typically, most empirical studies include some introduction to the research topic, an explication of the related literature, the design qualities used to study the topic, the results from the empirical analyses, and then some discussion of the implications and limitations of the empirical study. Although the research question is often physically placed after the literature review and just before the study design (often labeled "Procedures"), the influence of the research question is found in each of these various components of the study.

A scholar can consider each of these components in light of the eventual manuscript that will be constructed for the purposes of publication or dissemination to stakeholders. These components are also helpful heuristics in how one might construct a research question and the related empirical study. There is a reflexive relationship between what one shares as a result of an empirical study and the considerations in the development of that study.

For many scholars the introduction is tragically undervalued or at least misconceived. Most scholars are in agreement that the introduction hooks the interest of the reader, but in reality, the importance of the introduction is quite vast. In addition to drawing the reader in, the introduction should articulate why this particular area of inquiry is important. Furthermore, the introduction suggests the theoretical assumptions of the scholars. This pertains to the nature of the research question itself. For example, a school counseling scholar who is interested in how relationships with principals affect school counseling programs most likely has theoretical assumptions about school politics and authority. As such, when constructing a research question the scholar should be mindful that the introduction provides the reader with some insight about how the scholar thinks about the studied phenomenon.

In a similar way, the contents of the literature review are patently tied to the research question. The main purpose of a literature review is to inform the readers about the relevant, extant literature and, moreover, provide enough information to substantiate the methodological choices used to complete the study. The literature review should also provide the ground from which the results will be explained and contrasted to other findings in the Discussion section. With this in mind, the literature review should be primarily focused on an elaboration of the specific concepts embedded in the actual research question. For example, in a study of effects of a small-group counseling intervention, Lemberger and Clemens (2012) were interested in middle school students' changes in feelings of connectedness to aspects of the school environment. There are a number of concepts that are related to school connectedness, yet there is importance in the nuanced differences. In this way, the research question provides the specificity necessary to understand what was studied, why it was studied in the way it was, and how any results can be conceptualized.

The clearest example of the influence of the research question is how it affects the empirical design of the study. The research question dictates who will be studied (i.e., population and sample), what will be studied (e.g., the constructs, the intervention), and how it will be studied (i.e., the analytic procedures). For example, if a scholar is interested in how certain school counselor–facilitated consultation activities with teachers might affect pedagogy or students' experiences in the classroom, then that scholar will construct a research question and empirical design clearly tethered to each of these aspects. The sample might include certain types of teachers who are alike enough to compare their experiences and mitigate against any other explanations for the findings appropriately. Is it appropriate to construct a study and compare the experiences of more seasoned teachers versus novice teachers? Is there something about the consultation activities that are tailored specifically to a certain type of teacher? Are there certain units of measure that we would expect to change as a result of the consultation intervention? We would not necessarily expect that the consultation would change their eating habits, but we would expect that it might influence the types of verbal responses that they have to a child who is misbehaving in class.

Finally, the research question guides the way that any results from the empirical study are interpreted and discussed. Because school counseling is an applied science, many scholars feel compelled to offer suggestions for practice. Unfortunately, many times these inferences are outside of the parameters of what was or even what could have been studied. For example, if a scholar secured findings in support of a small-group intervention targeting elementary school students, it is impolitic to suggest that this intervention will yield similar results with adolescent students. It is plausible that findings under certain conditions can inform practices in other contexts, but such recommendations need to be proffered with a clear tactfulness and humility. Relatedly, just as the research question establishes the parameters of how results can be used, it also foretells the limitations of the study.

Qualities of an Effective Research Question

If a research question centers an empirical study, then it follows that there must be a range of qualities that make a particular question high- or lower quality. Although research theorists from various academic disciplines propose a variety of qualities for an effective research question, we suggest that school counseling scholarship in particular offers: (1) specificity, (2) innovativeness, (3) practicality, (4) relevance, and (5) coherence.

School counselors are under increasing pressure to provide evidence that their activities contribute to desirable student and school-wide outcomes (ASCA, 2019; Carey & Dimmitt, 2006; Zyromski & Mariani, 2016). In addition to external pressures, school counseling scholars and practitioners should be internally interested in the influence of their work and how results might rouse ongoing improvement. As such, an effective research question should be specific. For example, Harris and colleagues (2019) questioned whether school counselors' self-efficacy, multicultural competence, and perceptions of principal support and collaborative school climate predict perceived involvement in partnerships with families of color. In this question there exist specific constructs that were measured (e.g., self-efficacy, multicultural competence), specific qualities about the sample (e.g., school counselors), and specific details about the design and analysis features (i.e., predictor). The research question should be clear in a way such that the reader can anticipate with some precision the most necessary aspects of the topic and research design.

Although it is essential to produce a specific research question, one's efforts for specificity should not limit the utility of the question. It is possible that a seemingly well-constructed research question can be a tautology, which does seemingly answer the question but only does so because of the way that the question was presented. For example, in the broader psychotherapy literature there is a concern about which theoretical counseling orientation yields the most helpful and reliable results. Depending on how one proposes the research question, the results might erroneously privilege one theoretical approach and limit others. Consider that certain psychotherapy theories more closely adhere to psychological diagnoses, which in turn led to the creation of diagnostic instruments consistent with the language and assumptions of that counseling theory. If clients exposed to this theory-informed therapy perform better on an instrument designed to capture certain diagnostic symptoms, are we really answering the research question about what treatment is better, or are we answering another unasked question altogether—namely, how being a client of a certain therapy contributes to our comfort or acumen in responding to a certain type of instrument? Stated another way, do the respondents appear to have fewer diagnostic symptoms because the therapeutic intervention and research design are both tied closely to the theory that inspired these features? The end goal is not to confirm our assumptions and biases, but, rather, as scholars we want to be specific enough to know our results are truthful and reliable.

The second quality of an effective school counseling research question is that the question is generally innovative. As stated at the outset of this chapter, no research question or result should be considered conclusive; instead, it should be additive to a larger professional dialogue. By innovative we are not suggesting that a scholar pursue every newfangled concept, as there is little merit in knowledge for the sake of knowledge alone. By innovative we are suggesting that the research question can alter perspectives, provide new detail, challenge prior myths and suppositions, or even add subtle new dimensionality to established ideas or practice.

It should be noted that replication of past findings can be innovative. Performing research with a different student sample, using a different instrument, or even following the procedures identically can all be innovative depending on the intention of the research question. Consider the most extreme replication example, which is a scholar attempting to reproduce all features of a seminal empirical study precisely. If the research question is simply to repeat the study without a grander agenda, then this is probably not terribly innovative or contributory to the extant literature. But if the research question is to see if the results repeat so as to add further support for the initial findings, then this type of research question is potentially innovative. This is more than a mere semantic distinction, as it all attributes to the intent of the research question.

The third quality of an effective research question can be found in its practicality. For example, given the myriad context factors involved, many school counselors have trouble working in classrooms in a consistent manner. If your research question requires precise fidelity to the implementation standards for a classroom intervention, it might be impractical to pursue this particular research question with this particular school counselor sample. Another example might be the number of questions in a psychological instrument. Even if your instrument was appropriately normed on students at a certain grade level, if the time needed to complete the instrument does not fit within the allotted time you have in a classroom, then using that particular instrument would constitute an impractical practice. As a school counseling scholar, it is vital that one balances the desired empirical results with what is feasible in a research endeavor in your contexts.

The fourth quality of an effective research question has to do with its relevance to the field of school counseling. There are a great number of possible research questions with varying potential influence on the field. Within reason, most of these potential questions should be asked, and the results should be reported for consumers to integrate. However, when considering quality, there are certain research questions that by their nature might prove more influential or captivating to our constituents. For example, if you are a scholar who is working predominately with rural school counselors, it might be useful to target school concerns more endemic to rural environments. At the time of writing this chapter, we are in the throes of a global health pandemic and reminded of long-standing issues of racial and societal injustice; by the time of press and for many years after, school counselors will be performing their work with teachers and students who have had to adjust to these new realities. In turn, research questions that embrace the current educational and cultural zeitgeist might be more highly valued. It is important that a school counseling scholar consider what information is valued and perceived as relevant. It is also important for scholars to consider the audience to which their work speaks and to what end it might serve; generally speaking, scholarship that is relevant to the development of school counseling practices that improve the lives of young people and the adults who serve them will be appropriately lauded for its relevance and impact.

Finally, the fifth quality required of an effective school counseling research question is coherence. Consider Milsom and Morey's (2019) research question, "Are there significant differences in absences and grades between students in elementary schools that have implemented RAMP (Recognized ASCA Model Program) and those that have not?" (p. 2.). This is coherent because it identifies the units of measure (i.e., absences, grades), whose unit of measure is being used as a comparison in the analyses (elementary-aged students), what is being compared (i.e., a school counseling program's status relative to RAMP), and how the measurement units will be analyzed (i.e., a comparison of difference; later in this chapter we will describe this as a relational-type research question). Generally speaking, all quality research questions should inform the reader of the basic necessary ingredients to understand what is being studied and how the particular design approach contributes to relevant and applicable results. There is some variation in what is included in one particular research question versus another, but as general practice a scholar might want to include each of the following elements for coherence: (1) who is being studied, (2) how they will be studied (description, relationship, causality), and (3) what concepts are necessary to understand what was studied and the appropriateness of the design. A generic standard to consider is that both a novice and an expert should be able to read the research question and have some clear idea as to the intent and direction of the study.

Formulating a Research Question for School Counseling Scholarship

As suggested above, the best research questions have specific qualities. We assert that there are steps that scholars can follow in constructing a high-quality question for school counseling research. Although we believe that each step is indispensable in formulating an effective research question, we encourage the readers not to read the following steps as if they are discrete or linear. Instead, these steps are a collection of activities that can begin at any step, and a scholar can revisit and revise steps on many occasions, as necessary.

Step 1: Look Inward

In a previous paragraph, we suggested that a researcher's experiences and beliefs about school counseling can inform what questions one might pursue empirically. For example, when current school counseling professor Carrie Wachter-Morris was a counseling graduate student, she was confronted by a student's suicide ideation and her own feelings of uncertainty of how best to respond ethically. This early experience has influenced her work as a scholar, including a recent study wherein she and a colleague posed a number of research questions, including, "What are the prevalence rates of Self-Directed Violence (SDV) among youth in 8th through 12th grade within a school?" (Wachter-Morris & Wester, 2020, p. 111).

Schools and the people who inhabit them are incredibly complex. We encourage the reader to consider these complexities and note what things stand out, what patterns or curiosities arise, and what beliefs you may have about how school counselors can affect these complexities. Each of these foundational questions can serve as the impetus for a possible research question. For example, Blanco and colleagues (2019) asked two related research questions about the effectiveness of a 16-week child-centered play therapy intervention on the self-regulation and achievement outcomes on a group of 42 at-risk first graders. These researchers drew from their theoretical and practical experiences and responded to a perceived deficit in the standard schooling experience.

We encourage you to consider the following non-exhaustive list of questions that can help focus your experiences and beliefs in a manner that might contribute to the development of one or more compelling research questions:

(1) What are your beliefs or experiences about how school counseling might affect students? A classic illustration of this includes the many works of Greg Brigman and colleagues, who were interested in how students' exposure to the Student Success Skills program affects academic performance on a state-mandated achievement test (e.g., Brigman et al., 2007).

(2) What are your beliefs or experiences related to school counseling? For example, if you are interested in qualities about a school counselor, you might consider a study performed by Dollarhide and colleagues (2008) where they asked a group of 1st- and 2nd-year practicing school counselors about their identity and practices related to school leadership. Alternatively, you might be interested in the duties and influence of the school counselor like Bryan and colleagues (2009), who drew data from a national education database to answer the question "Who sees the school counselor for college information?" (p. 280).

(3) What are your beliefs about the various identities of students (e.g., social class, gender, race/ethnicity, special needs, age) and how such factors influence student outcomes (e.g., school behaviors, college pursuit)? Relatedly, what are your beliefs about how these various manifold identities intersect? For example, a school counseling scholar might pose the question to see if school counseling services affect college choice based on students' ethnicity, gender, or socioeconomic status (see Mulhern, under review).

(4) What are your beliefs or experiences related to school or other systemic factors on school counselors' or students' experiences? Dollarhide and Lemberger (2006) examined a number of research questions related to school counselors' and students' experiences of changes in services in response to changes in educational policy.

(5) Theory

Step 2: Look Outward

Given the profound influence that a school counselor can have on the lives of students and the cultures within entire school systems, it is crucial that we approach our practice and scholarship with an open awareness of the

Table 4.1. Look Inward

Authors' Example

I (Matthew) have a long-standing philosophical and practical belief that "To best prepare young children in poverty for later life challenges, professional counselors must make every attempt to improve social conditions; however, it is equally important that young children's internal capacities be strengthened either to accommodate improved social conditions or to maximize resilience in the face of persistent adversity" (Lemberger-Truelove et al., 2018, p. 289). I further believe that self-regulation and executive functioning skills—that is how a student activates internal regulatory skills for goal-directed behavior—coupled with how safe and contributory they feel in an environment lead to multiple desirable social outcomes like learning and healthy relationships. As such, there are three primary research questions that have served as the inspiration for most of the empirical studies I have completed in my career:

RQ 1: Does the Student Success Skills (SSS) intervention affect students' perception of connectedness to school?

RQ 2: Does the SSS intervention affect students' report of executive functioning skill?

RQ 3: Does the intervention affect students' performance on a standardized achievement measure?

Lemberger et al. (2015), p. 28.

---

various influences that affect our behaviors and concepts. Even the most well-intended and reflective school counselor will embody a number of biases and inclinations. The school counseling scholar is not exempt. To challenge our biases and therefore commit to work that is of greater relevance and integrity, we encourage you to consider a number of external influences in the construction of the research questions you pursue.

One primary external mechanism that needs to influence the construction of an effective research question is an awareness of trends found in the key contemporary literature. In addition to our own beliefs and experiences in the schools, what do our professional organizations suggest are required of a school counselor? For example, Wilkerson and colleagues (2013) were interested in how school counseling programs that were Recognized ASCA Model Programs (RAMPs) predicted students' annual academic performance outcomes. In addition to considering the conceptual recommendations tied to professional organizations such as the American School Counseling Association (ASCA), a researcher can look to the theoretical or empirical literature and identify trends or findings that can inform or even construe a question itself. Returning to the work of Greg Brigman and colleagues (2007), they consulted over 50 years of scholarship from a variety of disciplines, which in turn informed the construction of their school counseling intervention. As their work matured, they later examined how their school counseling intervention affected student development in the areas consistent with

Table 4.2. Strategies in Consulting the Literature

(1) Identify useful keywords.

(2) Start with the most relevant databases to search for your literature. For example, most university library systems have access to a great variety of relevant databases in addition to PsycInfo, ERIC, and Ebscohost.

(3) Consider incubators of school counseling resources, for example, the Center for School Counseling Outcome Research and Evaluation (CSCORE), the Collaborative for Academic, Social, and Emotional Learning (CASEL), ASCA, and state school counseling resources.

(4) Follow the breadcrumbs—who do the authors you are reading cite? Are there consistent author names or communities of scholars doing research related to your topic?

(5) What is the time period? Is a work still relevant if it is more than a decade old?

(6) Stay focused on the most relevant literature and watch out for the rabbit holes of unrelated literature; be open to diverse sources, but only when it is helpful and timely.

their initial literature searches (Webb et al., 2019). Finally, the literature itself can be a source of a research question; for example, Griffith and colleagues (2019) performed a systemic 10-year review of the school counseling intervention research to answer questions such as those about the number of intervention studies, features about designs, and where they were being published, among others.

In considering the literature, we do encourage a deep, primary competence in the school counseling literature in particular, but we also believe that it is important that school counseling scholars consider allied literatures as well. For example, in considering treatment outcomes across a variety of clinical and community settings, researchers have concluded that there are certain common features of effective counseling practice that contribute to client outcomes (e.g., Wampold et al., 1997). Given that these results were drawn almost entirely outside of school settings, a school counseling scholar might construct a research question to see if the same common factors predict desirable student specific outcomes. In addition to inspiring research questions, the extant literature might challenge a school counseling scholar to revise their assumptions. Relevant research areas to explore include career counseling, child and adolescent psychology, educational psychology, general counseling, mental health, school psychology, school social work, social justice education, and special education. We don't want to infer erroneously that the school counseling literature is insufficient, but the broader literature can certainly inform and inspire a great number of our specific research questions.

Beyond the literature, we encourage school counseling scholars to look outward to social trends and the needs of students and schools. Ideally, schools are intended to support the personal, social, and academic development for a range of students, yet there is evidence that schools have contributed to differing achievement, disciplinary, and social outcomes, especially for ethnic minority students (Merolla & Jackson, 2019). As education leaders, school counselors should commit to practices that affect learning climates and reduce gaps in outcomes (ASCA, 2019). Likewise, school counseling scholars should craft research questions that contribute to what is known about structural inequities in school systems and how interventions affect outcomes for the greatest diversity of students. Recent attention to antiracist education and counseling practices are clear examples of how school counseling scholars might challenge school inequalities (Holcomb-McCoy, 2021). One example research question is from Stickl Haugen and colleagues (in press), who completed a Delphi study to answer what should be included in a list of empirically based antiracist school counseling competencies. Drawing from responses offered by school counselors, directors, and counselor educators, the authors reported certain aspects of awareness, attitudes, knowledge, characteristics, and behaviors intended to dismantle racism and promote equity in schools. These externally focused research questions have the potential to affect broader policy and societal concerns, yet with pertinence that can affect the everyday experiences of educators and students.

We want to offer one more important consideration relative to the importance of looking outward. By nature, school counseling is concerned with intervening on behalf of students, educators, and other school stakeholders; therefore, the preponderance of our scholarship needs to have

Table 4.3. Look Outward

Authors' Example

In Table 4.1, I (Matthew) described my beliefs about how a school counselor can serve students and members of the school community. These beliefs are informed by a variety of sources, including empirical (e.g., Brigman et al., 2007) and theoretical counseling literature (e.g., humanistic and mindfulness-based interventions), as well as other sciences (e.g., neuroscience, evolutionary psychology) and prominent scholars (e.g., Bruce Perry, Alison Gopnik, Thomas Metzinger, John Powell, and Anil Seth). These literatures influence how I frame my research questions in a number of ways. For example, I am interested in the psychological and social mechanisms that can be applied in counseling practices and that have been consistently shown to be the most influential on a variety of positive student behavioral outcomes. From the literature, I was able to identify a 4-year longitudinal study on the effects of executive functioning on middle school students' academic achievement outcomes (Samuels et al., 2016).

clear implications for practice. This said, many of our empirical studies are designed in a way that is informative and yet not reflective of a specific counseling practice or intervention outcome. There is a pressure to make our work relevant. While this pressure is real, it is nonetheless essential that authors do not use findings from the outside literature to aid in the overextension of their own results. As stated, a research question inspires the empirical study design, and it establishes the boundaries of the implications that can be proffered in the discussion section when interpreting your findings. An appropriate way to use the related literature is to compare and contrast the findings that result from your current study. It is inappropriate to make leaps in interpretation simply because there is some marginal topical relatedness between your study and the literature you cite.

Step 3: Articulate the Research Question

One general motivation in looking inward toward one's suppositions pertaining to a topic and then extending outward toward the prevailing knowledge in the field is to ascertain a sense of one's position as a scholar. In other words, these steps toward a research question inform the scholar about what can be known about a given topic and how this can inspire a potential research question. Another motivation in these processes is to begin to whittle away at misconceptions or impractical ideas about a topic. For example, as a scholar you might be interested in the single definitive intervention that can work for all kids in all types of schools. When you look inward you might find that it is your own inclination to believe that "all kids are the same," causing you to neglect some of the cultural and psychological differences across children. In a similar way, after consulting the literature, you might find that there exists a paucity of evidence in support of a "silver bullet" intervention for all schools. This whittling away process is intended to make our research questions more precise and empirically plausible; the third tactic in constructing an effective research question further truncates our conceptions. Whereas looking inward and then outward generally pertains to the concept that underpins the research question, the third step pivots to a focus on what is empirically feasible—the school counseling scholar must consider what types of research questions can be asked and what qualities must be included to explore the topic systematically. In short, the third step is to consider the structure of and constraints to the research question itself.

The third step involves articulating your initial question. There is no ideal question, even after you accomplish each of the prior or subsequent steps. At this stage though, the agenda is to start to identify the words that most closely resemble the topic of interest, as inspired by what you found both inward and outward. While there is some utility in precision, now is not the time to get overwhelmed if you cannot find the perfect words; write your question and revise as needed.

Within this step the scholar must consider the various types of research questions, including descriptive, relational, and causal. Each of these three types of questions suggests different intentions for scholars, and the ways in which these different types of questions are posed in turn affect how empirical projects are designed and interpreted.

A descriptive research question is posed by a scholar who intends to elucidate a phenomenon or qualities about a phenomenon. Later in this textbook, colleagues will describe the differences between quantitative and qualitative approaches to design and analyses, but it is important to note that both traditions can be used for the purposes of a descriptive research question. For example, Hilts and colleagues (2019) proposed the following descriptive research question: "What do school counselors perceive as relevant obstacles to implementing a school counseling program that earns the RAMP designation?" (p. 2). These authors chose to utilize a type of qualitative approach called phenomenology, wherein they used interview questions to elicit the sampled counselors' perceptions pertaining to RAMP, and participants perceptions of procedural difficulties in procuring this status. Alternatively, if these scholars intended to answer a related descriptive question quantitively, they would have to revise their question slightly to something like "What is the frequency of certain obstacles that typically confront a school counselor who intends to implement a RAMP program?" In both examples, the intention is to identify qualities or occurrences in themselves, as opposed to how two or more qualities or events relate to one another or as one might predict the occurrence of the other.

A second type of research question is relational in nature. A relational question intends to provide the scholar with information about how two or more qualities or events interface with the other. For example, Cornell and Huang (2016) raised the question "Are the effects of an authoritative school climate confined to certain risk behaviors, such as those involving school behavior (e.g., fighting at school), or do they extend to a wider array of risk behaviors including those observed primarily outside of school, such as substance use?" (p. 2248). This research question is relational because the researchers were interested in how one quality (i.e., authoritative school climate) is tethered to certain student risk behaviors. In this example, the researchers used a cross-sectional research design, with data drawn from a single time period. In this way, there are associations between school climate and student risk behaviors, but it is inappropriate to suggest that one caused the other.

Table 4.4. Causal Language: One Example

Authors' Example

In my work, I (Matthew) want to show how a certain school counseling intervention has a causal influence on student outcomes such as changes in executive functioning, feelings of connectedness to the school, and academic achievement. For example, in proposing our third research question—"Does the intervention affect students' performance on a standardized achievement measure?"—we offer very plain language, and yet it is evident by the choice of the word "affect" that we are suggesting there is something about the particular intervention that will contribute to the desired student learning outcome.

Different from descriptive and relational research questions, a causal research question does attempt to answer whether one or more qualities or events causes or affects the manifestation of another theoretically related quality or event. In a classic study, Sink and Stroh (2003) asked, "Does school counselors' work in elementary schools with well-established CSCPs (Comprehensive School Counseling Programs) promote higher academic achievement in students?" (p. 351). By assigning a code for the amount of CSCP implementation, the authors found that highly implemented CSCPs had a causal link with academic performance for third- and fourth-grade students. Although there are likely to be a number of influences on the academic outcomes, the specific intent of the research question and the related design afforded the scholars compelling evidence to suggest that the school counseling program had some clear effect on the student outcomes.

Step 4: Establish a Research Community

Effective research is rarely accomplished in isolation. Most contemporary empirical studies are done by a group of scholars, including work performed together on a single study or a group of allied researchers who collaborate over many years and across multiple studies. There are many advantages to a communal approach to research, including the interchange of ideas, building off of each other's strengths, and protecting against each other's blind spots.

We encourage novice and even senior scholars to forge effective relationships with others working in similar topical and research design areas. Many scholars will already have a research community composed of relationships with mentors and colleagues. These preexisting relationships are incredibly important, and they should be valued and maintained. We also encourage scholars to cultivate new relationships. Who is asking similar questions? Are there scholars whose work inspires me? Although it can often be intimidating to cold-call another scholar, for the most part, people are excited and humbled by others who are interested in their work.

Another community of relevance to school counseling scholars is our community partners. McMahon and Patel (2019) suggest that it is best for school counseling scholars to include a team of their school and community members to assess who potentially benefits from the selected interventions. Similarly, Bowers and Lemberger (2016) posit that it is important to harmonize a research agenda with the needs of key stakeholders and students. There are a variety of community partners that a school counseling scholar should consider, including an advisory board, district research administrators, and student interest groups, among others. These groups of individuals can inspire ideas, help clarify the important needs of the school community, and advise whether certain research questions and designs are feasible. Furthermore, consulting community partners is a great way to generate an ongoing professional community that can help disseminate and implement any useful findings.

Step 5: Identify a Research Tradition and Analysis Plan

For school counseling scholars, there is an incredible diversity of research traditions and analysis plans that are pertinent to our work. To preface what will be elaborated on in more detail in subsequent chapters found in this book, it is important to recognize the primary distinction between the qualitative and quantitative traditions. Generally speaking, the function of qualitative research is to elicit the facets of a phenomenon or how individuals attribute meaning to that phenomenon. This is different from quantitative designs whereby the researcher aims to identify patterns or manipulate outcomes.

Table 4.5. Considerations Created by a Research Community

Authors' Example

As a scholar, I (Matthew) consider a variety of communities, including the K–12 students I work with, educators, graduate student trainees, and the broader school counseling profession. Each of these groups affects my research questions in a different way. With K–12 students, I want to pursue research questions that can have a positive influence on their lives without dictating adult-only outcomes for them. With educators, I am concerned about how the research question can be pursued in a feasible manner. For example, will the school counselor have access to these students during the school day? Will teachers be involved in any intervention so that there is co-regulation and reinforcement that might occur beyond the actual counseling contact? And to the broader academic community, I am interested in answering research questions that can affect how allied disciplines consider the usefulness and scope of school counseling.

Typically, with some nuanced exceptions that are beyond the scope of this overview, a qualitative study requires no prior formal hypothesis about the outcome of a study and instead attempts to provide the researcher with the ingredients to proffer a theory, whereas quantitative research requires the scholar to acknowledge and test a priori assumptions about an established theory.

There is no definitive algorithm for knowing how a particular research question might contribute to a certain research design or analysis plan. This said, there are a number of words that might be more closely associated with one tradition or plan. For example, when a scholar asks about the "effects" of a school counseling intervention on student-level outcomes, it is most likely a causal quantitative type of question. This is different from a qualitative question, whereby the question might be to describe the lived experiences of students who realized improved academic performance after participation in a school counselor–led small-group intervention.

We would like to offer one important caveat that occurs far too often in research, namely, the choice of a research tradition or analysis plan due to the scholar's preference or familiarity. Instead, it is important that the design of the study and how the data are analyzed align with the nature of the question, not the attributes or preferences of the scholar. It is equally important to not exceed one's resources or areas of competence, and to reconcile this tension we encourage scholars to hark back to Step 4 and find colleagues or research partners who might be able to lend methodological expertise to help construct a design more likely to answer the desired research question.

Step 6: Consider Alternative and Adjunctive Research Questions

Throughout this chapter we have discussed the construction of a single research question. This said, rarely does a project require a single research

Table 4.6. Analytic Considerations

Authors' Example
It is important to craft research questions that best serve the data. I (Matthew) have preferences for certain analytic approaches such as longitudinal and nested analyses (see Selig et al., 2017) because I believe that they uniquely suit school counseling. This said, I also believe that it is important to connect quantitative outcomes with qualitative experiences of the students. As such, in recent years I have made an effort to include both causal quantitative research questions and descriptive qualitative questions in my projects.

question, and, instead, there are often multiple questions that build off of or coordinate with the others. We encourage scholars to consider the benefits of posing each research question in a cogent yet thorough manner. For example, if a school counseling scholar is interested in what factors contribute to culturally diverse students' career interests, it is advisable to include a separate question for each anticipated research-related outcome. The first question might be "What influences do children from culturally diverse communities cite as most influential in career information?" A second question might be "What influences do children from culturally diverse communities cite as most influential in career choice?" Although these two questions are quite related, there is an important distinction in the subtle differences. By asking these two questions, we might be able to make initial qualitative inferences about how information is different from the actual choices made by students from a variety of cultural backgrounds.

Conclusion

As we close, we want to echo a point offered earlier in the chapter—there are many important research questions that school counseling scholars can ask. These questions have the potential to affect a great number of individuals and even entire school communities. This said, it should be noted that there are certain questions that are incredibly urgent and yet terribly underrepresented in the school counseling literature. We encourage each scholar to consider the importance of the counseling process and outcome research questions, as these types of studies contribute critical information about how best to provide interventions and counseling services that are most beneficial to our students. This, after all, is the purpose of the work.

In a recent 10-year content analysis of the most affiliated counseling journals, Griffith and colleagues (2019) found that less than 1% of the more than six thousand published articles were school counseling intervention studies. In that small group of studies, the preponderance of them were quasi-experimental, single-group, and pre/posttest design with a fairly small sample size. While it is infelicitous to discount the importance of these research designs, the school counseling profession needs more studies with empirical validity and generalizability.

Most research questions have an answer that is interesting to someone. This said, considering the state of the science, we highly encourage all readers to consider how their interests can be made into process- or outcome-related research questions. If school counseling is primarily a support profession, then we require evidence that our efforts are accomplishing our ambitions.

References

American School Counselor Association. (2019). ASCA National Model: A framework for school counseling programs (4th ed.).

Babbie, E. R. (2016). *The practice of social research* (14th ed.). Cengage.

Balkin, R. S., & Kleist, D. M. (2016). *Counseling research: A practitioner-scholar approach*. John Wiley & Sons.

Bardhoshi, G., Swanston, J., & Kivlighan, D. M. (2020). Social–behavioral stories in the kindergarten classroom: An app-based counseling intervention for increasing social skills. *Professional School Counseling, 23*(1), 1–14. doi:10.1177/2156759X20919374

Blanco, P. J., Holliman, R. P., & Carroll, N. C. (2019). The effect of child-centered play therapy on intrinsic motivation and academic achievement of at-risk elementary school students. *Journal of Child and Adolescent Counseling, 5*(3), 205–220. doi:10.1080/23727810.2019.1671758

Bowers, H., & Lemberger, M. E. (2016). A person-centered humanistic approach to performing evidence-based school counseling research. *Person-Centered & Experiential Psychotherapies, 15*(1), 55–66. doi:10.1080/14779757.2016.1139502

Bowers, H., Lemberger-Truelove, M. E., Whitford, D. K. (2020). Kindergarteners are ready to learn: Executive functioning and social-emotional effects for a pilot school counseling intervention applying Advocating Student-Within-Environment theory. *Journal of Humanistic Counseling, 59*(1), 3–19. doi:10.1002/johc.12126

Brigman, G. A., Webb, L. D., & Campbell, C. (2007). Building skills for school success: Improving the academic and social competence of students. *Professional School Counseling, 10*(3), 279–288.

Bryan, J., Holcomb-McCoy, C., Moore-Thomas, C., & Day-Vines, N. L. (2009). Who sees the school counselor for college information? A national study. *Professional School Counseling, 12*(4), 280–291.

Carey, J. C., & Dimmitt, C. (2006). Resources for school counselors and counselor educators: The center for school counseling outcome research. *Professional School Counseling, 9*(4), 416–420. doi:10.5330/prsc.9.4.b66gwmp0h64476h3

Cornell, D., & Huang, F. (2016). Authoritative school climate and high school student risk behavior: A cross-sectional multi-level analysis of student self-reports. *Journal of Youth and Adolescence, 45*(11), 2246–2259.

Dollarhide, C. T., Gibson, D. M., & Saginak, K. A. (2008). New counselors' leadership efforts in school counseling: Themes from a year-long qualitative study. *Professional School Counseling, 11*(4), 262–271.

Dollarhide, C. T., & Lemberger, M. E. (2006). "No child left behind": Implications for school counselors. *Professional School Counselor, 9*(4), 295–304.

Goodman-Scott, E., & Boulden, R. (2020). School counselors' experiences with the section 504 process: "I want to be a strong team member . . . [not] a case manager." *Professional School Counseling, 23*(1), Article 2156759X20919378.

Griffith, C., Mariani, M., McMahon, H. G., Zyromski, B., & Greenspan, S. B. (2019). School counseling intervention research: A 10-year content analysis of ASCA-and ACA-affiliated journals. *Professional School Counseling, 23*(1), 1–12.

Harris, P. N., Shillingford, M. A., & Bryan, J. (2019). Factors influencing school counselor involvement in partnerships with families of color: A social cognitive exploration. *Professional School Counseling, 22*(1), 1–10. doi:10.1177/2156759X18814712

Heppner, P. P., Wampold, B. E., Owen, J., Thompson, M. N., & Wang, K. T. (2016). *Research design in counseling* (4th ed.). Cengage Learning.

Hilts, D., Kratsa, K., Joseph, M., Kolbert, J. B., Crothers, L. M., & Nice, M. L. (2019). School counselors' perceptions of barriers to implementing a RAMP-designated school counseling program. *Professional School Counseling, 23*(1), Article 2156759X19882646.

Holcomb-McCoy, C. (Ed.). (2021). *Antiracist counseling in schools and communities.* American Counseling Association.

Lemberger, M. E. (2010). Advocating Student-Within-Environment: A humanistic theory for school counseling. *The Journal of Humanistic Counseling, Education and Development, 49*(2), 131–146. doi:10.1002/j.2161-1939.2010.tb00093.x

Lemberger-Truelove, M. E., & Bowers, H. (2019). An Advocating Student-within-Environment approach to school counseling. In C. T. Dollarhide & M. E. Lemberger-Truelove (Eds.), *Theories of School Counseling for the 21st Century* (pp. 266–294). Oxford University Press.

Lemberger-Truelove, M. E., Carbonneau, K. J., Atencio, D. J., Zieher, A. K., & Palacios, A. F. (2018). Self-regulatory growth effects for young children participating in a combined social and emotional learning and mindfulness-based intervention. *Journal of Counseling & Development, 96*(3), 289–302.

Lemberger, M. E., Carbonneau, K., Selig, J. P., & Bowers, H. (2018). The role of social- emotional mediators on middle school students' academic growth as fostered by an evidence-based intervention. *Journal of Counseling and Development, 96*(1), 27–40. doi:10.1002/jcad.12175

Lemberger, M. E., & Clemens, E. V. (2012). Connectedness and self-regulation as constructs of the Student Success Skills program in inner-city African-American elementary students. *Journal of Counseling and Development, 90*(4), 450–458. doi:10.1002/ j.1556-6676.2012.00056.x

Lemberger, M. E., & Hutchison, B. (2014). Advocating Student-Within-Environment: A humanistic approach for therapists to animate social justice in the schools. *Journal of Humanistic Psychology, 54*(1), 28–44. doi:10.1177/0022167812469831

Lemberger, M. E., Selig, J. P., Bowers, H., & Rogers, J. E. (2015). Effects of the Student Success Skills program on executive functioning skills, feelings of connectedness, and academic achievement in a predominantly Hispanic, low-income middle school district. *Journal of Counseling & Development, 93*(1), 25–37.

Maxwell, S. E., Lau, M. Y., & Howard, G. S. (2015). Is psychology suffering from a replication crisis? What does "failure to replicate" really mean? *American Psychologist, 70*(6), 487–498.

McMahon, H. G., & Patel, S. (2019). Who benefits? Adding inclusive innovation into the evidence-based school counseling research agenda. *Professional School Counseling, 22*(1b), 1–7. doi:10.1177/2156759X19834439

Merolla, D. M., & Jackson, O. (2019). Structural racism as the fundamental cause of the academic achievement gap. *Sociology Compass, 13*(6), e12696. https://doi. org/10.1111/ soc4.12696

Milsom, A., & Morey, M. (2019). Does RAMP matter? Comparing elementary student grades and absences in one district. *Professional School Counseling, 22*(1), 1–10. doi:10.1177/ 2156759X19847977

Mulhern, C. (under review). Beyond teachers: Estimating individual guidance counselors' effects on educational attainment. Working Paper.

Samuels, W. E., Tournaki, N., Blackman, S., & Zilinski, C. (2016). Executive functioning predicts academic achievement in middle school: A four-year longitudinal study. *The Journal of Educational Research, 109*(5), 478–490.

Selig, J. P., Trott, A., & Lemberger, M. E. (2017). Multilevel modeling for research in group work. *Journal for Specialists in Group Work, 42*(2), 135–151. doi:10.1080/01933922.2017.1282571

Silberzahn, R., Uhlmann, E. L., Martin, D. P., Anselmi, P., Aust, F., Awtrey, E., . . . & Carlsson, R. (2018). Many analysts, one data set: Making transparent how variations in analytic choices affect results. *Advances in Methods and Practices in Psychological Science, 1*(3), 337–356.

Sink, C. A., & Stroh, H. R. (2003). Raising achievement test scores of early elementary school students through comprehensive school counseling programs. *Professional School Counseling, 6*(5), 350–364.

Stickl Haugen, J., Bledsoe, K. G., Burgess, M., & Rutledge, M. L. (2022). Framework of anti-racist school counseling competencies: A Delphi study. *Journal of Counseling & Development, 100*(3), 252–265. https://doi.org/10.1002/jcad.12422

Wachter-Morris, C. A., & Wester, K. L. (2020). Functions and prevalence of self-directed violence in adolescence. *Journal of Child and Adolescent Counseling, 6*(2), 110–123. doi:10.1080/23727810.2020.1719352

Wampold, B. E., Mondin, G. W., Moody, M., Stich, F., Benson, K., & Ahn, H. N. (1997). A meta-analysis of outcome studies comparing bona fide psychotherapies: Empirically, "all must have prizes." *Psychological Bulletin, 122*(3), 203–215.

Webb, L., Brigman, G., Carey, J., Villares, E., Wells, C., Sayer, A., Harrington, K., & Chance, E. (2019). Results of a randomized controlled trial of the Student Success Skills program on grade 5 students' academic and behavioral outcomes. *Journal of Counseling & Development, 97*(4), 398–408.

Wilkerson, K., Pérusse, R., & Hughes, A. (2013). Comprehensive school counseling programs and student achievement outcomes: A comparative analysis of RAMP versus non-RAMP schools. *Professional School Counseling, 16*(3), 172–184.

Yarkoni, T. (2019). *The generalizability crisis.* PsyArXiv Preprints. https://psyarxiv.com/jqw35

Zyromski, B., & Mariani, M. A. (2016). *Facilitating evidence-based, data-driven school counseling: A manual for practice.* Corwin Press.

5

Developmental and Social Considerations When Conducting Research With Children and Adolescents

Taryne M. Mingo and Demetrius Cofield

Developmental and Social Considerations When Conducting Research With Children and Adolescents

This chapter will examine how the complexity of school settings contributes to challenges school counselor educators (SCEs) and school counseling doctoral students face when conducting research with children and adolescents in schools. We will also explore the implications of external social factors that impact research with children and adolescents across geographic location and grade level. A case study demonstrating how a doctoral student effectively organized and collected data while also considering the developmental and social contexts of school settings is explored. Finally, we will conclude with a review of ethical and boundary considerations for doing research with children and adolescents. The overall goal of this chapter is to encourage SCEs, as well as doctoral students in counselor education, to consider all aspects of children's developmental and social contexts prior to implementing research in school settings, and to engage in research practices appropriate for children and adolescents of all backgrounds. For the purposes of this chapter, the terms "SCE" and "school counseling doctoral student" will be collectively labeled as school researchers unless specified separately.

To provide practical applications for school researchers collecting data in a school setting, the first section of this chapter will incorporate my (Taryne Mingo) experiences of conducting research, grounded in an antiracism framework, across multiple schools as an SCE. I am a former elementary school counselor who conducted research in my respective school building that examined the racial identity development of students of color

Taryne M. Mingo and Demetrius Cofield, *Developmental and Social Considerations When Conducting Research With Children and Adolescents* In: *School Counseling Research*. Edited by: Brett Zyromski and Carey Dimmitt, Oxford University Press. © Oxford University Press 2023. DOI: 10.1093/oso/9780197650134.003.0005 in predominantly white academic settings (e.g., classrooms, cafeteria, playground). Two years later, in the role of an SCE, I found conducting research in schools where I was not known, as well as accessing the school's students, to be significantly more challenging. These challenges are explored in the next section of this chapter to illustrate the impact of common barriers to conducting social-justice-oriented research in schools as an outside researcher.

As a preview to considering how to navigate these challenges, I decided to recruit school counseling graduate students interning in elementary school settings, as both co-investigators and research participants, to be an alternate path to conducting my research in schools. This gave me access to students and allowed me to mentor my graduate students at the same time. The research study was titled "Elementary Student Racial Identity Awareness and Counselor-Trainee Cultural Consciousness Development." The first goal of the study was to have school counseling graduate students (counselor-trainees), in the role of co-investigators, examine racial identity awareness of elementary students through an expressive arts-style interview method. The second goal of the study was to explore how these school counselor graduate students, in the role of research participants, conceptualized the racial identity development in the elementary students whom they interviewed, and how they perceived their own cultural consciousness development in a group counseling setting. As mentioned in Chapter 1, our goal as school researchers is to be intentional and mindful about implementing antiracist and social justice-oriented practices. As an SCE, I want future school counselors who conduct research within school settings to be self-aware of one's own social contexts and prior experiences that may impact their relationships with students. The intersection of research roles and the attention to the conceptualization of racial identity across multiple participants and settings made the research both richer and more complicated to conduct. I served as the primary investigator for the study, and, as an SCE, still encountered a variety of barriers when having graduate students work as co-investigators with me to conduct research, particularly research grounded in antiracism, in their respective elementary internship sites.

The Complexity of School Settings

Research is recognized as an essential tool for the counseling profession (Guiffrida et al., 2011; Kaffenberger, 2012; Rowell, 2006). However, conducting research in schools can be a challenge due to the complexity of school personnel, school climate, school stakeholders, community relationships, and/or previous negative experiences with university-affiliated or outside researchers (Boyland et al., 2019; Bright, 2018; Chandler et al., 2018). From my (Taryne Mingo) experience as an SCE, I highlight three social-context barriers to implementing research in school settings in this section: (1) school faculty resistance, (2) inability to provide anonymity and confidentiality, and (3) time constraints. Navigating these barriers makes it more challenging to conduct research that respects the developmental and social contexts specific to children and adolescents in school settings.

As an example, one of my graduate students found removing children and adolescents from classrooms for interviews to be a challenge because teachers did not want their students to miss instructional time. In an effort to minimize teacher resistance or frustration, my graduate students felt tempted to rush through individual interviews with students to return them to class by an agreed-upon time. Providing enough time to respond to the questions of children and adolescents prior to conducting research can contribute to developing a safe environment for research participants to share personal information. Therefore, I reminded the graduate students assisting me with my research study not to yield to the pressure of classroom time constraints, and to be honest with school stakeholders about the requirements and benefits of conducting the research successfully. Respecting the amount of time necessary for children and adolescents to feel safe with the researcher can certainly present challenges in a school setting but is a necessary step in conducting quality research. Ignoring the developmental and social contexts of children and adolescents can lead to inadequate data due to data collection methods that are too focused on increasing the number of participants, getting results quickly, and, ultimately, promoting interventions that are not reflective of overall student experiences in school settings (Dahir et al., 2009; Dahir & Stone, 2009).

Barriers to Implementing Research in School Settings

Faculty resistance can come in the form of administration and/or teachers' direct actions to prevent school researchers from conducting research by verbally refusing the study or by creating barriers that prevent school researchers from conducting research successfully (Farber, 2006). These barriers can take the form of only allowing researchers to conduct the study in the presence of school faculty, teachers who only allow students to participate during recess or lunch, preventing researchers from conducting the study during school hours, or not providing space for researchers to maintain participant anonymity or confidentiality. The *inability to provide anonymity and confidentiality* to research participants, either due to lack of space or the presence of a faculty member, can bring many research studies to a screeching halt. *Time constraints*, such as collecting data during lunch or recess, have a doubly negative effect. First, it removes children and adolescents from already limited social interaction opportunities during the school day to meet the needs of the school researcher. Second, most lunch and recess time frames are approximately 25–30 minutes long. This is not long enough to promote a safe environment with the researcher, answer participants' questions about the study, or provide participants with enough time to respond to the researcher's questions without feeling rushed. Attempting to conduct research after school hours can skew data results to students whose parents can afford after-school care or students with personal transportation and, as a result, misrepresent overall student experiences within the school. As suggested in Chapter 1, school researchers should take all steps necessary to ensure that their evidence-based strategies or interventions are not simply a reflection of a privileged few that are not representative of the experiences or voices of everyone.

Therefore, it is recommended that school researchers have an in-person meeting with school administration to address these barriers, even if the study has been approved by the district and your university or college institutional review board (IRB). Some school districts have an online approval process for any research conducted within their district, and school researchers may only be notified of their study's approval via email or letter. We recommend that school researchers schedule an in-person meeting to discuss the full scope of the study, including data collection procedures pertaining to the level of faculty participation, necessary time with students, and the type of space required to complete the study successfully.

School researchers should emphasize the importance of participant anonymity where necessary. Ensure, also, that school administrators are aware of the possible negative impact of data results if these measures cannot be guaranteed for potential research participants. That stated, school researchers should also be prepared to delay or discontinue studies where school administrators are unable to provide necessary accommodations for the successful implementation of a research study. As mentioned earlier, inability to navigate these barriers may pressure school researchers to conduct studies void of the developmental and social considerations of child and adolescent participants and can potentially lead to outcomes or interventions that inaccurately reflect overall student experiences in school settings. An example of encountering such barriers is detailed in the following personal account as I attempted to carry out a study, which highlighted the importance of antiracism in classrooms, across multiple elementary school settings as a school counselor educator.

Upon receiving IRB approval for my (Taryne Mingo) research study, Elementary Student Racial Identity Awareness and Counselor-Trainee Cultural Consciousness Development, I confirmed the number of graduate students willing to conduct the study in their respective elementary school internship sites. Each graduate student was given a research packet filled with materials to conduct the study successfully, including permission forms for school administrators and parents. Of the four graduate students who accepted a packet, two graduate students reported back that the principal at their internship site refused to allow the study at their school. Evidently, the topic of the study was the basis of refusal. One principal refused the study for fear of potential backlash from parents if word got out about the topic of the study in their predominantly white school district. The second principal stated simply that he "did not want that drama here." Such responses demonstrate that school researchers who wish to conduct research in schools may face barriers to implementation not only due to faculty resistance, inability to provide anonymity or confidentiality, or time restraints, but also as a result of the research topic and the school's fear of exposure. Interestingly enough, the goal of my study was to promote antiracist educational settings by learning about the academic experiences of elementary students of color in a predominantly white school, so as to provide solutions for making their educational experience more welcoming and inclusive. Nonetheless, I had to also admit that learning about the experiences of students of color would mean exposing the schools' history of anti-Black policies and procedures. As a result, I lost both potential school districts, as well as the two graduate students as co-investigators, given that their role was tied to their internship site's participation in the study.

The Implications of External Social Factors on Research in School Settings

After successfully navigating barriers to research implementation, this chapter also advocates for a focus on developmental and social considerations to conducting research with children and adolescents to promote inclusive strategies and interventions within schools. The complexity of geographic location and grade level across school districts can have a unique impact on conducting research with children and adolescents in school settings (Hannon, 2016). This means recognizing that external social factors such as how school funding and resource availability may vary across location and grade level impact the school experiences of children and adolescents and can significantly impact the research process (Bright, 2018). Various educational studies have demonstrated how social factors like zip codes can affect the quality of education a child receives (Berg & Gleason, 2018). It may also impact the perspective of the researcher if the school is located in a zip code that is considered "less desirable" in comparison with other geographic locations. Therefore, the location of a child's school can contribute to external influences on their academic and social experiences and should be considered in the development of research studies and subsequent interventions. In addition, researchers should remain mindful of their own implicit biases that may force them to develop research founded in deficit perspectives.

Grade-level indicators should also be a concern for those conducting research in K–12 settings, not only for gauging cognitive ability in research participation, but also for external social factors specific to each developmental level. Conducting research on behalf of children and adolescents without considering age-appropriate data collection methods can lead to skewed and inaccurate data results. Conducting research with children and adolescents without recognizing external social factors that influence their daily school experience can lead to the spread of misinformation about those experiences. Therefore, school researchers must ensure that they are following protocols for data collection methods that are developmentally and socially appropriate, free from bias, and cognizant of external influences on the data collection protocol. The implications of external social factors, specifically, geographic location and grade level, are explored in more detail next.

Geographic Location

One social context consideration for school researchers who wish to conduct research in schools is geographic location. The location of a school has been frequently correlated with the amount of funding and resources a school is given and, as a result, can have a direct impact on the academic experience of its students (Fasasi, 2017). As an SCE, I often notice how school districts located in communities of high poverty or schools labeled as Title 1 are often least desired as potential internship sites or future places of employment by graduate students. In an effort to prevent ongoing bias and promote anti-racist support for K–12 students, I encourage reluctant graduate students to look at the historical impact on those communities and school districts and challenge the half-narrative perspective of K–12 student experiences that may be promoted in spaces of privilege. I encourage school researchers to do the same prior to conducting research in Title 1 schools to prevent deficit perspective-driven interventions and strategies. Therefore, school researchers must be mindful of how seemingly basic external factors, like geographic location, can play a central role in the results of a study. Rural, urban, and suburban school districts often have distinct differences that influence research, including access to resources and funding. For example, it may be prudent when conducting research in rural school districts to budget financially for providing transportation and meals to participants. Conversely, when conducting research in urban school districts, it may be prudent to plan for providing additional funding to the school to ensure access by students, teachers, and parents to the programming, as funding is historically strained in many urban school districts. Therefore, school researchers should consider when it is appropriate to provide resources to participants as part of their research process, in addition to any participation incentives. An example of carrying out these considerations is detailed in a personal account as I (Taryne Mingo) conducted a study in a rural middle school setting with limited resources as an SCE.

In an effort to build connections between community resources and parents of children in a rural, Title 1 school district as a counselor educator, I decided to collaborate with the school counselor to interview parents regarding their perception of resource accessibility within their community, while simultaneously holding a "Resource Fair" that offered dinner and childcare to any parent in attendance. We had agreed to host the event after school hours to increase parental turnout, specifically those parents who worked until after 5:00 p.m. The school counselor and I had also acknowledged the mutual benefit of the study. She could deepen her relationship with parents at the event, while I interviewed parents as an "impartial outsider." I contacted all local organizations and agencies across a range of services, from food pantries to free mental health services, based on a list provided by the school counselor. Eventually local agencies and community partners were invited to the school's resource fair to meet with parents from 5:00 to 8:00 p.m. As a researcher seeking the school's parents as participants, I recruited parents attending the resource fair and offered restaurant coupons to those who consented to participating in the 10-question survey about access to community resources. Recognizing limited transportation in this rural community, I negotiated with the school's principal to provide school bus transportation to and from the event. The negotiation meeting with the principal was a key factor for my study because while getting parents to complete a 10-question survey is inexpensive, access to parents relied heavily on the success of the event. Unfortunately, the event meant using the school's limited resources (e.g., use of school's building equipment, cafeteria, faculty pay for extended time related to transportation and childcare after hours). Therefore, I reached out to my school counseling graduate students to volunteer as hosts for the event, particularly graduate students who were seeking additional community involvement or indirect clinical hours toward their internship to limit the expenses of the school where possible. I also explained to the school administrator and school counselor the various benefits of having the event in the evening rather than during normal school operating hours based on building relationships with parents and teachers and, possibly, providing solutions to parents who felt disconnected from their child's school. Another benefit of the event was acknowledged by the school's teachers. Many of them, I discovered, had never met their students' parents in person, and, as a result, some teachers were able to use the event to schedule mini parent conferences. Perhaps the most beneficial outcome of the event was in challenging the myth that parents who rarely attended parent conferences during the school day "Did not care about their child's education." Teachers were able to interact with their students' families and see how passionately they cared about their child's academics once systemic barriers were removed. I could not think of a better way to interview parents on their perceived best strategies of connecting them to community resources, including their child's teacher, than to carry out one possible solution in real time.

Grade Level

It is clearly critical to consider the cognitive and developmental abilities of the participants being included in research studies in K–12 school settings. Data results could be negatively impacted if school researchers neglect to use developmentally appropriate methods of data collection with children and adolescents, particularly if research methods are combined with minimal self-reflection on behalf of the researcher as to whether the intervention is an appropriate method for children (Griffin et al., 2016). One-on-one interviews are a popular method of data collection for school researchers because they provide direct feedback from a targeted population source (Farber, 2006). Unfortunately, this can be challenging across grade levels, specifically with elementary students. Though sometimes also the case with middle and high school students, limited vocabulary and/or limited verbal expression is a frequent barrier when conducting one-on-one interviews with elementary students. In addition, school researchers conducting research with children should acknowledge power differentials in one-on-one child interviews (Griffin et al., 2016), which could influence responses from participants. Engaging activities allow participants to communicate freely about their experiences and can serve as an incentive for their participation. Incorporating expressive arts activities and games into group counseling sessions, especially at the elementary level, can allow for a fun and safe interviewing atmosphere. Therefore, creating a safe and interactive interview space that encourages alternative forms of communication such as expressive arts is recommended when using one-on-one interviews with elementary-aged children.

Student field observations, another method of data collection for school counselors, can be used across all grade levels and are considered a beneficial form of data collection when attempting to conduct research with limited adult interference. Through field observations, school researchers can observe the interactions among students in different social settings, as well teacher–student interactions. From these observations, the school researcher may be able to evaluate the level of social and emotional experience of participants in different areas around the school. Field observations, however, often rely heavily on adult interpretations of the child's behavior (Griffin et al., 2016). Therefore, they should be considered supplemental to other forms of data collection for a comprehensive perspective on analyzing data and understanding student experiences.

As mentioned earlier, group counseling sessions are great environments that, when organized properly, can encourage open communication in a supportive atmosphere, and they potentially provide significant outcome data that can contribute to future counseling interventions and strategies. Through counseling and psychoeducational-based group sessions school researchers can provide a safe, caring atmosphere for participants to share their experiences with an adult and among each other. For third- to fifth-grade students, 9–11 years of age, we recommend that school researchers incorporate engaging activities that include expressive arts, dance and movement, or sensory techniques to facilitate group discussion. Using group psychoeducational strategies, school researchers can empower older participants by teaching them new skills that give them strategies to address negative experiences in academic settings, such as being able to identify teachers they trust in the building. As an example of generating outcome data within a group setting, school researchers can have group members complete a pretest to analyze preconceived notions about their academic experiences. At the conclusion of the group, the school researchers can administer a posttest with the same questions to determine what percentage of students have learned new skills as a result of the group intervention. Incorporating written self-report instruments or one-on-one interviews at the conclusion of a group is another strategy to produce meaningful outcome data for older students but may not be developmentally appropriate for elementary-aged participants.

When using data collection methods across any grade level, it is also important to consider alternate factors that can have a significant impact on outcome data. For example, a participant who is not having a positive school experience may still not reflect positively on a post-test question related to that topic even after weeks of counseling group sessions. It may not be that the counseling group was ineffective for the student, but that they felt the group setting is not reflective of the classroom setting. Or the conditions that allowed the participant to have positive experiences in school may change because the counseling group is coming to an end. This could be a factor that is never mentioned by the participant in the group setting and may leave the school researcher wondering why outcome data results from the posttest are skewed or inconclusive.

Just as familiarity with students is important when conducting research, participants' trust in adults and other educators can be another significant factor when conducting research with children and adolescents across all grade levels. Developing a relationship with students prior to conducting research should be a goal, when possible, for those conducting research with youth in school settings. Where appropriate, it is best to allow opportunities for shared voice within your research with children. An example of this may be allowing participants to hear the recordings of their sessions and make changes where they deem necessary to the school researcher's notes. Another example, particularly for elementary-aged students, is to allow their drawings or paintings to be visual demonstrations of progress in your interviewing space and include them as part of your outcome data results when shared with school stakeholders.

Grade level within schools can be seen not only as potential identifiers of cognitive processing related to age, but also of each student's capacity to be involved independently in the research process. As mentioned earlier in this chapter some school researchers may have their research stymied because the administration only allows access to students after school hours. While this certainly impacts potential participants at the elementary level, school researchers may find there is more flexibility when it comes to accessing students at the high school level. Specifically, those students may have a degree of freedom to transport themselves, either by car or public transit, to and from school to meet with the school researcher. The following section provides an outline for conducting research in a school setting that incorporates consideration of students' external social factors into research design, research procedures, and data collection.

Considering Ethics and Boundaries When Conducting Research With Children and Adolescents

One of the most important aspects of conducting research is ethics. Chapter 3 of this text explores ethical research practice in depth, but here we will briefly explore ideas for taking student developmental level into consideration when thinking about ethics. Ethics within research establish principles meant to ensure morality and to prevent doing harm to research participants (Mcleod, 2015). When considering research with minors—children and adolescents under the age of 18—this becomes more essential and, in some ways, more complex. When doing research involving children and adolescents school researchers should ensure that any risk associated with the study is not greater than or an addition to their normal way of life (Mcleod, 2015). The American School Counseling Association's (ASCA's) *Ethical Standards for School Counselors* (2016) outlines a code of ethics for school counselors. Even though these standards are not specific to research, they provide a guideline for ethical considerations that can also be applied when conducting research in schools.

One of the most important ethical considerations when working with children and adolescents is consent, which becomes more detailed when conducting research with children. Obtaining consent can be a simple process when conducting research with adults, but working with children and adolescents can present challenges that may not be present with adult participants (Gallagher et al., 2010). Specifically, consent does not only involve the participant, but also their parents or legal guardians. When conducting research with children and adolescents it is crucial to have parental consent because children are not legally able to provide consent for research. Similar to working with adults, parents should be provided information about their child(ren)'s expectations as participants, as well as advantages and disadvantages of research participation. In some instances, parental consent alone can be enough depending on the child's age and developmental level. In other cases, working with children requires assent, in addition to parental consent, particularly when the child or adolescent is older and developmentally able to understand the study. Assent differs from consent because it is an agreement given by a participant under 18 to participate in the study even when they are not legally able to give consent (Chwang, 2015; Coyne, 2010). Obtaining assent should always be considered when conducting research with older children or adolescents even if they are developmentally capable of understanding the study. Furthermore, information provided when obtaining assent from a minor may differ from the information provided to their parents, using language more appropriate for the minor's age and developmental level. Though it may not be a legal requirement, obtaining assent when capable provides evidence of a more ethical study.

When conducting research with children and adolescents the most ethical option is to obtain both consent from the parents and assent from the child or adolescent (Chwang, 2015; Coyne 2010). Though it may appear important and ethical, assent is not always considered a legal requirement when conducting ethical research (Fisher, 2004). This can lead to issues concerning "non-agreeing children" participants in a study (Chwang, 2015). In some cases, utilizing non-agreeing children may be necessary for the study when it is best for the participants to be unaware and parental permission has been obtained. However, with no specific regulations to determine these ethical dilemmas, researchers like Chwang (2015) argue the need for clearer guidelines to be established that would ensure obtaining assent from youth participants unless proven to be more harmful to the study or participants.

As school researchers, it is also important to consider appropriate ethical boundaries when conducting research with students in school settings. We need to be mindful of the power dynamics between ourselves and a child participant (Coyne, 2010; Woodgate et al., 2017). Students may look to the school researcher as an authority figure and feel pressured to participate or feel they have no choice but to participate in a research study (Gallagher et al., 2010; Richardson, 2019). This pressure could also be felt if the student's parents push them to participate or they feel obligated to participate due to their parents (Richardson, 2019). This ethical dilemma becomes even more complex when the school researcher is conducting research with children of school faculty. It is not unheard of, especially in rural school districts, to see a significant number of children attending the same school where their parents are employed (Shepherd et al., 2013). As a result, school researchers may encounter potential ethical dilemmas and boundary concerns due to the proximity and role of the parents and guardians of minor participants. Considering the power differential between adults and children is not something that can be overlooked. The school researcher should take every step possible to ensure that the students can choose to participate or not, without coercion or pressure from authority figures.

Boundaries should also be considered when collecting data. Being mindful of the power differential and potential dual relationship, particularly if you serve as an internship doctoral student, should be considered and addressed when it comes to data collection. It is important to ensure that the child participant is as comfortable as possible disclosing information or actively participating in the study without reservation. In some cases, child participants may feel they cannot be completely honest out of fear of how their words or actions may be interpreted. A clear explanation of where and how data will be collected and used should be provided to the child participant if possible, in order to alleviate these concerns (Woodgate et al., 2017).

Confidentiality should also be considered and explained when conducting research with children and adolescents. This is where an ethical dilemma can present itself for doctoral students when it comes to their role both as a researcher and internship student (Richardson, 2019; Woodgate et al., 2017). Children may present information they may not want revealed to their parents, and the school researcher should provide an explanation of confidentiality prior to participating, as well as be mindful and moral when considering whether or not sensitive information should be reported (Woodgate et al., 2017). When it comes to maintaining confidentiality from the child's parents, the school researcher should always consider the best ethical decision to ensure the well-being of the child and recognize that some collected data may be best left unreported (Gallagher et al., 2010; Richardson, 2019). This stated, school researchers should be mindful of mandatory reporting laws and follow the necessary guidelines if information is presented by the child that must be reported by law or ethical codes. Boundaries should also be considered for the nonparticipating children involved in the research environment. In some cases, children may receive unwanted attention from their peers when being studied and potentially singled out. There are also situations that cause information to be presented or collected from other children who are not participating. Though there are no clear guidelines for these ethical scenarios, it is an ongoing debate within current literature and should be considered when ensuring ethical boundaries within a study by school researchers (Richardson, 2019).

School researchers are likely to find themselves conducting research and studying children and adolescents who come from different cultural backgrounds than their own. As educators and researchers, it is always important to be open and reflective when working with children of different cultural backgrounds. Bias on behalf of school researchers can negatively alter a study if the school researcher is not mindful of inherent biases that may come up before and during the study. It is always important to maintain a multicultural lens to ensure the use of appropriate language, racial and cultural boundaries, and appropriate interventions when researching children and adolescents from different cultural backgrounds.

In the research study example mentioned earlier in this chapter titled "Elementary Student Racial Identity Awareness and Counselor-Trainee Cultural Consciousness Development," graduate students who were racially/ethnically different from the elementary students interviewed were expected to have already developed a trusting relationship with those students prior to implementing the study. Having a preestablished, trusting relationship with students of color was a required aspect of the study for graduate students who would be asking Black and/or Latinx students about racial identity awareness. While parts of this chapter have focused on the impact of researcher bias on evidence-based interventions and strategies, school researchers must also consider how their participants' prior experiences with systemic oppression will be accounted for in data results as mentioned in Chapter 1 of this book. As an example, a white school researcher unaware of how racism has already influenced the life of a fifth-grade Black male student research participant, or who holds the common myth that "children are too young to understand racism or experience it firsthand," will inevitably be perplexed if the student is unwilling or unable to divulge authentic responses to interview/survey questions. We are not suggesting white school researchers should not interview students of color, but we want to highlight the influence of power dynamics and acknowledge the importance of a preestablished, genuine, and trusting relationship with children and adolescents for accurate data results in school settings.

As mentioned earlier, ASCA provides *Ethical Standards for School Counselors* (2016), which should be followed in all aspects of the role as a school counselor and school researcher. Close attention should be given to sections discussing consent, confidentiality, relationships, record keeping and working with underserved populations when conducting school counselor research. In addition, school researchers should always be familiar with all applicable ethical codes and state regulations as well as any guidelines provided by administration or IRB of your study.

Considering Developmental and Social Contexts of Conducting Research in Schools

The following case study describes a doctoral student's research study that actively incorporates developmental and social considerations during data collection with high school students in an urban school district. The case study is presented as a model for doing research in school settings to promote inclusive and developmentally appropriate data-informed interventions and strategies. In addition, school researchers are provided with strategies for working with schools, parents, or guardians, as well as the use of appropriate techniques and interventions when conducting research with children and adolescents.

Case Study

Jamal is a doctoral-level school counseling intern at a Title 1 high school. Within the first 2 months at his internship, Jamal notices that a significant number of students are dropping out of school. When he brings this observation up to his supervisor, she informs him of the increase in student dropout rates over the past few years, as evidenced by the school's database system. Jamal begins to take an interest in the school's high school dropout rate and initiates discussions with his supervisor about what they could do about the issue. Because his supervisor and other school counselor colleagues are stretched thin with a variety of program responsibilities, she suggests that Jamal do some exploration into the situation and identify some possible solutions.

After checking to make sure he is in compliance with his district's policies on conducting an internal study about student outcomes that will not be published, Jamal uses the school database to identify trends among students who have dropped out in the past year. Using this information, he works to identify students he believes are on the same trajectory based on the data collected, specifically looking at student GPA, students in remediation, and classes with a high rate of student failure. Jamal also plans to see if patterns exist in the school's demographic categories, such as race and class. Jamal recognizes that some students drop out of school to earn extra money for their families, so he will specifically focus on high school students identified as socioeconomically disadvantaged.

Jamal recognizes two external social challenges to his study. Many of the students who meet the eligibility requirements for his study work after school and rely on public transportation to leave campus. Therefore, meeting after school is not a possibility for his study due to the limited time availability of potential participants. The second challenge involves interviewing these students during the school day. Doing so would mean removing them from class instruction where they may already be struggling academically, and Jamal does not want his study to contribute further to academic barriers leading to student dropout. He decides to meet with the school's graduation coach to find the best scheduling windows to meet with these students, so he can conduct interviews without negatively impacting the students' academic and work-related obligations. Through collaboration with the graduation coach, he determines the first period of the day, a non-academic period known as homeroom, as the best time not only to interview students for his study, but also to provide resources. These resources would include providing a warm breakfast upon arrival to school, so they would not have to pay for breakfast in the school's cafeteria, and supplying bus transportation vouchers as incentives for their time and participation.

Jamal shares his research and related intervention proposal with his site supervisor and the school's principal. Upon approval, Jamal develops assent forms for potential research participants and consent forms for their parents and guardians. Within each form, Jamal provides a clear explanation regarding the purpose of his study, detailed procedures for implementing the study, and all risks and benefits associated with the study. To alleviate potential concerns from participants and their guardians, Jamal provides a copy of the semi-structured interview questions he will ask each participant and contact information for both him and his site supervisor to answer any additional questions.

Once he receives signed consent and assent forms, Jamal decides to schedule individual interviews with freshman, sophomores, and juniors to inquire about their grades and school engagement. As part of the study and mentioned in both consent and assent forms, Jamal also schedules meetings with participants' teachers to discuss their concerns about students who are failing in an effort to identify possible trends. After collecting the information from student and teacher interviews, Jamal compiles data and identifies trends among students and teachers, including racial and class demographics. At the end of his data analysis, Jamal identifies social and academic barriers contributing to students' inability to complete coursework and related choice to drop out of school. By examining interventions conducted with similar student populations shared on the ASCA website as well as published in the Journal of Professional School Counseling, Jamal identifies some options. He then develops a proposed model for integrated interventions to be implemented by teachers and staff within the school to decrease the student dropout rate. He presents his results as a formal presentation with his supervisor to the other school counselors and the administration to advocate on behalf of these students. The intended outcome of sharing his data analysis and intervention plan is to present student data that is correlated with dropping out, to identify some possible causes for the increased rates of student dropout in their building, and to suggest some research-based interventions that could help improve the situation. He also shares his findings with his university advisor with the hope of conducting a larger, more formal study for possible publication in the future—well aware that if he scales up the study or publishes any findings, he will need to meet both university and district policies for human subjects research standards (see Chapter 3 for additional details regarding the IRB process).

School, Parental, and Guardian Considerations

As a doctoral student researcher, Jamal must first explore all ethical considerations of his study prior to developing a method of data collection and recruiting participants. Remaining cognizant of the appropriate methods of data collection is important when conducting research with children and adolescents. Likewise, full disclosure of one's research questions, process, and procedures should always incorporate the permission of the school and students' parents or guardians prior to data collection, particularly when working with minors. Although the focus of the research study is within the role and responsibilities of a school counselor, he will still need to gain permission from within the school prior to conducting the study. This chapter recommends Jamal begin with permission from his site supervisor or the school's administration, and, upon approval, reach out to students' parents afterward. Parental consent is essential to research, as it provides proof that participants are voluntarily participating in the study and have been given enough information to have a thorough understanding of participant expectations and outcome goals (Coyne, 2010; Mcleod, 2015). Though consent is usually obtained through written consent forms, there are some cases when verbal consent can be appropriate, but this is typically utilized only if written consent is not accessible. Informed consent is a specific type of consent utilized in ethical research and ensures that the participants also understand the possible risks and benefits involved with the study (Coyne, 2010; Mcleod, 2015). Informed consent should be given before a participant begins involvement with research (Mcleod, 2015). This is explored further in Drs. Anita Young and Ileana Gonzalez's Chapter 3, focused on ethically navigating relationships in research development.

All research studies require IRB approval, and, depending on the type of consent agreed upon in the IRB, usually parental permission is required prior to mentioning the research activity or intervention to the student, even at the high school level. For example, research studies that involve students talking about sensitive topics such as sexual abuse, racial identity, gender identity, or religious practices typically require parental consent. These research topics can be particularly important when examining concerns pertaining to school climate, risks to marginalized students, or other social-justice-related advocacy efforts. Conducting research examining these concerns is within the realm of school counseling duties according to the American School Counseling Association (2019). Passive parental permission, allowing the student to participate unless a "Do Not Participate" permission form is signed, is not recommended. Providing assent forms to students prior to talking with them, individually or in a group, is another opportunity to build rapport with students and can assure them about the questions they will be asked and their right to opt out of the study if they choose to participate. A child or adolescent's developmental level is a significant factor that should be considered when determining and discussing assent. While it is essential that the adult providing consent have a thorough understanding of the study, the same method of providing this information may not be as effective when seeking assent from the underage participant. Children may need more detailed explanations, and the language and delivery of the information should be provided in a way that is developmentally appropriate (Woodgate et al., 2017). For this reason, it may be necessary to spend more time not only explaining research expectations, but also ensuring participant comprehension when seeking assent from child and adolescent research participants (Gallagher et al., 2010; Richardson, 2019).

Though high school students are developmentally and cognitively advanced in comparison with elementary-aged students, parental and guardian permission is still required in most research studies even if the student is 18 years of age. According to the Family Educational Rights and Privacy Act (FERPA), parents have the right to be informed about their child's educational records, which can include school counseling notes and activities, unless the student has transferred those rights from their parents upon turning 18 years old or is currently attending school beyond high school.

In the case study, Jamal conducted individual interviews with freshmen, sophomores, and juniors under 18 years of age to identify trends that led to school dropout. He conducted a study based on student information retrieved from the school's database system and school counseling sessions to decrease student dropout. The focus of the study was within the roles and responsibilities of the school counselor and did not involve students talking about sensitive topics. Given Jamal's role as a doctoral school counseling student intern, parental consent was necessary. If this study had been conducted by a school counselor who was employed by the district, it would not require parental and/or guardian permission. However, if the parents request information on the data obtained from the database and interviews, they are allowed access to them under FERPA regulations. For additional information on using data to build relationships with stakeholders in schools, see Steen et al.'s Chapter 2, "Access to Schools: Relationships With Stakeholders and Systems."

Appropriate Use of Techniques and Interventions

Self-reporting instruments are another useful form of data collection—particularly at the high school level when discussing career aspirations. Many school counselors use career-interest inventories with middle and high school students to determine their post-secondary aspirations. Aligning with this intervention, school researchers can then give students a self-report questionnaire that provides data about how many 11th- and 12th-grade students have a defined post-secondary plan as a result of taking this career-interest inventory. School researchers and school counselor partners can then identify the percentage of students without a defined goal and target this specific population through career consultation meetings. In order to provide these kinds of data-based, targeted interventions, it is crucial that students have a clear understanding of confidentiality and that they feel comfortable sharing their responses in a safe space.

Conclusion

This chapter examined how the complexity of school settings contributes to the barriers school researchers face when conducting social-justice-oriented research with children and adolescents. The ways that external social factors such as geographic location and student development level impact research in school settings were explored, and a case study demonstrating how a doctoral student addressed these challenges was included. This chapter concluded with a thorough review of ethical and boundary considerations for school researchers working with children and adolescents. As mentioned earlier, the goal of this chapter is to encourage school researchers to consider developmental and social contexts when conducting research with children and adolescents. School researchers are called to advocate for the profession of school counseling, advocate on behalf of all student populations and school districts, and learn how research can be used to produce appropriate antiracist school counseling strategies across developmental and social frameworks.

References

American School Counselor Association. (2019). The ASCA national model: A framework for school counseling programs (4th ed.). Alexandria, VA.

American School Counseling Association. (2016). *Ethical standards for school counselors.*

Berg, J. H., & Gleason, S. C. (2018). Come together for equity: Rework beliefs, actions and systems through professional learning. *The Journal of Staff Development, 39*(5), 24–27.

Boyland, L. G., Geesa, R. L., Lowery, K. P., Quick, M. M., Mayes, R. D., Kim, J., Elam, N. P., & McDonald, K. M. (2019). Collaborative principal-school counselor preparation: National standards alignment to improve training between principals and school counselors. *International Journal of Educational Leadership Preparation, 14*(1), 188–205. https://files. eric.ed.gov/fulltext/EJ1218852.pdf

Bright, D. J. (2018). The rural gap: The need for exploration and intervention. *Journal of School Counseling, 16*(21), 1–27. https://files.eric.ed.gov/fulltext/EJ1193574.pdf

Chandler, J. W., Burnham, J. J., Riechel, M. E. K., Dahir, C. A., Stone, C. B., Oliver, D. F., Davis, A. P., & Bledsoe, K. G. (2018). Assessing the counseling and non-counseling roles of school counselors. *Journal of School Counseling, 16*(7), 1–33. https://files.eric.ed.gov/fulltext/ EJ1182095.pdf

Chwang, E. (2015). Against harmful research on non-agreeing children. *Bioethics, 29*(6), 431–439. https://doi.org/10.1111/bioe.12117

Coyne, I. (2010). Research with children and young people: The issue of parental (proxy) consent. *Children & Society, 24,* 227–237. https://doi.org/10.1111/j.1099-0860.2009.00216.x

Dahir, C. A., Burnham, J. J., & Stone, C. (2009). Listen to the voices: School counselors and comprehensive school counseling programs. *Professional School Counseling, 12*(3), 182–192. https://doi.org/10.l5330/PSC.n.2010-12.182

Dahir, C. A., & Stone, C. B. (2009). School counselor accountability: The path to social justice and systemic change. *Journal of Counseling & Development, 87*(1), 12–20. https://doi.org/10.1002/j.1556-6678.2009.tb00544.x

Farber, N. K. (2006). Conducting qualitative research: A practical guide for school counselors. *Professional School Counseling, 9*(4), 367–375. https://doi.org/10.1177/2156759X0500900401

Fasasi, R. (2017). Effects of ethnoscience instruction, school location, and parental educational status on learners' attitude towards science. *International Journal of Science Education, 39*(5), 548–564. https://doi.org/10.1080/09500693.2017.1296599

Fisher, C. B. (2004). Informed consent and clinical research involving children and adolescents: Implications of the revised APA Ethics Code and HIPAA, *Journal of Clinical Child and Adolescent Psychology, 33*(4), 832–839. https://doi.org/10.1207/s15374424jccp3304_18

Gallagher, M., Haywood, S. L., Jones, M. W., and Milne, S. (2010). Negotiating informed consent with children in school-based research: A critical review. *Children & Society, 24,* 471–482. https://doi.org/10.1111/j.1099-0860.2009.00240.x

Griffin, K. M., Lahman, M. K., & Opitz, M. F. (2016). Shoulder-to-shoulder research with children: Methodological and ethical considerations. *Journal of Early Childhood Research, 14*(1), 18–27. https://doi.org/10.1177/1476718X14523747

Guiffrida, D. A., Douthit, K. Z., Lynch, M. F., & Mackie, K. L. (2011). Publishing action research in counseling journals. *Journal of Counseling & Development, 89*(3), 282–287

Hannon, M. D. (2016). Professional development needs of urban school counselors: A review of the literature. *Journal of Counselor Preparation & Supervision, 8*(2), 139–154. https://doi.org/10.7729/82.1171

Kaffenberger, C. J. (2012). A call for school counseling practitioner research. *Professional School Counseling, 16*(1), 59–62. doi:10.1177/2156759X1201600107

McLeod, S. A. (2015). *Psychology research ethics.* Simply Psychology. https://www.simplypsychology.org/Ethics.html

Richardson, T. (2019). "Why Haven't I Got One of Those?" A Consideration Regarding the Need to Protect Non-Participant Children in Early Years Research. *European Early Childhood Education Research Journal, 27*(1), 5–14. https://doi.org/10.1080/1350293X.2018.1556530

Rowell, L. L. (2006). Action research and school counseling: Closing the gap between research and practice. *Professional School Counseling, 9*(5), 376–384. https://doi.org/10.1177/2156759X0500900409

Shepherd, L. L., Read, K., & Chen, D. T. (2013). Children enrolled in parents' research: A uniquely vulnerable group in need of oversight and protection. *IRB: Ethics & Human Research, 35*(3), 1–8.

Woodgate, R. L., Tennent, P., & Zurba, M. (2017). Navigating ethical challenges in qualitative research with children and youth through sustaining mindful presence. *International Journal of Qualitative Methods, 16*(1), 1–11. https://doi.org/10.1177/1609406917696743

6

Using Assessment Instruments in School-Based Research

Timothy A. Poynton

Using Assessment Instruments in School-Based Research

Finding, selecting, and using assessment instruments are central aspects of school-based research, as it is those instruments that create answers to our research questions in tangible ways. Once you have your research question(s), the next step in the research process is to figure out exactly how you are going to answer those questions—and for quantitatively oriented research questions, this will involve the use and/or creation of assessment tools. But how do you figure out which instrument(s) to use? Where can you find reliable and valid assessments? How do you make sure that your assessment instrument is fair and equitable, and that it doesn't perpetuate cultural racism or other biases (Randall, 2021)? How do you know if the instrument will be useful for answering the research questions? Do you know how to use the instruments successfully in online and paper-based administration formats? And what if you cannot find an existing assessment to answer the research question(s) you have posed? The answers to these questions form the basis of this chapter, emphasizing how school counselors and school counselor educators (SCEs) can efficiently and effectively carry out high-quality research in schools.

Brief History of Assessment Instruments in School Counseling

While a thorough detailing of the history of school counseling is interesting and intriguing, it is beyond the scope of this chapter—but what was originally known as vocational guidance (Gysbers & Henderson, 2001; Parsons, 1909) evolved into the profession of school counseling as we know it today.

Timothy A. Poynton, *Using Assessment Instruments in School-Based Research* In: *School Counseling Research.* Edited by: Brett Zyromski and Carey Dimmitt, Oxford University Press. © Oxford University Press 2023. DOI: 10.1093/oso/9780197650134.003.0006

The early work of people doing school-counseling-like work in schools was career oriented, and a natural result of the industrial revolution that made occupational choice a social issue. This was the motivation for Frank Parsons's (1909) work in his seminal book *Choosing a Vocation*. A civil engineer by training, Parsons was interested in improving productivity in factories and soon realized that finding people who were interested in and talented at their jobs was a better way to improve worker productivity than changing the work environment. While Parsons did not develop any assessment instruments, he elaborated a process for choosing an occupation that emphasized knowing about oneself in relation to the world of work. Psychologists working for the military developed the Army Alpha and Army Beta tests (Yoakum & Yerkes, 1920)—assessments of cognitive ability—to help place soldiers effectively into military occupations during World War I. The Strong Vocational Interest Blank was developed by psychologist E. K. Strong to address a perceived shortcoming of the Alpha and Beta tests—that occupational success and satisfaction is more complex than cognitive ability alone can predict.

The vocationally oriented work of school counselors continues to this day, but as the counselors' roles have expanded over the years, so too have the assessment instruments available to support our research and evaluation efforts. Campbell and Dahir (1997) summarized progressive changes in the school counseling profession that had been occurring for decades with a set of national standards for the profession. These new standards were developed to describe the competencies students should develop as part of a school's comprehensive guidance and counseling program and included not just the career realm, but also the academic and personal/social realms. From an assessment tool perspective, this shift in school counseling practice from being mostly career oriented to having responsibility for supporting student competence in the academic and personal/social domains opened the door to more assessment instruments that are relevant to school counseling practice. What does this mean for you? This means that we can expect to explore and find assessment instruments from a wide range of disciplines in addition to school counseling—vocational psychology, youth counseling, cognitive psychology, education, school psychology, social work, and educational psychology, to name a few. Knowing that relevant assessment instruments can come from just about anywhere in school-based research is simultaneously comforting and overwhelming—it's good to know that we are likely to find a valid, reliable instrument somewhere, but the process of finding it can in fact be daunting. I am hopeful that the information provided in this chapter offers knowledge and, in turn, comfort for aspiring and current researchers in school counseling.

Assessment Instruments in the ASCA National Model

The American School Counselor Association (ASCA) National Model (ASCA, 2019) promotes the use of data primarily in the manage and assess sections for program planning, management, and evaluation purposes—goals that are different from the ones we are typically trying to achieve in school-based research. When we are collecting, analyzing, and interpreting data for evaluation purposes, the goals are related to assessing and improving the programs we are offering to students *in our school.* When we are using data for research purposes, the goals are related to creating generalizable knowledge *that extends our findings beyond the school(s)* we have collected data from. This is an incredibly important distinction, because it highlights the importance of *reliability* and *validity*, which play a much greater role in choosing assessment instruments for research purposes than evaluation purposes. For example, it may be perfectly acceptable in an evaluation context to create your own instrument to answer your evaluation questions. In a research context, however, instruments you create have unknown reliability and validity characteristics and therefore limit your ability to generalize findings beyond the sample you collected data from.

In spite of the fact that the goals of using data as described by the ASCA National Model (ASCA, 2019) differ from the goals we seek to achieve in school-based research, knowing how the ASCA National Model talks about data—and the assessments that make "data" tangible—is still important. It is important because the goal of school-based research, when conducted by SCEs, should involve translating our research findings into practice—and the ASCA national model (2019) provides an excellent framework for doing so.

To summarize briefly, there are three overarching, primary types of data described in the *ASCA National Model* (2019): Participation data, Mindsets & Behaviors data, and Outcome data. Participation data describe the "what" and the "who"—number of students, number of counselors, and/or the number of intervention sessions, for example. Mindsets & Behaviors data describe "information that shows what progress students have made toward attaining the ASCA Mindsets & Behaviors standards" (ASCA, 2019, p. 149) and may include survey instruments and other self-reported data to demonstrate attainment of specific standards. You can review the Mindsets & Behavior standards documents at https://www.schoolcounselor.org/getmedia/7428a 787-a452-4abb-afec-d78ec77870cd/Mindsets-Behaviors.pdf (ASCA, 2021). For example, a measure of College Knowledge (Poynton, Ruiz, & Lapan, 2019) could be used to assess standards B-LS-1 and B-LS-9 in the Career

Development Domain. If you are interested in exploring specific *competencies* related to the ASCA Mindsets & Behaviors standards, they are provided in a user-submitted, searchable database at http://www.schoolcounselor.org/learningobjectives. Finally, Outcome data are behaviorally oriented data points that can be used to assess measurable changes in student behavior. Outcome data draw on attendance, discipline-related information, grades, and other measures of academic performance and may include the use of assessment instruments. For example, a measure of reading literacy such as the DIBELS (University of Oregon, 2018) or standardized tests such as the ACT° and SAT° may be used to measure academic-related data points, while the number of days absent and number of suspensions can be used to measure attendance and discipline behaviors.

With this background, the rest of the chapter is structured to guide you through the assessment selection process using a series of questions to answer, outlined in Table 6.1. While I believe this structure can be useful across a variety of disciplines, the issues I raise and ideas I propose are grounded in the knowledge that you are someone with experience, interest, and/or knowledge of school counseling and are planning to contribute to the knowledge base informing our field through research with K–12 students in schools.

Table 6.1. Overview of Questions to Answer When Finding and Using Assessment Instruments in School-Based Research

Question to Consider	Aspects of Answer
What is the construct(s) related to my research question that I'm hoping to measure?	Qualitative and/or quantitative methods
How do I find assessment instruments?	Google, Google Scholar, peer-reviewed literature, Mental Measurements Yearbook (MMY)
How do I know if an instrument will be useful?	Reliability, validity
How do I identify bias in instruments?	Understand how bias manifests in assessment, and check.
How do I know if an instrument is relevant to my population of interest?	Make sure it was normed with a sample similar to your participants; check the ages it should be used with.
Can I use the instrument within the constraints of my project?	Resources (time, money), access to sample
How can I use assessment instruments effectively?	Paper vs. digital, planning for response rate reporting
What if I can't find what I need?	Developing your own assessment.

How Do I Choose an Instrument?

The assessment instrument(s) you use in your research is what brings your ideas to life and allows you to find the answers to your research questions. The emphasis in this chapter is on quantitatively oriented assessment instruments. This is not to diminish the importance of or utility in qualitatively oriented research and assessment—many research questions are best answered with a qualitative methodology! I am simply acknowledging here a focus of this chapter. To learn more about qualitative research and how it may help you in your school-based research endeavors, I encourage you to review Chapter 8 by Emily Goodman-Scott and Blaire Cholewa.

So, how do you choose an instrument? To illustrate what can sometimes be a meandering, iterative process, I will begin with a simple outline and then provide a real-life example. The first step entails coming up with your research question(s) (see Chapter 4 for additional details regarding constructing research questions). Then, consider how empirical data may be used to answer each research question. Once you have identified the constructs related to the research question, you can then think about how assessment instruments can be utilized. This part may take some time and requires revising and refinement as you explore options and possibilities. I would encourage you to stay true to your original research question(s) in spite of any preferences you may have for a particular methodology. Personally, I am a quantitatively oriented researcher—always have been. However, while conceptualizing the research questions for my dissertation, some of the questions were qualitatively oriented—and answering all of the research questions therefore required a mixed methodology. If your research questions are more about learning "why" and "how," chances are you will be best served by following a qualitative methodology. If your research questions are more about "how much" or "how many," you will be best served by following a quantitative methodology.

Let me use my own dissertation research to illustrate. In the early 2000s, I was a doctoral student seeking a meaningful research problem to solve. As a recently practicing school counselor, I was very interested in trying to find research I could conduct that might solve a practical problem for the profession. During this time period, the ASCA National Model was being introduced, and "using data" was a frequent topic of conferences and professional development workshops. After some hemming and hawing, I finally decided to evaluate the potential role of technology in facilitating data use by practicing school counselors. Specifically, my overarching research question was: Do professional development and access to technology increase school counselors' actual data use, and why or why not? This research question was translated into several testable hypotheses that were answered in a quasi-experimental design where exposure to conceptual knowledge about data use (e.g., terminology, application to practice) and a new technology application (EZAnalyze, www.ezanalyze.com) were varied among four groups (Poynton, 2005). The hypotheses (e.g., the group with hands-on practice in technology use will exhibit more data use 4 months post-instruction than the group with hands-on practice with action planning) were assessed using a mix of assessment tools, some developed specifically for use in this study (e.g., a statistics knowledge questionnaire based on the workshop's learning objectives) and some drawn from peer-reviewed literature (e.g., Bauman's [2004] research confidence and attitudes scale).

While the hypotheses (and the assessment instruments employed) were critical in helping to answer the original, overarching research question, "Do professional development and technology impact data use?," the "why or why not" part of the original research question could not be answered without hearing the participants' authentic voices. To do this, a focus group of study participants was convened approximately 6 months after they participated in the workshops, and open-ended questions were asked to guide discussion of barriers and facilitators to data use in school counseling practice. I know you are curious, so I'll share the gist of what I learned from my dissertation research. The quantitative results indicated that workshop participants gained knowledge, but the access to and knowledge of technology to facilitate data use did not impact actual data use in school counseling practice. The qualitative findings indicated that lack of time and knowledge were the most prominent barriers to data use, and that technology and access to useful data were the most prominent data use facilitators. The quantitative findings by themselves were lackluster in terms of answering the research questions; however, the qualitative data helped make sense of the quantitative findings by bringing participant voices to the numbers.

In terms of how I chose the instruments employed in my dissertation research, I first identified the constructs related to the overarching research questions, driven by both personal experience and an (extensive) review of the literature. With this information, I was then able to identify specific constructs to test, resulting in a series of hypothesis statements. Since I was seeking to evaluate the effect and effectiveness of a professional development workshop, I had to assess whether or not participants benefited from the workshop in expected ways—in other words, did participants learn anything in the workshop? Being physically present in the workshop does not mean participants gained any knowledge or skills, or changed their beliefs and attitudes, so measures were identified to assess attainment of the workshop's learning objectives (a knowledge-based multiple-choice assessment), and to assess whether or not participants' confidence in and attitude toward conducting research activities changed (a research confidence and attitudes scale; Bauman, 2004). These were administered in a pretest/posttest format.

To assess the impact of the professional development workshop on school counseling practice, two measures were employed. A measure of data use was developed, consisting of four quantitatively oriented items and two qualitatively oriented items, and this was administered at one month and 3 months post-instruction. The School Counseling Program Implementation Survey (SCPIS: Clemens et al., 2010) was also employed at pretest and 3 months post-instruction to see if more elements of the ASCA National Model were put in place as a result of the training. While comprehensive school counseling programs were not uncommon at the time the ASCA National Model® was introduced, the data use elements were arguably the most unfamiliar to practicing school counselors, so if the workshop was effective in helping school counselors use data, the logic was that we should also see increased scores on the SCPIS. As I was seeking to clarify the specific constructs through the literature review, I was also keeping an eye open for instruments other researchers used that might help answer my own research questions. As illustrated above, a mix of instruments—existing and new, quantitative and qualitative—were required to answer my research questions and test the hypotheses resulting from the overarching research questions.

Paying Attention to Potential Bias in Assessment

Any conversation about educational or psychological assessment necessarily must also consider the complex history of implicit and explicit bias in measurement, as well as the challenges of creating assessments that don't unintentionally perpetuate discrimination or marginalization. While a full discussion of this topic is outside the scope of this chapter, I do want to acknowledge that increasingly the field of educational assessment prioritizes being aware of how assessment instruments and their underlying constructs are intrinsically connected to the social and political contexts they were developed in, and how those contexts must be part of the decision about whether or not to use any particular instrument (Boateng et al., 2018; Inoue, 2015; Knoester & Au, 2017; Randall, 2021). There is tremendous possibility for students to misunderstand or misinterpret assessment items—which is not the same thing as not answering accurately or honestly. And the misunderstanding may be due to a lack of exposure to the content, to a unique interpretation, or to another factor altogether. As Randall (2021) asks, "We know that students—especially marginalized students—do not experience the world including schooling in ways that are context-free, so the question becomes *why do we insist that they experience their assessments in this way*" (p. 82). As you look at possible instruments for your research, it's always useful to ask yourself how these might be perceived by students taking them, how they might be biased, and how you can try to ensure that you are using them as consciously as possible.

How Do I Find Instruments?

Using Boolean Search Techniques to Find Relevant Information

Knowing how to search effectively for information using Internet-based resources is the first step in finding instruments for use in your research. Using Boolean operators provides a powerful way to refine the results of our search efforts and improve our chances of finding relevant information. There are just three Boolean search operators—AND, OR, and NOT—that most search engines and tools will recognize (for more information, see https://www.socialtalent.com/blog/recruitment/the-beginners-guide-to-boolean-search-terms). You can use these operators right in the main search query box or look for a link to an "advanced" option to help you construct search queries that will be understood by the tool you are using. When combined with other search techniques, such as placing terms in quotes ("") to narrow what you find or using a wildcard (*) to expand search results, you can greatly increase your chances of finding exactly what it is you are looking for. For example, let's imagine that you forgot about the bananas you bought last week and have decided to make banana bread instead of throwing them out. When you search *Banana Bread Recipe* on Google, you find about 460,000,000 matches. Yikes, that's a lot. As you are checking your ingredients, you realize that you do not have brown sugar but do have white sugar. You also do not want to use a recipe that calls for nuts. You could start to sift through the 460 million webpages Google found for you—or you can construct a better search query to find exactly what you are looking for.

To exclude web pages that contain a keyword on Google, you use the minus sign (−) directly in front of the search term to specify the NOT Boolean operator. So, to find recipes that do not contain nuts, you would add –*nut* to your search query. When you do this, you find that recipes with nuts such as almonds and pecans are still popping up, so you need to refine your search further by adding –*pecans* and –*almonds*. Since we don't have brown sugar, we want to exclude recipes calling for that as well, but typing –*brown sugar* will not work, as that will just exclude web pages that contain the word brown. To define a phrase to exclude, we wrap it in quotes, so to exclude the phrase "brown sugar," we would type –*"brown sugar"* to find recipes that do not call for brown sugar. Now, our new search query looks like this: *banana bread recipe AND –nut AND –pecan AND –walnut AND –"brown sugar."* This cuts the number of web pages Google has found down to about 201,000,000. Whew! While Google (and most search tools) are pretty good about placing the most relevant results first, you can be even more precise by making sure the words *banana* and *bread* always appear next to each other by placing them in quotes. Adding quotes around *"banana bread"* further reduces the number of web pages Google has found down to about 15,800,000—a substantial reduction!

As you begin going through the recipes to see what sounds good, you become open to the possibility of making banana muffins instead. So now, to search for both types of recipes, banana bread and banana muffin, we can use parentheses with the OR operator to find either type of recipe without nuts or brown sugar. When you type *banana (bread OR muffin) AND recipe AND –*nut* AND –pecan AND –walnut AND—"brown sugar,"* this adds about 6 million recipes. To summarize, we can use the AND and NOT operators to narrow our search results, and we can use the OR operator to expand our search results. We can also use the wildcard symbol (*) to expand search results (e.g., wom*n would return results including *woman* and *women*, and *counsel** would return counsel, counseling, counselor, and counselors), and quotes to limit results to include phrases with multiple words. Above, I provided an example of how to exclude a phrase using quotes (brown sugar). Another example of using quotes to limit search results may help to clarify this concept further. If you search for *personality assessment* on Google, this returns 312,000,000 web pages that contain the terms "personality" and "assessment." If we want to only include web pages that contain the exact phrase, we need to put the words of the phrase in quotes, so this would be typed as *"personality assessment."* When we do this, Google returns a mere 2,660,000 results. That's more than 99% fewer results than searching without quotes and represents a significant improvement in the relevance of the information you will find on those web pages.

Peer-Reviewed Literature

The peer-reviewed literature is an excellent place to find instruments for your consideration and often results naturally from efforts to refine and operationalize your constructs. Chances are you are familiar with databases such as PsycINFO and ERIC, but a database you may not be familiar with that is chock full of assessments is the Mental Measurements Yearbook (MMY), published by Buros every 3 years. The MMY contains information about a variety of assessments, along with two reviews from people in the field. You can find the MMY in both print and database form, and it is worth your time to review multiple editions of the MMY as only new and newly revised assessments are included in each edition. In my experience, the vast majority of assessments in the MMY have a cost associated with them. While we have all grown accustomed to finding what we want for free on the Internet, sometimes the best instrument we can use in our research is not free—consider supporting the instrument developer and publisher by using commercially available instruments, if they fit the context within which you are operating. A database similar to the MMY is the American Psychological Association's (APA's) PsycTests database. Like the MMY, APA PsycTests contains information about a variety of instruments that may be relevant to your research. Unlike the MMY, PsycTests is likely to contain more freely available measures and does not contain peer reviews within the database itself—although most entries link to a peer-reviewed journal article to get more detailed information and, oftentimes, access to the instrument itself.

While ERIC is freely and publicly available through the Institute of Education Sciences at the U.S. Department of Education, access to databases such as PsycINFO, JSTOR, Academic OneFile, and Academic Search Complete require a subscription. Fortunately, libraries at colleges and universities subscribe to many databases, and access is often available to alumni as well as current students, faculty, and staff. Many libraries use a service called EBSCOhost to provide access to multiple databases, and this can greatly facilitate your search endeavors by allowing you to search several databases at once. For example, at my university, I can search APA PsycTests, PsycINFO, Academic Search Complete, ERIC, MMY, and MEDLINE simultaneously. How? Instead of searching for each individual database in my library's list of resources, I first find EBSCOhost—and then within EBSCOhost, I can choose which databases to include in my search, as illustrated in Figure 6.1.

Access to all of this wonderful information, literally at your fingertips, can be overwhelming—so please, remember to use your Boolean search techniques to find the most relevant information! Within most of these databases are

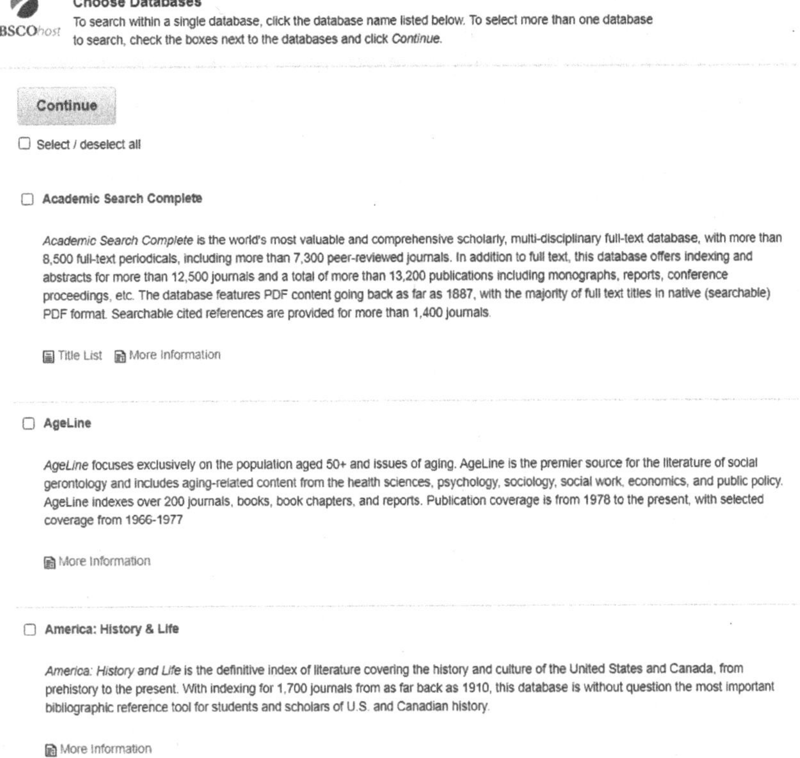

Figure 6.1 Choosing Databases in EBSCOhost.

additional options to help narrow and refine your search. For example, most databases allow you to limit your search results to peer-reviewed literature only, which would exclude books, chapters, and dissertations. You can also limit your search results by publication year in most databases and choose where to search for information (e.g., within the title, subject terms, journal name, or abstract, for example). On the other hand, if you are having some trouble finding what you are looking for, think about how you might expand your search by using different search terms (perhaps with the OR operator). If you are looking for an instrument to measure academic self-efficacy, for example, you might search for "academic self-efficacy assessment" OR "academic self-efficacy instrument." Feel free to use a thesaurus to help you come up with ideas for different search terms. Similarly, another way to expand your search is by closely examining the database information for relevant articles you do find. Examine the keywords and descriptors from those relevant articles and use them in subsequent searches.

While I have previously mentioned using Google to help you find assessments, I have not mentioned Google Scholar, where the search results are focused on findings from the scholarly literature. Many of the things you would find in the academic databases you will also find in Google Scholar, but you are also likely to find information that is often absent from those databases such as white papers and technical reports. Sometimes, Google Scholar can be connected to your university library, allowing you easy access to articles you find—it is definitely worth checking with your library to see if and how you can connect Google Scholar to your library's resources.

Other Places

While the above noted places are "tried and true" resources for finding assessments, this is the 21st century, and there are plenty of other places we can turn to for help on the World Wide Web. You are likely familiar with ResearchGate (www.researchgate.net), which is kind of like LinkedIn for researchers. I am personally not one to partake in social networking ... if you are, use whichever platform you like to ask for others' ideas. Another place to keep in mind is the Collaborative for Academic, Social, and Emotional Learning (CASEL; www.casel.org). In their Assessment Guide (measuringsel. casel.org/assessment-guide/) you will find more than 25 instruments that can be used to assess social-emotional learning (some require purchase).

K–12 schools are often swimming in data that can be used for research purposes, if you can obtain the appropriate permissions to gain access. For example, my research colleagues and I were able to access longitudinal data at the individual student level and connect it to data we collected. The study (Poynton & Lapan, 2017) consisted of a survey administered to graduating high school seniors, which we then connected to standardized academic achievement assessments they took as sophomores. We also were able to obtain college enrollment data from these same high school students approximately 18 months after graduating from high school to assess how well those planning to attend college achieved their postsecondary plans. Specifically, the 10th-grade assessments were the Massachusetts Comprehensive Assessment System (MCAS) English Language Arts and Math tests, while assessment of the transition into college employed National Student Clearinghouse (NSC) data. NSC data consist of enrollment verification information, allowing researchers to determine college/university attendance. We were able to access the MCAS, NSC, and other data (e.g., SES, IEP/504 status) by entering into a data-sharing agreement with our state's department of education. This saved us years of time while simultaneously increasing the volume and relia-bility of the data we obtained, as NSC data, for example, are easier to obtain than trying to follow up with students to obtain self-report data more than a year after graduating from high school. In addition to seeing how your state department of education might be able to help you access data they routinely collect, you can also form partnerships with school districts and explore how you might be able to access data they collect as well. Districts can vary tremen-dously in terms of how they collaborate with researchers, but they are often motivated to do so because they are keenly interested in learning more about how to help students succeed—which is very often a primary focus of our re-search efforts!

How Do I Know if an Instrument Will Be Useful in My Context?

When you find an assessment instrument that seems to fit your needs, the next step is taking a close look at the available information and materials to understand its potential strengths and challenges in relation to your specific research context. Answering the questions below can provide a step-by-step guide to help you think about what to consider to help you gain clarity and understanding of what the instrument is and perhaps is not. Please note, how-ever, that this is not meant to be a "checklist" that replaces your judgment and critical analysis of appropriateness. As noted in the *Standards for Educational and Psychological Testing* (American Educational Research Association, American Psychological Association, & National Council on Measurement in Education, 2014), there are no discrete and specific criteria that need to be met—but many things to consider as you make an informed decision about the instrument's appropriateness for use in your research context.

In no particular order, questions for you to consider as you evaluate the ap-plicability of an instrument to your research are:

Was the Sample Employed in the Instrument's Development Similar to Mine?

Ideally, instruments employed for research conducted in schools will have re-liability and validity evidence generated from samples that are like the one you plan to obtain—and doing so explicitly and intentionally helps you con-duct research aligned with social justice and antiracist research practices.

Finding instruments developed with participants similar to those available to you is often quite challenging given the diverse nature of students and the schools they attend. In addition to examining the demographic makeup of the samples employed in developing an instrument to assess the similarity of race/ethnicity, gender, and socioeconomic status with your intended sample, particular attention needs to be given to age in school-based research. There are huge developmental differences in many constructs across the K–12 years, and the instruments you employ may not work as intended if the sample you have is younger or older than the sample with which the instrument was developed. For assessments with younger, elementary-aged children, there can also be great diversity in reading ability. This could make an assessment normed with third and fourth graders potentially inappropriate for use with second graders, for example.

In general, you want to employ instruments that are accessible to as much of your intended sample as possible, so be sure you are using assessments with reading levels that are at least a few grade levels lower whenever possible. In a recent analysis of the readability of 20 different news sources (Tauberg, 2019), the Flesch–Kincaid grade level of the newspaper *USA Today* was calculated to be at approximately the 10th-grade level, while Breitbart and Politico were both calculated to be above the 12th-grade level, making *USA Today* more accessible to a wider swath of the population. In Microsoft Word, you can calculate the Flesch–Kincaid score if the instrument developers do not provide such information, but I would also recommend connecting with a reading or English teacher in the school, if possible, to get their input on the accessibility of the instruments you plan on using in your study.

Finally, consider the possible impact differing cultural contexts may have on the instrument(s) you plan on using. For example, has the instrument been translated into any other languages? If so, has that had any impact on the reliability and validity evidence? Could any items or aspects of the scale be misinterpreted? Check for content that reflects social norms for white, middle-class, American students rather than a more diverse population. Also, carefully review the items on the instrument to see if any of them exhibit cultural bias or lack relevance. Do any of the items assume, for example, that children come from two-parent households with a mother and father? Within the United States, there is a great deal of cultural diversity that can potentially influence how research participants perceive the meaning of items contained within an assessment. Instruments that ask about technology use often illustrate the need to examine the relevance of items. For example, are the types of technology referenced still in common use today? Even if you very carefully consider every aspect of how culture, gender, age, race, reading ability, relevance, etc., may influence participants in your study as part of the instrument selection process, it is still strongly recommended that you conduct a pilot study with the assessment(s) you plan on using to highlight any potential cultural bias or relevance issues before large-scale administration.

How Reliable Is the Instrument?

Reliability information is commonly reported by instrument developers, but there are several types of reliability to consider. *Test–retest reliability* is what most people think of when they think about reliability—but it is sometimes not reported because it can be challenging to obtain, and sometimes the construct itself may not be very stable over time to begin with. As the name implies, test–retest reliability requires two administrations of the same instrument, and the test–retest reliability is reported as the correlation between those two measures. If the instrument reliably measures whatever it is that it measures, it should have a high test–retest reliability coefficient. Many factors can influence the strength of a test–retest reliability coefficient—the nature of the construct being measured, the amount of time between administrations, and the nature of the sample employed, for example. I will not be providing any minimum or acceptable "cutoff scores" for evaluating test–retest reliability coefficients because of these somewhat thorny issues . . . but with that said, the expectation in social sciences is not to obtain a perfect correlation—.9 would be considered a strong correlation. We would expect, for example, the test–retest reliability of a speedometer to be much higher than that of a measure of student attitudes.

Another common form of reliability information provided by instrument developers is *internal consistency*—often expressed as a form of *coefficient alpha* such as Cronbach's Alpha (for Likert-type scales) or KR20 (for binary data). Without getting too far into the technical aspects of calculating internal consistency estimates, coefficient alpha is essentially derived from examining how well the individual items of an instrument correlate with each other, with estimates usually expressed as a decimal between 0 and 1. An often-cited cutoff point for acceptable reliability using Cronbach's Alpha is .7 (Nunnaly, 1978), but just because an instrument reaches this threshold does not necessarily mean all is well. Internal consistency estimates are pretty heavily influenced by the number of items in the scale/instrument—increasing the number of items leads to increases in coefficient alpha, even when the relations among items remain the same. Therefore, we would expect the internal consistency of a five-item subscale to be lower than the full 15-item scale the subscale is derived from.

Split-half reliability is another form of reliability information commonly reported by instrument developers, and like internal consistency estimates, is often reported because it is easy to obtain from a single administration of an instrument. Split-half reliability is calculated by splitting the instrument into two equal parts and seeing how well the halves correlate with each other. If the individual items of the assessment are all measuring the same construct, randomly splitting the instrument into two halves should produce a strong correlation. Split-half reliability is somewhat similar to *parallel forms reliability* in that the assessment is divided in two. However, parallel forms reliability differs in that the instrument is split and then administered to the same subjects at two different points in time—akin to test–retest reliability.

The final form of reliability we will review here—*inter-rater reliability* (or *inter-observer reliability*)—is not assessed in self-report measures. However, for instruments that are administered to observers (e.g., where parents or teachers report on a child's behavior, such as the Child Behavior Checklist; Achenbach & Rescorla, 2001), this is an important source of reliability information. For example, a reliable assessment of a child's behavior should produce similar ratings, regardless of who is completing the assessment. You will find inter-rater reliability reported as a correlation coefficient or (for categorical rating scales) the percent of agreement among raters.

While reliability information is important for helping you choose instruments appropriate for your context, it is just one piece of the puzzle. The fact is that an instrument can very reliably measure *something* without being meaningful . . . so how do we know if an assessment effectively measures what it is supposed to measure? By examining validity information.

What Kinds of Validity Evidence Are Available?

There are several types of validity evidence to look for when evaluating the appropriateness of an instrument for your research, and we can think of the differing types across three broad spheres—*construct validity, content validity,* and *criterion validity.* Generally speaking, validity in the measurement realm is concerned with how well an instrument actually measures what it intends to measure. Similar to how we approach evaluating the evidence supporting an instrument's reliability, a checklist to discern between acceptable and unacceptable levels of validity evidence will not be provided. Chances are good that assessments perfect for your research are not going to have evidence of every type of validity—your judgment is needed to evaluate the available evidence for the instruments under consideration to find the one(s) best suited to your goals and context.

Construct validity evidence is typically reported by instrument developers in terms of *convergent validity*, *divergent validity*, and other data demonstrating that the assessment behaves in theory-aligned ways. Convergent validity entails seeing how well a new measure of a construct correlates with existing measure(s) of the same construct. For example, if you are reviewing a new measure of anxiety, you would look for evidence of convergent validity by finding research where the new measure is administered alongside other, existing measures known to measure anxiety, and you would examine the correlations between them. Divergent validity (aka discriminant validity) takes the opposite approach and seeks to provide evidence of construct validity by demonstrating what the measure is not related to. We would look for evidence of divergent validity by finding research where the new measure is again administered alongside other instruments, and again examining correlations between the measures—except this time, divergent validity is demonstrated when low correlations exist in theory-aligned ways. For example, we would not expect a measure of anxiety to correlate well with a measure of emotion suppression (e.g., Doi et al., 2018), as theory does not support such a relationship. Factor analysis (both exploratory and confirmatory) is another common technique used by instrument developers to assess construct validity, as it can be used to explore and explain how individual items relate to each other in the context of the larger assessment.

Content validity is concerned with how well an instrument's items reflect the construct being measured. For example, a study skills assessment should contain items related to effective study skills and habits, and an instrument designed to assess school connectedness should contain items reflecting how connected students feel to various members of the school community. Content validity is often established through expert review, which can be formal (e.g., a Delphi study) or more informal (e.g., opinions sought from three people with expertise and knowledge). Sometimes, an instrument's developer is an expert themselves—in this case, you should look for evidence of their expertise, and how they describe the instrument's development. Content validity is similar to *face validity*, with a key distinction being that face validity is less formal and is concerned mostly with how well an instrument assesses a construct "on the face of it"—expert opinions not needed.

Criterion validity is concerned with how well an instrument is related to outcomes and most often comes in two forms—*predictive validity* and *concurrent validity*. Predictive validity examines the relationship between scores on the instrument and some future outcome. For example, the Graduate Record Examination (GRE) is considered to have good predictive validity of graduate school performance. Before you read on, please answer this question for yourself: What do you think the correlation is between GRE scores and doctoral students' overall grade point average (GPA)? Remember, the correlation should be large enough to justify "good" predictive validity. Let's compare your answer to what Kuncel et al. (2010) found in their meta-analysis of the GRE's predictive validity. For doctoral students, the raw correlation between GRE scores and overall graduate school GPA was .21 (verbal) and .20 (quantitative) (Kuncel et al., 2010). How does that compare with what you thought the correlation would be? I'll bet you thought the correlation should be larger. You may have heard the phrase "statistical significance does not imply practical significance," which is something I like to discuss with graduate students when teaching statistics, because the fact is that it is relatively easy to achieve statistically significant results if your sample is large enough—but that does not mean the finding is meaningful in terms of actual practice.

At this point, you might be wondering, why do graduate schools use the GRE as part of their admissions process when they only account for about 4% (.2 squared) of the variance in graduate school GPAs? The answer, I believe, lies in the complexity of the behaviors that need to be exhibited to achieve academic success in graduate school. A graduate school GPA consists of grades earned in all classes for the duration of the program and reflects not only verbal and quantitative reasoning ability (which were the GRE subtests employed in the meta-analysis), but many other things as well. Amount of time spent studying, self-regulation, peer and partner support, class attendance, prior learning in related subject areas, communication skills, number of hours spent working, and writing ability are all also very likely to influence a student's cumulative graduate GPA to some degree—but how would you measure all of these things in a way that is not too cumbersome as part of the graduate school application process? That, I believe, is why the GRE is such a common part of graduate school applications—and why the GRE is said to have predictive validity in spite of the relatively low correlations. Given the complex relationship of the behaviors that comprise a cumulative graduate school GPA, the fact that the GRE explains some of the variance makes it a meaningful predictor of potential graduate student success. It is also important to note that the GRE is not the only part of a graduate school application—undergraduate transcripts, recommendation letters, writing samples/personal statements, and interviews are also common, which (I hope) leads to appropriate use of the GRE in making graduate school admission decisions. Finally, I should point out that Kuncel et al. (2010) employed statistical corrections for measurement error that demonstrated that the average correlation between GRE subtests (verbal and quantitative) across three outcomes (1st-year GPA, overall GPA, and faculty ratings of students) was .30 for master's-level graduate students and .27 for doctoral students—a little higher than the uncorrected correlations.

The other form of criterion validity commonly reported is concurrent validity. Predictive validity is established by examining how well an instrument predicts a future outcome, and it therefore implies the measures are administered over some period of time. Concurrent validity, on the other hand, examines how well an instrument and outcome are related when both measures are administered at the same time. Extending our GRE example, concurrent validity could be determined by administering the GRE at the end of graduate school to compare with the cumulative GPA. In sum, instruments developed for use in schools should provide validity evidence to support that they measure the intended construct and are related to meaningful outcomes.

Can the Instrument Be Employed Within the Constraints of My Project?

Even if you have found instruments that were normed on a population similar to yours, have solid reliability and validity evidence, and clearly measure the construct you want to measure, there may be other obstacles to their use in your school-based research. Cost is, usually, a primary consideration. While I am a big fan of assessment instruments that are provided free of charge, I also recognize that there are times when paying for an instrument provides significant value—in terms of the construct you are measuring, confidence in the results you obtain, and the practical utility the assessment provides. For example, I was involved in a grant-funded project designed to help undergraduate electrical engineering students from the Boston Public Schools succeed in college and, ultimately, transition into the workplace (Shatz & Poynton, 2014). If you have access to information from the instrument developers, you can purposely select items from the larger assessment for inclusion in a shortened version. For example, if factor analysis findings are available, you can select the items with the highest factor loadings for use in a shortened version. If item-to-total (scale and/or subscale) correlations are available, you can select items with the largest correlations for use in your project. If you do choose to modify the length (and therefore the structure) of an assessment, plan on conducting analyses to assess the impact of the changes. At a minimum, assess changes to internal consistency (keeping in mind that coefficient alpha is likely to be lower as a simple function of there being fewer items). If you have the time and resources, it may be worthwhile to replicate other analyses the instrument developer(s) employed to investigate further how a shortened version of the original instrument affects its construct validity (e.g., exploratory and confirmatory factor analysis).

How Can I Use Assessment Instruments Effectively?

While most of this chapter has focused on helping you find assessment instruments and fit them into your school-based research, we will conclude with a few pragmatic thoughts on how you actually use the instruments you found. Do you plan on administering the instruments the old-fashioned way with paper-based assessments, or do you plan on administering digitally? If you have a choice and can administer either way, first review any information the instrument developers may have provided—did they administer digitally, on paper, or both, and do they provide any recommendations? There are pros and cons to each approach, and I'm not going to suggest one way is better than the other. A summary of the primary considerations is presented in Table 6.2, but I would like to elaborate on a couple of these issues.

Have you ever taken a web-based survey and been notified (or reprimanded) because you left a question blank? I have to admit I have mixed feelings about this . . . sometimes when I receive a message like this, I am thankful because I truly missed providing an answer I wanted to provide. Other times when I get this message, it irks me because I really don't want to answer the question.

Table 6.2. Comparison of Considerations When Choosing Using Paper or Digital Assessments

Paper-Based Assessments	Consideration	Digital Assessments
Familiar format to most participants	Format	May be unfamiliar to some participants
Cost associated with making physical copies	Cost	May have cost associated with digital survey provider
Each question technically optional	Response Choice	Technology can require question be answered before proceeding.
Data can be hand-tallied or coded into database for data analysis program.	Data	Data are in digital format ready for use in data analysis programs.
Anonymity and confidentiality are hard to guarantee.	Ethics	Anonymity and confidentiality are hard to guarantee.

This leaves me with needing to decide—should I answer the question to proceed, or abandon the assessment because I cannot leave it blank? If you create digital surveys, I encourage you to consider this issue—keeping in mind that with paper surveys, each question is technically optional, and there is no way to "force" people to answer. On the one hand, I totally get that the technology available in web-based surveys helps us get clean data (e.g., no one can circle halfway between 4 and 5, answers can be validated for quality) and can enhance the user experience (e.g., skip logic to move past irrelevant items, word replacement to personalize for each participant). On the other hand, we need to be mindful of how our use of digital survey features impacts the participants' experience. When I am developing web-based surveys, I only require answers to items related to the survey experience that are necessary for the survey to function correctly, such as skip logic items, and try to anticipate all the ways people may want to answer the item—including not wanting to provide any answer.

Another important consideration to succeeding in school-based research is explicitly including in your research plans how you will calculate the response rate. Determining response rates in school-based research when using paper-based assessments is usually fairly straightforward—simply determine how many surveys were returned, divide that by the number administered, and you have your response rate. However, when using web-based surveys, things can get a bit more complicated. For example, it is not uncommon for researchers using web-based surveys to encourage forwarding the link to others who may be interested, or even sharing the link on social media. For good news, of the published studies using online survey methodologies in four counseling journals, Poynton, DeFouw, & Morizio (2019) found that research with K–12 student participants yielded the highest response rates of any participant category. This is due, at least in part, to the nature of recruiting and survey administration in school-based research, where research participation occurs at the classroom or grade level. It may be helpful, and more accurate, to think of the response rate as a participation rate in school-based research. Regardless of what it is called, it is important to include when reporting research findings to help assess the possible presence of response/nonresponse bias.

What if I Cannot Find an Instrument That Accomplishes My Research Goals?

In spite of your best efforts using all of the tools and techniques mentioned in this chapter, you may find yourself unsuccessful in your instrument-seeking adventures. This is fairly common when you are doing intervention/program evaluation, when the goals and objectives of the intervention or program do not align well with existing measures. For example, in Poynton et al. (2006), we were evaluating the effectiveness of an intervention designed to improve problem-solving and logical reasoning with middle school students. We were able to employ some existing measures of academic problem-solving by using items from a state standardized test, and logical problem-solving using the Quizzle (Williams, 1976), but we were also interested in seeing how students' self-efficacy and problem-solving skill may have changed in relation to specific topics discussed over the course of the lessons contained in the intervention. This led to the development of an 18-item Problem Solving and Logical Reasoning (PSLR) survey directly tied to the intervention's learning goals, objectives, and activities, such as "I know how to begin solving a Math problem when it is given to me in class" and "When I am reading, I think about connections between what I am reading and events in my life." We administered the PSLR in a pre- and post-assessment design to help determine whether or not students benefited from the intervention in expected ways. When used to supplement the existing measures we employed in the study, our self-made measure helped paint a clearer evaluation picture than would have been possible if using existing measures alone.

Unfortunately, providing detailed information here on how to develop your own measure is beyond the scope of this chapter. However, excellent resources can be found with a well-constructed Google search and a visit to your library. For example, Dillman et al. (2014) provide an excellent treatment of survey item development, administration, and overall design, and I think it is written in an engaging, easy-to-follow manner. I would also encourage you to think about what other resources you may have available to you. For example, if you are affiliated with a college or university, are there colleagues who may have knowledge and expertise to support your instrument development endeavors? These colleagues may reside within your department or may be in another department—and they might just be interested in collaborating on a project like yours.

Conclusion

I see the assessment-finding endeavor described here as an exciting, constantly evolving process. With increasing amounts of information available literally at our fingertips and rapidly evolving technology, both the number and nature of assessments available are changing. How has the nature of assessment changed? In my opinion, we can use assessments in school-based research for more than just our data collection purposes—we should, at a minimum, share our findings about students with school personnel to help them learn things they may not have previously known. I would also encourage you to think of ways the assessments you employ might be used to help students themselves. For example, I have taken the college knowledge measure I developed (College Admissions Knowledge Evaluation; Poynton, Ruiz, & Lapan, 2019) and made it interactive, leveraging features available within most digital survey providers' platforms (e.g., Qualtrics). Each CAKE item is a knowledge-based, multiple-choice item with one right answer. In the interactive CAKE assessment, feedback is provided to respondents about whether or not they got the correct answer, and they are given additional information related to the correct answer. This allows the CAKE to potentially serve as both an assessment of college knowledge and an intervention to improve it. My research colleague and I employed a similar technique with the College and Career Readiness Counseling Support scales (CCRCS; Lapan et al., 2017), which consists of Likert-type items. Again, leveraging features of Qualtrics, we are able to calculate subscale and total scores immediately upon the participant's submission of the survey, which we then interpret for participants and make recommendations based on their answers.

I hope the information provided here helps you succeed in your school-based research endeavors. Now as much as ever, we need the knowledge that research with K–12 students can bring us, and the assessments you use significantly influence the value of the new knowledge. Choose well!

References

Achenbach, T. M., & Rescorla, L. A. (2001). *Manual for the ASEBA school-age forms & profiles.* University of Vermont, Research Center for Children, Youth, & Families.

American Educational Research Association, American Psychological Association, & National Council on Measurement in Education. (2014). *Standards for educational and psychological testing.* American Educational Research Association.

American School Counselor Association. (2019). *The ASCA national model: A framework for school counseling programs* (4th ed.). https://columbiacollege-ca.libguides.com/apa/booksandebooks#Book_corp_author.

American School Counselor Association (2021). *ASCA student standards; Mindsets and behaviors for student success.* https://www.schoolcounselor.org/getmedia/7428a787-a452-4abb-afec-d78ec77870cd/Mindsets-Behaviors.pdf.

Bauman, S. (2004). School counselors and research revisited. *Professional School Counseling, 7*(3), 141–151.

Boateng, G. O., Neilands, T. B., Frongillo, E. A., Melgar-Quiñonez, H. R., & Young, S. L. (2018). Best practices for developing and validating scales for health, social, and behavioral research: A primer. *Frontiers in Public Health, 6*, 1–18. https://doi.org/10.3389/fpubh.2018.00149

Campbell, C., & Dahir, C. (1997). *Sharing the vision: The national standards for school counseling programs.* American School Counselor Association.

Clemens, E. V., Carey, J. C., Ph.D., & Harrington, K. M. (2010). The school counseling program implementation survey: Initial instrument development and exploratory factor analysis. *Professional School Counseling, 14*(2), 125–134. https://doi.org/10.1177/2156759x1001400201

Dillman, D. A., Smyth, J. D., & Christian, L. M. (2014). *Internet, phone, mail, and mixed mode surveys: The tailored design method* (4th ed.). Wiley.

Doi, S., Ito, M., Takebayashi, Y., Muramatsu, K., and Horikoshi, M. (2018). Factorial validity and invariance of the 7-Item Generalized Anxiety Disorder Scale (GAD-7) among populations with and without self-reported psychiatric diagnostic status. *Frontiers in Psychology, 9*, Article 1741. https://doi.org/10.3389/fpsyg.2018.01741

Gysbers, N. C., & Henderson, P. (2001). Comprehensive guidance and counseling programs: A rich history and a bright future. *Professional School Counseling, 4*(4), 246–256.

Inoue, A. B. (2015). *Antiracist writing assessment ecologies: Teaching and assessing writing for a socially just future.* Parlor Press LLC.

Knoester, M., & Au, W. (2017). Standardized testing and school segregation: Like tinder for fire? *Race Ethnicity and Education, 20*(1), 1–14. https://doi.org/10.1080/13613324.2015.1121474

Kuncel, N. R., Wee, S., Serafin, L., & Hezlett, S. A. (2010). The validity of the Graduate Record Examination for master's and doctoral programs: A meta-analytic investigation. *Educational and Psychological Measurement, 70*(2), 340–352. https://doi.org/10.1177/0013164409344508

Lapan, R. T., Poynton, T. A., Marcotte, A., Marland, J., and Milam, C. M. (2017). College and career readiness counseling support scales. *Journal of Counseling & Development, 95*(1), 77–86. https://doi.org/10.1002/jcad.12119

Nunnally, J. C. (1978). *Psychometric theory* (2nd ed.). McGraw-Hill.

Parsons, F. (1909). *Choosing a vocation.* Houghton Mifflin Co.

Poynton, T. A. (2005). *Evaluating the effect and effectiveness of a professional development workshop to increase school counselors' use of data: The role of technology* [Unpublished doctoral dissertation]. Boston University.

Poynton, T. A., Carlson, M. W., Hopper, J. A., & Carey, J. C. (2006). Evaluation of an innovative approach to improving middle school students' academic achievement. *Professional School Counseling, 9*(1), 190–196. https://doi.org/10.1177/2156759X0500900309

Poynton, T. A., DeFouw, E. R., & Morizio, L. J. (2019). A systematic review of online response rates in four counseling journals. *Journal of Counseling & Development, 97*(1), 33–42. https://doi.org/10.1002/jcad.12233

Poynton, T. A., & Lapan, R. T. (2017). Aspirations, achievement, and school counselors' impact on the college transition. *Journal of Counseling & Development, 95*(4), 369–377. https://doi.org/10.1002/jcad.12152

Poynton, T. A., Ruiz, B., & Lapan, R. T. (2019). Development and validation of the college admissions knowledge evaluation. *Professional School Counseling, 22*(1a), 98–103. https://doi.org/10.1177/2156759X19834441

Randall, J. (2021). "Color-neutral" is not a thing: Redefining construct definition and representation through a justice-oriented critical antiracist lens. *Educational Measurement: Issues and Practice, 40*(4), 82–90.

Shatz, L., & Poynton, T. A. (2014). *Electrical engineering scholars at Suffolk University.* Sponsored by the National Science Foundation (Grant No. 1259529).

Tauberg, M. (2019, January 12). How smart is your news source? Readability analysis of 21 different news outlets. https://towardsdatascience.com/how-smart-is-your-news-source-1fe0c550c7d9

University of Oregon. (2018). *8th edition of Dynamic Indicators of Basic Early Literacy Skills (DIBELS®)*. University of Oregon. http://dibels.uoregon.edu/

Williams, W. (1976). *You're the detective when you solve Quizzles: Logic problem puzzles*. Dale Seymour Publications.

Yoakum, C. S., & Yerkes, R. M. (Eds.). (1920). *Army mental tests*. Henry Holt and Company. https://doi.org/10.1037/11054-000

7

Research Design

Quantitative Approaches

Catherine Griffith and Elizabeth Villares

Research Design: Quantitative Approaches

It bears noting at the outset that quantitative research can be intimidating. After all, most of us didn't become school counselors because we love numbers—we love people! We've found this to be equally true of school counselor educators (SCEs), scholars, and doctoral students: that even though conducting research is a significant part of our work, it is the drive to seek improvement in the day-to-day well-being of students and advocating for more equitable learning environments that is truly at the forefront of our minds. Quantitative investigations play a key—but secondary—role in that overarching sense of altruistic purpose. As counselors, it may even be helpful to take stock of your feelings about research and data. Discomfort, boredom, intimidation, and even resistance to conducting quantitative investigations are actually all quite normal in our profession. Some would even go so far as to characterize these types of projects as a troublesome nuisance only to be traversed on the road toward tenure (or graduation, or full professorship, etc.). Or perhaps you're like us, and you absolutely love research, but you shudder at certain aspects of the process (why don't manuscripts just write themselves?!). Whether you love or hate quantitative research, or more likely fall somewhere on the spectrum in between, it is our hope to at the very least make this work feel more *accessible*, and ultimately to develop an understanding that a passion for helping and quantitative data are in fact quite complementary.

Quantitative Data in School Counseling: The Bigger Picture

We would first like to set the stage by taking a moment to highlight the bigger picture of data, and the benefits of sharing information through numbers. It's

Catherine Griffith and Elizabeth Villares, *Research Design* In: *School Counseling Research*. Edited by: Brett Zyromski and Carey Dimmitt, Oxford University Press. © Oxford University Press 2023. DOI: 10.1093/oso/9780197650134.003.0007 easy to get lost in the weeds of all the minutia involved in carrying out a successful research project and forget that research findings can be a powerful tool for achieving meaningful outcomes, and that every data point potentially represents a life changed for the better. Never lose sight of the fact that data represent real people, real children, experiencing real issues!

In this era of accountability in education, school counselors are expected to engage in data-based decision-making and look to researchers in the field for guidance on key phenomena and evidence-based practices (EBPs). Furthermore, with time being at such a premium, school counselors need to know which endeavors will actually be worth their limited energy and resources, as they will be balanced with many other urgent demands. The need for quality data and a strong sense of which approaches are effective in schools have never been higher. At the same time, the distance between our scholarly knowledge base and what school counselors *need* to know is wide (Griffith et al., 2019; McGannon et al., 2004; McMahon et al., 2017; Ray et al., 2011; Whiston & Sexton, 1998). The evolution of our relatively young profession has resulted in a slowly growing body of empirical research that still has broad gaps. There are many opportunities for school counseling scholars to produce rigorous research that informs school counseling practice and preparation. Because numbers can serve as a common language between school counselors and other school-based personnel, our field (and subsequently the lives of children) benefit immensely from the availability of strong and compelling data specific to our profession.

We must also answer the growing call for antiracist, social-justice-focused research that leads to positive transformation at a systematic level. Such work requires a shift in focus from what's going "wrong" with individual students, to engaging in research that sheds light on school policies that leave students without the support they need to be successful. Antiracist research is emancipatory and abolitionist in nature (Dei, 2005), going beyond helping students merely to survive oppressive environments; rather, it sheds light on systems in which all students have what they need in order to thrive. Therefore, antiracist quantitative research is ultimately focused on a much bigger picture and can help us (Atkins & Oglesby, 2018; Carey & Martin, 2015; Dimmitt et al., 2007; Harrington, 2013; Holcomb-McCoy, 2007; Poynton & Carey, 2006; Zyromski & Mariani, 2016)

- become more aware of what strengths and weaknesses are present in school counseling practices rather than making assumptions;
- understand more deeply what about our work could be improved in order to support equity among all students;

Pop-Out 7.1. Pause and Reflect

Multiple studies have determined that we need more data directly from PK–12 participants themselves (vs. college students, other school counselors, and counselors-in-training), going so far as to label much of counseling research as "navel-gazing" and not particularly useful in generating transformational, social justice–focused change. After reading Chapter 2 ("Access to Schools: Relationships With Stakeholders and Systems"), what are your theories about why most of the research in our field does not include school-aged youth as participants?

BONUS: Identify someone you know who has conducted research in school settings. Ask them what they see as some of the barriers and hurdles to be navigated when conducting research with young people.

- uncover issues and inequities in schools that may have been previously invisible;
- get to the root of student issues at an individual, group, or schoolwide level;
- advocate for individuals and groups in more specific, tangible ways in a language that people in positions of power respect;
- strengthen our arguments for needed systemic change;
- effectively challenge and adapt existing policies to better serve students;
- influence the public policy at an even larger level that impacts the set priorities for school counselors' work in schools;
- . . . and certainly much more!

We cannot stress enough that given the scope of need, we need all hands on deck for this work. We need *you*.

What Will Be Covered and What Won't

Throughout this chapter you will notice that the majority of attention is placed on what tangible steps can be taken as you navigate the process of implementing a survey or intervention study. We aim to share information from as practical a lens as possible, focusing on real-life experiences, scenarios, and examples from actual published works. There are already so many excellent materials on the *general* process of quantitative research, so what will be unique about this chapter is the focus on the nuts and bolts of these endeavors and tips for how school counseling scholars can best implement these types of investigations. Therefore, the ideal audience for this chapter is someone who has taken at least one course on quantitative methods, has already done some prior reading on the foundations of empirical research, and who now would like to implement a school-based quantitative study. It is our hope that even if you already have some (or even substantial) research experience under your belt, you will still find information in this chapter that will help contribute to the quality of your future investigations. In service of this goal, the following topic areas are highlighted:

- a brief primer on quantitative research methods
- a discussion of the necessity of rigor coupled with the reality of feasibility
- practical considerations and boots-on-the-ground tips for the process of implementing different types of quantitative studies
- concluding thoughts and a call to action

In addition to assuming you have a basic understanding of the foundations of quantitative research, we also want to point you in the direction of related information covered elsewhere in this book. The full process of quantitative research has many components, and Chapters 2–6 of this book (i.e., "Access to Schools," "Ethical Research in Schools," "Research Questions," "Developmental and Social Considerations," and "Using Assessment Instruments"), as well as Chapters 12–14 (i.e., "Ensuring Treatment Fidelity," "Data Analysis," and "Bridging the Research-to-Practice Gap") give you the full picture for carrying out a quantitative study. Other forms of research and evaluation that include quantitative elements are covered in Chapters 9–11 ("Research Design: Action Research," "Single-Subject Case Study," and "Program Evaluation"). But if you haven't already read Chapter 1 ("A Framework for Conducting School Counseling Research"), then we absolutely suggest that you go back and read about important points to consider at the outset, especially those surrounding critical analysis of your intentions in conducting your research and the need for antiracist and social-justice-focused projects.

Finally, we should note that much of our content has been derived from what we think is helpful to share from our own education and ongoing professional development in research methods, but a good deal was inspired by actual experience. In fact, much of the useful information found here is the result of our many, many (many!) mistakes in implementing investigations at various stages, and the effort to continuously improve. And the rest can be attributed to what we have gleaned from brilliant colleagues and mentors, helpful research collaborations, and the ingenuity of our students, who have been generous in sharing helpful practices in the context of the ever-changing landscapes of PK–12 environments. Although the explicit purpose of this chapter is to describe a bevy of practical *how-tos* to keep in mind as you implement a study, the implicit purpose of this chapter is empowerment. Ultimately, we want you to see yourself as a researcher, someone who thinks, "*I can do this!*" We want you to know that quantitative research skills are sharpened by the DOING of quantitative research, as most of the learning in this area occurs via experience—mistakes and all.

Quantitative Research Basics

In a nutshell, quantitative research involves the collection and analysis of *numerical* data. Within the quantitative umbrella, there are four primary categories:

1. descriptive research (what the characteristics of something are)
2. correlational research (what the relationship between something and something else is)
3. quasi-experimental research (what the impact of something on something else is—without using random assignment of participants)
4. experimental research (what the impact of something on something else is—using random assignment of participants into treatment and control/comparison groups)

The first two categories (correlational and descriptive) are typically achieved via **survey research**, while the last two categories (quasi-experimental and experimental research) are grouped under the umbrella of **intervention research**. We will unpack the differences, practices, and unique usefulness of each of these methods later on in this chapter. Figure 7.1 provides a visual representation of types of quantitative research questions and their related designs.

The first question in the decision tree centers on whether you will be implementing a **treatment** or not. In school-based research, treatment usually means an intervention of some kind and is defined as "the assessment of a hypothesized causal impact of a specific practice, treatment, curriculum, or program on selected participant outcomes" (Griffith & Greenspan, 2017, p. 124). In other words, you want to determine the impact of something you or someone else has developed for those who engaged in it.

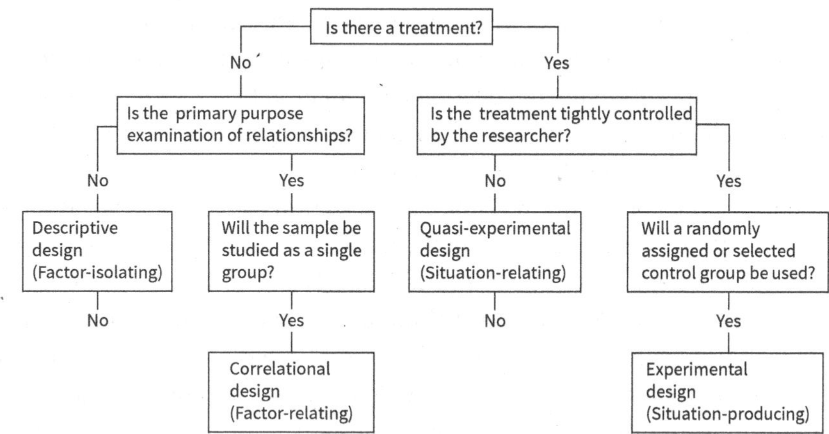

Figure 7.1. Decision Tree Matching Research Design to Category of Research Question
From Keele (2010).

In survey research, the primary focus is getting a sense of the descriptive characteristics of a population and/or construct, as well as the nature of the relationships between constructs and variables. In intervention research, descriptive data and relationships are also commonly explored but typically as secondary research questions.

One of the things we like about quantitative research is that even though these types of studies tend to take a lot of front-end planning in regard to implementation, once you've finished collecting your data, the analysis typically isn't too labor intensive (unless you're using a fancier approach like structural equation modeling, in which case you've got a lot of analysis work to do and godspeed). This differs substantially from qualitative research (the collection and analysis of *non-numerical* data such as interviews, observations, and artifacts), where the bulk of the complex work tends to occur during or after data have been collected.

The other thing we like about quantitative research is that—if the study design was robust enough—results may be considered more **generalizable** to broader populations. This means that you can take what was learned about the group of people within your study and can make reasonable assumptions of how what you have found may apply to similar groups of people or similar contexts. The stronger the methodological design, the wider the implications for the larger population and the greater the extent to which we can expect a given phenomenon to manifest in different settings. That said, please do not fool yourself into thinking that quantitative research is fully objective! As much as our engagement in the quest for truth involves numbers, people (and subsequently our subjective biases) heavily inform the process—from deciding what seems important as an initial research question to what seems valuable for publication during peer review. Quantitative research, despite its reputation as being more impartial than qualitative approaches, is also socially constructed throughout the stages of development, questioning, interpretation, persuasion, consensus, revision, and selection for publication (Ritchie, 2020). Quantitative data can absolutely become another tool of propagating systems of privilege and oppression. If we truly are to be agents of equity and change, as researchers we must think deeply about how our own biases are indeed impacting every step of the process. What issues are you seeing as important compared with others? Which voices and whose perspectives are informing your understanding of key constructs? What instruments have you selected and for which populations have they been normed? What is your unique sense of the meaning behind the data and implications for the school counseling profession? There is much to consider, and, frankly, everyone benefits when we enact the kind of depth of thought and cultural humility it takes to recognize where we need to improve, as we evolve from implicit to intentional in our methods.

Two Forces to Consider in School-Based Quantitative Research: Rigor and Feasibility

You may have noticed we've already used terms like **strong, rigorous,** and **robust** as qualifiers in quantitative research. All of these words refer to the general quality and subsequent generalizability of an empirical research study. In other words, the degree to which we have been able to reduce the impact of bias and error successfully in our investigation or not has a direct influence on the big question: *How much can we trust that these data actually represent the situation we hoped to explore?* To help answer this question, we look to issues of **validity,** the accuracy of instruments and subsequent findings (i.e., whether these measures accurately represent and identify the phenomena they are supposed to), and **reliability,** the consistency of results (i.e., whether these findings can be repeated). There are a number of ways to strengthen methodological rigor in the planning phases of a study, many of which are presented throughout this book. Typically, the more strictly planned and tightly controlled the study, the higher the rigor.

Do the phrases *strictly planned* and *tightly controlled* describe any school setting you've observed? Probably not! This is where the concept of **feasibility** comes into play when implementing quantitative research studies in school settings. A consideration of methodological feasibility has us contemplating questions such as: *Is this realistic? Are these reasonable expectations given the reality of the people and places this study involves?* Giving proper time and attention to the feasibility of your study is every bit as impactful on reliability and validity as methodological rigor, as it has everything to do with whether your study actually can be carried out as intended (see Chapter 12).

As you consider the research process ahead of you, know that these two forces will often be at odds with one another. Feasibility versus rigor more often than not represents a zero-sum game, and what you do in service of one will usually be at the cost of the other. Bowers and Lemberger-Truelove (2016) were keen to remind us that yes, as researchers we should be concerned with research designs that limit contaminations of data, but at the same time there are definite constrictions on how and what type of data can be reasonably collected in schools. We bring this all up because the consideration of these two forces—rigor and feasibility—should be at the forefront when planning your research study. This will also be an issue during implementation, as we have yet to see a research protocol be carried out perfectly start to finish in school settings with no adjustments needing to be made. Because of the inherent complexity and unpredictability of the environment, school-based researchers are constantly adapting to inevitable midstream changes in the plan (e.g., school schedule changes, logistical upsets, protocols being carried out incorrectly, recognition of missing voices, events that have residual effects on participant data, and on and on and on). We can be thoughtful about these potential hurdles in advance and as often as possible try to have the ability to pivot from our best-laid plans. This is a process that benefits immensely from

- being as clear and detailed as you can about your research process and goals at the outset,
- Assuming things will often take more time and resources than you would expect,
- incorporating flexibility into your research design,
- being empathetic and flexible to systemic challenges while also being mindful of pushing back against systems created to keep historically oppressed voices out of the research process, and
- using the relationships you've built with school personnel to navigate these challenges.

The big takeaway here is that disruptions to your research plan absolutely will happen. And though we don't want perfection, there is much you can do ahead of time to help ensure adequate—or even excellent—methodological

---

Pop-Out 7.2. Highlight: Common Markers of Rigorous Research

- Includes a large, diverse, and representative sample size
- Uses validated instrumentation that was normed with the current population being studied
- Incorporates random selection of participants
- Has low participant attrition
- Data collection involves more than self-report data.
- Establishes causality through baseline data and control group
- Uses appropriate/robust analysis (e.g., assumptions are met, data set is cleaned, confounding variables are accounted for, limitations are addressed)
- Results are replicated through multiple studies in different populations and settings.

Keep in mind: While it is helpful to have awareness of all the ways you can implement more robust research, there are very few studies in school counseling that meet all of these markers. Feasibility will likely get in the way of being able to incorporate every checkmark fully.

---

strength. Too much compromise in design quality can result in data you can't really trust. Be aspirational in your design, flexible in your adaptations, and transparent in the limitations section of your manuscript. And never forget, error is an ongoing and inevitable aspect of good research—each study is a stepping stone to lessons learned, greater rigor, and higher-quality data.

Getting Started: Foundations of Quantitative Designs

Most researchers find it helpful to break down the large and occasionally overwhelming work of beginning a new empirical investigation into bite-sized pieces. This also helps a great deal with intentionality in the process and serves as a highly detailed recipe of sorts that aids in implementing your study. As with any recipe, it bears considering what your ultimate goal is, distinct from other research projects you've carried out. You also want to give thought to how each stage of your implementation strategy informs the next, increasing specificity as time goes on. We find it helpful to think about the research process like an hourglass: You start by making your way through large swaths of information until you boil down to a very narrow research question and method that will best help you answer that question and then broaden out again as you think about the possible implications of your findings and next steps (Schulte, 2003).

Are you eager to start contemplating the methodological design for your quantitative research project? You're only truly ready if you have already completed the following:

1. Conducted a thorough literature review. Your literature review should help you determine what is already known on your topic of interest and what gaps in knowledge represent some possible next logical steps. Existing literature can also help you refine your study ideas by expanding your understanding of theoretical frameworks and providing support for the research methods you want to use. Critically consider the voices represented (or not) in the literature and actively seek out diverse viewpoints rather than those works with simply the most influence or number of citations.

2. Drawn from an observed area of interest and the existing literature to identify your research topics, questions, and hypotheses. Table 7.1 provides examples of methodological approaches and suggested research question stems.

3. Specified the purpose of your research (see Chapter 4). This critical step keeps researchers' efforts highly focused and organized during data analysis and write-up of results. It also provides clarity for communicating with key stakeholders.

4. Identified your constructs and variables of interest. **Constructs** are subjective and developed by researchers to represent simple or complex abstract concepts to be measured (Barrio Minton & Lenz, 2019). Anxiety, aggression, engagement, intelligence, and occupational satisfaction are examples of constructs. A **variable** represents an element or property that can vary. There are numerous types of variables, such as independent and dependent variables. **Independent variables** (IVs) are naturally occurring (e.g., age, demographic characteristics, ethnicity/race) or manipulated by the researcher (e.g., treatments, interventions, programs). **Dependent variables** (DVs) are influenced by or dependent on—hence the term—the IV (e.g., the participants' response to the treatment). Researchers often investigate how IVs influence or predict, explain, strengthen, or obscure DVs' relationships (e.g., **predictive, mediating, moderating, and confounding variables,** respectively).

5. Selected appropriate instruments to measure outcomes and your variables (see Chapter 6). Existing instruments will have reliable and valid estimates. If you have developed a measure or are planning to construct one, you need to describe how you will derive its reliability and validity estimates.

6. Assembled a research team. Team members may include colleagues, practitioners, supervisors, statisticians, and consultants. Your team members typically know the setting and research design, have content or statistical expertise, and have experience disseminating results. Their role in your study depends on the amount of support necessary to help navigate the research context and process. Conducting research is a complex process that involves deliberate planning, flexibility to manage twists and turns, and adaptability to address barriers to reach a successful conclusion. Working with a team helps you maximize your efforts and boost your confidence.

Several helpful texts (Balkin & Kleist; 2017; Barrio et al., 2019; Brace et al., 2016; Goodwin, 2010; Hancock et al., 2019; Sheperis et al., 2010; Wright, 2014) and of course the chapters within this book will help you think deeply about each research process stage. The absolute key here is to make sure you have engaged in all of the appropriate steps before determining your research design. All too often, we see folks using what could be labeled a *methods-first* approach, which does not help you arrive at the most needed or appropriate research questions. Although tempting, you should never start with *"I'd like to implement a survey"* or *"I'd like to design an intervention curriculum"* without a full examination as to whether the investigation of a given issue and the

Table 7.1. Methods and Sample Research Question Stems

Methodological Approach	Research Question Stem
Descriptive Research	What are the characteristics of . . .
	How often do . . .
	What percentage of time is spent on . . .
Correlational Research	What is the relationship between . . .
	How strong is the relationship between . . .
	What is the covariance of . . .
Intervention Research	What is the impact of . . .
	What is the effect of . . .
	What is the impact of X when compared with Y?

Note: X = independent variable. Y = dependent variable.

Pop-Out 7.3. Highlight: Anatomy of a Research Question

Great research questions not only inform the reader about the methodological approach but also contain information on the population, constructs of interest, instrumentation used, and any comparison/control groups involved. Here is the process broken down into a series of steps:

1. What is/are the . . .
   If descriptive research: . . . the characteristics OR . . . difference
   If correlational: . . . the relationship
   If intervention: . . . the impact of (describe intervention)
2. of/between/on . . .
   One group of people: . . . (population)
   Two or more groups: . . . (population) and (population)
3. who experience/rates of/who receive/on (construct of interest . . .
4. as measured by. . . (instrument used). Not comparing groups? Stop here.
5. when compared to (population).
   If control group: . . . who did not receive (intervention)
   If comparison group: . . . who received (other intervention or service)

This is really useful information not only for others to have clarity on an investigation, but also for researchers themselves to keep their efforts highly focused and in keeping organized during data analysis and when writing up results.

---

difference between what is known and what is unknown about that issue actually warrant that methodology. Remember the hourglass analogy: It starts with identifying a broader area or topic of interest, conducting a literature review, developing your research questions, and THEN deciding what specific method will best help you answer those questions.

Going back to the multi-pronged model posed at the beginning of this chapter, let's again look at common research designs that fit into the two broader categories of research that we've identified: surveys and interventions. Figure 7.2 highlights how the processes for both approaches are the same at the outset, branch out in how they are uniquely carried out, but align once again in the final stages of the research process. We will unpack the ample implementation considerations in two parts: Part I will outline pre-implementation planning in identifying your population of interest, inclusion/exclusion criteria, and selection of participants. Then in Part II we will expand on the characteristics of survey and intervention research during

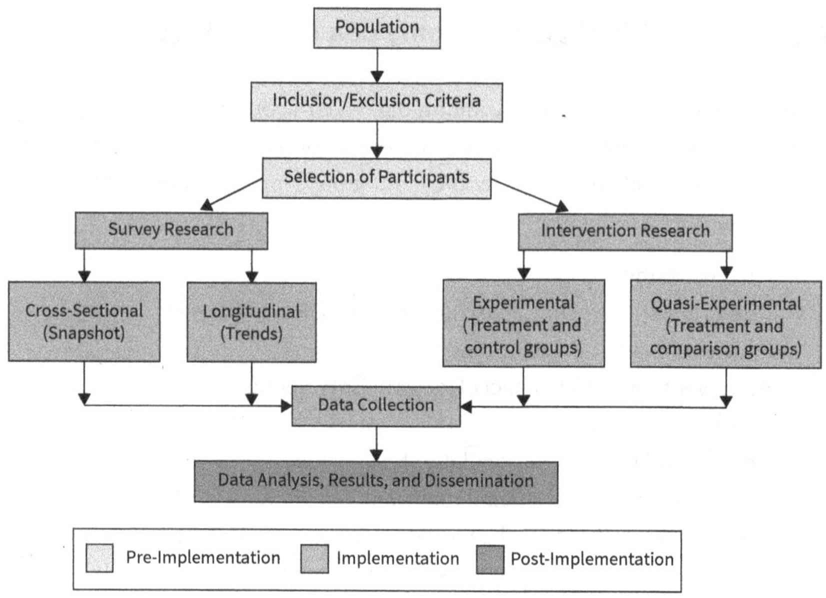

Figure 7.2. Flow Chart for Survey and Intervention Research

the implementation phase itself while making recommendations for sources and exemplary school counselor research to deepen your understanding of these designs. What follows will highlight practical information on applying the design sequence to solidify the methods for your own applied quantitative research study.

Implementation Considerations: Part I

It can be helpful to conceive of the implementation of your quantitative study as having two parts: (1) everything you do to prepare for your investigation after determining your research question(s), and (2) what you do during the study implementation to help ensure that the process runs as smoothly as can be managed. We'll start with the **pre-implementation phase** with our suggestions on how to best go about identifying and recruiting your study participants.

Also, we highly recommend that you take a quick (or not so quick) breather between this section and the upcoming Implementation Considerations: Part II. This is a lot of material to take in! Your brain will likely thank you if you give yourself a bit of space to think and reflect on the content from this section before moving on to the next.

Identify Your Population

Your **target population** serves the larger pool to which you intend to generalize your results and draw your participants. A population is an entire group of individuals and the subject of your study. For example, you might be interested in exploring the impact of a social-emotional learning (SEL) curriculum with elementary students. However, it's seldom feasible to implement a study involving the entire population, so instead you might select a smaller, representative sample from a diverse school district, school(s), or grade level(s). Therefore, your decisions to choose a representative group(s) depend on the resources (e.g., time, materials, funding, access to participants) you have at your disposal. Regardless, you want to base your rationale for targeting a specific group on the existing literature and be mindful of ethical considerations (see Chapter 3), so you can generalize your results to the population with confidence.

Pop-Out 7.4. Putting Your Study in Context: Is Your Population WEIRD?

Did you know that folks who are Western, educated, industrialized, rich, and democratic (WEIRD) represent approximately 80% of research study participants despite consisting of only 12% of the world's total population (Apicella et al., 2020; Henrich et al., 2010)? Furthermore, of these research subjects the vast majority are undergraduate college students enrolled in psychology courses (Henrich et al., 2010).

There is a lot to unpack here about ease of access to study participants, and what that might say about how applicable these study findings may be for minoritized individuals. Therefore, if you ultimately desire for your findings to be applicable with diverse populations, then your sample must be appropriately representative. If unable to do so, then ethically you should use qualifiers in how you describe your population. For example, expanding "in a sample of high school students" to be more specific could be: "in a sample of majority-white high school students in a suburban area or the Northeastern United States," or "in a sample of lesbian, gay, and bisexual youth" rather than "LGBTQ" if your population did not include transgender participants. But most preferable of all would be to be intentional about including a diverse and representative population in your study.

Determine Your Inclusion and Exclusion Criteria

Inclusion and exclusion criteria are a set of characteristics used to determine whether a participant is eligible for, or disqualified from, participating in your study. Setting these criteria helps you protect your resources (e.g., time, materials, funding, and the number of participants) and control the study's scope, recruitment strategy, and data collection. You also want to strike a balance between generalizing your results and minimizing bias.

Select Your Participants

Determine the Sample Size Needed

Participants (aka your sample) are essential to any study, but there are several factors involved in determining who is selected. To begin you must answer the question: *How many participants do I need*? There are two practical reasons you need to answer this question. First, to guard against **type I error** (saying there is an effect when there isn't) and, second, to prevent **type II error** (saying there's no effect when there actually is), you need to know how much power

---

Pop-Out 7.5. Research in Practice

Recently, Webb et al. (2019) published the results of a randomized control trial (RCT) study that examined the impact of the Student Success Skills intervention (Brigman & Webb, 2010). In this study, the researchers randomly assigned Grade 5 students attending 60 schools from two large school districts in Florida to treatment and control conditions. Therefore, the target population was Grade 5 students living in the two participating FL school districts' communities.

The researchers also defined the schools' characteristics and eligible students. For example, to qualify for inclusion, schools needed to employ a school counselor who agreed to deliver the intervention and have four general education classroom teachers willing to allow the counselor to conduct the classroom guidance lessons. The school counselors and teachers also had to complete all data collection and attend the professional development workshops. Conversely, the researchers excluded students if they had limited English language skills or if a disability prevented them from enrolling in general education classes. By establishing a clear set of criteria, the researchers focused their recruitment strategy on specific schools and students, thereby maximizing their effort and available resources.

you require to measure a statistically significant difference in your outcomes accurately. Keep in mind that in general, the higher the sample size, the greater the likelihood you will be protected from falsely rejecting or accepting your null hypothesis.

It's helpful to think of statistical power as a telescope. Gazing up into the evening sky you don't need a powerful lens to see the moon—it's clearly visible to the naked eye. In this analogy think of the moon as a very large effect size. There are, however, a great many smaller celestial bodies that require a stronger lens to be able to detect them. Just because some distant and smaller planets and stars aren't clearly visible to the naked eye doesn't mean they aren't there. Small effect sizes only need a more powerful telescope to be detected. One tool that can tell you how big your metaphorical telescope should be at the outset of your study is G*Power (www.gpower.hhu.de/), downloadable free-to-use software for calculating statistical power. Conducting an **a priori power analysis** is needed to determine how many participants you need to achieve your desired power, the probability of finding a true significance. To compute the a priori power analysis, you will need to input: (a) your desired alpha level (typically .05) and level of power (e.g., 80%); (b) your planned statistical test (i.e., t-test, analysis of variance, analysis of covariance, correlations, regression, logistics, proportions, chi-square, nonparametric equivalents); and (c) your estimated effect size (e.g., d, r, eta squared), and the software will produce the necessary sample size (N) required to help avoid type I or type II error.

Consider Your Sampling Procedures

Quantitative researchers use probability sampling methods to select their participants. Probability sampling methods include cluster random, opportunity, simple random, stratified random, systematic random, and volunteer sampling. You will need to use probability sampling if you want to generalize your results to your target population. Table 7.2 presents characteristics, strengths, and weaknesses for the probability sampling methods to take into consideration when making this decision. We also recommend Daniel's (2012) text, *Sampling Essentials: Practical Guidelines for Making Sample Choices* for a more thorough explanation of sampling.

Finalize Your Recruitment Strategy

Although your sampling method will inform how you go about recruiting participants, there are some additional considerations to keep in mind. For starters, you will be more successful in your endeavors to find participants if either you or a collaborator has established buy-in with the population of interest. The stronger the relationship, the more likely individuals are to agree to take part in the study and follow through with providing data. Therefore, if you find yourself conducting school-based research in an environment in which you are not employed, it is imperative that you link up with someone at the site (whether that be teachers, admins, or other counselors) who holds some degree of clout and positive influence in the recruitment phase. Chapters 2, 3 and 5 in this text also address this topic from various perspectives.

Table 7.2. Characteristics of Probability Sampling Methods

Sampling Type	Procedure	Strengths	Weaknesses
Cluster random sampling	Population is divided into subgroups or clusters, then randomly select entire cluster (e.g., classrooms).	• Easy to implement • Cost-effective	• Lowest precision
Opportunity sampling	Relies on participants who are available at the time • (e.g., speaking to students as they enter the cafeteria)	• Quick, convenient, and cost effective	• Can lead to researcher bias • Subgroups may be underrepresented.
Simple random sampling	Researchers use a population list and a random number to choose participants (e.g., random number generator).	• Best chance for an unbiased sample as everyone has an equal chance of being selected	• Requires knowledge of the population, access to data, and additional time to create a list
Stratified random sampling	Population is divided into subgroups and selected by equal percentages (e.g., 5% per subgroup).	• Researchers make a deliberate effort to achieve equal representation from each subgroup. • Highest precision	• Requires knowledge of the population, access to data, and additional time to create and divide the list into subgroups
Systematic random sampling	Prospective participants are ordered or ranked, then chosen by a regular interval (e.g., every 10th) until the sample size is reached.	• Can increase representativeness	• Does not give equal chance of selection
Volunteer Sampling	Relies on prospective participants to self-select	• Relatively convenient • No researcher bias	• Slower • Subgroups may be underrepresented and likely introduce a member bias.

A proactive approach to recruitment also goes a long way, and we recommend diversifying your methods in order to reach more folks within your population of interest. Consider both in-person methods such as visiting the site yourself to tell potential participants about your study directly as well as remote methods via emails, social media postings, media announcements, and good old-fashioned flyers. Participants who have already been recruited can also be helpful by providing referrals to more people who may fit your study criteria. All of this will of course be impacted by the desired size and scale of your study, your minimum target population size identified in your a priori analysis, and the stringency of your eligibility criteria. It is also safe to assume that you will encounter various hurdles during this phase of the process, so be wise and build a lot of breathing room into the research timeline, as recruitment almost always takes longer than originally anticipated.

Also, worth considering is whether to use incentivization or not. Examples typically include monetary compensation, gift cards, charitable donations, extra credit in courses/on assignments, meals/snacks, or lotteries for a bigger ticket item. Incentives should be used as token awards and not be so large that they are coercive in their influence. Furthermore, while incentives can certainly result in a higher rate of volunteers, they can also be a drain on your resources while potentially introducing participation bias. If you plan on using participant incentives to aid in recruitment and retention, you'll also want to make sure they are actually legal in your state. For example, you may see studies from time to time that say something along the lines of *five lucky participants will receive a $25 Amazon gift card!*" In California, however, this constitutes an illegal lottery if the only way to enter is to complete the survey. Overall, when it comes to recruiting, do your homework, develop a detailed plan at the outset, and anticipate that you will encounter curveballs during the process.

Strengthen Participant Retention

If you are considering conducting school-based research, you need to assume that you will experience some level of attrition. Attrition occurs when you lose participants and related data from your sample, a common occurrence when your research participants are PK–12 students. For instance, students might transfer schools, refuse to assent, drop out of the study, miss a round of data collection, or fail to complete all the items on your measure(s). Researchers planning intervention studies must also be concerned with how attrition can impact their group equivalency (e.g., treatment, control, or comparison groups). Generally, a low attrition rate is considered 5% or less, and more than 40% is deemed high (Puma et al., 2009). Ultimately, to mitigate data loss, you

---

Pop-Out 7.6. Highlight: Can You Spare a Dillman Dollar?

Have you ever received a survey in the mail and found a crisp dollar bill accompanying the instrument? This happened to one of the authors once in college, and it probably is the only survey-by-mail that she ever actually completed and returned. Don Dillman and his research team have conducted a vast number of studies focused on survey response rates over the years and have found that inclusion of a dollar or two in the mailout can have a profound effect. Whether it is through fostering a sense of obligation or just the novelty of it all, this token payment has been shown to increase response rates by 15%–20% (Dillman et al., 2014).

---

need to recruit more participants than your power analysis suggests, but how large you go will undoubtedly depend on your resources (e.g., time, effort, costs; da Silva Frost & Ledgerwood, 2020).

Additional steps to mitigate attrition include: (a) linking your study to trusted organizations and individuals known to participants; (b) offering accessible times and locations for the participants either to participate in the intervention and/or to complete your survey; (c) ensuring that any facilitators and/or instrument proctors have prior experience and training in creating a safe, nonjudgmental atmosphere for people to feel comfortable participating and providing data about themselves in; (d) providing reminders to individuals about participating in the study; (e) ensuring that any collaborators involved are committed to the project for the entire duration in order to maintain the continuity of the relationship with participants; (f) ensuring that the instruments are developmentally appropriate and understandable to your participants; and (g) marketing your study as something that can lead to positive change rather than addressing a deficit, which reduces stigma for participating (Davis et al., 2002; Robinson et al., 2007).

A word to the wise: peer reviewers will expect that you report the amount of attrition in your study and how you handled missing data in your analysis. Therefore, you need to document changes in your data and the procedures used to diminish any potential bias. The U.S. Department of Education, Institute of Education Sciences (IES), offers guidelines on how to calculate your attrition rates (Puma et al., 2009). When data are missing, researchers can use appropriate statistical methods such as imputation methods, maximum likelihood estimation, dummy variable adjustment, weighting methods, fully specified regression models, selection modeling, and pattern mixture modeling (Cook, 2020; Puma et al., 2009). Additional information

---

Pop-Out 7.7. Research Scenario

Ms. Quintero, a middle school counselor, wants to know how students rate their anxiety level after participating in a mindfulness intervention she has developed. To test the effects of the treatment (mindfulness lessons), she conducts a G*Power analysis (Faul et al., 2007).

She finds she needs a sample of 150 participants to find statistical significance, and after receiving the parent consent and student assent, she sorts them into two groups. Seventy-five students will receive the mindfulness program, while the other 75 students engage in the school's journal writing program (business as usual) for 30 minutes per week for the next 10 weeks. However, to measure the true effect of the intervention, she needs the differences between the groups to be insignificant so that the only measurable difference is the intervention being studied. She then accounts for the students' differences (e.g., demographics, socioeconomic status, achievement level) at baseline (before the pretest and intervention) by randomly assigning students to the group conditions.

Regrettably, by the time she collects her posttest data, she finds that only 54 treatment group students and 67 control group students completed all 10 weeks of their respective programs and the related study instruments. In this scenario, the attrition reduces Ms. Quintero's statistical power and likely changes the random differences between the groups, leading to a bias in the estimation of the intervention's effect, both of which diminish her chances of knowing whether the mindfulness program was actually responsible for influencing students' anxiety. Unfortunately, this scenario can happen to anyone, so to avoid this outcome, we recommend having a pointed recruitment plan and collaboration with school personnel to achieve a solution that meets the project and school needs (Bartlett et al., 2017).

---

on the participant recruitment and retention process can be found in the following resources:

- Bruzzese, J.-M., Gallagher, R., McCann-Doyle, S., Reiss, P. T., & Wijetunga, N. A. (2009). Effective methods to improve recruitment and retention in school-based substance use prevention studies. *Journal of School Health*, *79*, 400–407. https://doi.org/10.1111/j.1746-1561.2009.00427.x.
- da Silva Frost, A., & Ledgerwood, A. (2020). Calibrate your confidence in research findings: A tutorial on improving research methods and practices. *Journal of Pacific Rim Psychology*, *14*(14). https://doi.org/10.1017/prp.2020.7

- Faul, F., Erdfelder, E., Lang, A. G., & Buchner, A. (2007). G*Power 3: A flexible statistical power analysis program for the social, behavioral, and biomedical sciences. *Behavior Research Methods, 39*, 175–191.
- Schoeppe, S., Oliver, M., Badland, H. M., Burke, M., & Duncan, M. (2014). Recruitment and retention of children in behavioral health risk factor studies: REACH strategies. *International Journal of Behavioral Medicine, 21*, 794–803. https://doi.org/10.1007/s12529-013-9347-5.

Implementation Considerations: Part II

Did you take that break we recommend between this section and the last? We hope so, because this next part covers a great deal of territory and multiple methodological approaches under the quantitative umbrella. You will most definitely want a clear head for this next part, as we'll be addressing the following content:

- descriptive research
- correlational designs (including the differences between cross-sectional and longitudinal survey research
- intervention research (and within that, a great number of different experimental and quasi-experimental approaches)

So, are you well rested, fed, caffeinated, and in possession of a clear mind? If so, you're all set!

Non-Experimental Designs: Descriptive and Correlational Research via Surveys

There are multiple ways in which observing non-outcome-based quantitative data is helpful to the work of school counseling. Sometimes, as an observed need or gap in knowledge shapes into a research question, our aim may be to gather more information on a topic, population, or phenomena; learn how to solve a problem; shed light on existing inequities; improve current practices in schools; or understand the relationships between constructs. In such cases, implementing a non-experimental design, such as survey research, is appropriate. Surveys help researchers examine policies or program needs, evaluate program effectiveness, and generate new areas for research (Fink, 2017). Although surveys may include qualitative components, our focus is solely on those that involve numerically rated items.

Descriptive Designs

Sometimes it can be helpful to understand the what, how, who, when, and where without necessarily getting into the *why*. Researchers can benefit immensely from simply getting a snapshot and increasing their understanding of what currently exists. Descriptive research typically does not include independent variables, examination of relationships or causality, hypotheses, or theories. Instead, your research questions will mostly center on the characteristics of a population, environment, situation, or construct with regard to things like: (a) how often something occurs, (b) discovering central tendencies and variations to help understand what is common or more uncommon among your participants, and (c) discovering commonalities and differences between groups or with an established norm (Dulock, 1993). Data are often gathered through self-report but can also include observational data by teachers, caretakers, and counselors, as well as other regularly collected school data such as test scores, grades, attendance, discipline referrals, free and reduced lunch status, health, and climate surveys.

For example, say a researcher wants to determine the degree to which an achievement gap exists within her school district and decides to conduct a descriptive study. She begins by gathering demographic variables, such as students' race/ethnicity, gender, grades, grade level, test scores, attendance, and socioeconomic status (as measured by enrollment in the free-and-reduced lunch program), from the district database. Next, she combines the demographic data with advanced placement (AP) courses and special education services enrollment data. Finally, she surveys participants on the amount of time they spend weekly engaged in schoolwork, jobs, family responsibilities, and accessing resources. Once she has compiled her study data, she analyzes the data to report the frequency and percentages of her sample and measures of central tendency (e.g., means, median, mode, standard deviations) by her variables of interest to define the diversity and dispersion of the sample. Ultimately, this snapshot of information could help a great deal in identifying which specific groups of students need support and of what kind, which schools within the district are most in need, the degree to which support is needed, and when that help could be most effective (such as the transition between middle and high school). See Table 7.3 for reference for exemplary descriptive research.

Table 7.3. Purpose for Survey Design and Common Analyses

Type	Purpose	Common Statistical Approach	Exemplar Studies
Descriptive Surveys	Understanding program needs, program and subgroup characteristics, policy needs, and stakeholder satisfaction Evaluating program outcomes	Frequency and percentages Measures of central tendency (e.g., mean, median, mode, standard deviation) Measures of variability Measures of relationship	• Goodman-Scott et al. (2016) • Martin et al. (2009) • Mason et al. (2019) • National Center for Education Statistics (2003) • Sherwood (2010) • Sink & Yillik-Downer (2001)
Cross-Sectional Surveys	Understanding respondents' attitudes, beliefs, knowledge at a specific time Understanding the relationship between variables (e.g., influence, predictive)	Simple regression Multiple regression Logistical regression Hierarchical linear regression Canonical correlation Path analysis Structural equation modeling Chi-square	• Carey & Dimmitt (2012) • Gallo (2018) • Lapan et al. (2012) • Porter & Smith-Adcock (2016–2017) • Wilkerson et al. (2013)
Longitudinal Surveys	Understanding the change and prediction of data over time	Simple regression Multiple regression Logistical regression Hierarchical linear regression Canonical correlation Path analysis Structural equation modeling	• Bryan et al. (2012) • Cholewa et al. (2018) • Goodman-Scott et al. (2018) • Poynton & Lapan (2017)

Correlational Designs

Correlational research helps us understand the nature of relationships between variables, and, by definition, neither of those variables are manipulated by the researcher. Researchers may want to collect data on things like types and frequency of experiences, attitudes toward a construct, and severity of issues faced. The outcomes of these studies illuminate whether there is a positive correlation (an increase in one variable leads to an increase in another, with a perfect positive relationship having a coefficient value of +1.0), a

---

Pop-Out 7.8. Highlight: Research in Practice

Sherwood (2010), a school counselor from Georgia, gathered descriptive data using staff surveys, conducted qualitative interviews, and carried out researcher observations in service of a school counseling program evaluation at a PK–5 elementary school. The goals of the study were to determine staff members' perceptions of the school counseling program and their level of awareness of the role of the school counselor, and to identify program strengths and areas in need of improvement. Staff members included full-time general and special education teachers, early intervention teachers, support teachers, and administrators.

Fifty surveys were distributed during a staff meeting, and 31 were returned for analysis (62% response rate). The survey consisted of 10 items with a 4-point Likert scale (e.g., strongly agree, agree, disagree, and strongly disagree) and three open-ended questions. Follow-up interviews were conducted with nine volunteer staff members along with the notes from researcher's observations regarding repeated suggestions for program improvement. Results from the survey analysis revealed that of those surveyed, 65% strongly agreed the classroom guidance lessons and small groups were beneficial, the counselors responded to referrals in a timely manner, and they would recommend school counseling services to students and parents. Sixty-one percent strongly agreed the counselor was willing to collaborate with teachers to address student needs, 52% strongly agreed the small-group topics met the students' needs, and 32% felt the teachers were provided with appropriate follow-up information. Additionally, qualitative data suggested the staff perceived that the delay to providing follow-up information to staff was due to the school counselor's non-counseling-related duties.

As a result of the study, the school counselor decided to hold monthly grade-level meetings to share student concerns and to engage in a classroom guidance topic debriefing. The monthly meetings then led to increased consultation and collaboration with teachers and additional time for individual counseling with students.

---

negative correlation (an increase in one variable leads to a decrease in another, with a perfect negative relationship having a coefficient value of −1.0), or no correlation (the variables appear to have no impact on one another, with a coefficient value of 0). Within that −1.0 to +1.0 range, a value between ±.50 and ±1.0 is a strong correlation, a value between ±0.30 and ±0.49 is a medium correlation, and a value below ±.29 is a small correlation (Aggarwal & Ranganathan, 2016). There are two main types of correlational surveys, primarily distinguished by *time*.

Cross-Sectional Survey Studies

This approach involves collecting data during a single point in time, which could be within a single day, but for more rigorous research the window is more likely to occur within several weeks as you engage in recruitment rounds. It can be helpful to think of this method as something of a snapshot, helping you understand information about a population within a specific period. The main advantage of the cross-sectional method is that it tends to require relatively few resources and has a streamlined process. Findings from cross-sectional studies are helpful to school counselors when planning their comprehensive school counseling programs and policies. For example, Owen et al. (2020) examined how a nonrandom, national sample of high school seniors ($N = 2,901$; 4.5% response rate) who took the ACT college entrance exam in February 2018 prefer to receive college and career information. The brief, 5-minute survey was available for 2 weeks, and the participants did not receive incentives. The researchers then matched the completed surveys with the participants' ACT composite and subject scores to their self-reported race, gender, and parent income. Findings revealed that parents, friends, college admission counselors, and web searches were preferred modes of receiving college and career information. Low-income and first-generation students had higher positive correlations with perceiving school counselors as helpful sources, and email and one-on-one sessions were the preferred communication methods. While these findings cannot be generalized to other high school seniors outside of this study, school counselors can use this information to plan how to share their college and career knowledge. To address the lack of generalizability, counselors could survey their students to determine which services they would prefer. With their data, counselors can prioritize direct (small group, individual counseling) and indirect services (parent workshops, college admission visitors, college and career fairs). Additionally, counselors could prepare email templates and schedule a series of electronic communications (emails, blogs, newsletters) throughout the students' high school years.

Longitudinal Studies

Imagine if counselors could predict which students were more likely to struggle academically and behaviorally before entering high school. How could counselors use that type of predictive data to drive their program planning? Fortunately, by collecting data over time, school counseling scholars and practitioners can preventatively identify which students are most at risk, develop district/school-wide initiatives, deliver appropriate evidence-based interventions to support student growth and development, and evaluate program outcomes. Longitudinal surveys are a useful methodology for assessing participants over an extended period of time in order to help understand any trends in the data. These types of studies tend to be more involved and labor intensive, and some have even lasted for decades! Longitudinal studies allow researchers to quantify trends, identify behavioral changes and patterns, test theory, describe life events' progression, and justify interventions to meet population and community needs (White & Arzi, 2005). A researcher will use repeated measures throughout the length of the study and, unlike in cross-sectional research, has the option to adjust some of the variables being measured as data illuminate areas of interest over time. The longitudinal research about early warning indicators (EWIs; Gallup-Black & Sackman, 2015; Stuit et al., 2016) provides an example of the value of tracking participant behaviors and outcomes over a more extended period.

Attendance (missing more than 20 days), behavior (two or more mild or series infractions), and course performance (below reading or math grade level, grade retention, 2.0 GPA or less), also known as the ABCs, are highly predictive of high school completion (Bruce et al., 2011). Multiple longitudinal studies have revealed the predictive power of the ABC indicators across the PK–12 spectrum. Chang and Romero (2008) found that the combination of chronic absenteeism and living in poverty during the kindergarten year predicted students mostly likely to be at the lowest achievement level by Grade 5. Balfanz et al. (2007) followed nearly 13,000 urban middle school youth for 8 years and found that reported data for low attendance, misbehavior, and course failures were predictive of 60% of high school dropouts. Longitudinal studies of sixth graders in Philadelphia and Boston showed that students who failed English or math in the sixth grade rarely graduated (Balfanz & Boccanfuso, 2007; Baltimore Education Research Consortium, 2011). Conversely, Allensworth and Easton (2005) noted that freshman attending Chicago Public Schools were 3.5 times more likely to graduate if they: (a) earned at least five full-year credits and (b) did not receive more than one failing grade during a semester in Grade 9. While the ABCs have consistently been found to be predictive of a lower graduation rate, researchers who use this longitudinal data also suggest that EWIs can vary from one district to another. Therefore, they recommend analyzing data on prior cohorts to confirm the accuracy of indicators within the local context to explore underlying causes and to use multiple indicators to provide intensive supports from within a multi-tiered system of support (MTSS; Chang & Romero, 2008; Stuit et al., 2016).

Counselors interested in conducting longitudinal studies often use existing databases, many of which are available at the state and federal levels. The Education Technical Assistance Act of 2002 established funding for all 50 states, the District of Columbia, and five U.S. territories to help create Statewide Longitudinal Data Systems (SLDSs). The SLDSs store prekindergarten through postsecondary student data, including workforce data (U.S. Department of Education, n.d.). To date, the U.S. Department of Education's Institute of Education Sciences (IES) has awarded grants to 41 states to design and implement SLDSs.

The IES National Center for Education Statistics website (https://nces.ed.gov/surveys/) makes available additional programs, surveys, and databases to conduct longitudinal research, such as: (a) Assessments; (b) the Early Childhood Longitudinal Studies (ECLS) program, focusing on child development, school readiness, and early school experiences; (c) Common Core of Data (CCD), providing elementary and secondary information from public and private schools including School Level, Beginning Teacher and Staffing, Career/Technical Education, Rural and Urban Education, School Reforms, and more; (d) Postsecondary; (e) International; (f) Library; and (g) Resources.

This wouldn't be a chapter on quantitative methods if the standard public service announcement that *correlation is not causation* was not offered. So, remember that determining relationships between variables is quite different from establishing how one variable can impact another. Nevertheless, gathering data from multiple sources—students, teachers, caretakers, administrators—allows researchers to understand the trends in stakeholders' perceptions to guide the implementation of targeted interventions within comprehensive school counseling programs (Mariani et al., 2019). Table 7.3 provides an overview of the types of surveys, purpose, common statistical approaches, and exemplar studies.

Additional Considerations for Survey Research

Of great concern to survey researchers is the **response rate**. Generally, a response rate of 50% or higher is considered excellent in most fields (Nulty, 2008), and the higher the response rate, the less likely that response bias can impact the validity of your results. However, your response rate can depend on the participant group. For instance, requesting survey completion from children and adolescents could require an adult reading items to the students and validating that their responses are properly recorded. You might also consider distributing surveys at faculty and staff meetings, conferences, and workshops where participants can be verbally informed about the survey and given the opportunity to respond before the event ends, as these in-person approaches typically result in much higher response rates than other methods.

Though there is no substitute for a captive, in-person audience where response rates are more often the highest, hard-copy mailouts are the next best bet (Nulty, 2008). Despite the relative ease of implementing an online survey, the degree of participation tends to be relatively low. Internal online surveys within organizations (e.g., school sites you or a collaborator are affiliated with) tend to have an average response rate of 30%–35% (Baruch & Holtom, 2008; Nulty, 2008), while survey response rates among large, external populations (e.g., randomly selected folks with whom you have little affiliation) typically fall between 10% and 15% (Fan & Yan, 2010).

In general, however, the following are some empirically validated tips for increasing your overall response rates, reducing the number of individual missing items, and improving the accuracy of participant responses, adapted from the Tailored Design Method (Dillman et al., 2014):

- Give careful attention to the visual design and layout of the survey to establish clear organization of the information and an unambiguous navigational path. This can be accomplished using visual tools such as font size variations, brightness and color, selection of symbols (e.g., arrows, stop signs), spacing of text, alignment, and symmetry to encourage all respondents to process and interpret information in the same way.
- Plan on four to five carefully timed contacts to solicit responses. This may include (1) a pre-invitation to inform a potential participant that they will soon be receiving a survey to complete (recruitment phase); (2) the initial survey; (3–4) reminders if the survey has not yet been completed, spaced out by 1–2 weeks; and (5) a *last chance* contact with a final deadline.
- Use at least one special and standout form of contact if implementing through the mail (e.g., a postcard or a different size envelope with overnight delivery).
- Provide personalized correspondence that includes dates and is addressed to specific individuals if at all possible
- Place the demographic portion of the survey last, which facilitates participant engagement with and investment in the survey sooner. This will help with completion rates by reducing drop-offs as the survey goes on.
- Switch to another mode (e.g., mail, telephone, or email) for nonrespondents and use multiple attempts by the new method to obtain a response.

Experimental and Quasi-Experimental Designs: Intervention Research

We've been talking about non-experimental research so far, especially using surveys to gather various types of information about our variables of interest. In this next section, we will be focusing on intervention research. In a nutshell, experimental and quasi-experimental designs help researchers understand the impact of an intervention. Hence, intervention research is the science of cause and effect. This area of quantitative inquiry helps us determine the efficacy of something (e.g., treatment, curriculum, program, approach) and is thus likely to result in knowledge about more direct and tangible practices that have an impact on student outcomes (e.g., achievement, social/emotional and well-being, college and career readiness).

When designing and writing about your approach, you need to explain succinctly the intervention's purpose, who will receive it, what and when it will occur, why it needs to happen, and a rationale for whether or how the intervention might work in your setting. Additionally, you need to plan procedures for monitoring treatment fidelity (see Chapter 12; as well as Barrio Minton & Lenz, 2019). Conducting school counseling intervention research is both challenging and necessary. Whiston et al.'s (2011) meta-analysis of school counseling outcome research suggested the need for more targeted interventions at the middle and high school level. Additionally, researchers needed to expand their use of diverse outcomes, investigate the long-term effects of interventions implemented at the elementary level, and provide evidence to support the effectiveness of implementing comprehensive school counseling programs. In sum, to advance school counseling, we need to understand how to develop empirically supported interventions to influence students' academic, social-emotional, and career development positively (Whiston & Sexton, 1998; Whiston et al., 2011).

Despite this need, there is a dearth of intervention research in the school counseling field. For example, out of 6,656 articles published in American School Counselor Association (ASCA)- and American Counseling Association (ACA)-affiliated journals between 2006 and 2016, a mere 53 represented intervention research in school counseling (Griffith et al., 2019). That's .08 of the total, or less than 1%. At the same time, wanting to know which specific school counseling interventions result in the greatest gains in students' achievement was twice ranked by expert panelists as the number one priority for research in school counseling (Dimmitt et al., 2005; Villares & Dimmitt, 2017). So please, dear reader, accept this gentle nudge to consider gathering evidence of impact during your research endeavors. Not only is school-based and child-focused intervention research deeply needed, but there are few greater thrills as a researcher than actually putting something into practice and seeing how well it worked.

As for specifics, **there are two primary types of intervention research: experimental and quasi-experimental.** The main difference between the two is **randomization**, with only the random assignment of participants into groups constituting what is called a *true experiment*. Within this type of research, however, there are still a plethora of approaches with various pros and cons to consider.

Group Conditions

In experimental designs, the treatment is known as the independent variable (IV), and any participant who receives the IV is part of the **treatment group**. In the Webb et al. (2019) study, students in the treatment group received the Student Success Skills (SSS) classroom program (Brigman & Webb, 2010) whereas the students who did not receive the SSS program (IV withheld) were part of the **control group**. Several types of control group conditions are possible, which we briefly discuss below.

No-Treatment Control, Treatment-as-Usual Condition

When implementing studies in schools, researchers often use a **treatment-as-usual** approach because withholding a standard practice could present an ethical dilemma. For example, let's say a researcher wants to know if a new reading program can improve students' academic achievement. To maximize the contrast between the treatments, it would be best for students in the control group to not receive reading instruction. However, you could imagine the unnecessary harm or delay this could cause students. Therefore, the researcher needs to determine if it's practical to suspend or withhold any type of instruction or allow the standard instruction to continue (i.e., treatment as usual). If you do plan to take the treatment-as-usual approach, be sure to document what takes place to avoid introducing any potential confounding variables.

Wait List Control Condition: Control Group Participants Receive Delayed Treatment

Waitlist control groups help ease the dilemma of whether to withhold a potentially beneficial treatment from participants. In this design, participants are given the pretest measures along with the treatment group but are told their intervention will begin after some delay or when the treatment group has finished. In addition to being able to isolate the impact of the intervention during the initial phase of your study, waitlist control groups are beneficial if you have limited time to train implementers, data collectors, or intervention materials. For example, Lemberger et al. (2018) examined the academic growth of 193 Grade 7 Hispanic students' academic achievement scores, executive functioning, and sense of connectedness after participating in the SSS classroom program. The researchers used a multilevel, randomized control design. Six of 11 social studies classrooms were randomly selected to participate in the SSS intervention during the fall semester. The other five classrooms served as the waitlisted control group and did not receive the intervention until the following spring. To measure the differences between groups for the outcome variables, the treatment and control groups completed the pretests 1 week before the intervention and four cycles of state standardized tests (1 week before SSS, 3 weeks after SSS, 3 months, and 6 months after the SSS intervention). Thus, the waitlist control group completed the two pretest instruments and one state standardized achievement cycle before engaging in the SSS classroom program. Utilizing this design, the researchers could make comparisons between the groups without entirely withholding treatment from the control group, which could have unintentionally impeded their academic growth or social-emotional skill development (Lemberger et al., 2018).

Expectancy Control: Placebo/Blinded Condition

Researchers use **blinding** as a method of concealing whether a participant has been enrolled in the intervention group or the control group, in order to reduce participant bias, as the assessment scores of those in an intervention group may get a boost from expectancy alone. This approach can be more difficult to undertake in schools due to the obviousness of participants' awareness of taking part in an intervention or not; however, there is a potential for a researcher to train others in two distinct methods (intervention vs. alternative method or placebo). In this scenario, the participants would not be aware of which group is actually receiving the intervention under investigation.

Comparative Treatment Condition: Participants Receive Equivalent Intervention

In addition to control groups (or as close to you can get to a true control group in school-based settings), you may also be interested in how your intervention stacks up against other methods. Within a comparative treatment design the participants receive something different, but essentially equivalent to the main treatment group. Say, for example, you wanted to see how participant outcomes with a solution-focused curriculum fared against an approach with cognitive-behavioral foundations. Beware *the dodo bird effect*, however (a delightfully evocative term derived from a passage in Alice in Wonderland to describe the relative effectiveness of all major forms of therapeutic intervention; Wampold et al., 1997), and know that it may be difficult to detect differences between approaches unless the effectiveness of one over the other is particularly strong.

Comparison Condition

In a quasi-experimental study, participants who do not receive a treatment or intervention are part of the comparison group. The primary characteristic of this group condition is that participants are not randomly assigned, thereby eliminating the choice of being considered a control group. Comparison groups are often used in school-based research because true randomization is difficult to achieve.

Clusters: Reducing Contamination With Groups

When conducting experimental research in an education setting, researchers must consider whether participants who receive a treatment can share or **contaminate** participants who are not receiving the intervention or program with their new knowledge, beliefs, or skills. One way to control for contamination is to assign **clusters**—classrooms, grade levels, schools, or entire school districts, rather than individuals to the group conditions. Contamination makes it harder for the researcher to assess the full value of the intervention and opens up a greater possibility of **type II error**—a false negative. In terms of feasibility, it is a double-edged sword. On the one hand, the examination of naturally occurring clusters can reduce logistics around the need to separate individual participants. On the other hand, a study of this nature represents a larger-scale recruitment and sample size need, with top-level access required and significant logistics to consider. This is another reason why a strong school-based partnership is a must when conducting experimental design with clusters.

Randomized Controlled Trials

Randomized controlled trials (RCTs) are widely considered the gold standard in intervention research, and there's a key reason why. Because participants have an equal chance of being assigned to either the intervention group or the **control group** (participants who *don't* receive the intervention), this

> ## Pop-Out 7.9. Highlight: Do You Know the Origins of Randomized Control Trials?
>
> The first recorded instance of an RCT was carried out by Scottish naval physician James Lind in 1747. Interested in possible treatments for scurvy, he randomly assigned 12 afflicted sailors to six groups with different potential remedies. Two of the sailors recovered more quickly than the others after consuming lemons and oranges, which eventually led to a larger understanding that a lack of vitamin C in sailors' diets was the cause of this lethal ailment. A splash of lemon juice in your grog a day keeps the doctor away!

method cuts down on all kinds of threats to internal validity, thereby providing much stronger support for the causality of the intervention. In other words, we have greater assurance that the main difference between each group is whether they participated in the intervention or not, rather than other possible mitigating factors. This works because randomization accounts for equitable distribution between groups not only of known variables, but also of unknown **confounding variables** that could have a causal impact on results (e.g., maturation between the intervention's start and finish, community cultural factors, and untold others) as well as the equality of the degree of impact from nonspecific processes. Unmeasured confounding variables, such as merely receiving attention, being assessed, and having an expectation of what the outcome will be, can ultimately have big effects, so randomization is the cleanest way to even the playing field between participant groups.

Typically, researchers use **pretests** and **posttests** to determine the differences between the intervention and control groups. A good sign that randomization has served its intended purpose is to find no differences between groups after administering the pretest. If your intervention is effective, you will ideally find positive differences after administering the posttest. Figure 7.3 provides a helpful visual of this process, and we illustrate an example of randomization in the following research scenario.

If you recall from Table 7.2, there are a few different approaches to randomizing participants, for which we recommend checking out *randomizer.org*. This site provides some nifty tools, such as the ability to determine the number of sets you want to generate, how many numbers per set, the number range, and method of sorting, all in one fell swoop. Note that randomization should occur as close to implementation of the intervention as possible, after

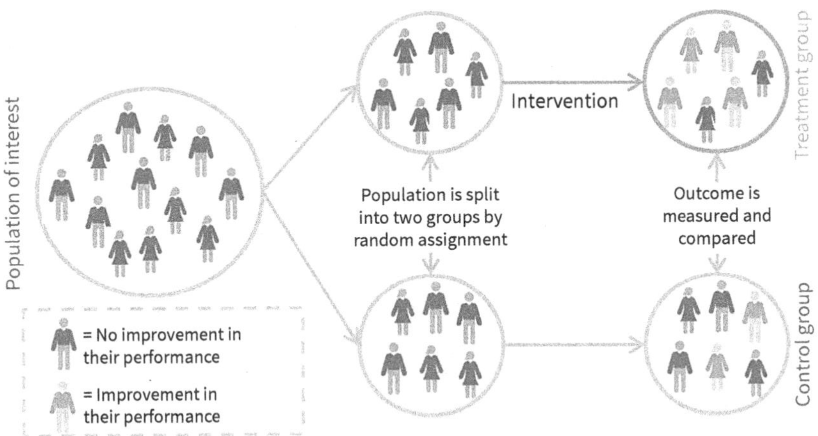

Figure 7.3. Visual Representation of the RCT Process
From Fyhn & Breining (2018).

pre-screening participants and after consent has been obtained. That way, you are more likely to avoid group imbalances from randomizing folks who were never actually going to take part in the study.

Randomized Groups Pretest–Posttest Design

Randomized Groups Pretest–Posttest designs, also known as efficacy studies, have gained increased attention in the field of education (Loeb et al., 2017); however, less have been reported in school counseling. The pretest–posttest design as depicted in Figure 7.3 is commonly used when conducting RCT studies and is an example of a treatment group receiving an intervention while the control group receives no treatment or placebo.

Other applications of the Randomized Groups Pretest–Posttest design would be to increase the number of levels (three levels) by adding a second type of treatment with one control (e.g., treatment 1 = SEL intervention; treatment 2 = tutoring; and control = no treatment). Another alternative is to introduce additional factors. In this case, a researcher would have two treatments (SEL intervention and tutoring) and two levels of intervention (5 weeks of classroom guidance lessons vs. 10 weeks of lessons). Researchers also refer to this design as **repeated measures** because the same participants are taking the study measures at multiple points throughout the study (i.e., pretest, posttest, follow-up). Table 7.5 provides an example of a between-groups factor design with two levels: treatment and control.

Pop-Out 7.10. Research Scenario: Conducting a Randomized Control Trial

Suppose you want to test, in an RCT design, whether your new *Mission You* classroom intervention will increase first-generation, low-income 10th graders' sense of occupational self-efficacy and improve their postsecondary decision-making. You plan to invite students attending the four high schools in a midsize, suburban community to participate in the intervention. For your two-condition, between-subjects study, the sample size required to detect a medium effect size of $d = .50$ with 80% power is about $N = 130$ (65 participants per group). Two school counselors from each school agree to complete the curriculum training and deliver six 45-minute, scripted lessons in all 10th-grade, general education, world history classes. The counselors will implement the program every Wednesday for 6 weeks, beginning the 1st week of September. The intervention will end 1 week before the district's annual College Readiness Assessment, which measures specific behaviors, academic and cognitive skills, and postsecondary and career interests related to college majors and occupations.

Two educators teach a minimum of four world history sections with 25 students in each class per school (e.g., one school, two teachers, 200 students). To avoid contamination, you match the schools by size, demographic, and teacher characteristics (age, gender, ethnicity, years of experience). You then retrieve students' Grade 9 achievement, attendance, behavioral, demographic, College Readiness Assessment scores (Grade 9 data = pretest scores), and world history course enrollment data for all eligible participants from the district database. Based on your matching, you randomly select a set of classrooms (one treatment and one control) to draw your sample from based on the eligibility requirement (first-generation, low-income students) using a randomization tool. To further mask participation, the school counselors, teachers, and students in the treatment group are informed of the new intervention and asked to provide consent/assent to use their attendance, GPA, and College Readiness Assessment data from Grades 9 and 10 to measure program effectiveness. However, neither the counselors, teachers nor students are aware if they are a part of the analysis sample. You follow the same procedures with the control group. While the treatment group receives the treatment, the control group counselors visit the world history classrooms every Wednesday and deliver the district-approved college and career lessons (i.e., treatment as usual). In January, you retrieve your samples' Grade 10 posttest data for analysis and train the control group counselors in the *Mission You* curriculum to begin implementation with their students.

Threats to Validity

Various factors can result in diminished confidence in a study's **internal validity** (the degree to which we can reasonably infer that any identified causal impact cannot be explained by factors other than the intervention) and **external validity** (the degree to which we can reasonably infer that the results of an investigation will also apply in other contexts; Shadish et al., 2002). Table 7.4 provides an example of how Webb et al. (2019) controlled for internal and external validity in the SSS RCT study with fifth graders.

Table 7.4. Sample Plan for Controlling for Threats to Internal and External Validity

Validity Type	Potential Threat	Approach to Minimized Threat
Internal	History	Random selection and assignment. Use of control group.
	Maturation	Random selection and assignment. Use of control group.
	Testing	Random selection and assignment. Use of control group. Long interval between testing. Use of school data and relatively nonreactive measures.
	Instrumentation	Standardized test administration of student measures. Standardized instructions to fifth grade teacher raters. Use of instruments with good reliability characteristics. Random selection and assignment. Use of a control group.
	Statistical regression	Random selection and assignment. Use of a control group.
	Mortality	Random selection and assignment. Use of a control group.
	Selection	Random selection and assignment (with large sample size). Use of a control group.
	Interaction of selection with previous six threats	Random selection and assignment. Use of a control group.
External	Interaction of selection and treatment	Random selection and assignment. Use of a wider range of schools. Use of covariate procedures will be employed to assure equivalence across groups.
	Interaction of setting and treatment	Multiple schools (settings). Random selection and assignment. Use of covariate procedures will be employed to assure equivalence across groups.
	Interaction of history and treatment	Random selection and assignment. Comparison of results to previous studies.

Note: Webb et al. (2019).

Consider the following sources for additional information:

- Cohen, J. (1988). *Statistical power analysis for the behavioral sciences* (2nd ed.). Lawrence Erlbaum Associates.
- Maxwell, S. E. (2000). Sample size and multiple regression analysis. *Psychological Methods, 5*, 434–458.
- Shadish, W. R., Cook, T. D., & Campbell, D. T. (2002). *Experimental and quasi-experimental designs for generalized causal inference*. Houghton Mifflin Co.

Quasi-Experimental Methods

This is an umbrella term for a larger array of methods to help determine the impact of an intervention. The key distinguishing feature between true experimental and quasi-experimental design is the use of random assignment. Even if you employ control groups, pre- and posttests, and fidelity logs, if there is not randomization of participants, your method is quasi-experimental. And while experimental designs are considered the strongest, there are lots of instances in school-based settings where quasi-experimental design will actually be the preferable approach. Random assignment is not always possible, but a quasi-experimental design can be robust enough to give a

---

Pop-Out 7.11. Research Reality: Can I Really Carry Out a Randomized Control Trial?

In our experience a lot of people assume that RCTs require a high level of expertise, must have huge sample sizes, and are incredibly costly. Fortunately, we can say from experience that none of that has to be true. The first author was a doctoral student when she set out to conduct her first RCT and was able to link up with others who had the needed expertise (in this case, her dissertation cochairs) to help guide the study. Furthermore, her a priori power analysis revealed that with her particular research conditions she only needed a minimum total sample size of 32 participants in the intervention group and control group. In terms of budget, she spent about $400 dollars, which mostly included postage to mail out three rounds of assessments to waitlist control group participants. Nowadays, Health Insurance Portability and Accountability Act (HIPPA)-compliant e-survey systems such as Qualtrics are more widely available and user friendly as well as less expensive!

reasonable amount of confidence in the causality of the intervention. For example, an RCT cannot be conducted if manipulation of the independent variable by researchers would be ethically unacceptable (e.g., randomly assigning students to a suspension and no-suspension condition), or practically not feasible (e.g., randomly reassigning students to one classroom vs. another for a portion of the school year). Ultimately there are several different means of implementing quasi-experimental research, and we will describe those that are the most common in school counseling literature.

Non-Equivalent Group Design

Quasi-experimental research using this design is more likely to draw upon naturally occurring groups such as existing classrooms. For example, a researcher may want to look at the impact of a teacher's use of a social-emotional curriculum compared with other classrooms that use another curriculum (comparison group) or are simply going about business-as-usual (control group). Though you lose some robustness and ability to infer full causality of the intervention itself on participant outcomes, this approach is much more palatable to both teachers and students who wouldn't want such a big disruption in their classroom structure for the purposes of a single research study.

We find the title *non-equivalent group design* to be something of a misnomer, as a key step is statistically demonstrating group equivalence at pretest. Keep in mind though that even though it appears you have group equivalence on the surface based on observable characteristics, only the randomization within experimental research helps reduce differences between groups that are hidden or latent.

Posttest-Only Design

Posttest-only designs are the most basic designs (see Table 7.5). In this case, the treatment is mostly an event, such as a natural disaster or illness, or an assessment that takes place immediately following an intervention to better understand your feelings about it. The design is helpful in generating hypotheses (Shadish et al., 2002).

Pretest–Posttest Design

Pretest–posttest designs are reported far more frequently than RCTs in school counseling research (Griffith et al., 2019). Take great caution in inferring causality of the intervention when using this method, as their defining characteristic is the absence of a control group. Therefore, bias of all kinds may be introduced into the process, and it is much more difficult to make a claim that the intervention was the cause for the outcome(s). So, when are these types of

Table 7.5. Examples of Quasi-Experimental Research Designs, Groups, and Implementation

Quasi-Experimental Research Design	Example of Group Condition and Implementation				
Nonequivalent Groups Posttest-Only Design	Treatment Group	NR	X	O	
	Comparison Group	NR	O		
Nonequivalent One-Group Pretest–Posttest Design	Treatment Group	NR	O	X	O
Nonequivalent Pretest–Posttest Design	Treatment Group	NR	O	X	O
	Comparison Group	NR	O	(Y)	O
Nonequivalent Interrupted Time-Series Design	Treatment Group	NR	$O_1 \ldots O_{20} \ldots X \ldots O_{21} \ldots O_{40}$		

Note: RCT = randomized control trial; R = random assignment; O = Pretest or posttest data collection; X = intervention applied; (Y) = intervention withheld or alternative applied; NR = nonrandom assignment; $O_1, O_{20}, O_{21}, O_{40}$ = data collection at week 1, 20, 21, and 40, respectively.

studies more appropriate? Namely, when the intervention is brief (and therefore less likely to be impacted by common threats to validity like issues with history or maturation). We also like to think of pretest–posttest studies as a less intensive approach that might provide helpful site-specific data for an intervention that has already been validated through a more rigorous, experimental process where you can have a reasonable degree of confidence in its effectiveness and generalizability of prior data. Lastly, pre–post data may be helpful in providing some support for the general process and/or theoretical underpinnings of an intervention approach prior to engaging in a much more time consuming or expensive experimental study, serving as sort of a pre-pilot pilot. Otherwise, you really do want a control group as a point of comparison as a bare minimum if the stakes are any higher. Table 7.5 provides examples of the common nonequivalent designs.

Additional Considerations for Intervention Research

As you design your intervention study, we recommend that you also consider the following elements:

- Create a reasonable timeline: Expect that the unexpected will happen and that you will encounter various hurdles at several points during your study. You're less likely to get derailed if you overestimate how long different stages will take and have a bit more breathing room in your process.

Pop-Out 7.12. Research Scenario Revisited for a Quasi-Experimental Design

---

In the previous scenario, we presented an example of how to test, in an RCT design, whether your new *Mission You* classroom intervention would increase first-generation, low-income 10th graders' sense of occupational self-efficacy and improve postsecondary decision-making. You randomized your groups using multiple techniques, such as matching schools and classrooms, random-sampling eligible students from classrooms using a randomization tool, and even masked participation.

The following school year, the counselors at one of the control group schools want to test, in **a quasi-experimental design**, whether the *Mission You* curriculum can positively impact their students' occupational self-efficacy and postsecondary decision-making. Assuming a two-condition, between-subjects study (d = .50, 80% power, N = 130), they assign one world history teachers' four classes to the treatment (n = 100 students) and the others to the comparison group (n = 100 students). In September, the *Mission You* school counselor delivers the six 45-minute, scripted lessons to the treatment group. A third school counselor, who has not received training, provides the district-approved college and career lessons (i.e., treatment as usual) to the comparison students. The counselors use Grade 9 attendance, GPA, and College Readiness Assessment data as pretest data and the Grade 10 data as the posttest to measure the group differences.

- Involve your site partners and stakeholders in the research design phase of your intervention study; otherwise, a lack of buy-in from your collaborators because they had no say and/or no interest in the findings can derail your study. Consider what data they may need and do what you reasonably can to incorporate these needs into your study if you want maximum collaboration (see Chapter 2).
- Improve treatment fidelity through manualization and training: Ideally there should be a standardized curriculum or manual that facilitators can refer to as they implement the intervention. In addition, fidelity improves when facilitators receive the same training.
- Track treatment fidelity: So many things can come up during the implementation phase, and only very rarely does everything go as intended. It can be really crucial information to know the degree to which the intervention was actually adhered to or not. For additional information on

this topic please reference Chapter 12, "Ensuring Treatment Fidelity and Clean Data Collection."

- Don't underestimate bias: It would be unwise to assume that there is minimal bias in quantitative research because it involves numbers. In fact, researcher bias is introduced at every stage of the process in the choices you make: The research questions we see as important, the constructs of interest we will assess, and in the meaning-making of our findings—all are influenced by our positionality. Indeed, we have a lot of lessons we could learn from qualitative approaches to scholarly inquiry, so we highly recommend reading Chapter 8, "Research Design: Qualitative Approaches."

We've certainly reviewed a lot when it comes to experimental and quasi-experimental research, but nothing creates a more tangible understanding of various methods within the intervention umbrella like perusing actual studies. Table 7.6 therefore serves as a quick reference to exemplar investigations within the field of school counseling by research design.

Table 7.6. Intervention Study Approaches and Exemplar Studies by Research Design

	Research Design	Common Statistical Approaches	Exemplar Studies
RCT	Clusters	Mixed, two-factor nested Analyses of variance Hierarchical linear model for multilevel analysis	Lemberger et al. (2015)
	Comparative treatment	Repeated measures Analyses of variance	Cerrito et al. (2018) Lan et al. (2019)
	Pretest–Posttest Design, Treatment as Usual	Repeated measures Growth modeling	Bardhoshi et al. (2018) Webb et al. (2019)
	Time-Series Design	Regression analysis	Lemberger-Truelove et al. (2018)
	Waitlist Control	Repeated measures Analyses of variance	Midgett et al. (2017)
Quasi-	One-Group Pretest–Posttest Design	Repeated measures Univariate and multivariate analyses	Zyromski et al. (2019)
	Comparison Pretest–Posttest Design	t-test Analysis of variance Multivariate analysis of variance Analysis of covariance	León et al. (2011) Schietz & Villares (2017)
	Interrupted Time-Series Design	Regression analysis	Howard & Ziomek-Daigle (2009) Lambie & Ieva (2012)

Collecting Data in Quantitative Research

Carrying out the data collection phase of a research study requires forward thinking and careful planning. Table 7.7 addresses some of the primary pros and cons within survey and intervention research for your consideration. Without stepping on the toes of other chapters in this book that address this topic, we do want to stress the importance of some additional key aspects in the process. Notably, be sure to provide training for any data collectors. You don't want to take for granted that boots-on-the ground folks will know exactly what to do and how to do it when it comes to data collection. Anyone

---

Pop-Out 7.13. Research Reality: Communication and Data Collection

The first author and a colleague were incredibly excited to have been granted permission to collect data at a very large conference for middle and high school–aged LGBTQ youth. They had formed a great relationship with the leader of the organization that put on this event and were given the green light to include a paper copy of the survey in all 3,000 attendees' welcome folders. They were pumped!

After a costly trip to the printers, they discovered that the surveys had not been collated and stapled as hoped for. Not to worry though, as they were told that the volunteer staff for the conference would already be doing similar organization for the rest of the welcome packet materials, so it wouldn't be a big deal to add collating the survey to their task.

Hurdle navigated! Or so they thought. Later that day they came to discover that only a small portion of the attendees ended up with full copies of the survey. Most had some pages but were missing others, others had no survey at all. And there was no way to know for sure just how many participants did not receive the full assessment. Because the researchers weren't there in person to communicate the expectations with the volunteers and provide guidance on how the surveys should be put together, it wasn't clear to the volunteers what to do. They did the best they could with the information they had, which was very little.

Ultimately this was a great lesson in not only the importance of attending to connection and buy-in from people at the top, but also the need to have that same collaborative relationship with the boots-on-the-ground folks who are helping you to implement your study. It was an immense amount of work building up to that particular study, and while it wasn't completely ruined, the researchers didn't end up with the dazzling amount of data they hoped they would. Lesson learned!

Table 7.7. Advantages and Disadvantages of Data Collection Methods for Survey and Intervention Research in Schools

Method	Advantages	Disadvantages
Survey Research	• Multiple survey formats (e.g., paper, electronic, mail) • Multiple standardized question types (e.g., forced-choice, open-ended, multiple choice) • Easier to obtain participant consent/assent • Easier to reach large samples • Easier to ask respondents about their attitudes, knowledge, and beliefs about sensitive topics • Easier to replicate and distribute • Easier to distribute to multiple subgroups at once • Easier to ensure questions are not skipped by mistake • Easier to download results for analysis • Can address multiple topics • Respondents can remain anonymous. • Respondents can work at their own pace.	• Assumes the respondent has a minimum reading and language ability • Assumes the respondent has access to the tools necessary to receive the survey (e.g., computer, mobile device) • Assumes the respondent is self-aware of their attitudes, beliefs, and behaviors • Can introduce respondent bias (e.g., social desirability) • May require multiple attempts/reminders to achieve a sufficient response rate • Limited generalizability • Items may be misunderstood • Cannot guarantee the respondent finishes answering all items (e.g., respondent may become fatigued) • Some items may be more time consuming to analyze (e.g., open-ended questions). • Difficult to calculate reliability and validity estimates for one-time surveys
Intervention Research	• Helps researchers make claims of causality • Helps researchers answer questions about effectiveness • Study protocols can be replicated. • Easier to control threats to internal and external validity • Expands knowledge of evidence-based programs • Trainers and participants gain access to new curriculums, programs, and treatments.	• Smaller samples can limit generalizability. • Can be time and labor intensive to train others to deliver the intervention (e.g., counselors, teachers) • Participants may be restricted by schedules, teacher assignment, school enrollment, thus limiting generalizability • Can be more labor intensive to obtain consent/assent • Introduces a researcher bias if the researcher delivers the intervention • Requires a strict timeline for implementation and data collection • May require the purchase of materials (e.g., curriculum, resources)

Note: Adapted from *Doing Survey Research: A Guide to Quantitative Methods*, by P. M. Nardi, 2018. Routledge.

who will be collecting data on your behalf should have a clear protocol, and if you ever can be available to help coordinate the process in person, you should.

For intervention research we recommend building in repeated measures if ever possible. In addition to pretests and posttests, midpoint assessments can also be helpful, especially for longer interventions. Not only do they increase the statistical power of your study (your ability to determine real differences between groups and avoid type II errors), but it can also give you a sense of the trajectory of your intervention outcomes. Furthermore, it can be incredibly beneficial to determine the degree of sustained impact: Implementing a post-posttest, as a follow-up in the weeks or months after the intervention, is highly recommended. These data can help determine the longitudinal impact of the intervention. If scores simply return to baseline after a short time, the intervention may not be worth the time and effort to implement.

Post-Implementation Phase: Analyze Data, Write Up Results, and Disseminate Findings

By this point a lot of the most time- and labor-intensive work is behind you when it comes to quantitative research. Tables 7.3 and 7.6 outline common data analysis approaches based on the method you use. Other chapters in this book provide full information about analyzing data and disseminating findings, so what follows is just a brief overview. But we do want to stress a couple of key ideas.

We can't say enough about the need to report **effect size** in intervention research. There is a world of difference between statistical significance (a measure of the likelihood that an observation was observed by random chance or not) versus practical significance (a measure of the degree of difference between observations, which is effect size). Whereas the slightest statistical significance can be detected if your sample size is merely large enough, it's the effect size that tells you—you guessed it—the size of the effect. For intervention studies in particular this is a very useful number, as it can help determine the all-important question as to whether all of the time, energy, money, and other resources put into an endeavor was actually worth it. Simply knowing whether a difference occurred or not is only part of the picture! Imagine, for example, that you've implemented an afterschool academic success curriculum that has a specific goal of raising state test scores.

Pop-Out 7.14. Pause and Reflect

What aspects of the quantitative research process outlined in this chapter make you nervous or would you like to know more about?

Now, take a moment to think about the people you have access to (colleagues/ peers, professors, practitioners) who seem to know a lot about different aspects of conducting research. With whom in this group might you be able to consult or collaborate? What next steps do you need to take to connect with those who can be helpful in your research process?

We all have our own unique research superpowers, and it's exceedingly rare that any one person has the entire breadth of knowledge or skill sets needed to implement a quality research study. Before you let a lack of knowledge or experience stop you, think about the people it would be helpful to link up with to help you fill in those gaps.

Fortunately, you have a lot of participants in your study, but, unfortunately, the curriculum costs half of the school counseling budget for the year and is fairly time intensive. Once you take a look at your data, you might be very excited to see a statistically significant difference in the intervention group with a p-value of .001. Hurray! But don't pop the champagne just yet, as an examination of the actual difference in test scores is only a 2-point difference out of 300, and thus a fairly miniscule effect size. Dang. But at the end of the day, it's better to have this information so you can look at potentially more successful interventions in the future. There are a number of ways to calculate effect size depending on methodological design (e.g., Cohen's d, eta-squared, partial eta-squared). Scholars also vary in their rationale for where the lines are in small-, medium-, and large-effect size benchmarks (Hill et al., 2008). We highly recommend reading Sink and Stroh (2006) and Watson et al. (2016) for more information on this process, as well as consulting with a stats expert to help determine what the best approach and interpretation for your specific study will be.

When it comes to disseminating your findings, we hope you'll keep *discoverability* in mind. In short, it can be very helpful to think like a reader and use searchable terms to help guide folks to your research. Similar to a well-constructed research question, a paper title that addresses the population, constructs of interest, and method used is extremely helpful (e.g., "Rural Elementary Students' Perceived Need for School Counseling

Services: Results From a Cross-Sectional Study," or "A Randomized Controlled Trial of Homeroom Education for Bystander Intervention in Bullying"). This makes for a lengthy title to be sure, but if your research is what someone needs to find, you've really upped the odds that it will end up in their hands.

Also, when it comes to dissemination, don't stop with your paper! Belser and Mason (2021) found that school counseling practitioners are far more likely to access your research through social media postings than through a peer-reviewed journal. There's a larger takeaway here also on the importance of considering layperson audiences in addition to scholarly publications and creating digestible reports that are more easily disseminated. Chapter 14 addresses this topic at length.

Concluding Thoughts

Let us circle back to The Bigger Picture that we initially shared at the beginning of this chapter. If you're anything like us, your head swirls with research possibilities, but also with occasional self-doubt as to your ability to carry out these types of projects. Common barriers for budding researchers or scholars hoping to up their game include a perceived lack of self-efficacy, perhaps a dash of boredom with the process, a heaping helping of imposter syndrome, and/or a keen ability to set unrealistically high bars as a starting point. Our challenge to you, however, is to set your focus on how research aligns with where your heart really is. Helping kids. Positive impact. Systems change. We simply cannot stress enough how high the need is for quality research focused on the needs of students and the work of school counselors. Don't forget the humanity behind your projects, and the opportunity to enact the kind of emancipatory research that centers minoritized students' experiences and can help to dismantle embedded inequitable structures. By setting your intention on the bigger picture, you may find it easier to take the steps needed in terms of expanding your own awareness, identifying collaborators and mentors, forming relationships with school-based partners, and carrying out the start-to-finish labor involved in a research project knowing the greater meaning that it potentially holds. And with each study you gain just a little more information, a little more acumen, and a little more belief in yourself and your abilities as a researcher to make the world a better, more equitable place for young people.

You. Can. Do. This.

References

Aggarwal, R., & Ranganathan, P. (2016). Common pitfalls in statistical analysis: The use of correlation techniques. *Perspectives in Clinical Research, 7*(4), 187–190. https://doi.org/10.4103/2229-3485.192046

Allensworth, E., & Easton, J. (2005, June). The on-track indicator as a predictor of high school graduation. Chicago: Consortium on Chicago School Research, University of Chicago.

Apicella, C., Norenzayan, A., & Henrich, J. (2020). Beyond WEIRD: A review of the last decade and a look ahead to the global laboratory of the future. *Evolution and Human Behavior, 41,* 319–329.

Atkins, R., & Oglesby, A. (2018). Interrupting racism: Equity and social justice in school counseling. Routledge.

Balfanz, R., & Boccanfuso, C. (2007). *Falling off the path to graduation: Middle grade indicators in [an unidentified northeastern city].* Center for Social Organization of Schools.

Balfanz, R., Herzog, L., & Mac Iver, D. J. (2007). Preventing student disengagement and keeping students on the graduation path in urban middle-grade schools: Early identification and effective interventions. *Educational Psychologists, 42,* 223–235.

Balkin, R. S., & Kleist, D. M. (2017). *Counseling research. A practitioner-scholar approach.* American Counseling Association.

Baltimore Education Research Consortium. (2011, February). Destination graduation: Sixth grade early warning indicators for Baltimore city schools their prevalence and impact. http://baltimore-berc.org/pdfs/SixthGradeEWIFullReport.pdf

Bardhoshi, G., Duncan, K., Erford, B. T. (2018). Effects of a specialized classroom counseling intervention on increasing self-efficacy among first-grade rural students. *Professional School Counseling, 21*(1), 12–25. https://doi.org/10.5330/1096-2409-21.1.12

Barrio Minton, C. A., & Lenz, A. S. (2019). *Practical approaches to applied research and program evaluation for helping professionals.* Routledge.

Bartlett, R., Wright, T., Olarinde, T., Holmes, T., Beamon, E. R., & Wallace, D. (2017). Schools as sites for recruiting participants and implementing research. *Journal of Community Health Nursing, 34*(2), 80–88. https://doi.org/10.1080/07370016.2017.1304146.

Baruch, Y., & Holtom, B. C. (2008). Survey response rate levels and trends in organizational research. *Human Relations, 61,* 1139–1160.

Belser, C. T., & Mason, E. C. M. (2021). A preliminary investigation of school counselors' attitudes and behaviors toward research and professional information seeking. *Professional School Counseling, 25,* Article 2156759X211042844.

Bowers, H., & Lemberger-Truelove, M. E. (2016). A person-centered humanistic approach to performing evidence-based school counseling research. *Person-Centered & Experiential Psychotherapies, 15,* 55–66. https://doi.org/10.1080/14779757.2016.1139502

Brace, N., Kemp, R., & Snelgar, R. (2016). *SPSS for psychologists (and everybody else)* (6th ed.). Routledge.

Brigman, G., & Webb, L. (2010). *Student Success Skills: Classroom manual* (3rd ed.). Atlantic Education Consultants.

Bruce, M., Bridgeland, J. M., Hornig Fox, J., & Balfanz, R. (2011). *The use of early warning indicator and intervention systems to build a grad nation.* https://files.eric.ed.gov/fulltext/ED526421.pdf

Bruzzese, J.-M., Gallagher, R., McCann-Doyle, S., Reiss, P. T., & Wijetunga, N. A. (2009). Effective methods to improve recruitment and retention in school-based substance use prevention studies. *Journal of School Health, 79*(9), 400–407. https://doi.org/10.1111/j.1746-1561.2009.00427.x.

Bryan, J., Moore-Thomas, C., Gaenzle, S., Kim, J., Lin, C.-H., & Na, G. (2012). The effects of school bonding on high school seniors' academic achievement. *Journal of Counseling & Development, 90,* 467–480.

Carey, J., & Dimmitt, C. (2012). School counseling and student outcomes: Summary of six statewide studies. *Professional School Counseling, 16,* 146–153. https://doi.org/10.1177/215 6759X0001600204

Carey, J. C., & Martin, I. (2015). *A review of the major school counseling policy studies in the United States: 2000–2014.* Research monograph. Ronald H. Fredrickson Center for School Counseling Outcome Research & Evaluation.

Cerrito, J. A., Trusty, J., & Behun, R. J. (2018). Comparing web-based and traditional career interventions with elementary students: An experimental study. *The Career Development Quarterly, 66*(4), 286–299. https://doi.org/ 10.1002/cdq.12151

Chang, H. N., & Romero, M. (2008). *Present, engaged, and accounted for: The critical importance of addressing chronic absence in the early grades.* National Center for Children in Poverty. https://doi.org/10.7916/D84B392G

Cholewa, B., Burkhardt, C. K., & Hull, M. F. (2018). Are school counselors impacting underrepresented students' thinking about postsecondary education? A nationally representative study. *Professional School Counseling, 19,* 144–154.

Cohen, J. (1988). *Statistical power analysis for the behavioral sciences* (2nd ed.). Lawrence Erlbaum Associates.

Cook, R. (2020). Addressing missing data in quantitative counseling research. *Counseling Outcome Research and Evaluation, 12*(1), 1–11. https://doi.org/10.1080/21501 378.2019.1711037

da Silva Frost, A., & Ledgerwood, A. (2020). Calibrate your confidence in research findings: A tutorial on improving research methods and practices. *Journal of Pacific Rim Psychology, 14,* Article e14. https://doi.org/10.1017/prp.2020.7

Daniel, J. (2012). *Sampling essentials: Practical guidelines for making sampling choices.* Sage.

Davis, L. L., Broome, M. E., & Cox, R. P. (2002). Maximizing retention in community-based clinical trials. *Journal of Nursing Scholarship, 34*(1), 47–53.

Dei, G. J. S. (2005). Chapter one: Critical issues in anti-racist research methodologies: An introduction. *Counterpoints, 252,* 1–27.

Dillman, D. A., Smyth, J. D., & Christian, L. M. (2014). *Internet, phone, mail, and mixed-mode surveys: The tailored design method.* John Wiley & Sons.

Dimmitt, C., Carey, J. C., & Hatch, T. (2007). *Evidence-based school counseling: Making a difference with data-driven practices.* Corwin Press.

Dimmitt, C., Carey, J. C., McGannon, W., & Henningson, I. (2005). Identifying a school counseling research agenda: A Delphi study. *Counselor Education and Supervision, 44,* 214–228.

Dulock, H. L. (1993). Research design: Descriptive research. *Journal of Pediatric Oncology Nursing, 10*(4), 154–157.

Fan, W., & Yan, Z. (2010). Factors affecting response rates of the web survey: A systematic review. *Computers in Human Behavior, 26,* 132–139.

Faul, F., Erdfelder, E., Lang, A. G., & Buchner, A. (2007). G* Power 3: A flexible statistical power analysis program for the social, behavioral, and biomedical sciences. *Behavior Research Methods, 39,* 175–191.

Fink, A. (2017). *How to conduct surveys: A step-by-step guide* (6th ed.). Sage.

Fyhn, J., & Breining, S. N. (2018, February 23). *Determining impacts of interventions.* Ramboll Group. https://ramboll.com/ingenuity/determining-impacts-of-interventions

Gallo, L. L. (2018). The relationship between high school counselors' self-efficacy and conducting suicide risk assessments. *Journal of Child and Adolescent Counseling, 4*(3), 209–225. https://doi.org/10.1080/23727810.2017.1422646

Gallup-Black, A., & Sackman, R. (2015). *From data to success: Using early warning indicators to shape interventions for students in the middle grades.* NFHI 360. https://www.fhi360.org/sites/default/files/media/documents/resource-ed-early-warning-indicators.pdf

Griffith, C., & Greenspan, S. B. (2017). Conducting outcomes research to identify efficacious and effective practices in school-based counseling. In J. C. Carey (Ed.), *International handbook for policy research in school-based counseling* (pp. 121–132). Springer.

Griffith, C., Mariani, M., McMahon, H. G., Zyromski, B., & Greenspan, S. B. (2019). School counseling outcome research: A 10-year content analysis of ASCA and ACA-affiliated journals. *Professional School Counseling, 23,* 1–12.

Goodman-Scott, E., Sink, C., Cholewa, B., & Burgress, M. (2018). An ecological view of school counselor ratios and student academic outcomes: A national investigation. *Journal of Counseling & Development, 96,* 388–398

Goodman-Scott, E., Watkinson, J. S., Martin, I., & Biles, K. (2016). School counseling faculty perceptions and experiences preparing elementary school counselors. *The Professional Counselor, 6*(4), 3030–307. https://doi.org/10.15241/egs.6.4.303

Goodwin, C. J. (2010). *Research in psychology. Methods and designs* (6th ed.). Wiley.

Hancock, G. R., Stapleton, L. M., & Mueller, R. O. (2019). *The reviewer's guide to quantitative methods in the social sciences* (2nd ed.). Routledge.

Harrington, K. (2013, November). *Getting to the heart of data-based decision making* [Keynote address]. Colorado School Counseling Association Annual Conference, Longmont, CO.

Henrich, J., Heine, S. J., & Norenzayan, A. (2010). The weirdest people in the world? *Behavioral and Brain Sciences, 33,* 61–83.

Hill, C. J., Bloom, H. S., Black, A. R., & Lipsey, M. W. (2008). Empirical benchmarks for interpreting effect sizes in research. *Child Development Perspectives, 2,* 172–177.

Holcomb-McCoy, C. (2007). School counseling to close the achievement gap: A social justice framework for success. Corwin Press.

Howard, A. K., & Ziomek-Daigle, J. (2009). School bonding, academic achievement, and participation in extracurricular activities. *Georgia School Counselors Association Journal, 16*(1), 39–48.

Keele, R. (2010). Quantitative versus qualitative research, or both? In R. Keele (Ed.), *Nursing research and evidence-based practice: Ten steps to success* (pp. 35–52). Jones & Bartlett Learning.

Lambie, G. W., & Ieva, K. P. (2012). Impact of a counseling ethics course on graduate students' learning and development. *International Journal for the Scholarship of Teaching and Learning, 6*(1), Article 12.

Lan, C.-W., Lightfoot, A., Gere, D., Taboada, A., Meyer, K., Harwood, J., & Milburn, N. G. (2019). Live or virtual? Comparing two versions of AMP!, a theater-based sexual health intervention for adolescents. *American Journal of Sexuality Education, 14*(3), 292–314. https://doi.org/10.1000/15546128.2019.1586270

Lapan, R. T., Gysbers, N. C., Bragg, S., & Pierce, M. E. (2012). Missouri professional school counselors: Ratios matter, especially in high-poverty schools. *Professional School Counseling, 16,* 108–116. https://doi.org/10.1177/2156759X0001600207

Lemberger, M., Carbonneau, K. J., Selig, J. P., & Bowers, H. (2018). The role of social-emotional mediators on middle school students' academic growth as fostered by an evidence-based intervention. *Journal of Counseling & Development, 96,* 27–40.

Lemberger, M. E., Selig, J. P., Bowers, H., & Rogers, J. E. (2015). Effects of the Student Success Skills program on executive functioning skills, feelings of connectedness, and academic achievement in a predominantly Hispanic, low-income middle school district. *Journal of Counseling & Development, 93,* 25–37.

Lemberger-Truelove, M. E., Carbonneau, K. J., Atencio, D. J., Zieher, A. K., & Palacios, A. F. (2018). Self-regulatory growth effects for young children participating in a combined social and emotional learning and mindfulness-based intervention. *Journal of Counseling & Development, 96,* 289–302. https://doi.org/10.1002/jcad.12203

León, A., Villares, E., Brigman, G., Webb, L., & Peluso, P. (2011). Closing the achievement gap of Latina/o students: A school counseling response. *Counseling Outcome Research and Evaluation, 2,* 73–86. https://doi.org/10.1177/2150137811400731

Loeb, S., Dynarski, S., McFarland, D., Morris, P., Reardon, S., & Reber, S. (2017). *Descriptive analysis in education: A guide for researchers.* (NCEE 2017–4023). U.S. Department of Education, Institute of Education Sciences, National Center for Education Evaluation and Regional Assistance.

Mariani, M., Sink, C., Villares, E., & Berger, C. (2019). Measuring classroom climate: A validation study of the My Child's Classroom Inventory-Short Form for Parents. *Professional School Counseling, 22, 1–14.* https://doi.org/10.1177/2156759X19860132

Martin, I., Carey, J., & DeCoster, K. (2009). A national study of the current status of state school counseling models. *Professional School Counseling, 12*(5), 378–386.

Mason, E. C., Griffith, C., & Belser, C. T. (2019). School counselors' use of technology for program management. *Professional School Counseling, 22,* 1–11. https://doi.org/10.1177/21567 59X19870794

Maxwell, S. E. (2000). Sample size and multiple regression analysis. *Psychological Methods, 5*(4), 434–458.

McGannon, W., Carey, J. C., and Dimmitt, C. (2004). *The current status of school counseling outcome research.* The Ronald H. Fredrickson Center for School Counseling Outcome Research and Evaluation.

McMahon, G., Griffith, C., Mariani, M., & Zyromski, B. (2017). School counseling intervention research on college readiness, college access, and postsecondary success: A 10-year content analysis of peer-reviewed research. *Journal of College Access, 3*(2), Article 3.

Midgett, A., Doumas, D., Trull, R., & Johnston, A. D. (2017). A randomized controlled study evaluating a brief, bystander bullying intervention with junior high school students. *Journal of School Counseling, 15*(9), 1–34.

Nardi, P. M. (2018). *Doing survey research: A guide to quantitative methods.* Routledge.

National Center for Education Statistics. (2003). *High school guidance counseling.* U.S. Department of Education. https://nces.ed.gov/pubs2003/2003015.pdf

Nulty, D. D. (2008). The adequacy of response rates to online and paper surveys: What can be done? *Assessment & Evaluation in Higher Education, 33,* 301–314.

Owen, L., Poynton, T. A., & Moore, R. (2020). Student preferences for college and career information. *Journal of College Access, 5*(1), 68–100.

Porter, J. R., & Smith-Adcock, S. (2016–2017). Children's tendency to defend victims of school bullying. *Professional School Counseling, 20*(1), 1–13. https://doi.org/10.5330/1096-2409-20.1.1

Poynton, T. A., & Carey, J. C. (2006). An integrative model of data-based decision making for school counseling. *Professional School Counseling, 10*(2), Article 2156759X0601000212.

Poynton, T. A., & Lapan, R. T. (2017). Aspirations, achievement, and school counselors' impact on college transition. *Journal of Counseling & Development, 95,* 369–377.

Puma, Michael J., Olsen, Robert B., Bell, Stephen H., and Price, Cristofer. (2009, October). *What to do when data are missing in group randomized controlled trials* (NCEE 2009-0049). National Center for Education Evaluation and Regional Assistance, Institute of Education Sciences, U.S. Department of Education. https://ies.ed.gov/ncee/pdf/20090049.pdf

Ray, D. C., Hull, D. M., Thacker, A. J., Pace, L. S., Swan, K. L., Carlson, S. E., & Sullivan, J. M. (2011). Research in counseling: A 10-year review to inform practice. *Journal of Counseling & Development, 89,* 349–359.

Ritchie, S. (2020). *Science fictions: How fraud, bias, negligence, and hype undermine the search for truth.* Metropolitan Books.

Robinson, K. A., Dennison, C. R., Wayman, D. M., Pronovost, P. J., & Needham, D. M. (2007). Systematic review identifies number of strategies important for retaining study participants. *Journal of Clinical Epidemiology, 60*(8), 757–765.

Schietz, R., & Villares, E. (2017). Effects of the girl squad curriculum on grade 5 females' transition to middle school. *Counseling Outcome Research and Evaluation, 8,* 2–14. https://doi.org/10.1080/21501378.2017.1327747

Schoeppe, S., Oliver, M., Badland, H. M., Burke, M., & Duncan, M. (2014). Recruitment and retention of children in behavioral health risk factor studies: REACH strategies. *International Journal of Behavioral Medicine, 21,* 794–803. https://doi.org/10.1007/s12529-013-9347-5.

Schulte, B. A. (2003). Scientific writing & the scientific method: Parallel "hourglass" structure in form & content. *The American Biology Teacher, 65*(8), 591–594.

Shadish, W. R., Cook, T. D., & Campbell, D. T. (2002). *Experimental and quasi-experimental designs for generalized causal inference.* Houghton Mifflin Co.

Sheperis, C. J., Young, J. S., & Daniels, M. H. (2010). *Counseling research. Quantitative, qualitative, and mixed methods.* Pearson.

Sherwood, H. (2010). Utilizing staff perceptions to guide and share future program planning. *GSCA Journal, 17,* 15–25. https://files.eric.ed.gov/fulltext/EJ909074.pdf

Sink, C. A., & Stroh, H. R. (2006). Practical significance: The use of effect sizes in school counseling. *Professional School Counseling, 9,* 401–411.

Sink, C. A., & Yillik-Downer, A. (2001). School counselors' perceptions of comprehensive guidance and counseling programs: A national survey. *Professional School Counseling, 4,* 278–288.

Stuit, D., O'Cummings, M., Norbury, H., Heppen, J., Dhillon, S., Lindsay, J., & Zhu, B. (2016). *Identifying early warning indicators in three Ohio school districts* (REL 2016–118). U.S. Department of Education, Institute of Education Sciences, National Center for Education Evaluation and Regional Assistance, Regional Educational Laboratory Midwest. http://ies.ed.gov/ncee/edlabs

United States Department of Education. (n.d.). *History of the SLDS grant program: Expanding states' capacity for data-driven decision-making.* Statewide longitudinal data systems grant program. https://nces.ed.gov/programs/slds/pdf/History_of_the_SLDS_Grant_Program_May2018.pdf

Villares, E., & Dimmitt, C. (2017). Updating the school counseling research agenda: A Delphi study. *Counselor Education and Supervision, 56,* 177–192. https://doi.org/10.1002/ceas.12071

Wampold, B. E., Mondin, G. W., Moody, M., Stich, F., Benson, K., & Ahn, H. N. (1997). A meta-analysis of outcome studies comparing bona fide psychotherapies: Empirically, "all must have prizes." *Psychological Bulletin, 122*(3), 203–215.

Watson, J. C., Lenz, A. S., Schmit, M. K., & Schmit, E. L. (2016). Calculating and reporting estimates of effect size in counseling outcome research. *Counseling Outcome Research and Evaluation, 7*(2), 111–123.

Webb, L., Brigman, G., Carey, J., Villares, E., Harrington, K., Wells, C., Sayer, A., & Chance, E. (2019). Results of a randomized controlled trial of the Student Success Skills program on grade 5 students' academic and behavioral outcomes. *Journal of Counseling & Development, 97,* 398–408. https://doi.org/10.1002/jcad.12288

Whiston, S. C., & Sexton, T. L. (1998). A review of school counseling outcome research: Implications for practice. *Journal of Counseling & Development, 76,* 412–426.

Whiston, S. C., Tai, W. L., Rahardja, D., & Eder, K. (2011). School counseling outcome: A meta-analytic examination of interventions. *Journal of Counseling & Development, 89,* 37–55.

White, R. T., & Arzi, H. J. (2005). Longitudinal studies: Designs, validity, practicality, and value. *Research in Science Education, 35*(1), 137–149.

Wilkerson, K., Perusse, R., & Hughes, A. (2013). Comprehensive school counseling programs and student achievement outcomes: A comparative analysis of RAMP versus non-RAMP schools. *Professional School Counseling, 16*(3), 172–184. https://doi.org/10.1177/2156759 X1701600302

Wright, R. (2014). *Research methods for counseling: An introduction.* Sage Publications.

Zyromski, B., & Mariani, M. A. (2016). *Facilitating evidence-based, data-driven school counseling: A manual for practice.* Corwin Press.

Zyromski, B., Martin, I., & Mariani, M. (2019). Evaluation of the true goals school counseling curriculum: A pilot study, *Journal for Specialists in Group Work, 44*(3), 170–183. https://doi.org/10.1080/01933922.2019.1634781

8

Research Design

Qualitative Approaches

Emily Goodman-Scott and Blaire Cholewa

Research Design: Qualitative Approaches

What is Qualitative Research?

Qualitative research aims to "illuminate complex phenomena in their settings, specifically as they relate to the daily lived experiences of individuals and groups" (Hays & Singh, 2012, p. 22). We unpack and expand upon this definition of qualitative research further, according to several seminal authors (Creswell & Poth, 2018; Hays & Singh, 2012; Hunt, 2011), as well as cultural, social justice, and antiracist considerations discussed here and throughout the chapter (e.g., Holcomb-McCoy, 2021; O'Hara et al., 2021; Polk et al., 2021; Wester et al., 2021):

- The **counseling profession values cultural competence, social justice, advocacy, and antiracism**; similarly, these same tenants are valued in counseling-related research. Thus, we acknowledge that all research, including qualitative research, is **multicultural** and **reflects the systems inherent in our society, including power, privilege, oppression, discrimination**, and so forth. As such, researchers must be mindful of their position of power within the greater society, as well as with regard to their research. How do the researcher's intersecting identities (e.g., race, ethnicity, class, education level, gender, language, social class, etc.) impact their research process? While qualitative research can be used as a method of empowerment, if not enacted with cultural competence and humility, research can serve as yet another tool of oppression and centering the dominant culture (e.g., white, middle class, ableist, heterosexual, cisgender, etc.). For more information we suggest: Holcomb-McCoy's book on antiracism in counseling (2021), O'Hara et al. (2021)

Emily Goodman-Scott and Blaire Cholewa, *Research Design* In: *School Counseling Research.* Edited by: Brett Zyromski and Carey Dimmitt, Oxford University Press. © Oxford University Press 2023. DOI: 10.1093/oso/9780197650134.003.0008 for multicultural competence in counseling research, and Wester et al. (2021) for innovation in counseling in qualitative research, specifically.

- According to multicultural and social justice counseling competencies (Ratts et al., 2015), **counseling researchers** should use quantitative and qualitative methods to: **highlight inequities** in counseling literature/practice; **examine how policies, norms, and values impact marginalized and privileged clients/students**; and use results to **advocate for systemic changes to address inequities.**

- In qualitative research we seek to **understand context and culture**, as well as inquire about **participants and phenomena in their natural settings.** Thus, **we do not necessarily aim for generalizability to a large sample** in the same way we do for quantitative research. For more information about the nuanced way of considering generalizability in qualitative research, please see Hays and McKibben (2021).

- Qualitative research is often **exploratory**, seeking a **rich, thick, in-depth perspective** of participants' experiences. As such, it often takes substantial time to gather and analyze qualitative data.

- **Philosophical assumptions** and **theoretical frameworks guide research questions** and methodology.

- **Researchers are the instrument of their investigations** and, as a result, describe their positionality in relation to the research and in relation to broader systems (i.e., reflexivity). As such, largely, researchers **attempt to bracket their perspectives**: recognize and then (as best they can), set aside their beliefs, perspectives, and biases while also acknowledging that some inherent beliefs, perspectives, and biases will always remain.

- The **qualitative research process is relatively flexible and fluid**, though there are also recommended steps for data analysis and steps to increase the rigor of the study (i.e., trustworthiness strategies).

- **Purposeful or purposive sampling is often used** to include participants who have experience with the phenomenon of interest.

- While interviews are often used, we are also seeing an increasingly wider **range of data collection strategies**, including photos, observations, social media analysis, document reviews, and so forth. While there are a range of methodologies that can highlight the voices of BIPOC and other oppressed groups, we've been hearing more recently about the power of photovoice and participatory action research, in particular. In this chapter we will use the term BIPOC at times, to reference Black, Indigenous, and people of color (BIPOC).

- While qualitative research is an **essential tool in understanding the experiences of those from historically oppressed populations**, it is also crucial that **the outcome of the research serves the participants**. As a start, researchers should share results with participants and partner *with* participants for actionable steps after the study, based on participants' wishes and perspectives.

Why Qualitative Research?

To provide some background about my journey: When I (Emily) was a school counselor, I worked at an incredible school and for a forward-thinking school district. Even with some of the best circumstances, I was still concerned that as a school counselor I wasn't able to fully do the work I was trained to do: focusing on academic, career, and social/emotional supports, including prevention and mental health. Thus, I saw firsthand the need for greater advocacy for the profession. As my principal said to me, "school counselors are so busy advocating for their students that they don't advocate for themselves enough." As a result, I moved from school counselor to school counselor educator (SCE) (e.g., faculty member) as a means to advocate for the school counseling profession on a larger scale. I'm grateful every day for the opportunity to impact the profession through teaching the next generation of school counselors and school counselor educators, engaging in professional leadership and service, and also advocating in a way that has become increasingly exciting to me: *through my research*. I am passionate about qualitative research in particular, because I have the honor to hear stories from the field, illustrate common themes across stories, and then share these stories at a national level through publications, presentations, advocacy, attempts at policy changes, and so forth. It is important to me that qualitative research is used to highlight the voices of those who may not necessarily be heard in our scholarship, including those practicing in the field, and those who have been historically oppressed. For instance, I believe our research should include the voices of practicing school counselors, as well as K–12 students, families, and community members. Too often research is conducted by and for those in academia and thus removed from our schools and communities, leaving out crucial voices. The recent reinvigorated racial justice movement has brought more mainstream awareness to systemic injustices that have been ever present in U.S. society, such as racism and white supremacy. **Qualitative research can be used as a tool for antiracism**: to seek out and hear the voices of those who have traditionally and systematically been marginalized, for the purpose of the researcher acting as a co-conspirator to prioritize the participant voice to raise awareness, and to advocate for removing systemic barriers and make systemic changes—and this work must be done alongside participants, rather than *for* participants.

I (Blaire) appreciate what Emily said about how she uses qualitative research as the basis for advocacy. I am drawn to qualitative research more pragmatically. I often find that the kind of research questions I am interested in are those that are best answered by qualitative methods. I was reflecting on this, and I think it is because as a school counselor I am drawn to hearing the voices of others. There is something special about getting to explore their experiences and actions in such an in-depth way, while also contributing to the body of research within the profession. Quantitative research has great value, but numbers cannot tell you the full story the way that people sharing their experiences, perceptions, feelings, and actions can.

Understanding the "full story" has become increasingly more meaningful to me as we face the pandemic of continued racial injustice. Qualitative research has the potential to elevate the voices of historically oppressed groups, particularly BIPOC, and can unveil systems of oppression when it is conducted with intentionality and attention to mitigating further harm. Additionally, qualitative research also can change us both personally and professionally. A qualitative study by Williams, Byrd, and Washington (2021), "Challenges in Implementing Antiracist Pedagogy into Counselor Education Programs: A Collective Self-Study," has rocked me to my core. It has left me to reckon with how so many of my practices as a counselor educator have been rooted in whiteness, despite perceiving myself as social justice oriented and equity focused. I am now taking active steps to engage in deep, painful reflection, as well as starting the journey to decolonize my pedagogy and my interactions. Qualitative research is POWERFUL—it can change lives and be used to dismantle oppressive systems. I am proof of this.

Purpose of Chapter

While there are a plethora of excellent articles and books providing detailed background information on qualitative research, this chapter is not necessarily one of those resources. Rather than describing *what* is qualitative research, **the purpose of this chapter is to describe *how* to conduct qualitative research, providing practical, concrete examples** from our own work, as well as the work of others. However, we will provide a wealth of resources for you to refer to, for further reading (e.g., see Table 8.1 and other examples throughout the chapter). To provide an overview, the current chapter is broken into four primary sections:

- Planning for Qualitative Research: Where to Start
- Data Collection and Analysis

- Concluding Steps: Writing Results for Publication
- Avoiding Pitfalls in Qualitative Research

In addition, when describing how to conduct qualitative research, **we will highlight three recently published school counseling studies** throughout this chapter, each demonstrating a different approach or data analysis method (see Table 8.1):

- Grounded theory: Gray and Rubel (2018): "Sticking Together: The adolescent experience of the group cohesion process in rural school counseling groups"
- Phenomenology: Havlik et al. (2018): "Do whatever you can do to try to support that kid: School counselors' experiences addressing student homelessness"
- Thematic analysis (TA): Goodman-Scott (2019a): "Enhancing student learning by building a caring climate": School counselors' experiences with classroom management"

Planning for Qualitative Research: Where to Start?

There is a common misconception that qualitative research is simply about conducting interviews, organizing the content into themes and subthemes, and then writing up the results for publication. For instance, we are often asked the following question from colleagues and doctoral students: *"I did a number of interviews on [insert school counseling topic]. Now I want to code the*

Table 8.1. Qualitative Resources by Approach and General Methods

Approach.	Grounded Theory	Phenomenology	Thematic Analysis
Sample School Counseling Study:	Gray & Rubel (2018)	Havlik et al. (2018)	Goodman-Scott (2019a)
Further Reading by Approach:	Clarke (2005) Charmaz (2014) Corbin & Strauss (2015) Flynn & Korcuska (2018b) Glaser & Strauss (1967) Strauss & Corbin (1990)	Flynn & Korcuska (2018a) Moustakas (1994) Van Manen (2014)	Braun & Clarke (2006) Braun & Clarke (2012) Clarke & Braun (2018)
Further Reading on Methods:	Creswell & Poth (2018); Denzin & Lincoln (2011); Flynn et al. (2019); Hunt, (2011); Hays & Singh (2012); Hays & Wood (2011); Lincoln & Guba (1985); Patton (2014)		

data and submit for review . . . what are my next steps?" However, qualitative research is not something you wake up and just *do*. The reality is, rigorous qualitative research is much more purposeful and complex and takes careful, advance planning.

To assist with my own qualitative research, I (Emily) created a "Qualitative Planning Guide," which I started sharing with close colleagues and doctoral students casually, then more formally, at the 2019 Evidence-Based School Counseling Conference's Research Day. Please see the "**Qualitative Planning Guide**" (Table 8.2; Goodman-Scott, 2019b). Hence, when generally thinking about a potential research topic and research questions that lend themselves to a qualitative approach, **we suggest drafting answers to this planning guide, as a preparation tool**. This guide is something you can use at the beginning of your study for planning and revisit throughout your process, including to assist you to write up the study for publication. While qualitative research is a flexible and fluid process, we also want to **plan and implement key elements within our investigations purposefully and proactively**.

In addition to ensuring we attend to important criteria within our qualitative research, it's crucial that these criteria are aligned with each other, or epistemologically consistent throughout the research design, also known as **methodological coherence or congruence** (*terms that are often used interchangeably within qualitative research*; Creswell & Poth, 2018; Hays & Singh, 2012; Hays & Wood, 2011). Planning for your study in advance also helps you to consider alignment thoughtfully, or coherence and congruence across the study. As qualitative research is not a linear process, we suggest reviewing and revising your planning guide throughout your study, as needed, knowing that the order of these steps may vary.

In addition, as noted in the introduction to this chapter, all research, including qualitative, is multicultural (O'Hara et al., 2021). Thus, in planning and implementing studies, cultural considerations should be infused throughout all aspects of the study, such as the research design, interview questions, data analysis, researcher reflexivity, trustworthiness, and so forth (O'Hara et al., 2021; Wester et al., 2021). As such, cultural considerations will also be woven throughout this chapter. Additionally, in their book on antiracism, Holcomb-McCoy (2021) posits that in addition to cultural considerations, counselors must go one step further, **to focus on antiracism**. Multiple chapter authors in Holcomb-McCoy's book speak to interrogating how the counseling profession is steeped in colonialism, whiteness, and white supremacy (Polk et al., 2021; Washington et al., 2021). Polk et al. specifically addresses white supremacy culture in counselor education scholarship, citing a focus on objectivity, traditional research methodologies, and "little emphasis on qualitative

Table 8.2. Goodman-Scott Qualitative Planning Guide (2019b)

Topic/Content	Researchers' Notes
1. Philosophical Assumptions *What are your philosophical beliefs? How do these impact your research? Including: ontology, epistemology, axiology, rhetoric, methodology.*	
2. Research Paradigms/Frameworks Belief systems, based on philosophical assumptions. *What paradigms/beliefs/theoretical orientations guide your research? Examples: Positivism, Post-Positivism, Social Constructivism, Critical Theory, Feminism, Queer Theory, Disability Theory, etc.*	
3. Traditions/Approaches Methodological approaches/design strategies are based on paradigms. Examples: *Case Study, Grounded Theory, Phenomenology, Consensual Qualitative Research, Thematic Analysis, Ethnography, Participatory Action Research, etc. Briefly state: Why was this tradition/approach used in the study?*	
4. Topic, Purpose, and Goals of Study *Examine research; what are gaps in literature? How can you address this gap?*	
5. Research Questions Often: *what/how* questions; broad; specific to approach	
6. Sampling and Recruitment *What type of: Sampling? Inclusion criteria? Sample size? Recruitment strategies?*	
7. Data Collection *List: type of data (e.g., type of interview, interview questions, interview length, use of protocols, etc.).*	
8. Data Analysis *List the data analysis steps and cite accordingly.*	
9. Trustworthiness Strategies *What trustworthiness strategies will be used?*	
10. Researcher Reflexivity *Describe: researchers' role in the study; their experiences in relation to the study's phenomena/participants; any other related background, biases, assumptions, reactions, etc.*	
11. Findings *What will you include in the findings? For example, write up the narrative to explain the results, including a thick, rich description and illustrative quotations.*	

Other Notes:

Note: Steps 1–5 do not occur linearly; rather, they are considered and created in tandem and inform one another.

and participatory research" (p. 164). As antidotes, Polk et al. suggest requiring an acknowledgment of author positionality, more expansive views of acceptable forms of inquiry, increased focus on action, and a decreased focus on generalizability within our scholarship, among others. This chapter will explain the ways in which qualitative research can align with these antidotes when conducted with rigor and intentionality.

Next, we will delve into the contents of the planning guide, while keeping in mind the need for coherence/congruence, cultural considerations, and anti-racism throughout.

Planning

The first five steps in the planning guide mutually shape each other (see Figure 8.1): (1) philosophical assumptions, (2) research paradigms/frameworks, (3) research traditions/approaches, (4) topic, purpose, and goals of the study, and (5) research questions. These five steps, described next, are based on recommendations from a variety of scholars (e.g., Creswell & Poth, 2018; Denzin & Lincoln, 2011; Hays & Singh, 2012; Hunt, 2011; Patton, 2014). Many of these concepts will be mentioned only briefly in this chapter, and thus we recommend reading these referenced sources for more information.

Step 1: Philosophical Assumptions

When starting a qualitative study, scholars suggest first **examining your philosophical assumptions, and how these beliefs impact your research.**

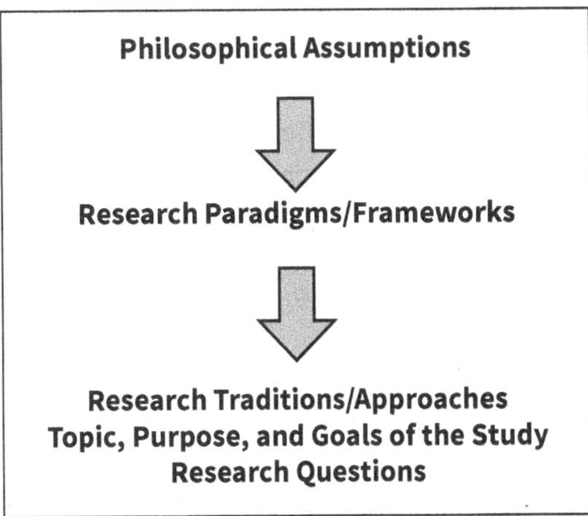

Figure 8.1. The First Three Steps of Planning

We also suggest that your philosophical assumptions take into account your perspectives on culture and antiracism as well. This includes the following:

- Ontology: *What is the nature of reality? Is there one reality? Multiple realities? What dominant and oppressed systems shape one's perspective of reality?*
- Epistemology: *What is the process of knowledge? Is knowledge limited or unlimited?*
- Axiology: *How do researchers' values impact their investigation? Is the researcher objective or subjective? What are their values, biases, assumptions?*
- Rhetoric: *How are data presented? In the researcher's voice? Participant's voice?*
- Methodology: *What research procedures/processes are used? Inductive or deductive methods?*

Step 2: Research paradigms/frameworks

As a result of your philosophical assumptions, consider your belief systems. Specifically: **What paradigms/beliefs/theoretical orientations guide your research?** Examples are listed below, though they are not exhaustive:

• Positivism	• Feminism
• Post-Positivism	• Queer Theory
• Social Constructivism	• Disability Theory
• Critical Race Theory	• And others
• Critical Theory	

Step 3: Traditions/Approaches

The research tradition/approach you use is based on the chosen paradigm/framework for the current study. For instance, social constructivism (which includes the belief in multiple, contextual realities) may lend itself well to a variety of qualitative traditions/approaches that seek out and therefore acknowledge the existence of a range of participants' unique experiences. Important to note, Critical Race Theory (which posits that racism is inherent to systems, structures, and interactions in the United States; Bell, 1995) is well suited to approaches listed below. Examples of qualitative traditions/approaches you may consider include:

• Grounded Theory	• Consensual Qualitative Research
• Phenomenology	• Ethnography
• Thematic Analysis	• Participatory Action Research
• Case Study	• And others

We want to note that while the approaches listed above are those that are most regularly and traditionally cited in our field, many are developed by white, cis-gender men. When deciding on research traditions and data analysis (see Step 8), we ask researchers to consider reading and utilizing work from scholars from a range of intersecting identities. And we acknowledge this practice as a work in progress for us authors. We are working to extend our knowledge of and advocate for the acceptance of additional qualitative approaches. For instance, I (Emily) started reading a book that was published recently, *Recovering Black Storytelling in Qualitative Research: Endarkened Storywork* by Toliver (2021, p. V). The author notes that

> this book decenters traditional, white-centered qualitative methods and utilizes Afrofuturism as an onto-epistemological tool and ethical premise. It asks researchers to consider how we move forward in data collection, data analysis, and data representation by centering how Black girls reclaim and recover the past, counter negative, and elevate positive realities that exist in the present, and create new possibilities for the future.

Hence, in using an antiracist lens, it is important to consider which scholarly voices and perspectives are represented, prioritized, and centered in research methods, and which voices are not. And we look for research methods and strategies for data analyses that expand beyond the dominant cultures.

Step 4: Topic, Purpose, and Goals of the Study

When deciphering a study's topic, purpose, and goals, it's important to examine the existing research to determine:

- **What are existing gaps/needs in the literature?** (this drives your **topic**)
- Whose **voice is present or privileged** in the literature? **Whose voice is absent?** Are there publication barriers and advantages that contribute to the research that is published in our journals?
- **How can you address these gaps/needs?** (this drives your **purpose and goal** statements)

It is important to **consider the topic and purpose of your study within the context** of the **previous literature,** as well as **trends in the field, the voices privileged and absent (both researcher and participant/subject), and how the study can advance the profession.** For instance, I (Blaire) published a consensual qualitative research project in 2020 exploring how school counselors enact multicultural education behaviors and the barriers that prevent school counselors from implementing multicultural education. At the time, this topic was important because of the increase in hate crimes and discrimination that had been reported in the media and research. Our hope was for the study to provide examples of how school counselors can enact multicultural education behaviors in response to and in prevention of injustices while acknowledging they may face obstacles in the process. Similarly, in 2020, I (Emily) published a study on school counselors' experiences with Section 504 plans. My interest for this was sparked due to hearing a number of practitioners vocalize their increased 504 responsibilities, and then seeing the lack of related relevant literature.

Step 5: Research Questions

Research questions are based on the (a) topic, purpose, and goals, and also they are aligned with the (b) tradition/framework chosen. Qualitative research questions are broad, and typically open-ended questions that often begin with *what* and *how*. For more information on aligning your research question to your research design, please see Chapter 4, "Research Questions That Contribute to Sound Study Designs for School Counseling," by Dr. Matthew Lemberger-Truelove and Citlali Molina.

Important to note: These first five steps do not occur in a linear fashion but, rather, mutually shape each other. To provide an example, based on my thematic analysis on classroom management (Goodman-Scott, 2019a), please see Table 8.3.

Next, please see Table 8.4, in which we portray aspects of these five steps, in relation to the three research traditions that are the focus of this chapter: grounded theory, phenomenology, and thematic analysis. We will be including content from the three sample research studies in tables throughout this chapter.

Data Collection and Analysis

Step 6: Sampling and Recruitment

Before recruiting participants or collecting data, in accordance with **ethical research practices**, researchers must first secure approval from their Institutional Review Board, also known as an IRB. In addition, research that is conducted with school staff or students during school hours, on the school premises, or by similar means, typically requires additional permission from

Table 8.3. Planning for a Qualitative Study: Example from Goodman-Scott (2019b)

Planning Step	Description
Research Topic:	I reviewed the existing research on school counseling classroom management, learned of the significant dearth of literature, and thus decided on a **research topic: classroom management.**
Purpose and Goals of the Study:	Next, I defined the **purpose and goals** of the study: – **To gain an increased understanding of school counselors' experiences regarding classroom management.** – **My hope was that the results may provide practicing school counselors with information and examples as well as build a foundation for future research.**
Philosophical Assumptions:	I considered my **philosophical assumptions** (though not included in the article, due to space constraints): – Ontology: Reality is subjective, comprised of many contextual perspectives. – Epistemology: Knowledge is unlimited and created through the research process and the researcher–participant relationship. – Axiology: Individuals' reality is colored by their values and assumptions (hence, the importance of bracketing the researchers' experiences and biases, to remain focused on the participants' experiences). – Rhetoric: Data are presented in the first person, noting the researcher is an instrument of the research process; however, participant quotes are heavily used, to provide a thick, rich description of their accounts, using participants' voices. – Methodology: Aligned with a qualitative approach, I used an inductive approach: starting with a broad, general research question (rather than a deductive approach that starts with a hypothesis).
Research Paradigms/ Frameworks:	In examining the **research paradigms/frameworks**, I subscribe to a social constructivist perspective, acknowledging multiple, subjective realities.
Research Tradition/ Approach and Research Question:	I simultaneously conceptualized the **research tradition/approach** (thematic analysis), as well as the **research question** (*What are school counselors' experiences with classroom management?*).

Note: Coherence/Congruence: Throughout this process, I ensured **alignment**, or methodological **coherence/congruence**, across all aspects in this planning phase. Ensuring this coherence/congruence often includes consulting with a range of qualitative texts, such as those we recommend at the start of the chapter.

the school district's research office, as well as the building's administrators. For more information on IRB and district research approval, please see Chapter 3 by Drs. Anita Young and Ileana Gonzalez: "Ethical Research in Schools: Navigating the IRB Process at the District and University Levels."

As you prepare to recruit participants and collect data, it's important to consider this: Who can best answer your research questions? If the answer is

Table 8.4. Examples of Philosophical Assumptions, Research Paradigms/Assumptions, Goals, and Research Questions in Some Qualitative Approaches

Approach:	Grounded Theory	Phenomenology	Thematic Analysis
Common Philosophical Assumptions and Research Paradigms/ Frameworks:	Philosophical assumptions and research paradigms/frameworks will vary, based on the specific type of Grounded Theory being used (e.g., Glasserian, Straussian, or constructivist).	Philosophical assumptions and research paradigms/frameworks will vary, based on the specific type of Phenomenology (e.g., transcendental, hermeneutical, etc.).	Thematic Analysis (TA) can be applied across a range of epistemological and theoretical assumptions/frameworks. It is not limited in this area, but both a theory and philosophical underpinning are necessary, as TA is not atheoretical.
Goals:	Create a theory grounded in participants' experiences/views, describing the *how* of actions or procedures.	Describe the essence of participants' in-depth lived experiences with a given phenomenon.	Overarching term for data analysis focused on determining patterns or themes across data that answer a specific research question.
Research Questions:	Often includes *how* questions.	Often includes: *What are participants' experiences with . . .*	Research questions are flexible: can be broad and exploratory, or narrow and more specific.
Sample Research Question:	Gray & Rubel (2018): How do adolescents experience the group cohesion process in school counseling groups in a rural setting?	Havlik et al. (2018): What are the central experiences of school counselors who work with students experiencing homelessness? What are the school counselors' perceptions of their role and challenges in working with children experiencing homelessness?	Goodman-Scott (2019a): What are school counselors' experiences of classroom management?

Note: Citations: Braun & Clarke (2006); Charmaz (2014); Clarke & Braun (2018); Corbin & Strauss (2015); Creswell & Poth (2018); Glaser & Strauss (1967); Hays & Singh (2012); Hays & Wood (2011); Moustakas (1994); Strauss & Corbin (1990).

an individual with one or more historically oppressed identities, can the research questions be answered without causing further oppression or harm? Qualitative research often uses **purposeful sampling**, also known as **purposive sampling**, meaning that participants are purposefully selected based on their experience with a given phenomenon (Patton, 2014). As a result, it's crucial to provide a thick, rich description of participants in your write-up (e.g., demographics and information relevant to the research question, like years of experience), so the reader can have a full picture of your sample (Hunt, 2011). In order to define the bounds of your purposeful/purposive sample, you need to create **participant inclusion criteria**, defining the key criteria required for participants to take part in your study, as well as a rationale for this set of criteria (Hays & Singh, 2012). In Table 8.5, see examples of participant criteria from our sample studies.

In regard to **sample size**, qualitative studies are **typically smaller than quantitative studies, though there is little consensus on an exact number of participants** for each approach. This makes sense, given the fluid and flexible nature of qualitative research. Thus, scholars' suggestions on sample size can vary. On one hand, Hunt (2011) relayed that sample size doesn't matter in qualitative studies, as long as the researchers provide a thorough rationale for why and how participants were selected, as well as an in-depth description of data collection. At the same time, other scholars have provided more specific recommendations (e.g., Corbin & Strauss, 2015; Creswell & Poth, 2018; Hays & Singh, 2012; Hays & Wood, 2011; Moustakas, 1994), some of which are dependent on your research tradition/approach (see Table 8.5). Overall, we suggest **providing a citation and a rationale for your given sample size based on your specific tradition/approach.**

Next, just as important as deciding who to include in your study is to determine **participant recruitment**. We have recruited participants in a range of ways: social media announcements in closed school counseling groups, email LISTSERVS, and digital platforms (e.g., the ASCA Scene). We have also recruited from conference attendees and reached out to school districts directly, including district-level and school-level administrators. Ultimately, while there are many strategies for recruiting participants, we suggest carefully considering how to access participants who meet your participant inclusion criteria, and how to ethically work within the guidelines of your partnering school districts. This topic is one that requires much more discussion and can be found in Chapter 2 by Dr. Sam Steen et al.: "Access to Schools: Relationships with Stakeholders and Systems."

Table 8.5. Sampling and Inclusion Criteria by Qualitative Approach

Approach:	Grounded Theory	Phenomenology	Thematic Analysis
Sampling/ Participant Inclusion Criteria:	Purposeful/purposive to theoretical sampling Including participants who have taken part in a process related to a central phenomenon Data collection and data analysis are recursive; thus, as concepts emerge, more data are sought in relation to those concepts.	Purposeful/purposive Participant must have experienced the phenomenon and is willing to engage in in-depth conversation, as part of study.	Any; however, homogenous samples enhance theme generation in small samples.
Sample Size:	Sample size is guided by theoretical saturation, not a specific number of individuals. Theoretical saturation: keep sampling until you no longer obtain new theoretical information for categories and themes. General guidance is 20–30 participants	Sample size varies. In the literature we commonly see 10–12 participants and thus aim for something similar.	Sample size varies. While not typically defined, suggested sample sizes for "small projects" are: $N = 6$–10 interviews $N = 2$–4 focus groups $N = 10$–50 participant generated text (Braun & Clarke, 2013)

Sample Studies:	Gray & Rubel (2018):	Havlik et al. (2018):	Goodman-Scott (2019a):
	Inclusion criteria: (a) middle school or high school adolescents who had experienced cohesion in school counseling groups, (b) groups occurred in a rural setting more than 5 miles from an urban area	Inclusion criteria: (a) current employment as a full-time school counselor in an elementary, middle, or high school in or around the specific city; (b) at least 2 years of experience as a school counselor; and (c) at least two students experiencing homelessness presently or within the last 2 years on the participant's caseload	Inclusion criteria: (a) school counselor, (b) self-identified as having classroom management experiences
	Sample size: $N = 7$	Researchers attempted to recruit a heterogeneous sample by targeting both male and female participants and school counselors who worked across different settings.	Sample size:
	Recruitment: Researcher contacted school counselors, administrators, and districts within her network in her state to gain access to adolescents meeting the criteria.	Sample size:	Archival survey data:
		$N = 23$	$N = 200$ randomly selected cases from ASCA data set
		Recruitment:	Focus groups:
		Researchers focused on a large metropolitan area that, which had been documented as having an increased number of those who experienced homelessness. Thus, researchers believed school counselors in this area would have a likelihood to serve students experiencing homelessness.	Total $N = 21$
		Researchers first reached out to school counselors they were familiar with and, then engaged in snowball sampling to gain information on other pertinent school counselors.	Focus group 1 = 11;
			Focus group 2 = 10
			Recruitment:
			Survey: ASCA sent out a survey to its members asking about their experiences with classroom management. Provided researcher with de-identified data.
			Focus group: Researcher contacted registrants of a statewide, day long school counseling training program to volunteer to participate in a focus group during the lunch break.

Note: Citations: Braun & Clarke (2012); Braun & Clarke (2013); Corbin & Strauss (2015); Creswell & Poth (2018); Glaser & Strauss (1967); Hays & Singh (2012); Hays & Wood (2011); Moustakas (1994).

When considering recruitment and engaging in data collection, it is important that we as researchers do not just quickly enter a system for a study and "take" (i.e., gather data) and then abruptly leave. How can we be intentional about building relationships and trust through your research? How might the results of our study benefit the participants—and be shared and discussed with participants? What do our participants' want to see happen with the results, as follow-up from the study? Do the participants want to engage in advocacy by sharing the results with key partners? For instance, after I (Emily) completed a study on school counselors' experiences with 504 plans and distributing the results with school counselors, some of the participants asked that I share the results with their district-level supervisor, as a means of advocacy. In hindsight, I could have also offered to meet with the participants, to discuss how we could advocate together, and how I could support their advocacy efforts. And as such, I would be working alongside the school counselors (i.e., participants), informed by their perceptions, needs, and recommendations, about how best to relate the findings.

Additionally, in discussing participant recruitment, it is also important to be mindful of how power dynamics impact both recruitment and then participation (O'Hara et al., 2021). For instance, I (Emily) coauthored a phenomenological study in 2020/2021 (led by Dr. Jennifer Betters-Bubon). We recruited school counselor educators (SCEs) to participate in focus groups on a politically charged topic; as such, the research team talked at length about how to increase potential participants' feeling of safety during interviews. However, we noticed after recruitment and data collection that we had several SCEs volunteer to participate and then decline the actual focus group attendance. Upon closer examination, it appeared that the majority of those were faculty identified as BIPOC and/or as pre-tenure faculty members. In reflecting on these demographics, we wondered if these potential participants declined participation due to power imbalances in the focus group, and perhaps a lack of professional safety. Consequently, when recruiting for studies on sensitive topics in the future, we will offer both individual and group interviews, and perhaps focus groups based on academic rank or similar participant demographics, to decrease the power imbalances inherent in focus groups. Also, using an antiracist lens, we must also simultaneously work to examine, interrogate, and alter the greater systems in place that lead to power imbalances across BIPOC and junior faculty.

In sum, there is much to consider regarding sampling and inclusion: from logistics to cultural and antiracist considerations. We have created Table 8.5 to provide examples of sampling, participant inclusion criteria, sample size, and recruitment strategies, highlighting the three sample studies.

Step 7: Data Collection

After all your careful planning, you now have an opportunity to gather rich, in-depth data to explore your research questions(s). There are a variety of data sources in qualitative research and which ones you choose are often influenced by your research tradition and research questions. Some of the most common types of data include:

- Individual interviews: Through a series of interview questions, researchers gather information about participants' experiences and perceptions, responses to, or relationship with a certain phenomenon. A researcher may interview an individual once, or multiple times (Creswell & Poth, 2018). Depending on your topic and research question, you might consider interviewing students, caregivers, administrators, teachers, etc.

- Focus group interviews: Focus groups allow researchers to engage multiple participants about their experiences simultaneously. In this synergistic approach, participants' responses build off one another, encouraging participants to recall and share their stories, building upon the interactions of group members (Hays & Singh, 2012; Kreuger & Casey, 2014). The focus groups you create might include any of the individuals indicated above.

- Participant observation: Researcher(s) immerse themselves in the lives/experiences of the participants by engaging in their day-to-day activities as relevant to the study. Thus, researchers focus on "participant and setting characteristics and behaviors," interacting with the participants, and taking field notes (Hays & Singh, 2012, p. 224). Researchers can also be complete observers in which they minimally interact with and try to go unnoticed by the participants (Creswell & Poth, 2018). As you consider your own school counseling–centered studies, this may be observing classroom lessons, multidisciplinary meetings, staff meetings, students at recess, professional development events, etc.

- Document review: Researchers gather relevant public and private documents related to the research question, which could include but is not limited to diaries, notes, and emails (Creswell & Poth, 2018; Hays & Singh, 2012). Within the context of school counseling research, you may also consider lesson plans, forms, calendars, student records (e.g., attendance, academics, discipline), staff procedures, policy manuals, etc.

- Audiovisual material: Researchers gather audiovisual materials including photos, participant artwork, social media posts, and websites (Creswell & Poth, 2018). For example, as a school counseling–focused researcher, you could analyze students' drawings or photos around a particular topic or examine the social media posts of practicing school counselors pertaining to a given phenomenon.
- Open-ended survey responses: Researchers can collect open-ended survey questions as part of a qualitative inquiry. These open-ended survey responses can be used as the primary source of data analysis or could be used in triangulation with other data collected (e.g., see Goodman-Scott, 2019a).
- Other: There is a range of types of data that can be collected and triangulated with school-based qualitative research, in addition to those mentioned here. During the June 2021 *Teach-In on Antiracism* hosted by American University, Dr. Lynetta Henry, of Fairfax County Public Schools (Virginia) provided examples of collecting school-based data, using an antiracism lens. She shared that when noticing a gap in enrollment in Algebra 1 in eighth grade, between Black and Hispanic eighth-grade students and their white counterparts, the school asked the Black and Hispanic students specifically for their input on the reason for this trend—then used these data to inform school staff, and in their school decision-making, thus gathering partner voices (e.g., student, families, community members), and prioritizing their perspectives. She also suggested an *empathy interview* in which school staff engage in informal, anecdotal interviews to listen empathetically to partners (e.g., families/ parents/guardians), to understand their perspectives better on key topics, trends, or situations. Both of these examples are additional data, from an antiracist lens, that can be triangulated with other forms of qualitative data (e.g., interviews).

Overall, collecting multiple sources of data, and triangulating the results, is a strategy for increasing the rigor or trustworthiness of the study, a topic to be discussed further later in this chapter.

The most common data type across counseling research is individual interviews. **Interviews can be conducted in person, on the phone, or via a videoconferencing platform, and in some cases via chat or email** (Creswell & Poth, 2018). When interviews take place orally, a recording device is used, and researchers create a transcript of each interview for data analysis. To guide the interviews, researchers develop open-ended questions to elicit participants' experiences, meaning making, perceptions, etc., and these questions are put into an interview protocol. Questions may aim to elicit information about the participant's background, experience, opinions or values, knowledge, and feelings (Hays & Singh, 2012).

In this process, the researchers' positionality becomes important, particularly if conducting research with historically oppressed populations. It is necessary to consider how aspects of one's identity and the questions posed may privilege the dominant identities in our society, as well as perpetuate racist or patriarchal processes in which the person in power, in this case the researcher, is taking from the participant for their own gain. As such, it is important to acknowledge the inherent power imbalance between the researcher and the participant (Hays & Singh, 2012). Consequently, some scholars suggest that qualitative researchers create an opportunity for the interviewees to ask questions of the interviewer/research (see "Interactive Interviewing" in Hays & Singh, 2012). By sharing information about yourself and engaging in two-way communication, you can slightly flatten the hierarchy and space between researcher and participant. Further, Hays and Singh (2012) suggest including participants as much as possible in design decisions and the interpretation of the data to mitigate power imbalances as well.

There are three kinds of interviews: **structured**, **semi-structured**, and **unstructured**. As their names suggest, they become increasingly less rigid as you move from structured to unstructured interviews. **Structured interviews** have strict interview protocols that include a set number of questions asked in a particular order. **Semi-structured interviews** have a set of questions that act merely as a guide. There is variability in which questions are ultimately asked and additional questions or probes are added based on the progression of the interview (Hays & Singh, 2012). **Unstructured interviews** are more typical in the context of participant observation, with questions emerging based on the surrounding context (Hays & Singh, 2012). You might find that you have a difficult time getting unstructured interviews approved by some IRBs, as they want to know what you will be asking to assess the risk to participants (see Chapter 3). Regardless of the interview type, after transcribing interviews we recommend providing participants with an opportunity to review their transcript (e.g., member checking; described subsequently) so that they can add to, modify, or further explain anything that they have said. This not only adds to the rigor of the study (see Steps 9 and 10 in this chapter) but also can serve to empower the participants in the research process.

You might be wondering, "How long do the interviews have to last?" It depends! As you can imagine, the **interview length is influenced by your research approach/tradition**, your **research topic, and your research question**(s). For example, given the nature of phenomenological studies and the aim to truly understand the participant's experience with a phenomenon, longer interviews are expected. It would be difficult to convince a reviewer that you truly understood a school counselor's experience of participating in active shooter drills with a 15-minute interview. Other factors that may influence interview length include the age and developmental level of participants, the topic of exploration, the interviewer's ability to establish rapport with the participant, and their use of prompts (e.g., "Tell me more" and "Can you give me an example?"). For example, youth tend to provide shorter responses to interview questions as compared to adults, who are often more verbal and descriptive. Further, when interviewing teachers, you may find that their busy schedules preclude them from sitting down for a long, in-depth interview. As such, you may plan for your interviews to be shorter, or to interview teachers on more than one occasion.

We created Table 8.6 to help differentiate the research traditions in terms of the types of data collected, the types of interview questions, and interview length, while also referencing our sample studies.

Tips and tools during data collection. Now that we've described data collection steps, we will suggest related tips and tools that we've found helpful over the years.

- When recording qualitative interviews, we suggest **using two recording devices**; it's imperative to have a backup in case of a malfunction. We also recommend carrying extra batteries/charging options. While it doesn't happen often, we've had a few cases where one recording device ran out of battery or otherwise failed to record properly. Thankfully, backup options have been lifesavers. We have also found video platforms like Zoom to be especially helpful, and some have built-in transcription options.
- As school counselors, we value connection and relationships. I (Emily) especially appreciate qualitative research because during interviews, I develop a rapport with participants as I hear their stories. Thus, similar to counseling, **relationship and rapport are important in qualitative data collection**. In order to collect participants' authentic experiences and perspectives, they must feel comfortable sharing during the interview. When starting each interview, I spend a few minutes intentionally building rapport and connecting with participants, to help them feel comfortable and build trust. Again, this underscores the importance of trying to address the power imbalance by creating bi-directional communication (Hays & Singh, 2012).
- The goal of interviews is typically to obtain a rich, in-depth account of participants' experiences and perceptions. As such, when conducting interviews, we use counseling skills to encourage participants to expand

Table 8.6. Types of Data, Interview Questions, and Interview Length by Approach

Approach:	Grounded Theory	Phenomenology	Thematic Analysis
Type of Data:	Interviews, participant observation, and artifacts/texts	Interviews Can be supplemented by observations, documents, etc.	Any type of data (interviews are common)
Types of Interview Questions:	Open-ended general questions that attend to a range of experiences and some narrow questions attending to individual's specific experience. Probes and follow-up questions are common.	Broad, open-ended, semi-structured interview questions; often few broad questions (e.g., 1–2), with follow-up probes, as necessary.	Not specified
Interview Length:	To our knowledge, interview length is not necessarily specified by approach. However, for adequate depth and richness, the literature often suggests interviews are 60–90 minutes, unless study purpose, research design, participants, or contexts dictate otherwise.		
Sample Studies:	Gray & Rubel (2018): Data collection: in-person interviews Interview length: three, 30 minutes or less because of developmental level. Six of the seven participants participated in three interviews; the seventh participated in two interviews. Researchers felt they reached theoretical saturation after three rounds of interviews. Interview Questions: "How did you experience the school counseling group (including both positive and negative experiences)?" "How would you describe what it's like to belong to a school counseling group, and how would you describe what it's like to not belong to a school counseling group?" Note. The above only represents 2 of 7 of the interview questions	Havlik et al. (2018): Data collection: phone and in-person interviews, as well as public documents (e.g., McKinney Vento training documents, online resources, protocols, etc.) Interview length: Ranged from 20 to 80 minutes. (Every study has limitations; while this is a strong study, best practices instead suggest 60- to 90-minute interviews for a phenomenological investigation.] Interview Questions: "In general, what has your experience been like working with students who are homeless?" "What are the biggest challenges you faced?" Note: The above represents 2 of the 10 interview questions	Goodman-Scott (2019a): Data collection: open-ended survey responses and focus group interviews Interview length: 60 minutes for each focus group Open-Ended Survey Question: "What's your best tip for working with disruptive students during your classroom lessons?" Interview Questions: "What's your best tip for working with disruptive students during your classroom lessons?" "When you think of classroom management for school counselors, what comes to mind? How does that look?" "Tell me about gaining classroom management skills"

Citations: Braun & Clarke (2006); Braun & Clarke (2013); Charmaz & Belgrave (2012); Clarke & Braun (2018); Creswell & Poth (2018); Hays & Singh, 2012; Hays & Wood (2011); Moustakas (1994).

on their responses, getting beyond their surface-level answers. For instance, **to encourage in-depth interview responses, we use counseling skills** such as: listening, purposeful silence, summarizing, reflecting their meaning and feeling, asking probing questions, and so forth. Reflecting participants' meaning is a trustworthiness strategy (described later) and also provides participants with power during the interview, to provide feedback regarding whether the researcher's understanding accurately reflects the participant's intended meaning.

- When interviewing participants, it's normal to have reactions to their responses. For instance, because of participants' interview responses, I (Emily) have felt excited, inspired, moved, and angered. However, **as a qualitative researcher I am a tool of the investigation and typically aim to bracket, or set aside, my personal thoughts and feelings**, as best I can to focus on my participants' voices. Thus, **when conducting interviews, it's important to present neutrally**: neither praising nor disparaging participants' responses. We also recommend asking neutral, open-ended questions and refraining from leading questions.

- While we attempt to bracket, we also must acknowledge that we are cultural beings who can never fully separate ourselves from our intersecting identities. And these identities influence all aspects of the study. Thus, when conducting research, it is important to be cognizant of how our intersecting identities influence our role in recruiting and interviewing participants.

- We **collect demographics** in different ways. At times, we include a brief electronic survey before the interview that includes consent, interview availability, contact information, and demographic questions. At other times, we may ask demographic questions at the end of the interview. Largely, this depends on the context, situation, and researchers' preferences.

For more tips and tools, please see the following:

- Appendix A: Qualitative Interview CheckList: This provides a step-by-step guide to setting up and conducting qualitative interviews, as well as the transcription and member checking process.
- Appendix B: Interview Protocol: This interview protocol lists steps to complete immediately before, during, and after conducting a qualitative interview.
- Appendix C: Data Collection Log: Researchers can use this log to track the status of their data collection process; this is especially useful when data collection is being completed by a team of researchers.

Step 8: Data Analysis

Analyzing qualitative data is an exciting part of the process, as you get a chance to answer your research questions by diving into the data you worked so hard to gather. When we talk about qualitative data analysis you will hear words like *codes, themes, categories, domains, horizonalization, and codebooks.* Which terms you hear may depend on your research approach; however, **all qualitative data analysis aims to make meaning of the data through intentional steps and processes.** In its most simplified form, this involves first organizing and then examining text and audiovisual material so that you can label "chunks" of data with terms or phrases often called *codes* (Hays & Singh, 2012). You then examine the codes for themes or patterns to determine how they fit together, **using a management system** (often called a *codebook*) that helps list codes and patterns (Hays & Singh, 2012). For a more in-depth, general explanation of qualitative data analysis, see Chapter 13 by Drs. Mullen and Limberg. For the purposes of this chapter, we will focus on highlighting some of the key components of data analysis in grounded theory, phenomenology, and thematic analysis.

Grounded Theory

To explore the research questions for my dissertation, I (Blaire) used a grounded theory approach, thus grounded theory data analysis has a special place in my heart. Given that I was still naive in the qualitative research process, I clung to the specific step-by-step procedures for data analysis in grounded theory. In Straussian grounded theory analysis, there are **three specific phases involved in coding the data (open, axial, and selective)** and a key process that researchers engage in called the **constant comparative method** (Glaser & Strauss, 1967). This results in an emergent theory describing the phenomenon of focus, which often includes a figure or diagram to explain the theory (Creswell & Poth, 2018).

Below we outline the data analysis steps that most closely align with Straussian grounded theory analysis.

- Review Data: Start by reading through the transcripts/field notes and familiarizing yourself with the data.
- Open Coding: This first step of coding involves looking at the data broadly and assigning codes to segments of data (e.g., a phrase, a sentence, or a couple of sentences) as you create categories of information.

You might assign your own words or use the participant's words (also called in vivo codes). Codes that are similar are grouped into a category (Creswell & Poth, 2018; Hays & Singh, 2012; Corbin & Strauss, 2015).

    a. You want to keep what grounded theory calls *theoretical memos*, which document your reflective process regarding the codes, categories, and their relationship to one another (Corbin & Strauss, 2015).

- Constant Comparative Method: As you continue to collect and analyze data, constantly compare instances within each code for similarities and differences to begin refining the code and its properties. Additionally, you will compare open codes to one another for similarities and differences (Creswell & Poth, 2018; Glaser & Strauss, 1967).

- Axial Coding: Based on your open coding, identify a category central to the phenomenon of study (sometimes called the *core phenomenon*); this will be the axis. Next return to your open codes and categories and determine categories that relate to this selected core phenomenon. Strauss and Corbin (1990) recommend you look at the following types of categories:
  - Causal conditions: Factors that cause the core phenomenon
  - Strategies: Actions that occur because of the phenomenon (strategies), conditions that influence the strategies
  - Contextual and intervening conditions: Situational contexts that impact the strategies
  - Consequences: Outcomes of using the strategies

  You may find that in this stage you will combine categories into larger categories with subcategories. You may visually represent the axial codes at this stage, called the *axial coding paradigm*, depicting how the categories relate to the core phenomenon (Creswell & Poth, 2018; Strauss & Corbin, 1990).

  a. Continue with theoretical memos.

  b. Saturation occurs when new data no longer provide information to refine and define the categories or add to the developing theory (Corbin & Strauss, 2015; Hays & Singh, 2012).

- Selective Coding: Examine your axial codes and determine how the categories interrelate as you look for patterns and sequences within them. As Creswell and Poth (2018) state, "the researcher may write a 'story line' that connects the categories" (p. 89).

- Figure Creation: Develop a figure to represent visually the relationships among and between the categories based in the data (Creswell & Poth, 2018).

Phenomenology

As we mentioned at the beginning of the chapter, phenomenology aims to provide a description of participants' lived experience of a certain phenomenon that really gets at the essence of this experience across participants (Creswell & Poth, 2018). I (Emily) have used it to explore a variety of topics from social stories to school counseling advocacy. Remember, unlike grounded theory, theory development is not the goal. Instead, there is an **exploration of the subjective and objective experiences of the phenomenon to find what participants have in common** (Creswell & Poth, 2018). Given this drive for the essence of the experience, it is important that the data analysis strategies focus on both *what* participants experienced and *how* they experienced it (Moustakas, 1994). For the purposes of this chapter, we present Moustakas' (1994) steps for data analysis for transcendental phenomenology.

1. *Epoché* or Bracketing: To begin, you must clearly articulate your own biases and assumptions related to the phenomenon of interest (Moustakas, 1994). This allows you to fully acknowledge and set aside your biases and assumptions in order to focus on the participants' lived experiences with a new perspective (Creswell & Poth, 2018). This is an ongoing process, as you must continue to bracket your assumptions throughout the study.
2. Horizonalization: Next, read through a transcript and identify relevant quotes, sentences, or units of meaning, called *horizons*, and list them in a separate document. These should be non-repetitive and non-overlapping (Moustakas, 1994).
3. Clustering Horizons: Organize or cluster the horizons into themes, and repetitive statements are removed (Moustakas, 1994).
4. Textural and Structural Descriptions: Using the clustered themes write textural descriptions and structural descriptions (Moustakas, 1994). **Textural descriptions** describe **what** participants have experienced and "strives to understand the meaning and depth of the essence of the experience" (Hays & Singh, 2012, p. 355). **Structural descriptions** relate to **how** participants experienced the phenomenon. More specifically, think of this in terms of how the context and setting impacted the participants' experiences of the phenomenon (Creswell & Poth, 2018).
5. Essence: Last, the textural and structural descriptions are used together to write the essence, or the overarching common experience of the phenomenon (Moustakas, 1994).

Thematic Analysis

Braun and Clarke (2012), two of the researchers who really codified thematic analysis, describe thematic analysis as **"an entry into a way of doing research that otherwise can seem vague, mystifying, conceptually challenging, and overly complex"** (p. 58). So, the good news is that thematic analysis is geared toward beginning qualitative researchers. It does not mean that it is easy and that you can analyze data haphazardly, but it does offer flexibility (Braun & Clarke, 2006, 2012). As noted earlier in this chapter, thematic analysis should only be used with a research paradigm serving as a theoretical framework (e.g., constructivist, social constructionist, feminism theory) to guide research questions, interview questions, etc. (Clarke & Braun, 2018). With these considerations established and data collected, you are ready to engage in the six phases of thematic analysis.

1. Become Familiar with Data: Actively read through the entire data set while taking notes on what you are noticing (Braun & Clarke, 2006). If you conducted interviews, you may even consider listening to the recordings (Braun & Clarke, 2012).

2. Generate Initial Codes: Start by applying codes to extracts of the data that address the research question (Braun & Clark, 2006). It is possible for the same segment of data to be coded more than one time if it is relevant. Begin by making a list of the code names and the subsequent extracts.

3. Search for Themes: Once all the data have been coded, begin sorting the codes into themes, considering relationships between codes as well as overlap (Braun & Clarke, 2006, 2012). You may decide that certain codes should be collapsed and that some codes cluster together around a central idea or feature, thus indicating a pattern. As you identify themes, consider how they relate to one another, "like the pieces of a jigsaw puzzle" (Braun & Clarke, 2012, p. 65). In this phase you may also determine that there are main themes but also related sub-components called subthemes (Braun & Clark, 2006, 2012). At this time, you may find it helpful to create a thematic map of the themes and how they relate to one another (Braun & Clark, 2006, 2012), much like a concept map, or you may want to create a table that delineates your themes and the related codes and data extracts (Braun & Clarke, 2012).

4. Review Potential Themes: Next, read the data extracts associated with each theme to determine if the theme fits the data (Braun & Clarke, 2012). Also examine the working list of themes to determine whether there are enough data to support themes, if themes should be combined,

Table 8.7. Data Analysis Steps by Approach

Approach:	Grounded Theory	Phenomenology	Thematic Analysis
Data Analysis Steps:	Straussian Grounded Theory 1. Open coding 2. Axial coding 3. Selective coding Constant comparative method; saturation; theoretical memos	Moustakas (1994): Transcendental Phenomenology 1. Bracketing assumptions 2. Read transcripts; horizontalization. 3. Horizons clustered into themes. 4. Write textural and structural descriptions. 5. Write the essence. Goals: Move from narrow to general.	Braun & Clarke (2006, 2012): Thematic Analysis 1. Read the data. 2. Generate initial codes. 3. Search for themes. 4. Review themes. 5. Define and name themes. 6. Write the report.

Note: Citations: Braun & Clarke (2006); Braun & Clarke (2012); Moustakas (1994); Strauss & Corbin (1990)

or if themes should be separated (Braun & Clarke, 2006). Next, look at the entire data set and whether the themes accurately portray the data, and then determine if your thematic map reflects the data set, adjusting accordingly (Braun & Clarke, 2006).

5. Define and Name Themes: Identify what is specific and important about each of your themes and what data they represent, choosing a name that exemplifies this. Your themes should have a singular focus, relate but not overlap, and answer your research question (Braun & Clarke, 2012). You can determine this by writing a narrative explanation of each theme, which helps to establish themes and subthemes further (Braun & Clarke, 2006).

6. Produce the Report: In this last step, tell the story of the data within the themes and as they relate to each other (Braun & Clarke, 2006). You will want to use rich data extracts from the data to illustrate the theme and explain to the reader how and why the extract is significant (Braun & Clarke, 2012).

For a list of the data analysis steps by approach, see Table 8.7.

Steps 9 and 10: Trustworthiness Strategies and Researcher Reflexivity

In qualitative research, we as the researchers have the privilege of serving as the instrument to explore the phenomenon of interest. **We are an intimate part of the entire research process** including choosing the topic, collecting data (e.g., interviewing participants), analyzing the data, and writing up the results. As such, the research process can reflect our culture, intersecting identities, thoughts, emotions, personal experiences, beliefs and biases, all of which can influence our interactions with and interpretations of the data (Hays & Singh, 2012; Kline, 2008). This is not considered a limitation in qualitative research. Instead, we employ **specific strategies as a means of transparency and minimizing the impact of our own biases** as we strive to convey the "truthfulness of [the] findings and conclusions based on maximum opportunity to hear participants' voices in a particular context" (Hays & Singh, 2012, p. 192). These strategies relate to what qualitative researchers call *trustworthiness*.

Lincoln and Guba (1985) developed four criteria of trustworthiness (credibility, transferability, dependability, and confirmability) to evaluate qualitative research. These are referred to repeatedly in counseling and education-based qualitative textbooks (e.g., Creswell & Poth, 2018; Hays & Singh, 2012).

- Credibility: This criterion parallels internal validity in quantitative research. It relates to the accuracy of the findings based on how the study was conducted and on the perceptions of those who participated in the study (Lincoln & Guba, 1985).
- Transferability: This criterion mirrors that of external validity or generalizability in quantitative research. However, qualitative research does not aim for generalizability. Instead, transferability relates to describing the research process in depth, particularly the participants, their context, and settings such that a reader can determine the "degree of similarity" between the study and their own group and setting of interest (Lincoln & Guba, 1985, p. 297).
- Dependability: This criterion is most similar to reliability in quantitative research. You can think of it as relating to the clear steps that researchers articulate related to their data collection, analysis, and interpretations such that another researcher is clear as to exactly how it progressed and can make judgments accordingly (Lincoln & Guba, 1985). Perhaps more clearly stated, "consistency of findings across time and researchers" (Hays et al., 2016, p. 174). Thus, for a study with high dependability, we'd expect similar findings among researchers within and across studies.
- Confirmability: This criterion is much like the concept of objectivity or neutrality in quantitative research (Lincoln & Guba, 1985). With confirmability we ensure that the findings are rooted in the data and not based on the researchers' own perceptions (Lincoln & Guba, 1985).

Now that we have articulated trustworthiness criteria, you might be wondering: How can I engage in the research process in such a way to increase trustworthiness? The good news is that there are a set of trustworthiness strategies that researchers can employ to increase the rigor of their studies purposefully (Hays & Singh, 2012; Hays et al., 2016; Lincoln & Guba, 1985). Some of the strategies even attend to more than one criterion (see Table 8.8). Your selection of trustworthiness strategies is often influenced by your qualitative approach to ensure coherence/congruence (Hays & Wood, 2011) as well as to establish rigor by using as many strategies as possible. There are so many trustworthiness strategies that a whole chapter or even book could be committed to their full description; however, our goal is to define each of the strategies briefly, designate to which criteria they align according to Lincoln and Guba (1985), and indicate how our sample studies used them where applicable (see Table 8.8). For more information regarding employing specific trustworthiness strategies, please see Chapter 13 of this book by Drs. Mullen and Limberg.

Given that reflexivity is one of the most popular trustworthiness strategies utilized in qualitative counseling research (Hays et al., 2016), we want to provide a bit more background. Reflexivity can be best described as self-reflection and includes the "monitoring throughout the research process of the assumptions and relationships the researcher has with the topic, sample, and site" (Hays et al., 2016, p. 175). It can be conceptualized as the framework in which the research study is viewed (Hays & Singh, 2012; Stake, 1995). Therefore, when sharing your research, it is important to convey your reflexivity clearly to the audience, through what is often called a "reflexivity statement" or "subjectivity statement." This provides the audience with an explanation of the researchers' roles in the study, their backgrounds, and their experiences with the study's topic (Hunt, 2011). At times this reflexivity statement can also include researchers' biases and assumptions (Hunt, 2011). Thus, when we think of comprehensive reflexivity statements, we think of those that include the following:

1. The researcher(s)' demographics as they relate to the focus of the study
2. Researcher(s)' personal experience with the phenomenon of focus
3. Researcher(s)' biases and assumptions

Below is an example of the reflexivity statement from Goodman-Scott (2019a):

I, the researcher, am a counselor educator specializing in school counseling. I have previous experience as both a school counselor and a special education teacher in a self-contained setting. I identify as a White woman of European descent. As a result of my professional experiences, I entered this study with assumptions and biases regarding school counseling classroom management. For instance, as a practicing

Table 8.8. Trustworthiness Strategies

Trustworthiness Strategy	Description	Trustworthiness Criteria	Trustworthiness in Sample Studies (According to Authors)
Reflexivity	A process of self-reflection by the researchers that can include reflexive journaling, field notes, and memos. This can be communicated by the researcher's reflexivity statement in the manuscript.	Credibility Dependability Confirmability	Gray & Rubel: First author journaled on previous experiences, engaged in reflective discussions with second author, and double-checked ideas that paralleled their own assumptions to ensure participant voice. Also included a reflexivity statement including both authors' race/ethnicity, age, gender, their expertise in group counseling, and their school counseling work experience Havlick et al. bracketed their assumptions, took field notes after each interview, 2nd–5th author shared insights with 1st author after interview, engaged in reflexive journaling. Goodman-Scott stated axiological assumptions and used journaling, field notes, and reflective discussions with peer debriefer/external auditor. Also included a reflexivity statement describing her gender and race/ethnicity as well as her work experience and relationship with classroom management.
Triangulation	Using multiple data sources, multiple researchers, and/or data methods to support the findings.	Credibility Dependability (methods)	Gray & Rubel triangulated data across the three interviews and across diverse participants. Havlick et al. triangulated data analysis across researchers. Goodman-Scott triangulated survey data and focus group data and triangulated data across focus groups.
Thick Description	In-depth description of the entire research process (sampling, participants/settings, data collection, data analysis steps), the participants' accounts [e.g., direct quotes], and the research setting.	Transferability	Gray & Rubel provided detailed descriptions of participants and context. Goodman-Scott used an audit trail and provided in-depth description of the research process and results.

Member Checking	Asking study participants to confirm the accuracy of the transcripts, coding, findings, etc. This can include checking their interview transcript, how the emergent themes reflect their experiences, and researcher conclusions.	Credibility	Gray & Rubel consulted with participants regarding the transcriptions and coding. Goodman-Scott sent participants their transcripts and drafted results section asking for feedback.
Audit Trail and External Audit	Audit trail: maintaining evidence of your research process including but not limited to: interview protocols, raw data (e.g., transcripts), field notes, reflexive journals, memos of data analysis decisions, etc. External audit: having an individual external to the study review the coherence of the study, examine researcher bias, evaluate the method implementation, ensure that the findings are based on the data and the accuracy of themes. Basically, they review the audit trail.	Credibility Dependability Confirmability	Havlick et al.: An individual with qualitative data analysis experience and experience working with students going through homelessness reviewed transcripts and final themes. (Important to note: best practices suggest that an external audit be more comprehensive and include more of what is described in the audit trail description in the column to the left. It may also include an examination of the horizons as well as the textural and structural descriptions. Goodman-Scott: Advanced doctoral student compared the audit trail with the findings.
Prolonged Engagement	Spend extensive time with the participants to build trust, learn the context and setting, and thus be able to reflect the phenomenon better.	Credibility	Gray & Rubel: First author interviewed participants approximately 3 times.
Peer Debriefing	Engaging with a peer to critically unpack the researcher(s)' biases, research process and interpretation of the data, as well as talking through hypotheses	Credibility	Gray & Rubel presented their theory to three school counselors and one counselor educator for feedback. Havlick et al. discussed findings and reflexive journals with those external to the study. Goodman-Scott met with an advanced doctoral student to discuss methods and findings.
Negative Case Analysis	Constantly examining the data for disconfirming examples of your developing themes and making subsequent revisions.		Havlick et al. looked for disconfirming evidence during theme exploration.

Note: Citations: Hays & Singh, 2012; Hays et al., 2016; Lincoln & Guba, 1985.

school counselor, I had limited training in classroom management and was therefore self-taught. Thus, as a school counselor educator, I am biased toward including classroom management strategies in both my teaching and supervision. (p. 5)

Researcher reflexivity must also be done in the **context of the particular study,** and the **population in which you are studying.** This includes the use of **cultural humility, the awareness of power dynamics, and potential for trust or distrust between the research team and the potential participants.** For instance, consider a lead researcher who identifies as of European-descent, White, cisgender, heterosexual, highly acculturated to dominant U.S. cultures, speaking English as a first language, male, and a doctoral-educated researcher—who is seeking to interview K–12 students and family members who are Latinx, multilingual, speaking Spanish as a first language, and in a school community with a high rate of families receiving free and reduced lunch. Power and cultural considerations are crucial in this circumstance. When reaching out to potential participants, will the researcher appear to be a safe outlet for the students and families to confide in during an interview? And in all actuality: *is* the researcher a safe outlet? *Is* participating in the study safe and beneficial to the participants? And taking it one step further, the lead researcher must ask themselves, *What is the purpose of the research?* Will the research be used for the researcher's benefit—for accolades and publication? Or will the research be used to prioritize the voice and experience of the sample, and to share the results in a way directed by the participants? In this example, the research team should spend considerable time in self-reflection as to the purpose of the study and the potential impact on the participants. If the study is to benefit the sample, the lead researcher may consider strategies to decrease participant risk and increase their comfort and safety. In their article, O'Hara and colleagues (2021) outline a **number of related strategies for decreasing the power imbalance in research,** such as adding research team members who are part of the historically oppressed populations, as well as partnering with the participants regarding how to use the results of the study.

Concluding Steps: Writing Results for Publication

Step 11: Writing the Results

After collecting and analyzing the data, you are ready for the final steps of your qualitative study: writing the results and submitting for publication. Completing the planning checklist has assisted me (Emily) in writing manuscripts, including the Methods and Results sections. I appreciate having key aspects of my study housed in one document, which I update throughout the research process.

Qualitative results include commonalities as well as differences across approaches. To start with commonalities: We suggest that the presentation of the **results demonstrate coherence/congruence with the rest of the manuscript,** as well as include **cultural and antiracist considerations utilized throughout the study.** Thus, if you conduct a thematic analysis and create themes and subthemes, then those themes and subthemes should be presented in the results. Next, broadly speaking, **in qualitative results, researchers typically list and describe themes and subthemes, providing participant quotes** to illustrate those themes and subthemes. Providing these participant quotes ensures a thick, rich example, which is a hallmark of qualitative research. It also allows readers to ensure that researchers are staying true to the data, thereby limiting researcher bias. Typically, when conducting qualitative research, we have so many quotes to choose from to illustrate each theme/subtheme that it can be challenging to decide which to use! Often writing the results is a process of continuing to pare down the existing quotes, to choose a few for each theme or subtheme.

At the same time, the results will also be different, based on approach. For more information on the differences in results by approach, please see Table 8.9; we also provide a more in-depth example of results, from one of our featured studies, subsequently.

Next, we'll **demonstrate excerpts of results, from Havlik et al.'s (2018) phenomenology.** To start with, the researchers provided an overview of the two overarching themes of their study and outlined how they would present those themes. Please see the text below. We added boldface, for emphasis:

> *During the interviews, participants shared their personal experiences working with students experiencing homelessness. Through data exploration, the **researchers identified two general themes across participants:** (a) school counselors as the first line of support and (b) the desire to help while feeling helpless. **The two themes and subsequent subthemes are summarized below with quotations from the interview transcripts.** (p. 52)*

Next, Havlik and colleagues named, then described, their first theme (in bold), followed by a participant quote (we added bold to the quote) to illustrate the theme. Then they unpacked the participant quote further, through additional narrative:

Table 8.9. Presenting Results by Approach

Approach:	Grounded Theory	Phenomenology	Thematic Analysis
Presenting Results:	Report the model developed. Illustrate axial and selective codes.	Present the essence of participants' lived experiences, comprised of textural and structural descriptions.	Present themes, including the meaning and content.
Notes:	Narrative, explaining results Thick, rich portrayal of results, including illustrative quotes		

Note: Citations: Braun & Clarke (2006); Hays & Wood (2011); Moustakas (1994); Strauss & Corbin (1990).

First Line of Support

The participants explained that their roles in working with students experiencing homelessness primarily included addressing students' basic needs and then referring them to other resources, such as school social workers or homeless liaisons to provide more comprehensive support. Because basic needs, such as food, clothing, and shelter, overshadowed educational and emotional needs, participants recognized that they had to initially ensure these needs were met before others could be addressed. These needs were often extensive, requiring partnerships within and outside of the school to help. As an example of how this process may play out in a school, Participant 14 shared:

We have a charter school, so the kids all wear a uniform. So, if they are missing a piece of their uniform, it's my job to make sure we can provide it for that child. If they're needing food outside of the home, 'cause we provide breakfast and lunch for the kids, but if there's not enough food where they are staying, we provide them with food or the resources to go to a food bank so that they can get food.

In this sense, participants seemed to be the first line of support in the school, determining how to best serve students, and then directing support to others when necessary. (p. 52)

After naming and describing a theme, the researchers then named and explained a corresponding subtheme (in bold), this time including multiple participant quotes, as examples:

Addressing basic needs. Participants felt the basic needs of students experiencing homelessness took precedence over all other needs (i.e., emotional and educational). Basic needs described by participants included those areas considered necessary for students to attend and to be successful in school. Participants mentioned providing transportation, clean clothes (e.g., uniforms), school supplies, free and reduced lunch, and school dues. Participant 13 said she kept a closet of supplies available for *students: "If we see there is a need for it . . . clothing, such as uniforms, sneakers, and cap and gown cost for graduating seniors. We have a stock. Like, we have a closet full of binders, folders, school bags, pens, notebooks." Title I funds were frequently cited as an important source for providing basic needs for students. Participant 6 mentioned that her school got funding to provide for basic needs such as "socks, shoes, and stuff like that." She stated that her school was able to provide each student who qualified with $100 to meet specific basic needs. (p. 52)*

Now that we've provided examples of how to write up the results of a qualitative study, our last consideration is to be **mindful of manuscript length**. We've found that counseling journals tend to require that manuscripts are no more than 20–25 pages in length, which may or may not include references and the cover page. Thus, we need to **be extremely frugal with our use of space**, especially given that qualitative research is known for utilizing thick, rich descriptions of the method and results. As such, some journals may offer flexibility in length (e.g., granting an additional one to two pages) for qualitative studies; this may require respectfully reaching out to the journal editor or editorial assistant, to inquire.

Another option, when appropriate, is **dividing one qualitative data set into two manuscripts**. Hunt (2011) described publishing multiple articles from one qualitative study, and we have experience doing this as well. However, there are several important considerations. First, we recommend that the results can be separated completely (hence, removing all overlapping content between the two manuscripts), and that each set of results and each manuscript can stand on their own. Hence, we need to be mindful to avoid the ethical conundrum of piecemealing. Next, when the two sets of results are unique from each other, this means the literature review and discussion sections will also be distinct from each other. While the two method sections will include the same content, researchers should be mindful to vary their write-up as much as possible. Lastly, Hunt (2011) recommends that each study note that the present results are from a larger qualitative data set and describe the overarching study. While separating results across two manuscripts is an option we've used, we've done this sparingly. This decision depends on the depth and breadth of the results, and how they fit together, as a whole.

Avoiding Pitfalls in Qualitative Research

As we wrap up the chapter, we will emphasize key points by noting common mistakes to avoid when conducting qualitative research:

Common Mistake #1: Lack of Alignment/Coherence/ Congruence Across the Study

Examples:

- The paradigm and research questions are unaligned. Example: using a positivism paradigm (i.e., one universal truth), yet conducting a study on participants' unique perceptions.
- The tradition/approach is not congruent with data collection strategies. Example: facilitating a phenomenological study (i.e., in-depth interviews to understand participants' lived experiences), but utilizing short interviews (e.g., 15 minutes).
- The tradition/approach and results are not in alignment. Example: conducting a grounded theory study, but a theory is not described in the findings.
- The tradition/approach and the data analysis are incongruent. Example: completing a phenomenological study using grounded theory data analysis strategies.

Common Mistake #2: Shallow Data Analysis

- When we (Blaire and Emily) completed our first phenomenological studies, we each separately received feedback that our themes were very similar to our interview questions. For instance, during interviews, we may have asked participants about their challenges with a phenomenon, and then one of the themes was *challenges*; we did this for several other interview questions as well. The editor challenged each of us to dig deeper into the data: to look for themes across and beyond the interview questions. Thus, our research teams spent a few months re-analyzing the data. This is a common mistake in qualitative research: lack of a thorough or comprehensive data analysis. To truly immerse yourself in the data, qualitative data analysis takes substantial time, thought, and effort and creates new meaning.

Common Mistake #3: Lack of Description, Depth, and Citations

- We commonly see qualitative articles submitted for review that lack key aspects such as leaving out Trustworthiness sections or Reflexivity statements. Similarly, we have also seen articles with very limited descriptions (e.g., listing the data analysis steps briefly, rather than describing these in depth).

- When I (Emily) was a novice researcher, I found my interviews were more surface level, and I got shallow answers. I've since learned to use my counseling skills more purposefully during interviews (e.g., reflection, listening, summarizing, probing questions, silence) in order to gain a richer, more in-depth account of participants' experiences and perceptions.
- We've seen authors state they are using an approach (e.g., case study) but not cite, define, or describe the approach in the article.

Common Mistake #4: Overreaching in Implications and Limitations

- When writing up the study, be mindful to avoid widely posing recommendations and implications, as the goal of qualitative research is not generalization. For instance, when conducting a qualitative study, which typically has a small number of participants, it is not appropriate to make generalizations and implications for a large population. We (Emily and Blaire) attempt to write tentative implications (e.g., "In light of the results, practicing school counselors may want to consider . . . ").
- We often see researchers list the "small" sample size as a limitation for their qualitative study. In fact, we've even had editors/reviewers ask us to include this in our limitation sections as well. However, qualitative studies purposefully have a relatively small sample, to provide an adequately rich account. Describing sample size as a limitation merely because the numbers are smaller than in quantitative research is inappropriate and speaks to using a quantitative lens for qualitative research.

Conclusion

We have covered a lot of ground in this chapter. We situated qualitative research as powerful methodology that can raise up the voices of historically oppressed populations if implemented thoughtfully and with awareness of own's own positionality, biases, power, etc. Further, we provided a brief introduction to qualitative research, including (a) how to begin and plan for a study, (b) data collection and analysis, (c) strategies for writing and publishing qualitative research, and (d) common mistakes to avoid. Throughout the chapter we highlighted three studies to demonstrate three different qualitative approaches: grounded theory, phenomenology, and thematic analysis. As we noted at the beginning, the purpose of this chapter is to share practical tools and strategies for *how* to conduct qualitative research. Thus, we also included a wealth of resources, for more in-depth reading on qualitative research. While we have shared tips, tools, and strategies in this chapter, we want to end with relaying more about our motivation and passion for qualitative research.

Final Reflections

As I (Emily) mentioned at the start of this chapter, I appreciate qualitative research as a powerful means to advocate for not only the school counseling profession, but also groups who have been traditionally oppressed in K–12 education: gaining insight from K–12 students, families, and community members.

To provide an example of advocacy for the profession: Student lockdown drills have become increasingly implemented in the United States yet have been anecdotally scrutinized as potentially harmful and even traumatic for students and school staff. Due to a lack of research on the topic, a colleague and I completed a study on school counselors' experiences with lockdown drills (Goodman-Scott & Eckhoff, 2020). According to results, many school counselors in our study were concerned with their roles in lockdown drills, described negative reactions from students, staff, and school counselors, as well as challenges with communication, procedures, school culture, and so forth. In short, the results of this study were quite troubling. In response, my colleague and I are using the results to provide education and advocacy pertaining to lockdown drills. Specifically, we are sharing the results and implications of our study in the following ways:

- Presenting at a national counseling conference and a state-level school safety conference
- Presenting to local school board members, educators, and community members, hosted by a local school safety coalition
- Created a policy statement that was disseminated to state legislators
- Co-wrote an editorial/opinion article for a national education outlet

Thus, I had the incredible privilege to hear school counselors' accounts of lockdown drills and share these experiences across a variety of audiences, in an effort to raise awareness and hopefully instill change on several levels of education and policy.

Final Thought

In sum, we hope you have a better understanding of the beauty, complexities, and rigor of qualitative research, and that you have gained concrete tools to help you proactively plan for and carry out future qualitative investigations. In addition, we hope you have seen the power of qualitative research within the school counseling profession as a tool for both education and advocacy for systemic change, as well as to share the stories and experiences of individuals in historically oppressed groups. And finally, we hope you finish this chapter excited about qualitative research as a tool for strengthening the school counseling profession.

References

Braun, V., & Clarke, V. (2006). Using thematic analysis in psychology. *Qualitative Research in Psychology, 3*(2), 77–101. https://doi.org/10.1191/1478088706qp063oa

Braun, V., & Clarke, V. (2012). Thematic analysis. In H. Cooper, P. M. Camic, D. L. Long, A. T. Panter, D. Rindskopf, & K. J. Sher (Eds.), APA handbooks in psychology®. *APA handbook of research methods in psychology*, Vol. 2. Research designs: Quantitative, qualitative, neuropsychological, and biological (pp. 57–71). American Psychological Association. https://doi.org/10.1037/13620-004

Braun, V., & Clarke, V. (2013). *Successful qualitative research: A practical guide for beginners.* Sage.

Charmaz, K. (2014). *Constructing grounded theory* (2nd ed.). Sage.

Charmaz, K., & Belgrave, L. L. (2012). Qualitative interviewing and grounded theory analysis. In J. F. Gubrium, J. A. Holstein, A. B Marvasti, & K. D. McKinney (Eds.), *The SAGE handbook of interview research: The complexity of the craft* (2nd ed., pp. 347–366). Sage.

Clarke, A. E. (2005). *Situational analysis: Grounded theory after the postmodern turn.* Sage.

Clarke, V., & Braun, V. (2018). Using thematic analysis in counselling and psychotherapy research: A critical reflection. *Counselling and Psychotherapy Research, 18*(2), 107–110. https://doi.org/10.1002/capr.12165

Corbin, J., & Strauss, A. (2015). *Basics of qualitative research: Techniques and procedures for developing grounded theory* (4th ed.). Sage.

Creswell, J. W., & Poth, C. N. (2018). Qualitative inquiry & research design: Choosing among five approaches (4th ed.). Sage

Denzin, N. K., & Lincoln, Y. S. (Eds.). (2011). *The Sage handbook of qualitative research* (4th ed.). Sage.

Flynn, S. V., & Korcuska, J. S. (2018a). Credible phenomenological research: A mixed-methods study. *Counselor Education and Supervision, 57*(1), 34–50. https://doi.org/10.1002/ceas.12092

Flynn, S. V., & Korcuska, J. S. (2018b). Grounded theory research design: An investigation into practice and procedures. *Counseling Outcome Research and Evaluation, 9*(2), 1–15. https://doi.org/10.1080/21501378.2017.1403849

Flynn, S. V., Korcuska, J. S., Brady, N. V., & Hays, D. G. (2019). A 15-year content analysis of three qualitative research traditions. *Counselor Education and Supervision, 58*(1), 49–63. https://doi.org/10.1002/ceas.12123

Glaser, B., & Strauss, A. (1967). *The discovery of grounded theory: Strategies for qualitative research*. Sociology Press.

Goodman-Scott, E. (2019a). Enhancing student learning by "building a caring climate": School counselors' experiences with classroom management. *Professional School Counseling, 22*(1), 1–12. https://doi.org/10.1177/2156759X19852618

Goodman-Scott, E. (2019b, March). How to write and publish qualitative research: Questions and conversations. Evidence-Based School Counseling Conference. Research day.

Goodman-Scott, E., & Eckhoff, A. (2020). School counselors' experiences with lockdown drills: A phenomenological investigation. *Journal of Counseling and Development, 98*(4), 435–445. https://doi.org/10.1002/jcad.12345

Gray, T. M., & Rubel, D. (2018). "Sticking together": The adolescent experience of the cohesion process in rural school counseling groups. *Journal for Specialists in Group Work, 43*(1), 35–56. https://doi.org/10.1080/01933922.2017.1370049

Havlik, S. A., Rowley, P., Puckett, J., Wilson, G., & Neason, E. (2018). "Do whatever you can to try to support that kid": School counselors' experiences addressing student homelessness. *Professional School Counseling, 21*(1), 47–59. https://doi.org/10.5330/1096-2409-21.1.47

Hays, D. G., & McKibben, W. B. (2021). Promoting rigorous research: Generalizability and qualitative research. *Journal of Counseling & Development, 99*(2), 178–188. https://doi.org/10.1002/jcad.12365

Hays, D. G., & Singh, A. A. (2012). *Qualitative inquiry in clinical and educational settings*. Guilford Press.

Hays, D. G., & Wood, C. (2011). Infusing qualitative traditions in counseling research designs. *Journal of Counseling and Development, 89*(3), 288–295. https://doi.org/10.1002/j.1556-6678.2011.tb00091.x

Hays, D. G., Wood, C., Dahl, H., & Kirk-Jenkins, A. (2016). Methodological rigor in journal of counseling & development qualitative research articles: A 15-year review. *Journal of Counseling and Development, 94*(2), 172–183. https://doi.org/10.1002/jcad.12074

Holcomb-McCoy, C. (Ed.). (2021). *Antiracist counseling in schools and communities*. American Counseling Association.

Hunt, B. (2011). Publishing qualitative research in counseling journals. *Journal of Counseling and Development, 89*, 296–300. https://doi.org/10.1002/j.1556-6678.2011.tb00092.x

Kline, W. B. (2008). Developing and submitting credible qualitative manuscripts. *Counselor Education & Supervision, 47*(4), 210–217.

Kreuger, R., & Casey, M. A. (2014). *Focus groups: A practical guide for applied research* (5th ed). Sage.

Lincoln, Y. S., & Guba, E. G. (1985). *Naturalistic inquiry*. Sage.

Moustakas, C. (1994). *Phenomenological research methods*. Sage.

O'Hara, C., Chang, C. Y., & Giordano, A. L. (2021). Multicultural competence in counseling research: The cornerstone of scholarship. *Journal of Counseling and Development, 99*(2), 200–209. https://doi.org/10.1002/jcad.12367

Patton, M. Q. (2014). *Qualitative research & evaluation methods: Integrating theory and practice* (4th ed). Sage.

Polk, W., Savitz-Romer, M., & Brion-Meisels, G. (2021). Dismantling white supremacy in school counselor training programs: Preparing to enact antiracist practices. In C. Holcomb-McCoy (Ed.), *Antiracist counseling in schools and communities* (pp. 151–181). American Counseling Association.

Ratts, M. J., Singh, A. A., Nassar-McMillan, S., Butler, S. K., & McCullough, J. R. (2015). Multicultural and social justice counseling competencies. Retrieved from http://www.counseling.org/docs/default-source/competencies/multicultural-and-social-justice-counseling-competencies.pdf?sfvrsn=20

Stake, R. E. (1995). *The art of case study research.* Sage.

Strauss, A., & Corbin, J. (1990). *Basics of qualitative research: Grounded theory procedures and techniques.* Sage.

Toliver, S. R. (2022). *Recovering Black storytelling in qualitative research: Endarkened storywork.* Routledge.

Van Manen, M. (2014). *Phenomenology of practice: Meaning-giving methods in phenomenological research and writing.* Left Coast Press.

Washington, A., Byrd, J. A., & Williams, J. M. (2021). Decolonizing the counseling canon. In C. Holcomb-McCoy (Ed.), *Antiracist counseling in schools and communities* (pp. 17–31). American Counseling Association.

Wester, K. L., Wachter Morris, C. A., Turstey, C. E., Cory, J. S., & Grossman, L. M. (2021). Promoting rigorous research using innovative qualitative approaches. *Journal of Counseling and Development, 99,* 189–199. https://doi.org/10.1002/jcad.12366

Williams, J. M., Byrd, J. A., & Washington, A. (2021). Challenges in implementing antiracist pedagogy into counselor education programs: A collective self-study. *Counselor Education & Supervision, 60,* 254–273. https://doi.org/ 10.1002/ceas.12215

Appendix A

Goodman-Scott Qualitative Interview Checklist (2019b)

- Has participant met inclusion criteria, and are they willing to speak for [insert amount of time] on topic?
- Has participant completed the informed consent?
- Has participant completed the demographic questionnaire?
- Confirm with the participant: time, date, interviewer, and interview method (in-person, phone, video, etc.).
  - Send a reminder via email one week in advance, and then the day before (ideally in the morning)
- When audio recording the interview:
  - Use a primary recording device and a back-up. Bring extra batteries or a charger.
- Where will audio recordings be saved? Ensure this is in compliance with IRB approval.
  - Decide on uniform naming of data files, across participants/interviewers that lists the participant number (e.g., PA01), the interviewer (e.g., EGS), and the date (e.g., 5.02.2020), such as PA01.EGS.5.02.2020.
- How will interviews be transcribed?
- After transcription, interviewer reads transcript:
  - Ensure accuracy of content (reminder: sometimes transcription services do not understand professional acronyms (e.g., ASCA, RAMP, CACREP)
  - Blind the transcript, removing identifying information (e.g., names, schools, cities, etc.)
  - Highlight any words/phrases in question, that you'd like the participant to review
- Send the transcript to participant for member checking
  - See sample member checking email (below)
  - If participant does not respond within the timeframe, send another email reminder a few days before the due date, then a final email reinforcing that the participant is confirming the accuracy of the transcript.

Sample Member Checking Email:

Greetings _________,

Thank you again for our conversation <u>last month/week</u> regarding [insert interview topic]. I really appreciated your unique insight and the work you've done on behalf of our field: thank you. Attached is the transcript from our interview, which I attempted to mask (e.g., taking out identifying information, such as names and locations). I also have questions regarding a few phrases, which are highlighted.

Sometime in the next month, if you don't mind, please read through the transcript, and let me know (a) if you have any corrections, (b) if I need to further mask/blind content, or (c) if there is anything you'd like to expand on further. If I don't hear from you, I'll assume you do not have any corrections and expansions, and you agree with the content of the transcript. I also have highlighted words that I could not determine in the event you can fill that in.

Please let me know if you have any questions. Thank you again for your participation in this important study!

Sincerely,

[insert name]

- After member checking is complete, put the final transcript in the designated location, modifying the title of the document accordingly (e.g., PA01.EGS.3.15.2019. MemberChecked)

Appendix B

Goodman-Scott Interview Protocol (2019b): [Insert Title of Study]

(to be completed by researcher conducting each interview)

Interviewer's name:
Participant's pseudonym:
Participant's assigned ID:
Interview date:
Interview start and stop time:
Interview location/type (e g , phone, in-person, video web conferencing, etc.):
Interviewer completed field notes (to describe facts, context, logistics, etc.):
Interview completed reflexive journal (to describe reactions/biases/experiences):
Date of interview transcription:
Date(s) transcription sent to participant (initial and reminder):
Date participant confirmed member checking:
Follow-up questions needed for subsequent interview:

Interview Protocol

Note: Before starting the interview, briefly greet the participant and try to connect with them/build rapport. Thank them for their expertise and passion, and for volunteering to be a part of this important study.

Introduction

Thank you for agreeing to speak with me about [insert topic]. I imagine you are extremely busy, and I appreciate you taking the time to talk to me today.

Before we get started, I would like to confirm that you are comfortable with the informed consent document you signed, and to see if you have any questions [field participant questions and remind participant of key points, from informed consent].

The interview should last about [insert time] minutes and will be recorded for later transcription. If at any time you wish to stop the interview or to not answer a question, you are completely free to do so without penalty. I will take all necessary precautions to protect your anonymity, the anonymity of your school district, school, and students. After the interview is transcribed, I will blind any identifying information and email the transcribed interview back to you to see if you would like to change, clarify, or add anything.

Also, participants often use a pseudonym, such as a favorite name, that I can use during our interview. Is this something you'd like to use?

Before I hit the record button and we begin the interview, do you have any questions?

Qualitative Interview Questions

Note: Suggestions when interviewing: use your counseling skills, reflecting feeling and content to help clients expand, summarizing, probing, etc. If engaging in a semi-structured interview, start with planned questions, then ask follow-up probes based on the content/direction of the interview. Last, when asking and responding to questions, aim to remain somewhat neutral, rather than reinforcing/praising their responses.

Interview Questions

1. *Insert*

After Asking All Interview Questions:

Thank you again for helping us better understand [insert topic]. This interview will be transcribed over the next several weeks, and we will email it back to you, in case you would like to change, clarify, or add any information. Also, if we have any additional questions at a later time, would you be willing to have brief conversation?

Turn off recording device when the call ends.

Usually When I Finish the Interview, I Reserve 30 Minutes To Do the Following:

- Save both audio files (primary and backup), send the audio file for transcription
- Complete field notes
- Complete reflexive journal
- Complete any additional steps noted on this Interview Protocol sheet

Appendix C

Data Collection Log (Goodman-Scott, 2019b)

Participant Identifier	Name	Pseudonym	Met Inclusion Criteria	Consent Completed	Email Address	Phone Number	Availability for Interview	Interviewer	Interview Scheduled and Method	Status of Interview	Status of Member Checking
PA01. EGS.5.02.2020	R. W.	Archie	Yes [elaborate]	Yes: 4/15/2020	RW@gmail.com	111-111-1111	Monday and Tuesday, 9–12 pm	EGS will conduct interview	5/2 at 9 am PST; sent a Zoom link	Interview completed 5/2; interview transcribed 5/3; transcription checked for accuracy and blinded by 5/10	Transcript sent to participant 5/10; sent reminder 6/5; participant sent feedback 6/7. Member checking complete and file saved.
Insert other PAs here and below.											

9

Research Design

Action Research

Jennifer Betters-Bubon, Holly Kortemeier, and Chia Vang

Research Design: Action Research

Introduction

Each day, educators, including school counselors, balance a multitude of responsibilities—counseling students in crisis, handling scheduling changes, conducting transcript credit checks, meeting with teachers, and communicating with parents/caregivers. According to the American School Counselor Association (ASCA) National Model (2019), school counselors design and deliver comprehensive school counseling programs that impact student outcomes, providing direct and indirect services while working toward educational and systemic change. At the same time, they are charged with assessing their program and interventions to determine which aspects of their programs are working and measuring their impact. One common way educators assess their actions and impact is through action research. Action research is defined as a "research method for systematically and intentionally studying issues related to practice" (Manfra, 2019, p. 3). Emerging from the field of education, action research provides a framework through which educators can approach real-life and classroom-based problems. Thus, action research fits well within the field of school counseling and provides opportunities for school counselor educators (SCEs) to partner with school counselors. The **purpose of this chapter** is to provide you, the reader, with knowledge that will allow you to engage in action research. In other words, we provide a step-by-step guide for planning an action research study. To that end, we have organized this chapter to include:

1. a **description** of action research, including why it emerged as a research design and how it differs from other approaches (*the what and why*)

Jennifer Betters-Bubon, Holly Kortemeier, and Chia Vang, *Research Design* In: *School Counseling Research.*
Edited by: Brett Zyromski and Carey Dimmitt, Oxford University Press. © Oxford University Press 2023.
DOI: 10.1093/oso/9780197650134.003.0009

2. a detailed explanation of the **action research process**, including planning, observation, reflection, and sharing results (*the how*)
3. a **case study** delineating the process along with a **step-by-step action research guide**

We utilize examples from school counseling literature throughout to highlight studies that bring action research to life. We also provide scenarios from the field to help you move from theory to practice. Let's turn our attention to learning about *the what* behind action research.

What Is Action Research?

Before further defining action research, we ask you to consider the following scenario:

The above scenario provides a brief snapshot into questions school counselors ask on a continual basis, as well as central questions school counselors have about their programs. As a future researcher in the field, you may recognize potential areas for program assessment and evaluation. At the same time, you likely recognize how difficult it can be for individuals in the field to engage in this research. Throughout this chapter, we will encourage you to consider how to partner with school counselors and educators to engage in action research to answer questions, such as: **How are students different as a result of school counseling programs? How are educational interventions impacting outcomes for all students? How can questioning systems (e.g., staff policies and procedures) in the school create lasting equitable change?** We will return to Quinn later, but first, let's further define action research and examine the *what* behind it.

Action research is defined as systemic inquiry, often conducted by educators, to study schools, teaching, and learning (Mills, 2011) and includes a focus on transformative change (Rowell et al., 2015). Action research is often guided by questions about practice, similar to the questions Quinn asked in the scenario above and includes simultaneous action and reflection. Action research is process oriented rather than answer oriented and is personal, as it involves identifying the reasons for the action, acknowledging the researcher's values. Throughout, researchers gather and interpret data to determine if reasons and values are being fulfilled. Action research moves beyond professional practice "which emphasizes the action but does not always question the reasons and motives" (McNiff & Whitehead, 2009, p. 20). Take a look at the descriptors in the box below:

Pop-Out 9.1. Case Example: Quinn

Quinn is a white elementary school counselor in a school with a predominantly white student population with an all-white staff. Early Monday morning, Quinn (they/them/their) arrives at school. As they walk toward their office, a staff member stops by to share that a family with three students was evicted from their home over the weekend. Quinn thanks them for the information, enters their office, listens to three voicemails, quickly browses 20 unread emails, and reviews their planner for the week. Quinn begins to prioritize their work:

- *The family who was evicted from their home: What is the best way to reach them? How can we support the three children who may be arriving at school in 30 minutes?*
- *Voicemail from a teacher about a racial incident: Specifically, a student in her class called another student a derogatory name. While the principal handled the situation, they wish to talk with Quinn about how to support the students in the classroom best.*
- *Upcoming diversity lessons, part of the school's universal MTSS core curriculum and taught by social studies teachers the next week: Do the lessons feature culturally responsive examples/materials and focus on realistic life skills related to diversity?*
- *Meeting with the reading interventionist about a new literacy curriculum: How will Quinn advocate for the necessity of an equitable program that recognizes the views and voices of all people, including students of color and an emerging population of Latinx students whose first language is Spanish?*
- *The district's student services team meeting on piloting a universal screening tool for select grades: How will we work as a team to support students who are identified as currently experiencing high levels of mental and emotional stress? How will students' caregivers be informed of these findings?*

Pausing for a few moments, Quinn considers: Am I using my time in the best way possible? Am I positively influencing individual children, classrooms, caregivers, staff, our school, and community? Are there ways in which my program and interventions could be modified or changed to better impact the well-being of all students, staff, and families?

Pop-Out 9.2. Action Research Is

- *Systematic*: Action research is intentional and requires inquiry that moves beyond casual problem solving.
- *Cyclical:* Action research includes a series of action steps, such as questioning, observing, and reflecting.
- *Iterative:* Action research is a fluid process during which individuals can expect to acquire additional questions and move between questions, observations, and reflection.
- *Applied*: Action research can be used for "real-life" questions and educational problems (e.g., Is this small group having an impact on student behavior?).
- *Collaborative:* Participants are part of the action research process.

As you can see from the definition and description, action research moves beyond day-to-day problem-solving to include a systematic and ongoing inquiry. How does this look in practice? Perhaps a high school counseling team notices an ongoing pattern of disengagement among ninth-grade students as they transition from middle to high school. To conduct action research, they may identify a research question such as: what factors impact students' successful transition from eighth to ninth grade? They may partner with a local SCE to examine the research related to school engagement and design research questions. Together, the school counselor and SCE would gather additional data: Which students are most disengaged? How is disengagement communicated? Where does disengagement occur? They would create an action plan that details an intervention or action they wish to take and then they would act on that plan. Throughout, they would make systematic observations while gathering data, continuously referring back to the purpose of their research. After implementing the intervention, they would reflect upon the results and share their findings with partners. In short, they would move through action research like the cycle outlined below (Figure 9.1).

The action research process consists of planning, implementing, analyzing data, reflecting on results, and sharing these results (Manfra, 2019; Figure 9.1). Of note, this cycle may not be linear—instead, action research involves moving fluidly between steps. Let's look at an example from school counseling literature below:

While the steps in the research snapshot are described in list form, the school counselor in this scenario engaged in continuous reflection on her practice, modifying her actions (e.g., discontinuing a homework club location

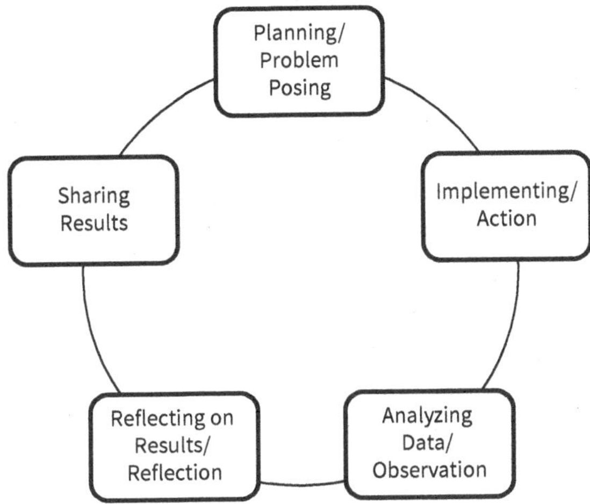

Figure 9.1. The Action Research Process
From Manfra (2019); Rowell et al. (2015).

that students did not attend, and adding additional options for caregiver voice). She collaborated with individuals well versed in research and intervention to enhance the actions she took within the partnership to impact student outcomes. Utilizing action research allowed the school counselor to impact systemic change for students and families by sharing the results with participants and partners and allowed the SCE to share best practices with individuals in the field.

Action Research Versus Quantitative Research

It is important to recognize how action research differs from other forms of research. Whereas traditional research is objective focused, finding answers and results, action research is process focused, seeking answers for relevant and sometimes practical questions in education and the community (Table 9.1). Action research is often considered to be a subset of qualitative research (see Chapter 8), which differs from traditional quantitative research.

Within action research, the researcher is in the middle of the problem and associated research question, which requires time, commitment, and collaboration with individuals in the social context. This differs from traditional quantitative research, which requires researchers to remain neutral and uninvolved. Action researchers "do not claim 'neutrality' but rather account for their position in the action and inquiry on answers versus questions and

Pop-Out 9.3. Research Snapshot

Betters-Bubon and Schultz (2018), an SCE and school counselor, used action research in implementing a school–family–community partnership to increase Latinx student achievement.

1. Planning: Jenny Schultz, school counselor, along with a team of educators from her school identified a clear achievement gap between Latinx students and white students. Recognizing that her perspective would shape her understanding, she talked with Latinx families in the community. In doing so, she asked family and community members for their ideas in supporting student success in school.

2. Implementing/Action: After doing home visits alongside the school principal, she learned that students and families would access a homework club in the community. She worked with community members to find different spaces, secured grant funding to pay teachers, and talked with students about the homework club. She collaborated with a local SCE to consider ways to assess the impact of the homework club. The SCE served as a sounding board throughout the process and helped create surveys for students, staff, and families.

3. Observing: She noted that approximately 45 students attended the homework club with an average of 34 students participating regularly. Data indicated that 80% of the second-through-fifth-grade students who lived in the neighborhood attended the homework club at least twice. Parents responded positively through feedback surveys distributed at the end of the school year.

4. Reflecting: She continued to modify the program as she implemented. Initially, she offered two separate locations for the homework club. Finding students only accessed the club directly in their apartment complex, she stopped using the other location. She also learned from caregivers about additional opportunities for increased engagement. Jenny continued to collaborate with individuals at the university—master's level students provided evidence-based academic interventions at the homework club, collecting data on student outcomes.

5. Implementing/Action (again): With additional ideas and feedback from staff, families, and individuals at the university, she started a caregiver group, Correr la Voz (Spread the Word), to bridge the home/school gap and build up the capacity of Latinx leaders within the caregiver community.

6. Sharing Results: Jenny shared her results with her school team as well as with the school board, advocating for the work to be fully integrated into the budget. She was successful, and the program continued to grow and develop in subsequent years. Along with the SCE, she wrote an article for publication outlining the leadership skills needed to develop a successful school–family–community partnership.

Table 9.1. Action Research Versus Quantitative Research

Action Research	Quantitative
Process-oriented: Seek to find explanations for specific educational/practice questions.	Answer-oriented: Seek to find explanations for existing phenomena.
Personal/Participatory	Removed
Context-dependent	Objective
Reflective	Numbers-driven
Practice-based	May be practice based
Engaging in action to create new knowledge	New knowledge

Pop-Out 9.4. Thought to Application

Take a step back and consider the complex issues happening with educational practice today. What is a pattern or ongoing issue that you notice with students, in classrooms, or within the school as a system? Write down the problem in as much detail as possible. Discuss the problem with a fellow student, researcher, or SCE that you know to conceptualize the problem further. Then consider: What are the advantages of using action research? What are disadvantages? What other voices might need to be included in the research?

---

the level of involvement on the part of the researcher" (Rowell et al., 2015, p. 255). In this way, researchers must continually be aware of how their perspectives and biases might shape the questions they ask as well as subsequent approaches and interventions.

Before we move into more specifics about how to do action research, let's briefly examine the history of action research, including how it emerged as a research design and how it is utilized in education and school counseling.

Why Did Action Research Emerge as a Form of Study?

Social psychologist Kurt Lewin coined the term *action research* in the 1930s in an effort to apply practical problem-solving strategies in post–World War II America (Mills, 2011). Since that time, action research has been embraced by researchers from diverse fields all over the world, including many areas of social science. Action research was quickly welcomed in the educational field due to its practicality, as it allowed the educator-researcher to derive findings that would lead to specific, individualized change in their educational environment rather than arrive at another researcher's conclusion, which would require a general application to the very distinct contexts other educators worked in (Ferrance, 2000).

Action research is particularly well suited for the school counseling field due to its focus on a **systems perspective**. As SCEs, we are familiar with bioecological theory (Bronfenbrenner, 1994), which posits that development takes place through complex proximal processes between individuals and their environments. Many of us can acknowledge the ways in which individuals are impacted by and have an impact on their micro-, meso-, exo-, and macro-systems. For example, we recognize that students' success or failure in school may be impacted by the extent to which families and teachers agree and communicate—an interaction that takes place within a student's mesosystem. Given the complex systems that are present in schools, school counseling scholars have proposed an ecological school counseling approach (McMahon & Mason, 2019; McMahon et al., 2014), which focuses on multiple layers to understand best how to facilitate student development. Thus, students are best understood within the framework of the multiple ecosystems of which they are a part (Figure 9.2).

At the center of the ecosystem are students, who bring experiences, personalities, learning styles, and trauma histories. Classrooms impact students by forces such as class climate, teaching style, and communication between individuals. The school itself impacts students and classrooms

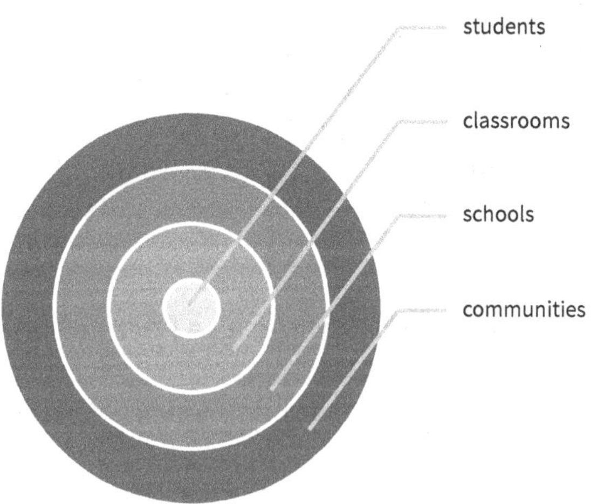

Figure 9.2. Nested Ecosystems Impacting Students
Adapted from Manfra (2019).

through the mission, vision, structure, curricular guidelines, and schedule. Finally, the community, which includes school funding and location (e.g., urban, rural, suburban) and access to community resources, influences all other systems (Manfra, 2019). Thus, action research can focus on each of these layers (Manfra, 2019) with study within the individual, school system, and community levels (McMahon et al., 2014).

To be sure, action research has been used within the field of school counseling for many years to assess problems, collect data, advocate, and collaborate with partners. Scholars in the field have made the call for collaborative action research, involving multiple partners, school counselors, counselor educators, and preservice school counselors to work toward school improvement and to demonstrate our impact (Mason & Uwah, 2007). Others argue that action research is the means to connect practice and additional practitioner-based research (Kaffenberger, 2012), to bridge the gap from graduate school to practice (Young et al., 2014), and to do so while being grounded in social justice (McAteer, 2021). As such, in the following section we detail the action research process, describing *how* SCEs and scholars can collaborate with school counselors to utilize this approach in schools.

Action Research Steps

As mentioned earlier in this chapter, action research includes systematic procedures that school counselor researchers use to engage in thoughtful and purposeful planning and reflection. Let's take a detailed look at each of the action research steps—**planning, action, observation, reflection, and results sharing**. To bring these steps to life, we will highlight Quinn, the school counselor from the scenario at the start of the chapter. In addition, at the end of each step, we highlight specific school counseling research literature. Finally, we created Appendix A, a step-by-step guide that consists of ideas and questions to consider as you move through the action research process yourself.

Step 1: Planning

Action research starts with **planning**, which requires time and energy. Given the level of detail within this section, we have divided it into substeps: problem identification, gathering information, choosing a research approach, and planning for data collection.

Problem Identification

The first step in action research requires that you determine the **essential problem to study**. Because action research is grounded in experience, this step requires you to be thoughtful of relevant and essential problems in the school and community. As an SCE initiating an action research project, it is imperative that the needs and preferences of the partner practitioners be prioritized while keeping the demands of effective research practices in mind. SCEs play an important role in highlighting aspects of social justice, including which voices are amplified as part of the research process and which voices are silenced.

With the plethora of problems in schools and communities, it is important to spend a significant amount of time **narrowing the focus**. To engage in problem identification, we suggest examining data and engaging in conversation related to the problem of interest. Different data sources can include:

- school or district outcome data (e.g., discipline, GPA, college and career readiness outcomes)
- school or district school counseling program data (e.g., gaps or disproportionality in programs/services)
- universal screening data
- formal or informal needs assessment or feedback (e.g., parent survey, student climate survey)
- qualitative interviews with school teams (e.g., student services teams, multi-tiered system of support (MTSS) teams, professional learning communities, etc.), teachers, caregivers, etc.

Pop-Out 9.5. Case Example: Quinn

In the introduction, Quinn recognizes a number of problems at the start of their day. Time was needed to tune into the most significant issue at hand. Quinn gathers information on the student information system about racial incidents and recognizes the overarching need for staff to become more culturally responsive, specifically with regard to race. After taking a moment to process the serious emotional and mental effects that racially charged conflicts could have on the school community, especially students, families, and staff of color, Quinn decides to partner with a previous professor from their counselor education program to further examine and gather additional information.

A common misconception is that action research is the same as problem-solving. Let's consider a school counselor who experiences ninth-grade disengagement during a goal-setting lesson. Upon leaving the classroom of students, she might consult with a colleague about how to change the lesson to increase engagement. Similarly, a school counselor might collaborate with the MTSS team to create action steps to decrease fighting on the playground. Both examples outline the excellent problem-solving skills that are critical parts of the school counselor role; however, **neither would be considered action research** given a lack of ongoing planning, observation, reflection, and results sharing. Further, neither school counselor constructed a research question or engaged in ongoing information gathering as we discuss below.

Gathering Information and Writing a Research Question

As an SCE, you provide critical expertise related to data gathering, analysis, and critical thinking about both the research process and the possible outcomes. As you narrow an area of focus, we recommend that you further define the problem by examining the research literature. For example, conduct a literature review, examine current trends in the field on professional email LISTSERVs, engage with social media groups, or examine presentations from recent conferences. Then, in collaboration with the school team, conduct a **gap analysis**, defining the difference between what is currently in place compared with the desired result (Manfra, 2019).

As part of gathering information, it is also important to **examine your own beliefs**. Similar to examining your philosophical assumptions when engaging in qualitative research, action research requires that individuals consider their worldview or epistemology, as it can influence the questions asked, as well as the chosen approach. This is a good reason to have collaborators across roles and from outside the school district, as each can provide useful, different

---

Pop-Out 9.6. Thought to Action

Consider a problem that is impacting student, staff, or family wellness within school communities. Reflect and answer: **What is the current reality?** Write down the reality in as much detail as possible. Then, reflect and answer: **What is the ideal reality?** Again, write down your response in as much detail as possible. What do you notice? Share the results with a colleague or peer to gain their perspective, insight, and ideas. Consider gaining ideas from individuals outside of the educational staff to include students, families, and community members.

Table 9.2. Theoretical Frameworks for Action Research

Framework	Key Assumptions
Postpositivism	Knowledge as external; use of data collection methods that predict or provide way to analyze
Interpretive/Constructivist	Understand how knowledge is constructed by individual or individuals; recognize multiple perspectives.
Critical theory/ Poststructuralism	Empowerment, change, identifying and resisting oppression
Critical race theory	Inclusion of race in definition of individual and group experiences; acknowledgement of racism
Feminist theory	Focus on women's diverse situations within societal and local contexts; collaborative creation of knowledge
Queer theory	Examination and deconstruction of categories

Note: Adapted from Manfra (2019).

perspectives. Common philosophical lenses used in educational research are described in Table 9.2. As you gather information, notice which theoretical approach aligns with how you are approaching the problem and consider how that might impact the actions you take.

Within action research, individuals take an active stance on the construction of knowledge and the above lenses help action researchers see the world from a new vantage point. Only with a clear sense of their worldview can you write a strong and concise research question. Chapter 4, "Creating Research Questions," in this book provides a plethora of information on how to write thoughtful research questions.

Choosing an Approach

Once you finalize a research question, you can move to choosing the action research approach that best answers the question. Action research approaches (Table 9.3) vary based on types of questions asked as well as the anticipated level of engagement with partners and/or participants. For example, when your research questions are about counseling programs or practices, the approach would fall toward an **educational or practical approach** whereas questions about systemic or societal change would be **critical** in nature.

Within each approach, the level of participation and involvement among participants can vary. Action research that includes significant participant voice is called **participatory action research (PAR)**. In PAR, researchers and participants work collaboratively to develop goals and methods, participate in the gathering and analysis of data, and implement the results in a way that promotes change in the lives of those involved (Reason, 1994; Kidd & Kral, 2005). You likely notice the alignment of participatory action research and the critical action research approach listed in Table 9.3.

Pop-Out 9.7. Case Example: Quinn

Let's consider how Quinn approached gathering information and writing a research question. Before fully diving into the depths of action research, Quinn considered their personal perspective and how that might influence further steps. Quinn is a white, nonbinary individual in their late 20s. They grew up in a small, predominantly white town and are now working in a predominantly white, rural community. While Quinn possessed foundational knowledge of equity and culturally responsive practice, they realized there is always room to improve and continue gaining knowledge.

Quinn then talked to the dean of students, collecting data on the five discipline reports in which white students have used racial slurs. Additionally, Quinn consulted with the student services team and administrators at the weekly meeting. The team wondered if school staff are adequately equipped to handle racial conflict among students, as it appeared many of the racial conflicts could have been handled more effectively. Finally, Quinn narrowed the goal to focus on the disturbing trend and reduction of racial slurs among students. Quinn consults with their SCE partner, gathering evidence-based activities and strategies that might be used to enhance staff cultural knowledge. The specific research question they ask is: *How will coordinated staff development about antiracism impact school staff knowledge and skills and acceptance among students?*

Table 9.3. Action Research Approaches

	Practical Action Research	Critical Action Research
Description	*Practical action research* is the study of a local problem or specific situation.	*Critical action research* is research that involves mutual involvement, change, and a process that promotes personal growth.
Focus	Counseling or educational practice	Social issues/systems that impact individual lives
Implementation	Individual or team approach	Shared power with participants
Role of researcher	Reflects on a practice or approach	Reflects on self, including knowledge, skills, and values while working with others
Sample studies	Jones et al. (2019)	Edirmanasinghe & Blaginin (2019)

Note: From Creswell (2012) Griffin (2019); Manfra (2019).

In recent years, **youth participatory action research (YPAR)** has emerged as a way to provide students with power and voice within the group process. In YPAR, youth, alongside the researcher, identify and investigate issues that are of direct interest and concern to them (Ozer, 2016). The adult researchers act as facilitators and collaborators, conscious of the power differential, examining power structures unspoken within the youth's choice of topic (Cook & Krueger-Henney, 2017). YPAR is particularly relevant within the school counseling field given the call to be social justice– and multicultural leaders and their role in supporting traditionally marginalized youth (e.g., Levy et al., 2018; Cook et al., 2019). The inherent inclusion of student voice within YPAR allows students to see themselves as both creating and taking in knowledge (Smith et al., 2014). There are additional ethical concerns when engaging in this research approach, including consent, confidentiality, anonymity, and remuneration (Cullen & Walsh, 2019); thus, should you wish to engage in this work, a thoughtful plan and consultation with institutional review boards (IRBs) is required from the onset. For additional information on PAR, readers are directed to Cox et al. (2021), Griffin (2019), Smith et al. (2014), and Kidd & Kral (2005).

Planning for Data Collection

The methods for data collection are similar to those of other research designs. The types of data collected will be dependent on the research question and lens through which you designed the study. For example, open-ended questions tend to lend themselves to qualitative data collection efforts while

---

Pop-Out 9.8. Case Example: Quinn

Quinn's professional and personal background have equipped them with knowledge about equity, empathy, and, most importantly for this project, race. Specifically, Quinn recently took part in an antiracist book group facilitated by BIPOC school counselors in a nearby school district. Through that work, they recognized the power of focused dialogue and discussion on race and racial identity.

As such, Quinn chooses to act first at the staff level to create systemic change. Providing professional development to staff on antiracism and racial conflict may have a direct impact on students. Quinn decides to take a practical action research approach to first assess staff knowledge and awareness of their own racial identities, cultural self-awareness, and implicit bias. In collaboration with the school administration and student services team as well as the SCE, they plan to implement monthly book discussions on the book *White Fragility* (DiAngelo, 2018).

more focused questions may lend themselves to quantitative data collection. Because both of these approaches are covered elsewhere in this book (Chapter 7, "Research Design: Quantitative Approaches," and Chapter 8, "Research Design: Qualitative Approaches"), we provide an overview of the types of data you can collect within an action research framework in Table 9.4.

The importance of taking time to outline what types of data you wish to collect, as well as how you will collect it, cannot be overlooked. As such, when you engage in the data collection planning process, ask yourself the following (Mertler, 2017):

- Why am I collecting these data?
- What exactly am I collecting?
- Where am I going to collect data from and for how long?
- When am I going to collect data and for how long?
- Who is going to collect data?
- How will the data be collected, displayed, and protected?

Prior to implementing action research you will need to gain approval from students, caregivers, administrators, and/or colleagues. In fact, as an SCE, you should move through the formal process of IRB approval because action research involves human subjects. Depending on the nature of the research, action research studies are often considered exempt, falling within education research or research conducted in established or commonly accepted educational settings. Despite being exempt, ethical scholars ensure that action research is conducted with permission and consent of those involved, following the ethical guidelines of the profession (ASCA, 2018). Please also refer to Chapter 3, "Ethical Research in Schools."

Finally, we have reached the end of the first step of action research, the **planning stage.** This stage can be lengthy given the substeps: **problem**

Table 9.4. Data Types

	Quantitative		Mixed Methods	Qualitative	
Type of data	Observations	Interviews	Document analysis; existing data	Checklist, rating scales, tests, pre/posttests	Surveys, questionnaires
Examples of data collected	Field notes, journals	Individual, Focus groups	Review of educational records; student work samples	Standardized tests	Existing school climate survey, web-based survey

Note: From Mertler (2017); Fraenkel & Wallen (2003).

Pop-Out 9.9. Case Example: Quinn

In collaboration with the school team and SCE, Quinn plans to uses discipline data focused on student racial incidents and pre/posttest data before and after each staff development meeting. They construct the questions around staff knowledge, skills, and attitudes related to racial identity and their feelings that emerge during the discussions. They create a short permission slip for the start of the pre/posttest, which they provide to teachers via Google Forms.

---

identification, gathering information and writing a research question, choosing an approach, and **planning for data collection**. We recommend that you move slowly through this process, particularly if this is your first action research study. Don't be afraid to reach out to others for help, as thoughtful planning during this stage will help facilitate a smooth process in the following steps. Before we move to **Step 2: Implementing/Action**, let's look at examples from school counseling research to highlight the planning process.

Step 2: Implementing/Action

After determining the desired approach, researchers can move into the action, or active, phase of action research. Action involves doing something, often in collaboration with participants, to learn or create change. Action can include, but is not limited to, implementing an intervention (e.g., classroom social-emotional [SEL] unit, small-group curriculum, staff development presentation, community activities), engaging in discourse (e.g., interview or group work with community members, students, caregivers), or analyzing existing data. Throughout the action stage, you collect data and engage in reflective practices related to the process. Please know that the action stage of action research can be a bit messy. Action research involves real-life situations, which are often unpredictable.

The level of required rigor within your study is dependent on the type and purpose of action research. A practical study focused on changing an individual counseling program may require less rigor than a study that is designed for professional presentation or publication. At the same time, we share with you Table 9.5, which includes strategies that may help you be more systematic and, thus, more rigorous in your implementation of action research.

Before turning to **Step 3: Analysis**, we highlight an action research study conducted by an SCE and school counselor, focusing on increasing acceptance and support for transgender and gender-nonconforming students.

Pop-Out 9.10.   Research Snapshot

Action Research Step	Description
Problem Identification Gathering Information and Constructing a Research Question	Jones et al. (2019) conducted action research in a middle school setting. Two teachers and the school counselor collaborated for their **identification of a problem**: the transition from sixth grade to higher grades was marked with increased academic pressure and expectation to which students responded with anxiety. Because they wanted to help students acknowledge their anxiety and learn to navigate it, they further **defined the problem** by **gathering information**: They reviewed student records and noted many students struggled with formal tests and talked with students to understand their anxiety. In that process they recognized that they could further define the problem into the following **research question**: *What factors influence student anxiety surrounding tests?*
Choosing an Approach and Data Collection	Bowers et al. (2020) used a practical action research framework to analyze an intervention with kindergarten students in response to school administrators' desire for additional preventative services. Upon learning about the students and the school, they developed two research questions based on a Ready to Learn (RTL) Intervention aimed at understanding intervention interactions among staff and changes in executive functioning skills of kindergarten students. Members of the research team, which included three SCEs and the school counselors at the school site, took a **mixed methods** approach. They utilized **quantitative data collection techniques.** They used parent ratings scales (Social Skills Improvement System [SSIS] Rating Scales [Gresham & Elliott, 2008] and Behavior Rating Inventory of Executive Function, Second Edition [BRIEF-2] [Gioia et al., 2015]). Teachers completed pre- and posttest surveys. Additionally, they collected **qualitative data** by taking observational field notes for all 25 RTL sessions, including quotes from students, counselors, and teachers, as well as behavioral observations of individual actions and classroom climate.

Pop-Out 9.11. Case Example: Quinn

Quinn develops a workshop and facilitates a discussion with all teachers at their grade-level team meetings the following week. They intentionally decide to provide this staff development in more personal settings given their belief that relationships are critical to change. In addition, Quinn wants staff to feel safe enough to share their experiences, biases, and questions in a smaller group setting. As such they take part in the discussion, sharing vulnerability and their own learning related to race and racial inequality rather than remaining in the presenter role. Quinn collects pre/post-data with each team.

Table 9.5. Strategies to Increase Rigor

Strategy	Practice	Questions to Consider
Experience	Previous experience with the cyclical nature of action research	*What training or experience qualifies you to engage in this work? How can you partner with others who have action research experience?*
Prolonged engagement and persistent observation	Active engagement; do not limit the time spent in observation.	*How will you ensure adequate, intentional engagement with the phenomena of study?*
Repetition of action research cycles	Engage in multiple iterations—use earlier cycles of the action research process to inform subsequent cycles.	*How will you move through multiple cycles of action–observation–action–observation?*
Diverse case analysis/ Triangulation of data	Include multiple voices in the study; utilize multiple data sources in analysis.	*Are you including multiple voices in the study? Are you examining multiple sources of data to understand the results best?*
Contextualization	Results should be reflective of participant experience and perspective.	*How will you maintain participant voice and language?*

Note: Adapted from Mertler (2017), Mills (2011), and Stringer (2007).

Step 3: Analyzing/Observation

As you act, you collect data and engage in analysis. Action research is cyclical; thus, analyzing and observation may take place **while** you are acting (e.g., intervening, etc.). In fact, you will move back and forth from Step 2 through Step 4—implementing, analyzing, reflecting—often simultaneously. Similar to previous steps, the process is grounded in the research questions as well as the types of data you collect. As you saw above, action research can focus on informal methods of gathering data (e.g., pre/posttests,

Pop-Out 9.12. Implementing/Action	
Action Research Step	**Description**
Implementing/Action	Mason et al. (2017) highlighted the importance of using collaborative action research models that include SCEs and school counselors. Within their article they highlight a case study in which an elementary school counselor led a staff development presentation on the needs of gender-nonconforming and transgender students. The school counselor then partnered with an SCE to design a formal qualitative research project to learn more about staff's attitudes and the meaning they took from their experiences with the presentation. Both projects informed the school counselor on staff knowledge and recommendations for future professional development.

conversations with parents/caregivers, staff, students, etc.) as well as formal methods (qualitative data, quantitative data, or both), and how you analyze data in this step can vary. The process may change as information is gathered, and the needs of the participants are prioritized over any initial plan for the study. Thus, if an intervention is discovered to be particularly effective, the plan might be to implement it with more students immediately, even if that disrupts the process of comparing groups. The well-being of the students is what matters most.

As social justice change agents, school counselors and SCEs must reflect on their own worldviews and biases while engaging in data analysis. First and foremost, it's critical to remember that individuals in the field of school counseling are called to be social justice leaders, with an expectation that they address issues of "power, privilege, and oppression impacting students" (Ratts & Greenleaf, 2017, p. 2). Further, school counselors must be willing to serve as leaders and advocates for students and families that are traditionally marginalized within schools and communities and address systemic inequities.

As such, within action research, school counselors and SCEs should analyze data from a social justice perspective—attempting to uncover aspects of the sociocultural contexts that may impact individuals within schools (Betters-Bubon et al., 2019). In a recent YPAR study, for example, Smith & Hope (2020) analyzed how Black boys make sense of race, identity, and oppression

---

Pop-Out 9.13. Case Example: Quinn

Two weeks after the staff presentations, Quinn analyzes results from the staff pre/posttest with the dean of students. They note an increase in staff knowledge about how to intervene in racial conflict and improved comfort level in talking about race in the classroom. Quinn analyzes teacher responses to the short-answer questions about their comfort level and feelings, looking for themes. They note the discomfort many teachers felt at the start of the presentation and how information helped empower them to stand by and for students. Quinn also gathers discipline data on a weekly basis and finds that younger white students (grades K–2) have continued to make racially insensitive remarks while there were small changes for older students, which provides additional questions within the research. Quinn again collaborates with their SCE colleague to ensure intentionality within the data analysis.

---

in a suburban high school. Through an after-school small group involving photovoice, researchers noted a change in narrative from deficit to achievement among youth in the study. Thus, analysis should involve examining the participant data as well as how the data are situated in the complex systems of families, schools, and communities. The following questions can help you in your analysis:

- What are the data telling me about the level of the problem?
- What voices were included in the data collected? What voices were absent?
- What additional data do I need to understand the problem fully? How can I further engage with community members and allies?
- How much power do I have within this problem? Who else has power?

Take a look at how Quinn integrated quantitative data, (pre/posttests, discipline data) along with qualitative data (short-answer responses from teachers on pre/posttests) in the case example below.

Above all, we want to emphasize intentionality in your analysis. Give yourself time and space to devote to examining the data you collect. To dive further into specific types of analysis, we direct you to Chapter 7, "Research Design: Quantitative Approaches," and Chapter 8, "Research Design: Qualitative Approaches." Note in the research snapshot below how the co-researchers and middle school students first conducted interviews with parents and then analyzed themes found within the interviews.

Pop-Out 9.14. Analyzing/Observation

Action Research Step	Description
Analyzing/ Observation	In an excellent example of YPAR, the eighth-grade school counselor recruited 30 Latina students to participate in a club, #CHICAS. Each letter in Cientificas, Heroes, Inteligentes, Confidente, Activistas, Son˜adores (CHICAS) stood for Spanish terms, chosen by the girls. The co-researchers, Edirmanasinghe and Blaginin (2019), brainstormed some of the concerns with the #CHICAS, determining that lack of parental outreach from the school was a factor in how engaged students were in school. The co-researchers and the girls interviewed parents, analyzed the results, and presented them to partners. The school community responded by sending information home to parents in English and Spanish, providing interpreters at school events, and recognizing Hispanic heritage activities. The students involved also became involved in leadership opportunities in and beyond the school.

Step 4: Reflecting on Results/Reflection

Reflection involves examining the results of data analysis, interpreting the results, and drawing initial conclusions. To facilitate this process, Manfra (2019) suggests asking a series of questions:

- What did I intend to do?
- What seemed to be the outcomes of my action?
- How do I know this occurred?
- What additional or new questions do I have?
- What are my next steps?

As in previous steps, this step is most effectively done in consultation and collaboration with others. Action steps may require you to move outside of your traditional role and collaborate with partners to ensure equitable educational opportunities for all students (Griffin & Steen, 2011). Let's examine how Quinn engages in reflection alongside of the SCE in the case example.

In example Pop-Out 9.15, Quinn reflects on their actions, seeing success with the intervention with staff. At the same time, because student behavior continued for a subset of students, Quinn modifies the initial research question to include parents/caregivers in the next iteration of the action research

Pop-Out 9.15. Case Example: Quinn

After reflection on the data, Quinn and SCE colleague reconsider how to use their time, knowledge, and skills to eradicate the student-to-student racial conflicts occurring in the school. They note success with staff, and older students, yet continuing conflict among younger students. Quinn gathers additional data through further conversation with students and staff, finding that students do not know the meaning of the phrases they are saying to their classmates. Rather, they are repeating phrases that their caregivers say at home. Quinn wonders if a similar approach to what was provided to teachers would work with caregivers. Quinn also wonders about the specific targets of the racial slurs and how to ensure they feel safe and accepted at school.

Quinn recognizes the power that parents/caregivers have and sought their involvement. They modify the research question: *Will universal teaching about antiracism to school staff, **students, and parents** reduce racial conflict among students? Further, will providing students of color with mentors help them feel safer in our school?*

Further, Quinn creates an initial action plan that included steps for follow up: quarterly parent nights, sponsored by the parent–teacher organization, to include:

- speakers of color
- a school climate survey designed to ascertain which students feel accepted and safe at school
- a mentorship program for students of color with high school and middle school students

Pop-Out 9.16. Reflecting

Action Research Step	Description
Reflecting	Goodman-Scott and Carlisle (2014) outlined an action research case study focused on how school counselors can use social stories within a comprehensive school counseling program. Within the case study, the school counselor took action by implementing social stories in weekly meetings with a student on the autism spectrum. They outlined the social story sequence and reflected how school counselors can integrate social stories in their intervention work. In addition, they highlighted decreases in the student's behavioral referrals and the need for one-on-one counseling.

cycle. Quinn continually looks for ways to improve outcomes for students who identified as Black, Indigenous, and People of Color (BIPOC) and works to engage multiple voices in the process. Let's examine one more example of the reflection stage from school counseling research.

Step 5: Sharing Results

Similar to other research approaches, action researchers are expected to share research findings as the final step in the cycle. Findings should be shared with participants, peers, school staff, and other partners, as well as with other professionals, including those whose knowledge and beliefs differ from yours (Rowell et al., 2015). In the case example below, Quinn shares the results with multiple partners. Note how Quinn sharing results does not end the action research process. Rather, through the sharing of results, Quinn hopes to move through the action research process again—this time on a systems level.

School counselors and SCEs have options when it comes to how they share results of action research. On a practical level, school counselors can utilize the flashlight method (Hatch, 2013). This method encourages school counselors to focus on or shine the light on important program activities and highlight specific results. Action research results can also be shared at state school counseling association conferences or through state counseling association accreditation or recognition (e.g., Wisconsin School Counselor Program Accountability Report; WSCPAR). Finally, school counselors and SCEs can share their research in formal publications. Many journals highlight

---

Pop-Out 9.17. Case Example: Quinn

Quinn prepares a presentation for administration and student services staff at the weekly team meeting. In addition to presenting the initial problem, the action steps, and data, Quinn presents next steps within their presentation. Specifically, they considered how these efforts could be improved and how to continue conversations on race and equity. After the presentation, Quinn makes a plan to share the work, process, and findings with district-level administrators to create system change at other school levels. In addition, Quinn plans to share the results with caregivers from diverse backgrounds to include their voice and analysis in subsequent steps. Quinn and the SCE partner discuss how to translate the research into a conference proposal for the state conference and formalize the next iteration of action research for publication.

Pop-Out 9.18. Sharing Results

Action Research Step	Description
Sharing Results	Levy et al. (2018) put youth as experts, alongside their school counselor, in a critical cycle of mixtape creation using hip-hop song construction. This mixtape was grounded in a topic of importance within the youth community (e.g., psychological health and well-being, social/environmental factors, academic issues, etc.). Students were encouraged to engage with their community and share their findings (e.g., final mixtape) publicly. Additionally, the findings were written up in manuscript form, published in the journal *Professional School Counseling*.

Pop-Out 9.19. Thought to Action

Consider the partners who might benefit from learning of your progress and the findings of your action research. Make a list. Who did you include? Did you ensure that diverse perspectives were included?

---

action research, including the *Action Research Journal* and *Educational Action Research*, as well as the flagship journal for the American School Counselor Association (ASCA), *Professional School Counseling*. See the resource list at the end of the chapter for additional journal ideas and action research readings.

In the research snapshot below, results sharing extended beyond specific school staff to include community members and later professional publication.

Given the plethora of ways in which to share results, we direct you to Chapter 14 for additional information on how to share results in a variety of formats and approaches.

Action Research in School Counseling

With a clear sense of the action research process, let's return to examples from school counseling literature, specifically examining how school counselors

Table 9.6. School Counseling Action Research—Selected Examples

Title	Level	Context Focus	Description
"Tackling Male Underachievement: Enhancing a Strengths-Based Learning Environment for Middle School Boys"	Middle School	Individual	Clark et al. (2008) examined small-group interventions with middle school boys to help address the gender achievement gap. The study led to overall positive results with a decrease in discipline referrals and increased positive attitudes toward school.
"Action Research Shows Group Counseling Effective with At-Risk Adolescent Girls"	High School	Individual	Zinck & Littrell (2000) conducted an action study on a school counselor–led 10-week small-group intervention with at-risk females that appeared effective in promoting positive behavioral change.
"School Counselor Action Research: A Case Example"	Elementary School	Classroom	Luck & Webb (2009) utilized an action research model to evaluate the effectiveness of the Student Success Skills intervention in fourth- and fifth-grade classrooms.
"Preventing and Responding to Bullying: An Elementary School's 4-Year Journey"	Elementary School	Schoolwide	McCormac (2014) evaluated a schoolwide anti-bullying curriculum called Steps to Respect (STR) over the span of 4 years. Results indicated a decrease in bullying and increased trust in reporting bullying behavior to adults.
"Utilizing a Practitioner-Led Action Research Study to Improve Urban Students' College Readiness and Pursuit"	High School	Schoolwide	Yavuz (2019) utilized a critical action research approach to examine a Comprehensive College Readiness Access and Success Program (CCRASP) for preparing students for postsecondary success.
"The Counselor as Advocate for English Language Learners: An Action Research Approach"	High School	School & Community	McCall-Perez (2000) studied a counselor partnership with a larger nonprofit to support students who were identified as English language learners (ELL) through counselor support, promotion of cross-cultural training, and student advisement within a multi-year project.

and SCEs can utilize action research across the educational ecosystems to ignite change. We provide a table of examples that include a focus at the individual, classroom, and school/systems levels (Table 9.6).

Action research is an approach that leads to social change. By examining the examples in Table 9.6, note how collaboration between school counselors/

educators and SCEs created best practices for students, schools, and the larger community (Rowell, 2006). SCEs, in concert with school counselors and educators in the community, can examine the impact of school–community partnerships or small-group counseling interventions. We hope you see how you can do the same! Again, we direct you to the step-by-step action guide (Appendix A) and to Table 9.7, which provides a summary of the steps Quinn followed in their action research. Start at the beginning and **plan**—*define a problem* within local school districts or within the larger school community. *Gather information* to define further the *research question* that will guide your work. *Choose an approach*, which is dependent upon the level of involvement of your participants and then *plan for data collection*. Expand your view of data, knowing it can include interviews, journal entries, pre/posttests, surveys, and so much more. With a plan in place, you can move to **implementation** and **action**. Engage in the work, knowing that you will **analyze/observe** and **reflect** throughout the process. Throughout these steps, collaborate with others, seeking input and assistance as needed. Finally, **share your results**, which can be a presentation or a published manuscript. We are excited for all that you may discover along the way.

Action Research: Chapter Conclusion

Action research is a useful approach to help SCEs assess best practices in schools and communities. In this chapter, we provided: (1) *The what and the why* of action research; (2) a detailed explanation of the **action research process**, including planning, observation, reflection, and sharing results (*the how*), highlighting a case example; (3) a **step-by-step action research guide**. As school counseling scholars, we know the importance of assessing student and program outcomes within a comprehensive school counseling program (ASCA, 2019), and now, more than ever, school counselors are challenged not only to demonstrate how their programs impact student outcomes but also to ensure that systems that exist allow *all* students to succeed. Action research is a useful research approach for SCEs to use within schools and can serve as a useful tool for you in your future and current role as you work to change systems for students, families, staff, and the community.

Table 9.7. Step-by-Step Action Research Guide: Case Example

Overview of Case Study

Quinn is a white elementary school counselor in a school with a predominantly white student population with an all-white staff. Early Monday morning, Quinn (they/them/their) arrives at school. As they walk toward their office, a staff member stops by to share that a family with three students was evicted from their home over the weekend. Quinn thanks them for the information, enters their office, listens to three voicemails, quickly browses 20 unread emails, and reviews their planner for the week. Quinn begins to prioritize their work:

- *The family who was evicted from their home: What is the best way to reach them? How can we support the three children who may be arriving at school in 30 minutes?*
- *Voicemail from a teacher about a racial incident. Specifically, a student in her class called another student a derogatory name. While the principal handled the situation, they wish to talk with Quinn about how to support the students in the classroom best.*
- *Upcoming diversity lessons, part of the school's universal PBIS (Positive Behavior Intervention and Supports) core curriculum and taught by social studies teachers the next week: Do the lessons feature culturally responsive examples/materials and focus on realistic life skills related to diversity?*
- *Meeting with the reading interventionist about a new literacy curriculum: How will Quinn advocate for the necessity of an equitable program that recognizes the views and voices of all people, including people of color?*
- *The district's student services team meeting on piloting a universal screening tool for select grades: How will we work as a team to support students who are identified as currently experiencing high levels of mental and emotional stress? How will students' caregivers be informed of these findings?*

Pausing for a few moments, Quinn considers: Am I using my time in the best way possible? Am I positively influencing individual children, classrooms, caregivers, staff, our school, and community? Are there ways in which my program and interventions could be modified or changed to impact the well-being of students, staff, and families better?

Planning

Problem identification	Examine data. Talk with partners (school staff, parents, students, community members).	After reflection on the many problems that emerged that Monday, Quinn chose to focus on the number of recent student conflicts that were racist in nature. Quinn gathers information on the student information system: • Six incidents in the last month included: name-calling, physical altercation, deliberately isolating others or leaving them out of play, based on race. • Staff responses by the teacher assistants and teachers' system included problem solving between students and calling parents; however, there was not a focus on the race of individuals. All were treated as isolated incidents, not part of a bigger problem. Quinn recognizes there have been many other, similar instances that have occurred that semester. After taking a moment to process the serious emotional and mental effects that racially charged incidents could have on the school community, especially students, families, and staff of color, they decide to partner with an SCE from their counselor education program to examine and gather additional information.

(continued)

Table 9.7. Continued

Gathering information	Gather more information. Gap Analysis: • What is the current reality? (Examine additional data, talk with partners, engage in needs assessment.) • What is the ideal reality? (Read literature, reflect on epistemology, talk with partners.) Pose and refine the research question.	Quinn talks to the dean of students, who reports white students have used racial slurs six times during the fall semester. Quinn collects grades and students who were targeted. They more fully examine the response to the incidents by school staff. Quinn consults with the student services team and administrators at the weekly meeting. The team wonders if school staff are adequately equipped to handle racial conflict among students, as it appeared many of the racial incidents could have been handled more effectively. Quinn reflects on the context of the school and community. Quinn is a white school counselor in a school with a predominantly white student population with an all-white staff. The school is located in a rural area, approximately 30 minutes from the closest major, diverse city. Quinn reflects on their approach as a school counselor, recognizing that equity is a key value of importance, and conducts a gap analysis, noting the ideal school environment for all students would be inclusive and safe in nature. Finally, Quinn narrowed the goal to focus on the disturbing trend and reduction of racial conflict among students. Quinn consults with their SCE partner, gathering evidence-based activities and strategies that might be used to enhance staff cultural knowledge. The specific research question they ask is: *How will coordinated staff development about antiracism impact school staff knowledge and skills and acceptance among students?*
Choosing a research approach	Decide on level of impact. • Practical vs. Participatory Decide on level of participation among those impacted. • Define the level of involvement of participants in the design, and analysis.	Quinn's professional and personal background has equipped them with knowledge about equity, empathy, and, most importantly for this project, race. Specifically, Quinn recently took part in an antiracist book group facilitated by BIPOC school counselors in a nearby school district. Through that work, they recognized the power of focused dialogue and discussion on race and racial identity. As such, Quinn chooses to act first at the staff level to create systemic change. Providing professional development to staff on antiracism may have a direct impact on students. Quinn decides to take a practical action research approach first to assess staff knowledge and awareness of their own racial identities, cultural self-awareness, and implicit bias. In collaboration with the school administration and student services team as well as the SCE, they plan to implement monthly book discussions on the book *White Fragility* (DiAngelo, 2018).

| *Planning for data collection* | Construct a **data collection plan**, including the specific type of **qualitative** or **quantitative** methods. Answer the following questions:
• Why am I collecting these data?
• What exactly am I collecting?
• Where am I going to collect data and for how long?
• When am I going to collect data and for how long?
• Who is going to collect data?
• How will the data be collected, displayed, and protected? | In collaboration with the school team and SCE, Quinn uses discipline data focused on student racial incidents and pre/posttest data before and after each staff development meeting. They construct the questions around staff knowledge, skills, and attitudes related to racial identity and their feelings that emerge during the discussions. They create a short permission slip for the start of the pre/posttest that they provide to teachers via Google Forms. |

Action

| | Take action (e.g., intervention, small group, focus group, survey, event, etc.).

Collect data as action is taken. | Quinn develops a workshop and facilitates a discussion with all teachers at their grade-level team meetings the following week. They intentionally decide to provide this staff development in more personal settings given their belief that relationships are critical to change. In addition, Quinn wants staff to feel safe enough to share their experiences, biases, and questions in a smaller group setting. As such they take part in the discussion, sharing vulnerability and their own learning related to antiracism rather than remaining in the presenter role. Quinn collects pre/post-data with each team. |

(continued)

Table 9.7. Continued

Observation

Analyze data. • Qualitative data analysis may include observations, interviews. • Quantitative data analysis may include checklists, rating scales, pre/posttest, surveys, questionnaires. Questions to ask: • What are the data telling me about the level of the problem? • What voices were included in the data collected? What voices were absent? • What additional data do I need to fully understand the problem? • How much power do I have within this problem? Who else has power?	Two weeks after the staff presentations, Quinn analyzes results from the staff pre/posttest with the dean of students. They note an increase in staff knowledge about how to intervene in racial conflict and improved comfort level in talking about race in the classroom. Quinn analyzes teacher responses to the short-answer questions about their comfort level and feelings, looking for themes. They note the discomfort many teachers felt at the start of the presentation and how information helped empower them to stand by and for students. Quinn also gathers discipline data on a weekly basis and finds that younger white students (grades K–2) have continued to make racially insensitive remarks while there were small changes for older students, which provides additional questions within the research. Quinn again collaborates with their SCE colleague to ensure intentionality within the data analysis.

Reflection	
Reflect on key takeaways: • What did I intend to do? • What seemed to be the outcomes of my action? • How do I know this occurred? • What additional or new questions do I have? • How can I further engage with community members and allies? • What are my next steps? Create an action plan outlining next steps. Note: Action, observation, and data analysis do not occur as a discrete step; rather, as you observe through the action stage, you will engage in continual reflection, allowing for modification and changes in response.	After reflecting on the data, Quinn and their SCE colleague reconsider how to use their time, knowledge, and skills to eradicate the student-to-student racial conflicts occurring in the school. Through further conversation with students and staff, Quinn realizes students do not know the meaning of the phrases they are saying to their classmates. Rather, they are repeating phrases that their caregivers say at home. Quinn wonders if a similar approach to what was provided to teachers would work with caregivers. Quinn also wonders about the specific targets of the racial slurs and wishes to ensure they feel safe and accepted at school. Quinn recognizes the power that caregivers have and seeks their involvement. The research question is modified to *Will universal teaching about race and race conflict to school staff,* ***students, and parents reduce racial conflict among students?*** Further, *will providing students of color with mentors help them feel safer in our school?* Further, Quinn creates an initial action plan that includes steps for follow-up: quarterly parent nights, sponsored by the parent teacher organization, to include speakers of color, a school climate survey designed to ascertain which students feel accepted and safe at school, as well as a possible mentorship program for students of color with high school and middle school students.

(continued)

Table 9.7. Continued

Results Sharing

Delineate the ways to share results: local presentation, newsletter, academic journal. Translate the results into a suitable format: • PowerPoint • Formal report • Oral presentation • Email/Letter **Share results and celebrate the work** (before starting another iteration of action research!).	Quinn prepares a presentation for administration and student services staff at the weekly team meeting. In addition to presenting the initial problem, the action steps and data, Quinn presents next steps within their presentation. Specifically, they considered how these efforts could be improved and how to continue conversations on race and equity. After the presentation, Quinn makes a plan to share the work, process, and findings with district-level administrators to create system change at other school levels. In addition, Quinn plans to share the results with caregivers from diverse backgrounds to include their voices and analyses in subsequent steps. Quinn and the SCE partner discuss how to translate the research into a conference proposal for the state conference and formalize the next iteration of action research for publication.

Resources

Books

Efron, Sara Efrat, and Ruth Ravid. (2019). *Action research in education: A practical guide.* Guilford.
Manfra, M. (2019). *Action research for classrooms, schools, and communities.* Sage.
Mertler, C. A. (2017). *Action research: Improving schools and empowering educators.* Sage.
Mills, G. E. (2011). *Action research: A guide for the teacher researcher* (4th ed.). Pearson.

Journals

Action Research Journal: https://journals.sagepub.com/home/arj
Action Learning: Research and Practice: http://www.tandf.co.uk/journals/actionlearning
Canadian Journal of Action Research: http://cjar.nipissingu.ca/index.php/cjar
Educational Action Research: http://www.tandf.co.uk/journals/reac
Inquiry in Education: https://digitalcommons.nl.edu/ie/

Websites

http://www.aral.com.au/resources/index.html
https://pd.madison.k12.wi.us/node/341

References

American School Counselor Association. (2018). ASCA *ethical standards for school counselor education.* https://www.schoolcounselor.org/getmedia/44f30280-ffe8-4b41-9ad8-f1590 9c3d164/EthicalStandards.pdf
American School Counselor Association. (2019). *ASCA National Model: A framework for school counseling programs* (4th ed.).
Betters-Bubon, J., Kortemeier, H., & Durkin-Smith, S. (2019). Culturally responsive MTSS: Advocating for equity for every student. In E. Goodman-Scott, J. Betters-Bubon, & E. Donohue (Eds.), *The school counselor's guide to multi-tiered systems of support* (pp. 298–329). Routledge.
Betters-Bubon, J., & Schultz, J. W. (2018). School counselors as social justice leaders: An innovative school–family–community partnership with Latino students and families. *Professional School Counseling, 21*(1b), 1–11. https://doi.org/10.1177/2156759X18773601
Bowers, H., Lemberger-Truelove, M. E., & Whitford, D. K. (2020). Kindergartners are ready to learn: Applying Student-Within-Environment Theory to a school counseling intervention. *The Journal of Humanistic Counseling, 59*(1), 3–19. https://doi.org/10.1002/johc.12126
Bronfenbrenner, U. (1994). Ecological models of human development. In T. Husen & T. Neville Postlethwaite (Eds.), *International Encyclopedia of Education* (Vol. 3, 2nd ed.). Elsevier. (Reprinted in *Readings on the development of children*, 2nd ed., pp. 37–43, by M. Gauvain & M. Cole, Eds., 1993, Freeman.)
Clark, M. A., Flower, K., Walton, J., & Oakley, E. (2008). Tackling male underachievement: Enhancing a strengths-based learning environment for middle school boys. *Professional School Counseling, 12*(2), 127–132. https://doi.org/10.1177/2156759X080 1200203

Cook, A. L., & Krueger-Henney, P. (2017). Group work that examines systems of power with young people: Youth participatory action research. *The Journal for Specialists in Group Work, 42*(2), 176–193. https://doi.org/10.1080/01933922.2017.1282570

Cook, A. L., Ruiz, B., & Karter, J. (2019). "Liberation Is a Praxis": Promoting college and career access through Youth Participatory Action Research. *School Community Journal, 29*(2), 203–224. http://www.schoolcommunitynetwork.org/SCJ.aspx

Cox, R., Heykoop, C., Fletcher, S., Hill, T., Scannell, L., Wright, L., Alexander, K., Deans, N., & Plush, T. (2021). Creative action research. *Educational Action Research, 29*(4), 569–587. https://doi.org/10.1080/09650792.2021.1925569

Creswell, J. (2012). *Educational research: Planning, conducting, and evaluating quantitative and qualitative research.* Pearson.

Cullen, O., & Walsh, C. A. (2019). A narrative review of ethical issues in Participatory Research with young people. *YOUNG, 28*(4), 363–386. https://doi.org/10.1177/1103308819886470

DiAngelo, R. (2018). *White fragility.* Beacon Press.

Edirmanasinghe, N., & Blaginin, K. (2019). Demystifying the research process: A career intervention with Latinas. *Professional School Counseling, 22*(1b), 1–6. https://doi.org/10.1177/2156759X19834433

Ferrance, E. (2000). Themes in education: Action research. *Brown University: Educational Alliance, 34*(1), 1–33.

Fraenkel, J. R., & Wallen, N. E. (Eds.). (2003). *How to design and evaluate research in education.* McGraw-Hill.

Gioia, G. A., Isquith, P. K., Guy, S. C., & Kenworthy, L. (2015). *BRIEF-2: Behavior rating inventory of executive function.* Psychological Assessment Resources.

Goodman-Scott, E., & Carlisle, R. (2014). School counselors' roles in creating and implementing social stories to serve students with Autism Spectrum Disorder. *Professional School Counseling, 18*(1), 158–168. https://doi.org/10.1177/2156759X0001800108

Gresham, F. M., & Elliott, S. N. (2008). *Social skills improvement system: Rating scales manual.* NCS Pearson.

Griffin, D. (2019). The uses of qualitative research methods in school counseling. In G. W. Noblit (Ed.), *Oxford Research Encyclopedia of Education* [online publication]. Oxford University Press. https://doi.org/10.1093/acrefore/9780190264093.013.548

Griffin, D., & Steen, S. (2011). A social justice approach to school counseling. *Journal for Social Action in Counseling & Psychology, 3*(1), 74–85. https://openjournals.bsu.edu/jsacp/article/view/337/319

Hatch, T. (2013). *The use of data in school counseling: Hatching results for students, programs, and the profession.* Corwin Press.

Jones, T., Riggs, A., & Kuo, N. (2019). Helping middle school students acknowledge and navigate anxiety: An action research. *Current Issues in Middle Level Education, 24*(2), Article 2. https://doi.org/10.20429/cimle.2019.240202

Kaffenberger, C. J. (2012). A call for school counseling practitioner research. *Professional School Counseling, 16*, 59–62. https://doi.org/10.1177/2156759X1201600107

Kidd, S. A., & Kral, M. J. (2005). Practicing participatory action research. *Journal of Counseling Psychology, 52*(2), 187–195. https://doi.org/10.1037/0022-0167.52.2.187

Levy, I. P., Cook, A. L., & Emdin, C. (2018). Remixing the school counselor's tool kit: Hip-hop spoken word therapy and YPAR. *Professional School Counseling, 22*(1), 1–11. https://doi.org/10.1177/2156759X18800285

Luck, L., & Webb, L. (2009). School counselor action Research: A case example. *Professional School Counseling, 12*(6), 408–441. https://doi.org/10.1177/2156759X0901200609

Manfra, M. (2019). *Action research for classrooms, schools, and communities.* SAGE Publications.

Mason, E. C. M., & Uwah, C. J. (2007). An eight-step action research model for school counselors. *Georgia School Counselors Association Journal, 14*, 1–5.

Mason, E. C. M., Springer, S. I., & Pugliese, A. (2017). Staff development as a school climate intervention to support transgender and gender nonconforming students: An integrated research partnership model for school counselors and counselor educators. *Journal of LGBT issues in counseling, 11*(4), 301–318. https://doi.org/10.1080/15538605.2017.1380552

McAteer, M. (2021). Critical issues in socially just action research. *Educational Action Research, 29*(4), 505–509.

McCall-Perez, Z. (2000). The counselor as advocate for English Language Learners: An action research approach. *Professional School Counseling, 4*(1), 13–22.

McCormac, M. E. (2014). Preventing and Responding to Bullying: An Elementary School's 4-Year Journey. *Professional School Counseling, 18*(1), 1–14. https://doi.org/10.1177/2156759X0001800112

McMahon, H. G., & Mason, E. C. M. (2019). Ecological school counseling. In C. Dollarhide & M. Truelove (Eds.), *Theories of school counseling for the 21st century* (pp. 241–265). Oxford University Press.

McMahon, H. G., Mason, E. C. M., Daluga-Guenther, N., & Ruiz, A. (2014). An ecological model of professional school counseling. *Journal of Counseling & Development, 92,* 459–471. https://doi.org/10.1002/j.1556-6676.2014.00172.x

McNiff, J., & Whitehead, J. (2009). *You and your action research project* (3rd ed.). Routledge.

Mertler, C. A. (2017). *Action research: Improving schools and empowering educators.* Sage Publishing.

Mills, G. E. (2011). *Action research: A guide for the teacher researcher* (4th ed.). Pearson.

Ozer, E. J. (2016). Youth-led participatory action research: Developmental and equity perspectives. In J. Benson, *Advances in child development and behavior* (vol. 50, pp. 189–207). Elsevier. https://doi.org/10.1016/bs.acdb.2015.11.006

Ratts, M. J., & Greenleaf, A. T. (2017). Multicultural and social justice counseling competencies: A leadership framework for professional school counselors. *Professional School Counseling, 21*(1b), 1–9. https://doi.org/10.1177/2156759X18773582

Reason, P. E. (1994). *Participation in human inquiry.* Sage.

Rowell, L. (2006). Action research and school counseling: Closing the gap between research and practice. *Professional School Counseling, 9*(4), 376–384. https://doi.org/10.1177/2156759X18773582

Rowell, L. L., Polush, E. Y., Riel, M., & Bruewer, A. (2015). Action researchers' perspectives about the distinguishing characteristics of action research: A Delphi and learning circles mixed-methods study. *Educational Action Research, 23*(2), 243–270. https://doi.org/10.1080/09650792.2014.990987

Smith, C. D., & Hope, E. C. (2020). "We just want to break the stereotype": Tensions in Black boys' critical social analysis of their suburban school experiences. *Journal of Educational Psychology, 112*(3), 551–566. https://doi.org/10.1080/10888691.2019.1630277

Smith, L., Beck, K., Bernstein, E., & Dashtguard, P. (2014). Youth participatory action research and school counseling practice: A school-wide framework for student well-being. *Journal of School Counseling, 12,* 1–31. http://jsc.montana.edu/articles/v12n21.pdf

Stringer, E. (2007). *Action research* (3rd ed.). Sage.

Yavuz, O. (2019). Utilizing A Practitioner-Led Action Research Study to Improve Urban Students' College Readiness and Pursuit. *Necatibey Faculty of Education Electronic Journal of Science & Mathematics Education, 13*(1), 1–30. https://doi.org/10.17522/balikesirnef.511509

Young, A., Gonzales, I., Owen, L., & Heltzer, J. V. (2014). The journey from counselor-in-training to practitioner researcher. *Professional School Counseling, 18*(1), 217–226. https://doi.org/10.1177/2156759X0001800120

Zinck, K., & Littrell, J. M. (2000). Action research shows group counseling effective with at-risk adolescent girls. *Professional School Counseling, 4,* 50–59. https://www.jstor.org/stable/i40102870

Appendix A

Step-by-Step Action Research Guide

Step 1: Planning	
Problem identification	Examine data. **Talk with partners** (school staff, parents, students, community members).
Gathering information and writing a research question	Gather more information. Gap Analysis: • What is the current reality? (Examine data, talk with partners, engage in needs assessment) • What is the ideal reality? (Read literature, reflect on epistemology, talk with partners) **Pose and refine the research question.**
Choosing a research approach	Decide on level of impact: • Practical vs. Participatory Decide on level of participation among those impacted: • Define the level of involvement of participants in the design and analysis
Planning for data collection	Construct a **data collection plan,** including the specific type of **qualitative** or **quantitative** methods. Answer the following questions: • Why am I collecting this data? • What exactly am I collecting? • Where and when am I going to collect data and for how long? • Who is going to collect data? • How will the data be collected, displayed, and protected?

Step 2: Action	
	Take action (e.g., intervention, small group, focus group, survey, event, etc.). Collect data as action is taken.

Step 3: Observation	
	Analyze data: • Qualitative data analysis may include observations, interviews. • Quantitative data analysis may include checklists, rating scales, pre/posttest, surveys, questionnaires. Questions to ask: • What are the data telling me about the level of the problem? • What voices were included in the data collected? What voices were absent? • What additional data do I need to understand the problem fully? • How much power do I have within this problem? Who else has power?

Step 4: Reflection	

Reflect on key takeaways:
- What did I intend to do?
- What seemed to be the outcomes of my action?
- How do I know this occurred?
- What additional or new questions do I have?
- How can I further engage with community members and allies?
- What are my next steps? Create an action plan outlining next steps.

***Note**: Action, observation, and data analysis do not occur as a discrete step; rather, as you observe through the action stage, you will engage in continual reflection—allowing for modification and changes in response.

Step 5: Results Sharing

Decide how to share results: presentation, community meeting, newsletter, academic journal

Translate the results into a suitable format:
- PowerPoint
- Formal report
- Oral presentation
- Email/Letter

Share results and celebrate the work (before starting another iteration of action research!).

10

Single-Case Research Design

A Practical Option in School Counseling Research

Dee C. Ray

Single-Case Research Design: A Practical Option in School Counseling Research

Traditional research design is based on the comparison or aggregation of group data, that is, comparing means of groups of participants in quantitative design or developing consensus of themes in qualitative design. Focus on the individual person is rare in research yet exists as the cornerstone of concern for most counselors: "Does the counseling intervention in which I am engaging make a difference for this child/adolescent/student?" Single-case research design (SCRD) is one method that addresses individual or single-group-level change, giving voice to both the quantitative and qualitative aspects of growth anticipated in the practice of counseling. SCRD is a research design methodology that allows for the tracking of change over time for a single student, or single cohort of students, in order to determine effectiveness of intervention. Such designs concentrate on causal inference by means of pairing change with intervention in the context of time (Kazdin, 2011; Riley-Tillman et al., 2020; Vannest et al., 2013). Hence, SCRD is particularly positioned as a useful tool for school counselor scholars in their quest to provide interventions that make a difference to individuals and groups of students.

SCRDs are beneficial to the school counselor scholar primarily as a way to demonstrate the effectiveness of intervention. In addition to the benefit of attributing intervention to outcome in SCRDs, there are several other advantages to the SCRD in the school setting. SCRD offers a quantitative method of tracking change without the requirement of large groups of participants or the need to randomize participants into lesser interventions or no-intervention groups. In quantitative designs, the principal method of determining effectiveness of intervention is randomized controlled trials

Dee C. Ray, *Single-Case Research Design* In: *School Counseling Research.* Edited by: Brett Zyromski and Carey Dimmitt, Oxford University Press. © Oxford University Press 2023. DOI: 10.1093/oso/9780197650134.003.0010

(RCTs). These trials necessitate random assignment of large groups of participants to multiple conditions, which may be waitlist or placebo groups, wherein students will not receive intervention. Alternatively, SCRDs are efficient, avoiding the use of excessive resources or delaying interventions for long periods of time. Another benefit of SCRD in the school setting is the flexibility of design, a feature not characteristic of typical quantitative designs (Riley-Tillman et al., 2020). The individual nature of SCRD allows the school counseling researcher to start, stop, or modify intervention according to the specific needs of the student. The initiation, discontinuance, or modification is built into the design itself through the application of intervention phases. This feature allows the school counseling researcher to meet the student at the individual level yet still allow for an experimental application of research. Finally, a substantive benefit of SCRD is that the focus on individual process allows for the recognition of marginalized children within the school system and the environmental factors or systemic barriers that may influence their social-emotional wellness and behaviors.

The Case for Single Case

My interest in SCRD emerged as a result of my research in counseling intervention, specifically play therapy. In exploring the most credible research designs to infer causality, I discovered two methods. The first was the RCT, which involved substantial resources and funding but is considered the most reliable form of research to match outcome with intervention. I vigorously pursued RCT research, which resulted in multiple studies demonstrating the effects of play therapy, with almost all of my RCTs conducted in school settings. The second method that emerged as credible in establishing causality was SCRD. Over the last 15 years, I have worked on over a dozen published SCRDs, using varying designs within the family of SCRDs, mostly conducted in school settings (e.g., Schottelkorb & Ray, 2009; Swan & Ray, 2014; Ware Balch & Ray, 2015).

SCRD provides a road to causality when resources are limited, yet I prefer SCRD for other, more clinical reasons, especially when compared with RCTs. In SCRD, the individual student participant is of the highest concern. As a counselor, I want to know if the intervention I am using is making a difference for the child I am serving. SCRD gives me that opportunity. And unlike most quantitative designs, SCRD allows for flexibility in the provision of intervention. If the intervention appears to have positive results but the child needs more sessions for optimal results, as an SCRD researcher, I can extend the intervention phase to allow for more sessions. If the child appears to be deteriorating, I can discontinue one phase and move to another phase of intervention. I know what outcomes are being affected by the intervention on a daily, weekly, or session basis. In my perspective, this is an optimal way to practice counseling, as single-case design allows for particular attention to client care (Kazdin, 2011). SCRD provides a means for individual counselors to track progress of individual or single units of students.

What Is SCRD?

The first challenge in embracing SCRD is to clarify what it is not. SCRD is not a case study. Counseling literature is replete with case studies of clients wherein counselors engage in descriptive exploration, sometimes with accompanying bits of data, of counseling relationships. Case studies can also be presented as rich designs in the qualitative framework for understanding counseling (Creswell & Poth, 2018) in which counseling researchers present thematic qualities of a counseling relationship. Case studies help counselors understand the intricacies of counselor, client, and relationship dynamics through thick description and provide deep consideration of how counseling and change may take place. However, case studies do not allow for causal inference from a research perspective (Tate & Perdices, 2019). When a counselor describes change in working with a student, that description is influenced by multiple subjective factors, such as the counselor's perspective and experience, the relationship with the student, or the student's contextual factors. The subjectivity involved in case studies precludes conclusions of causality. This is the main difference between an SCRD and a case study. The purpose of this chapter is to present the mechanics of SCRD in order to provide the reader with a method to determine causality. If the reader is interested in presentation or analysis of case studies, I recommend exploration of research methods specific to case studies (see Creswell & Poth, 2018; Hayes & Singh, 2012).

If SCRD is not a case study, the next logical step is to define the characteristics of SCRD that separate the design from others. As implied in the title, SCRDs are designs that track change of individual participants. Less clear is that SCRDs can also be used to track change of single-cohort groups of students, such as a group of 20 seventh graders who are participating in a particular counseling curriculum. Additionally, SCRDs rarely involve only one participant. Typically, researchers involve multiple participants, usually a minimum of three, when engaging in SCRD.

Understanding SCRD requires definitions of multiple terms specific to the design. Perhaps the acquisition of SCRD language is one obstacle to adopting the design due to the need for counseling researchers to engage in new terminology specific to design application. The following are a few terms to get us started.

SCRD: SCRD is a broad term that encompasses the use of continuous assessment of target behaviors for individuals or single units of participants in order to infer that participant change is a result of intervention. SCRDs are also referred to as single-subject designs, N-of-1 trials, and single-case experimental designs (SCEDs).

SCED: SCED is a specific implementation of SCRD in which particular criteria such as number of data points, standardization of assessment, integrity of intervention protocol, stability of phases, and visual analysis are applied to ensure credibility of design and outcome.

Phase: A phase is a discrete period of time within SCRD in which intervention or no intervention occurs but in which data are collected.

Baseline: Baseline is a phase within SCRD in which no intervention occurs. Baseline is commonly referred to as A in SCRD.

Intervention: Intervention is a phase within SCRD in which a well-defined intervention protocol is conducted with a participant (or single unit of participants). A single intervention may be noted as B phase. Different and subsequent interventions are noted with succeeding letters, such as C, D, etc. For example, in A phase, a student receives no intervention. Following A phase, the school counselor may use five sessions of motivational interviewing with the student referred to as B. Following B, the school counselor begins a new phase using teacher consultation regarding the student who would be referred to as C. The counselor then ends intervention but continues to collect data in a new baseline phase, A, resulting in an SCRD of A-B-C-A. In SCRD, the intervention is the independent variable.

Target Behavior/State: The target behavior is the behavior or state of being that is of particular interest to the school counselor. In other words, progress regarding the target behavior is the goal of the counseling intervention. The target behavior may be changes in specific behaviors or more internalized states such as anxiety, depression, self-esteem, or sense of social belonging. In SCRD, the target behavior is the dependent variable.

Three Characteristics That Define SCRD

Kazdin (2011) noted three unique characteristics of SCRDs that define the methodology, including continuous assessment, baseline data, and stability of performance within phases. In SCRD, the counselor researcher identifies a particular target behavior or state, such as attention, self-concept, behavior disruptions, or depressive symptoms, that serves as the focus of intervention. The researcher then seeks to monitor the target behavior through consistent and frequent collection of data throughout the SCRD in order to ascertain change. Continuous assessment involves multiple data points collected through standardized methods. For example, a school counselor may administer a self-esteem measure to a student every week over the course of an SCRD. Continuous assessment takes place throughout all phases of the SCRD, including baseline. The collection of baseline data is integral to inferential causality. In SCRD, the researcher collects data prior to introduction of intervention. During this baseline phase, the counselor researcher is monitoring the target behavior by data collection methods such as observations, self-reports, or teacher or parent reports. Finally, the ability to infer change associated with intervention relies on stability of performance within phases of the SCRD. In baseline phase, the researcher is seeking stability in order to demonstrate that there is no change or that the target behavior is worsening without intervention, while in intervention phases, the researcher is monitoring a reliable trend of change.

The Baseline Phase

Although there are three distinctive characteristics of SCRD, the collection of baseline data is especially critical to the implementation of the design. In the baseline phase, the researcher **establishes the conclusion that the target behavior is not subject to change through other everyday occurrences without intervention.** It is this baseline phase that allows for causal inference later in the design. For example, second grader Liam is referred for frequently disrupting the classroom. Instead of immediately working with Liam, the school counselor provides Liam's teacher with a daily checklist in which the teacher tally-marks the number of times Liam disrupts the class for a two-week period. At the end of two weeks, the school counselor now has 10 data points to graph. For these 10 data points, the disruptive behaviors range between 5 and 8 times each day, establishing a fairly consistent pattern of disruption. The school counselor now knows that Liam regularly disrupts the classroom on average 5–8 times a day. The school counselor also knows that passing of time, maturation of Liam, typical responses by the teacher or other students, or other disciplinary actions are not making a difference in Liam's disruptions. When the school counselor implements an intervention, she will continue to have the teacher fill out the daily checklist and will be comparing all subsequent data points with the original baseline graph. It is through this comparison that the school counselor will be able to determine the effectiveness of intervention. If the school counselor chose to intervene immediately, there would be no way to know if intervention was uniquely effective or if other events occurred that made a difference. Frequent and consistent baseline data collection is the SCRD's effort to address internal validity threats that prevent causal inference. Internal validity concerns may include maturation (i.e., things get better because time passes), history (i.e., other events occur between measurements), testing (i.e., effect of administering an assessment multiple times), or statistical regression to the mean (i.e., extreme scores that move closer to the mean in second testing; Tate & Perdices, 2019). Without baseline data in SCRD, there is no way to infer that change can be attributed to intervention.

Figures 10.1–10.3 provide examples of baseline data using the Liam example. Both Figures 10.1 and 10.2 present a stable baseline. In Figure 10.1, Liam stays within the consistent range of 5–8 disruptions each day. Following Day 2, Liam's disruptions remain on the high level of 6–8 with a continued stability of later days being in the range of 7–8, indicating that Liam's disruptions are not decreasing. The researcher can conclude from Figure 10.1 that Liam's behaviors are remaining fairly consistent in the range of 6–8. In Figure 10.2, the example shows a stable trend of Liam's disruptions wherein Liam's disruptions are showing a stable increase over the days measured. The researcher can conclude from Figure 10.2 that Liam's disruptive behaviors are increasing over time. Both Figures 10.1 and 10.2 can be considered stable because the researcher can now compare subsequent phase data to the consistent pattern established in either example. However, Figure 10.3 presents

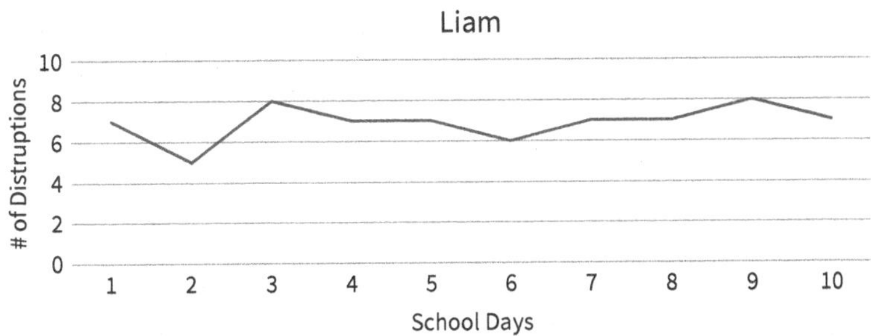

Figure 10.1. Stable Baseline for Liam: Example A

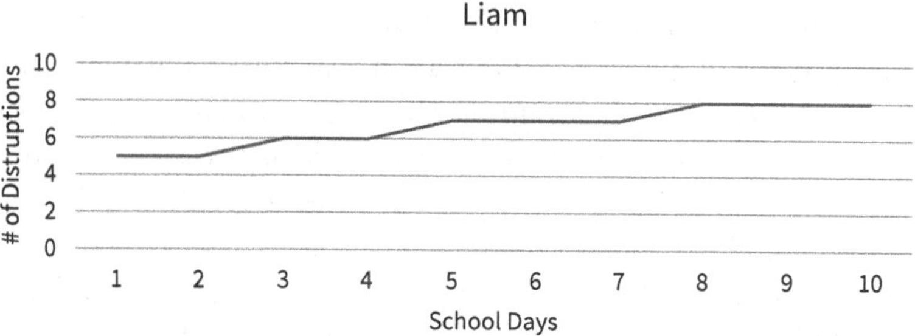

Figure 10.2. Stable Baseline for Liam: Example B

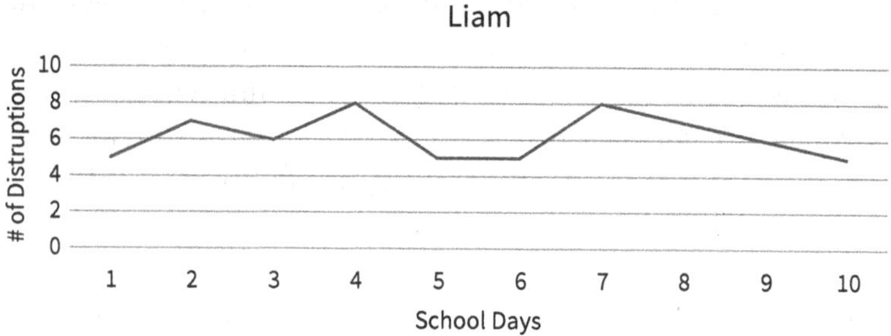

Figure 10.3. Unstable Baseline for Liam: Example C

an example of an unstable baseline. Although all data points are still within the same range of 5–8 disruptions, there is variability without a consistent pattern. In addition, the last three data points in Figure 10.3 indicate that Liam's disruptions are decreasing. If there is no definitive pattern or if there is a decrease in problem behaviors in the baseline phase, the researcher will be unable to determine if intervention is making a difference or if Liam's behavior is sporadic and subject to change for multiple other reasons.

Baseline Examples

In addition to the essential requirement to include baseline data in order to infer causality, the collection of baseline data is probably the most controversial aspect of SCRD. A baseline phase necessitates the delay of intervention. In the previous example, in the real world, Liam's teacher is most likely very frustrated; Liam is not successfully meeting academic markers, and classmates' learning may be impeded by his behavior. When the school counselor responds with "Let's take two weeks to collect data," administrators or Liam's teacher may be less inclined to support such an effort. In schools, the moral imperative is to apply intervention when needed. However, an alternative perspective may be that the school counselor is uncertain of the implications or effectiveness of certain methods. Or possibly, an administrator has been skeptical or unsupportive of the school counselor's methods. Baseline data collection will allow the school counselor to know and demonstrate the impact of intervention, which is beneficial for Liam and for children who subsequently present with disruptive problems. The two weeks of Liam's continued problem behaviors may be worth the delay in the long run. Each school counselor researcher will need to make this judgment call on a case-by-case basis. A child who is truly in immediate crisis would not be an ideal candidate for SCRD.

A Word About Credibility and Single-Case Experimental Designs

The purpose of this chapter is to provide the reader with a practical resource for conducting SCRDs within the school counseling field. As provided in the aforementioned description and characteristics of SCRDs, unique features include experimental qualities of baseline data collection, continuous assessment, and phases of stability to correlate intervention with outcome. Beyond the general description of SCRD, criteria are applied by researchers to determine the rigor and validity of design in order to meet the standards of a SCED. Although there is no singular agreed-upon set of criteria (Tate & Perdices, 2019), several researchers have proposed standards for recognition of SCEDs (Ledford et al., 2018). Experimental design criteria for SCED are focused on the replication of phases (introduction and withdrawal of intervention); data points (sufficient number of data points to establish stability); and/or participants, behaviors, or settings (repeating the effect of intervention across participants, behaviors, or settings). Table 10.1 presents criteria from two prominent frameworks in determining the validity of SCEDs: What Works Clearinghouse (Kratochwill et al., 2010) and Council for Exceptional Children (CEC, 2014).

The criteria applied to the determination of SCED quality is rigorous and may extend beyond the resources of the school counseling researcher. Specific criteria such as the use of observers and observations to collect data may not be practical or desirable for the school counseling researcher who is interested in assessing the impact of intervention on children's internal states or perceptions of parents and teachers in their interactions with children. The purpose of sharing this quality indicator information is to inspire as much rigor as possible in SCRDs, knowing that real-life implementation may limit some aspects of validity.

Table 10.1. Abbreviated Criteria for Organizational Frameworks Determining Rigor for Single-Case Experimental Designs (SCEDs)

What Works Clearinghouse (Kratochwill et al., 2010)	Council for Exceptional Children Standards for Evidence-Based Practices in Special Education (CEC, 2014)
"Meets Standards" Requirements	*Quality Indicators*
Intervention must be systematically manipulated by the researcher (initiated, withdrawn, or modified in phases).	Sufficient information on participants to provide eligibility for generalization
More than one rater measures target behavior in continuous assessment.	Description regarding roles and features of the intervention
Interrater reliability is established on at least 20% of data points in each phase.	Assessment and report of treatment fidelity
Interrater agreement must meet 80% threshold for agreement or 60% for Cohen's kappa.	Evidence of adequate internal reliability (i.e., score reliability coefficient $\geq$ .80, interobserver agreement $\geq$ 80%, kappa $\geq$ 60%)
Design must include at least three attempts to demonstrate an intervention effect at three different points in time or with three different phase repetitions.	Design controls for threats to internal validity using replication, withdrawal, or alternating designs.
Designs must meet a threshold of data points: • Reversal /withdrawal (e.g., ABAB) design must have a minimum of four phases per case with at least five data points per phase. • A multiple baseline design must have a minimum of six phases with at least five data points per phase. • Alternating treatment design needs five repetitions of the alternating sequence.	The design must include a baseline of at least three data points, and each subsequent phase includes at least three data points.
• Documentation of the consistency of level, trend, and variability within each phase • Documenting the immediacy of the effect, the proportion of overlap, the consistency of the data across phases in order to demonstrate an intervention effect, and comparing the observed and projected patterns of the outcome variable	Study provides graph in order to use traditional visual analysis techniques (i.e., analysis of mean, level, trend, overlap, consistency of data patterns across phases).

SCRD Designs

The A-B design is the cornerstone of SCRD (Ray, 2015) yet is not considered an experimental design due to lack of ability to confirm that change is attributable to intervention. Such attribution requires replication of the effect through repeated introduction of conditions that establish patterns of change.

Within the family of single-case research, there are multiple types of experimental design that can be classified into four broad categories, including withdrawal/reversal, multiple baseline, alternating treatment, and changing criterion designs. In the interest of clarity and brevity, I will present the characteristics of each category in Table 10.2.

In order to select the appropriate SCRD design, characteristics of the design in the context of types of intervention and target outcomes are considered. The most commonly employed SCRD is the withdrawal/reversal design in which intervention is introduced and withdrawn repeatedly in order to ascertain the effects of each phase. The withdrawal design is predicated on the assumption that the target behavior is subject to reversal upon removal of intervention. For example, when a teacher praises a student, the student will re-focus on schoolwork, yet when the teacher ceases to praise the student, the student will remain distracted. In the context of most counseling interventions, the intention of the counselor is to provide an intervention that has lasting impact, such as increased social skills or improved self-concept. In SCRD, this impact is referred to as a carry-over effect (Barlow et al., 2009) and interferes with SCRDs that require reversibility of the target behavior. Both withdrawal and alternating treatment designs require reversibility and therefore may be inappropriate designs for many counseling interventions. Changing criterion

Table 10.2. Categories and Characteristics of Single-Case Experimental Designs (SCRDs)

Design Category	Description	Limitations of Use
Withdrawal/ Reversal	Phases involve the repeated introduction and withdrawal of intervention. Examples: A-B-A, A-B-A-B.	Withdrawal of intervention may be unethical; target behavior must be reversible.
Multiple Baseline	Design involves the replication of A-B phases across participants, settings, or behaviors.	Participants or behaviors may not be independent from one another; baselines may be prolonged.
Alternating Treatment	Different interventions are rapidly alternated for a single participant following the baseline phase in order to compare effect of multiple intervention or components of interventions. Example: A-BC-A-BC-A.	Target behavior must be reversible; interaction between treatments may obfuscate interpretation.
Changing Criterion	Based on operant conditioning, intervention is intensified or decreased in each phase following baseline in order to meet preestablished phase criteria for the target behavior (Tate & Perdices, 2019).	Difficulty in establishing appropriate criterion levels; changes in behavior that exceed criteria

designs are heavily reliant on behavioral operant conditioning principles and may also be less desirable for counselors engaged in relationally based counseling interventions designed to affect internal states.

Although school counseling researchers may use any of the SCRDs described, multiple baseline designs are notably well positioned for use with counseling interventions (Ray, 2015). In multiple-baseline designs, the researcher manipulates the process of replication by instituting more than one baseline (typically three or more) during the design implementation. In other words, the researcher will collect data during baseline phases for multiple participants, or for multiple behaviors for one participant, or across multiple settings for one behavior for one participant. Multiple baseline designs are considered evidence based due to replication features. In multiple baseline studies, the counselor applies the A-B phases with multiple participants, settings, or behaviors. Use of the A-B design prevents the need to withdraw intervention, allowing the school counselor to continue services once intervention is introduced. When applying multiple baselines across behaviors, the counselor will target multiple behaviors with the same intervention, demonstrating repeated effects with different behaviors for a single participant, such as collecting data on attention, hyperactivity, and completion of assignments for each participant during design implementation. The application of multiple baselines to settings involves the tracking of a target behavior for a single participant across different settings as a result of intervention, such as collecting data for an individual student at school, at home, and during an extracurricular activity. Multiple baselines across participants signifies that the counselor will employ A-B design with multiple participants targeting the same behavior/state, such as collecting the same data for five students who start intervention at different times. When implementing a multiple baseline design across participants, often the design of choice for mental health intervention, the baseline is extended for each replication in order to demonstrate repeated similar outcomes. The extension of baselines may be especially challenging for school counselors who have limited timelines in the school year or who may have immediate concerns about a student's target behavior or internal state. A multiple-baseline design is used as the primary example in this chapter to demonstrate implementation of single-case design.

How to Conduct an SCRD

The following section presents step-by-step guidelines on how to conduct an SCRD. I have introduced these steps, or variations of, in previous literature on implementation of SCRD (Ray, 2015; Ray et al., 2010; Ray & Schottelkorb, 2010; Ray & Stulmaker, 2016). In order to illustrate the steps, I will expand on the example of Liam for each step of the process.

Step 1: Define the Research Question/Identify Dependent Variable

The basic SCRD research question is "Is Intervention Q effective in the reduction of the target behavior for a particular set of students?" The SCRD research question involves specification of the participants, target behavior, and intervention (Wolery et al., 2018). Secondary questions might include: "What is the impact of Component M within Intervention Q?," "To what degree does Intervention Q reduce the target behavior?," or "At what point does the target behavior demonstrate reduction after implementation of Intervention Q?" Questions in SCRD are related to intervention effectiveness, implementation of intervention, and timing of intervention. Some examples from school counseling might include: "Is child-centered play therapy effective in improving self-regulation among second graders?," "Does the Second Step Violence Prevention Program result in decreased incidents of aggression among a class of eighth graders?," or "Does the group component of a cognitive-behavioral therapy intervention result in immediate improvement of social belonging perceptions among 10th-grade girls?" As indicated by the example questions and consistent with experimental intervention design, SCRD research questions ask for a yes or no response. The outcomes of SCRDs indicate support or nonsupport for interventions or components within interventions.

Example. As the school counselor, I have a scheduled meeting with the second-grade teaching team which consists of five second-grade teachers. In this meeting, three of the teachers are frustrated with a few children who are "acting out" in class. I asked them to specify what they mean by acting out. They provide examples of children who burst out verbally or physically in the middle of lessons or quiet times, annoy other students by taking their things or talking to them, run around the room at random times, and start arguments with other students or with the teacher. The teachers share their discipline techniques, which sound reasonable but are not working with these particular students. As a school counselor who conducts play therapy, I hypothesize that group play therapy may be helpful for these children to increase self-regulation. I develop the research question "Is group play therapy effective in the increase of self-regulation and reduction of disruptive behaviors among second-grade students who are disruptive in the classroom?"

Step 2: Identify Participants

Inherent in the title, SCRD requires only one participant. However, the ability to match intervention with outcome credibly typically requires recruitment of multiple participants. Replication of effects is a hallmark of SCRD, and therefore, the ability to repeat demonstration of outcome across multiple participants adds substantial credibility to the design. Multiple-baseline participant designs require replication across a minimum of three participants, with a preference of some researchers for four or more (Barlow et al., 2009; Gallo et al., 2013; Kratochwill et al., 2010; Tate & Perdices, 2019). Additionally, it is not uncommon for participants to drop out during the implementation of the study. In schools, children may move or be sent to alternative placements, especially if you are working in highly mobile schools or with children with significant behavioral problems. The identification of 4–6 student participants (I always recommend 6) is typically sufficient to ensure that the study will end with at least three participants.

Another consideration regarding selection of participants and SCRD is identifying students who are as similar as possible in presentation. The ability to generalize findings is dependent on the homogeneity of the participants, specifically regarding presenting problems, in order to apply outcomes to children who present similarly. For example, I would want to identify participants who have similar depression symptoms or who are all physically aggressive. Ideally, I am also searching for participants for whom I can affirm independence of intervention effects. For example, I would avoid recruiting siblings in order to avoid the possible internal threat of current family dynamics that may interfere with interpretation of outcomes. In schools, it is possible that this might be true for students who have the same teacher. It can also be useful to try to ensure that your sample has a mix of student ethnicities and races and has diversity for gender, but that may not always be possible depending on the presenting issue, the size of the sample, and the students who are referred or recruited to the study. Alternatively, the school counselor may want to observe effect of an intervention on a group of marginalized students (e.g., students experiencing racism, ableism, gender bias) and choose to limit participants to students within that group in order to explore fully the intersection of systemic barriers and a proposed intervention. Finally, the individualized nature of SCRD requires that the researcher is familiar with the background and current circumstance of the participants. The SCRD researcher conducts interviews and collects background information with the participants if age appropriate and with parents and teachers. This qualitative information may be used to interpret variations in data at a later point. Exploring and providing a rich description of each participant is another way for the school counselor to uncover systemic barriers that have impacted the student up to this point and may impact the student's response to intervention.

Example. After talking with the second-grade teachers, I asked them to refer the particular students for whom they have concerns to me. I specifically asked them to identify only students who have verbal and physical outbursts with little provocation, verbally or physically annoy other students, and are argumentative. After defining these criteria, the four teachers referred eight children. One teacher referred three students, two teachers referred two, and one teacher referred one. After talking with the teachers, the teacher who referred three students indicated that she was quite frustrated with one of the referred students due to his inability to sit still and his being in constant movement, yet he responded compliantly when she requested he do so. Based on this description, I ruled him out for being part of the study but did provide recommendations to the teacher and parents to help with attention and hyperactivity. I then contacted each of the parents of the remaining seven students to explain the study and the intervention. Upon receiving informed consent from parents, I then conducted interviews with the parents about each child's background. One parent indicated that their child had experienced multiple adverse life events that resulted in a PTSD diagnosis. Due to the apparent complex trauma experienced by this child, I ruled out the possibility of this child participating in the study, provided the parent with referrals for counseling, and offered to see the child weekly if outside counseling was not an option. This resulted in six children whose parents consented and seemed appropriate for the study. Of the six children, two sets of two children were in the same classroom, and the remaining two were in different classrooms, resulting in the involvement of four teachers. All referred children were boys. (Note: If results of this study are intended to be disseminated, the researcher needs approval through an IRB to ensure the safety and health of human subjects in research. See Chapter 3, written by Young and Gonzalez, for additional details regarding ethics and IRB requirements.)

Step 3: Choose a Measurement/Instrument

The measurement of the dependent variable in SCRD is vital to the continuous assessment characteristic of the design. The measurement of the dependent variable must be valid, reliable, able to be administered frequently, and practical for the setting. Because SCRD is intended to be an experimental design, the researcher seeks to use measurements that have been determined to be valid and reliable through standardization procedures. SCRD researchers are particular proponents of observation measures for overt behaviors. As stated earlier, SCEDs employ the use of blind raters that have established interobserver agreement or reliability. Although measurement of observed behaviors by objective raters is preferable for some researchers (Kratochwill et al., 2010), school counselors are often more concerned with internal states (i.e., thoughts and feelings) that are not observable. Self and other-reports, sometimes referred to as indirect measures (Kazdin, 2011; Tate & Perdices, 2019), can be used to measure participants' perspectives on how they are doing. The caveat to using these types of measures is to ensure that the assessment has been validated through reliability procedures for the population the school counselor is serving. It is particularly important for the school counselor to ensure that measurements do not perpetuate stigmatization of marginalized groups. The school counseling researcher is cautioned to read through assessment manuals to affirm validation procedures for any assessment that is used in SCRD. Although it may be tempting to create an assessment of one's own, validation is poor for such a measurement, negating the ability to interpret the data. One resource for finding credible assessments is the assessment guide available through the Collaborative for Academic, Social, and Emotional Learning (CASEL) at https://measuringsel.casel.org/access-assessment-guide/.

A challenge to the identification of measurements is the frequency with which assessments must be administered in SCRD. The school counselor researcher is charged with the obligation to identify assessments that can be administered on a session, weekly, or sometimes daily basis. I have experienced this requirement of assessments to be one of the most challenging aspects of SCRD. One suggestion is when identifying an instrument, the researcher may contact the author of the instrument to clarify the frequency at which the assessment can be administered. If supported by the author's research, the SCRD researcher may choose to modify administration directions. For example, if a protocol instructs the participant to "identify the intensity of the following emotions in the last 2 weeks," with the assessment author's permission, the SCRD researcher may change the prompt to "identify the intensity of the following emotions in the last 2 days."

Example. In order to address the research question on the effectiveness of group play therapy on self-regulation and reduction of disruptive behaviors, I pursued two types of measurements. For the measurement of self-regulation, I selected the standardized assessment Social Emotional Assets and Resilience Scales (SEARS; Merrell, 2011), which has a subscale for self-regulation and has both a teacher and parent form. The SEARS can be administered frequently, and I intended for both the teacher and parent to fill out the SEARS on a weekly basis. For the measurement of decrease in disruptive behaviors, I created a tally mark checklist for each teacher. Each time the student exhibited one of the identified behaviors (i.e., verbal or physical outburst, verbal or physical annoyance of other students, or argumentativeness), the teacher placed a tally mark for that day. I used the sum of the daily tally marks for data points. Although using blind raters or establishing interrater agreement among teachers would be preferable for credibility of data, I determined that this was impractical based on lack of funding to pay observers and lack of time from teachers to engage in interrater agreement procedures. For the purposes of brevity in this example, I will only be graphing the disruptive behavior data. However, the SEARS data would be graphed in the exact same procedure as illustrated with the disruptive behavior.

Step 4: Define the Intervention/Independent Variable

SCRD requires that the intervention be well defined and described in procedures. A published protocol is preferable but thick description may suffice (Kratochwill et al., 2010). Experimental designs are predicated on the assumption that the protocol can be replicated in other studies with other participants, hence the need for detailed description. The SCRD researcher is expected to address thoroughly the role of the intervention agent (e.g., school counselor), training necessary for intervention, procedures for intervention, and procedures for determining intervention fidelity (i.e., ensuring the counselor is following intervention procedures).

Example. As the school counselor, I have selected five sessions of group play therapy as the intervention to study. Because "group play therapy" is a broad term, I will specifically provide child-centered group play therapy (CCGPT; Ray, 2011), which is an evidence-based intervention with a written protocol for delivery of services. I am certified as a child-centered play therapist, indicating that I have received additional training in the approach beyond my master's degree, and my school counseling certification. In order to establish fidelity of intervention, I will video-record the sessions (as explained in my informed consent to parents) and ask a fellow certified colleague to randomly select 10 of my sessions and use the CCGPT fidelity checklist to ensure that my intervention meets protocol standards.

Step 5: Select the SCRD

As previously presented, the SCRD researcher chooses a specific design within the family of SCRDs. Among the choices are the withdrawal/reversal, multiple-baseline, alternating treatment, and changing criterion designs. The choice of design may be impacted by several factors, including available time, severity of problem, intervention type, or the rigor needed for reporting results. If the school counseling researcher has 10 weeks left in the semester, extending baseline in a multiple-baseline design may be ill-advised because weeks for intervention will be limited. A decision to use multiple baselines may also be influenced by the severity of the problem exhibited by the child. If the baseline demonstrates that the child's target behavior is worsening, delaying intervention in order to meet study protocol standards may not be a workable plan. Intervention type may be another consideration for a school counselor who is interested in only exploring the effects of one holistic intervention (i.e., an intervention that is not organized into time components). In this case, an alternating treatment design is unwarranted. Finally, the school counseling researcher may be affected by the rigor necessary for stakeholders. In some cases, the researcher may be reporting to a principal who only needs to see evidence that the student is improving, thus warranting a simple A-B design in which the school counselor demonstrates the student's regression before the intervention but improvement during the intervention. This can be especially powerful if the school counselor can demonstrate change for three to six children. Yet, in other cases, the school counseling researcher may intend to report to the school board or other researchers, as in a peer-reviewed forum. In these cases, the school counseling researcher may select an SCED design that meets criteria for replication standards.

Example. As the school counselor, I experienced that my administrators, including my principal and counseling director, were unsupportive of using play therapy in the schools. In order to address their concerns, I decided to use the What Works Clearinghouse (Kratochwill et al., 2010) criteria for experimental designs and opted for a multiple-baseline-across-participants design. I hoped that the use of an evidence-based design would convince administrators of credibility of results if group play therapy demonstrated effectiveness.

Step 6: Establish a Baseline

Earlier in the chapter, I discussed the significance of establishing a baseline in SCRDs. I continue to emphasize this point. ***Interpretation of outcome can only occur when a stable baseline has been established.*** In my experience, researchers struggle with the baseline requirement and will often attempt to cut it short before stability is reached or impulsively move to intervention based on a need to help. The lack of stable baselines is noted in the research literature and serves to discredit the interpretation and implication of results (Vannest et al., 2013). If a researcher is opposed to baselines, SCRD is not a good match.

Example. In the example, I have asked the teachers to tally-mark disruptive behaviors every day for a minimum of 10 school days. Because I am using

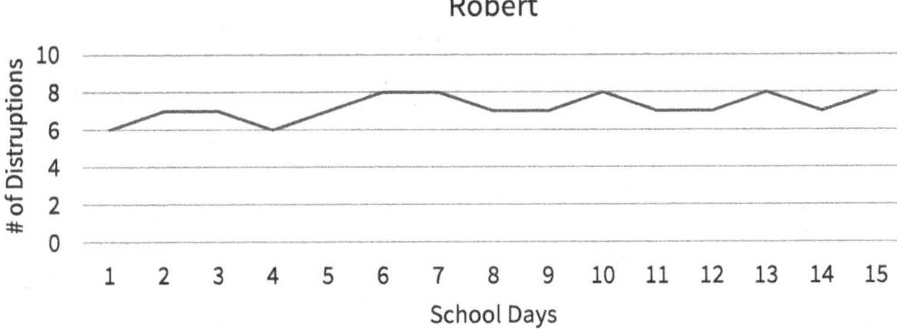

Figure 10.4. Robert's Stable Baseline

a multiple baseline across participants design, I plan to stagger implementation of intervention for two participants at a time in random order. For two participants randomly selected, I will begin intervention if the 10 days demonstrate a stable baseline. For two participants randomly selected, I will begin intervention at the end of a 15-day baseline. For the final two participants randomly selected, I will begin intervention at the end of a 20-day baseline. In the end, if baselines are stable, I will begin intervention at 2 weeks, 3 weeks, and 4 weeks, respectively. In the event of unstable baselines, I will extend baselines until stability is reached. As examples, I present two stable baselines within the example study. Liam was one of the first two participants, and his baseline was demonstrated in Figure 10.4. Robert was a participant in the second group of two participants. Figure 10.4 depicts his stable baseline.

Step 7: Implement Phase Protocol and Measure at Multiple Points

Following the establishment of the baseline, the SCRD researcher is ready to implement the phase protocol while also continuing to collect data at established time intervals. The intervals between data collection remain consistent across all phases of the study. In other words, if the researcher collected data one time per week during baseline, they would continue to collect data weekly across the intervention phases. SCRD researchers specify the need for three data points for each phase at a minimum, but five or more is more typical and considered to be evidence based (Kratochwill et al., 2010). Vannest et al. (2013) recommended a minimum of nine. The purpose of multiple data points is to establish a trend in each phase. Rarely will three points of data indicate a trend, especially in counseling interventions, whereby immediacy of effect may be delayed due to the intrinsic nature of counseling impact.

Another consideration in study protocol implementation is the flexible nature of SCRD. SCRD researchers create a protocol plan prior to studying implementation, but if issues arise regarding intervention, the protocol may be modified to address the outcomes indicated during the study. For example, a participant may demonstrate a noticeable improvement in the 7th of 8 sessions. The SCRD researcher may choose to extend the intervention phase by two additional sessions to determine if the improvement is stable and/or continues. Such flexibility works within SCRD because the researcher is continuing to collect data at the same frequency across all phases even when shortened or lengthened. During the implementation of phase protocol, the researcher is graphing the data at each collection point in order to monitor variability and stability. Unlike group experimental studies, SCRDs require immediate recording and presentation of data to determine continued phase protocol implementation.

Example. In the example, I have planned a phase protocol for implementation of intervention phases across participants in coordination with data collection. Table 10.3 presents the protocol implementation plan. Five days each week, data will be collected with the disruptive behaviors tally mark checklist, resulting in five points of data per week.

Step 8: Data Analysis and Interpretation

Within SCRD, visual data analysis is the preferred and most frequent method of interpreting outcomes attributed to intervention (Barton et al., 2018; Riley-Tillman et al., 2020). Graphic display of data across phases is the basis for analysis. Therefore, graphs are a required component to the understanding and reporting of outcomes. Upon visual inspection of graphs, Kratochwill et al. (2010) proposed four steps and six variables that require consideration to interpret results. The four steps include *documentation of a predictable baseline pattern, examination of data within each phase to assess patterns, comparison of data between phases to assess the effect of intervention,* and *integration of data*

Table 10.3. Group Play Therapy Multiple-Baseline Protocol

Participant	Week								
	1	2	3	4	5	6	7	8	9
Liam	A	A	B	B	B	B	B		
Miguel	A	A	B	B	B	B	B		
Robert	A	A	A	B	B	B	B	B	
Samuel	A	A	A	B	B	B	B	B	
Alex	A	A	A	A	B	B	B	B	B
Carlos	A	A	A	A	B	B	B	B	B

Note: A = no intervention; B = group play therapy 1× per week.

across all phases. The four steps require that the researcher ensure through inspection of data that a stable baseline was established and then continue to compare data within each phase, between each phase, and across all phases. The analysis of data across the four steps includes six variables under inspection. Table 10.4 provides a brief description of the six variables.

In the case of Liam, Figure 10.5 shows data points across A-B phases. In the A baseline phase, Liam's level is 6.9 daily disruptive behaviors while in the B intervention phase the level is 3.85, indicating a substantial reduction in average disruptive behaviors. The diagonal line in Figure 10.5 indicates a steep

Table 10.4. Six Variable Considerations for Visual Inspection of Single-Case Design Graphs

Variable	Definition
Level	Mean of each phase
Trend	Slope of the data
Variability	Amount of difference between the trend line and each individual data point within a phase or range of data points within a phase
Immediacy of Effect	The point at which change is observed once intervention is introduced
Consideration of Overlap	Data points in the intervention phase that are the same or worse than data points in the baseline phase
Consistency of Data Patterns	Data pattern is replicated across phases, participants, settings, or behaviors.

Source: Kratochwill et al. (2010).

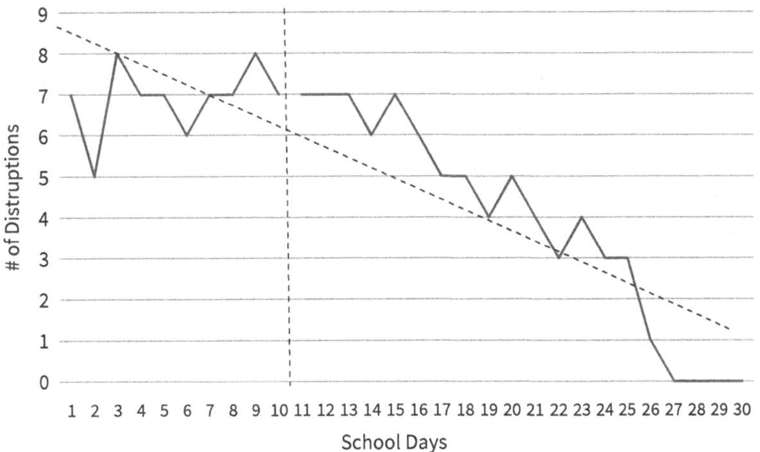

Figure 10.5. Liam's Graph for Visual Analysis

slope across A-B phases, demonstrating a trend of reduction during the intervention phase. Variability between data points is consistent with the trend line indicating a consistent pattern of reduction.

The three remaining variables under consideration include immediacy of effect, consideration of overlap, and consistency of data patterns across similar phases. A unique feature of SCRD is the concern regarding when change starts to take place once intervention is introduced, referred to as **immediacy of effect**. Relationally oriented counseling interventions focused on internal states of being are likely to have a delayed effect, yet SCRD allows the counselor to observe when effects start to take place. In Liam's case, the downward trajectory starts to be observable around data point 15, which would be a week after the first group play therapy session, indicating that Liam started to show a reduction in disruptive behaviors a few days after his first session. In examination of **consideration of overlap,** data points in the intervention phase that are the same or worse than data points in the baseline phase indicate that intervention is not consistently effective. In Liam's case, the second data point was his lowest in baseline at 5 disruptions. In the early intervention phase, there are several data points that are equal to or above 5, yet after data point 20, all data points are below 5. Data point 20 coincides with the 2nd group play therapy session, indicating that after the 2nd group play therapy session, Liam's disruptive behaviors never reached the same number as any point in the baseline phase. The final variable for consideration is consistency of data patterns across similar phases. This particular variable is representative of the use of replication in SCRD to establish validity of findings. If using an A-B design, there is no ability to examine consistency of data patterns across replication of effect because there is no replication. In the case of Liam, if I used only his data, an A-B design, I would be unable to conclude validity across replication because there was only one intervention phase used with one participant. However, if I use a multiple baseline design and examine the effect across multiple participants, I can establish a pattern of replication of results.

Example. For my play therapy SCRD with a focus on disruptive behaviors, I used a multiple baseline across participants design to establish a pattern of replication. Figure 10.6 presents data on three participants, one from each pair randomly assigned to intervention initiation at different points. I used data for three participants as a brief example. If I were reporting on the full study, I would provide the graphs for each of the six participants. Figure 10.6 clearly depicts that level changes, trend lines, low variability, reasonable immediacy of effect, and low overlap of data points are consistent across replication among participants, indicating that outcomes are most likely explained by implementation of intervention.

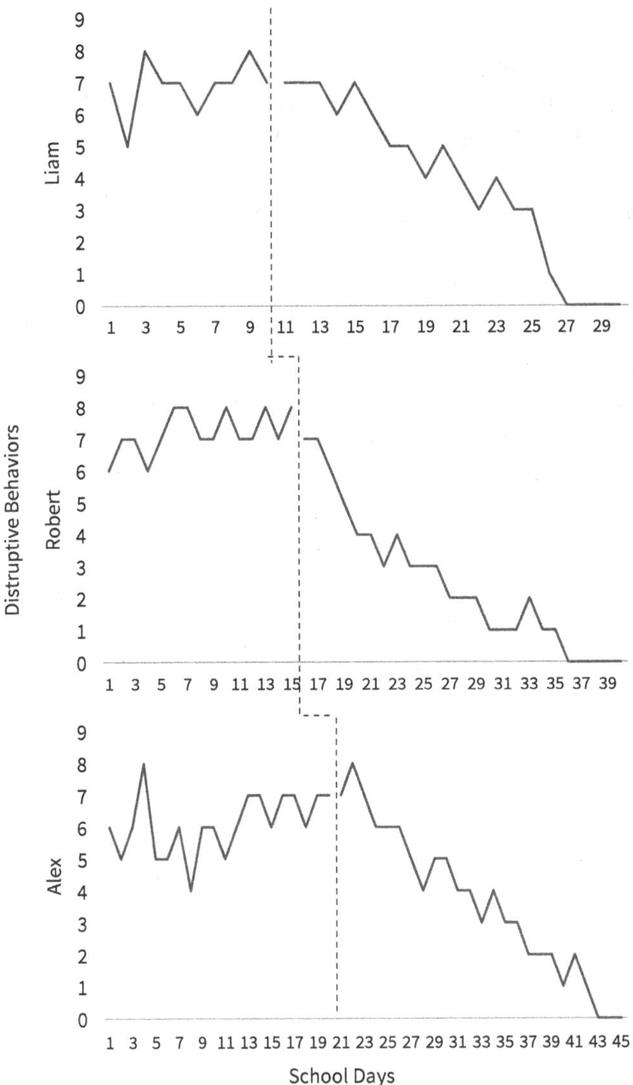

Figure 10.6. Multiple Baseline Results from Play Therapy Example, Society for Research in Child Development (SCRD)

A Few More Considerations Regarding Interpretation

Among SCRD researchers, there is a lack of agreement regarding the use of statistical analysis, effect sizes, and even descriptive statistics for the purposes of interpreting data (Barton et al., 2018; Kazdin, 2011; Riley-Tillman et al., 2020; Vannest et al., 2013). Some advocate for the reporting of means to establish level, while others caution against it. Some propose using the R-statistic to establish slope, while others argue that the lack of sufficient data points contraindicates the use of a parametric analysis. The list of disagreements is long and can be followed in historical and current literature on SCRD (Burns et al., 2014; Maggin et al., 2019). Effect sizes constitute a particularly controversial subject among SCRD researchers. In an effort to provide a statistical analysis that will lead to conclusive evidence of effectiveness, SCRD researchers have engaged in the development of multiple effect sizes. Tate and Perdices (2019) identified 12 types of effect sizes focused on non-overlap methods and debated in the literature regarding their validity and use for interpretation. The advantages of non-overlap methods are that they can be used with data that do not meet parametric standards of normality or independence and typically can be calculated by hand, absent complex mathematical equations. A few frequently used effect sizes in SCRD research include split-middle trend line, percentage of non-overlap data, percentage of data exceeding the median, percentage of all non-overlapping data, non-overlap of all pairs, improvement rate difference, and Tau-U. Explanation, calculation, and advantages/limitations of each of these effect sizes is beyond the scope of this chapter. Resources that may be helpful in seeking effect size application to SCRD include Parker et al. (2011), Tate and Perdices (2019), and Vannest et al. (2013).

Although SCRD researchers are not in agreement regarding use of statistical analysis in the interpretation of data, they are in agreement regarding the primacy of visual analysis. The use of visual analysis contributes to the accessibility of SCRD to everyday practitioners. As illustrated throughout this chapter, if a school counseling researcher has access to Microsoft Excel, SCRD data analysis is straightforward and easy to apply. Riley-Tillman et al. (2020) provide simple and detailed instructions on how to create SCRD graphs in Excel so that school counselors can clearly track data, create graphs, and interpret results. And finally, Kratochwill et al. (2010) provide guidance on interpretation of visual analysis by designating at least three demonstrations of intervention effect with no demonstration of no effect as strong evidence, at least three demonstrations of intervention effect with at least one demonstration of no intervention effect as moderate evidence, and less than three demonstrations of intervention effect as no evidence. These guidelines clarify that the school counseling researcher can provide strong evidence of intervention effectiveness if the SCRD includes replication across phases, participants, or behaviors. Table 10.5 provides multiple examples of SCRDs conducted in schools examining the effects of differing interventions. In these examples, I attempted to provide a variation of participants, interventions, designs, and data collection methods.

Table 10.5. SCRD Examples in Literature

	Ware Balch & Ray (2015)	Collier-Meek et al. (2017)	Meany-Walen et al. (2017)	Allen et al. (2019)	Taylor & Hill (2017)
Research Focus	Effectiveness of child-centered play therapy on the social-emotional competencies of children with autism spectrum disorder (ASD)	1. Do emailed prompts improve teachers' treatment integrity to the class-wide student intervention? 2. Do emailed prompts improve teachers' rates of praise and decrease teachers' rates of corrective statements? 3. Does implementation of the class-wide student intervention result in an increase of class-wide levels of academic engagement and a decrease of class-wide levels of disruptive behavior?	1. Is Adlerian play therapy effective in increasing children's on-task behaviors? 2. Is Adlerian play therapy effective in decreasing total problems? 3. Is Adlerian play therapy effective in reducing children's symptoms of ADHD?	Investigate the efficacy of the resilience education program (REP), a targeted intervention for students with internalizing problems.	1. Are daily behavior report cards (DBRC) an effective intervention for improving behavior during extended school year services for young students with intellectual and developmental disabilities (IDD)? 2. Can teachers of young students with IDD effectively implement DBRCs as a behavior intervention during Extended School Year (ESY) services?
SCRD	Multiple baseline	Multiple baseline	A-B-A	Multiple baseline	Changing criterion
Participants	Five participants with ASD 6–8 years old	Four teachers	Two participants 7–8 years old	Three participants 10–11 years old	Four participants with IDD 6–7 years old
Data Collection	Weekly SEARS parent form (Merrell, 2011)	Objective rater observations	Objective rater observations	Objective rater observations	Teacher checklist
Outcome	Play therapy beneficial for three participants by increasing social-emotional competencies and mixed results for two participants	Improved implementation of behavior intervention for 3 of 4 teachers who received emailed prompts. Increases in praise, decreases in corrective statements, and corresponding improvements in student outcomes were noted.	Play therapy very effective for one participant for on-task behavior, total problems, and ADHD scales across intervention and follow-up. Effective for second participant in intervention phase for on-task behavior and ADHD scales.	REP intervention resulted in decreased internalizing behaviors and increased social engagement for 2 of 3 participants.	All four students increased appropriate behaviors. Teachers positively implemented the behavioral intervention with fidelity.

Conclusion

The understanding and implementation of a single design can be a particularly helpful research tool for the practicing school counselor. As school systems seek to identify children in need of services matched with effective intervention, single-case design offers a data-based method for determining utility and viability. Within the multi-tiered system of support (MTSS) model used in school settings, SCRD can play a featured role in determining timing and level of support intervention. The continuous assessment of single units of students can be especially useful in determining the effectiveness of Tier 1 interventions wherein a school counselor may track the impact of a specific counseling program intended for all students. By following a single group of fifth graders prior to, during, and following implementation of a guidance curriculum, a school counselor can demonstrate the curriculum as effective in decreasing conflicts among students. For fifth graders who seem unresponsive to the general counseling curriculum, the school counselor may implement Tier 2 and Tier 3 interventions for small groups or individual students and track progress through SCRD to determine response to intervention. An MTSS requires the use of evidence-based methods to determine eligibility and account for intervention effectiveness (Riley-Tillman et al., 2020). SCRD provides a procedure for enacting and implementing MTSS with integrity and credibility.

Among the varied research designs available to the school counseling researcher, SCRD stands out as a design that is practically applied, is resource sensitive, and assesses effectiveness of intervention. Within the context of the MTSS approach to responding to needs of students, SCRD provides a procedure for determining what interventions are making a difference across tiers of support. Perhaps, most importantly, SCRDs allow the school counselor to explore the impact and outcomes of interventions for individual students, answering the age-old research question of what works for whom. SCRD is particularly well suited for school counselors to identify needs and intervention practices that work for marginalized students or students for which historically racist or oppressive systems have gone unidentified as contributors to academic and social-emotional challenges. In an era where school counselors are compelled to advocate for interventions that meet the social-emotional needs of all students, SCRDs provide an advocacy tool that can support the everyday efforts of the counselor in the role of meaningfully serving students.

References

Allen, A. N., Kilgus, S. P., & Eklund, K. (2019). An initial investigation of the efficacy of the resilience education program (REP). *School Mental Health: A Multidisciplinary Research and Practice Journal, 11*(1), 163–178. doi:10.1007/s12310-018-9276-1

Barlow, D., Nock, M., & Hersen, M. (2009). Single case experimental designs: Strategies for *studying behavior for change* (3rd ed.). Pearson Education.

Barton, E., Lloyd, B., Spriggs, A., & Gast, D. (2018). Visual analysis of graphic data. In J. Ledford & D. Gast (Eds.), *Single case research methodology: Applications in special education and behavioral sciences* (3rd ed., pp. 179–214). Routledge.

Burns, M., Kratochwill, T., & Levin, J. (2014). *Single-case intervention research: Methodological and statistical advances.* American Psychological Association.

Collier-Meek, M., Fallon, L., & DeFouw, E. (2017). Toward feasible implementation support: E-mailed prompts to promote teachers' treatment integrity. *School Psychology Review, 46*, 379–394. doi:10.17105/SPR-2017-0028.V46-4

Council for Exceptional Children. (2014). Council for Exceptional Children standards for evidence-based practices in special education. Retrieved from https://exceptionalchildren.org/sites/default/files/2021-04/EBP_FINAL.pdf

Creswell, J., & Poth, C. (2018). *Qualitative inquiry & research design: Choosing among five approaches* (4th ed.). Sage.

Gallo, K., Comer, J., & Barlow, D. (2013). Single-case experimental designs and small pilot trial designs. In J. Comer & P. Kendall's (Eds.), *The Oxford handbook of research strategies for clinical psychology* (pp. 24–39). Oxford University Press.

Hayes, D., & Singh, A. (2012). *Qualitative inquiry in clinical and educational settings.* Guilford Press.

Kazdin, A. (2011). *Single-case research designs: Methods for clinical and applied settings* (2nd ed.). Oxford University Press.

Kratochwill, T., Hitchcock, J., Horner, R., Levin, J., Odom, S., Rindskopf, D., & Shadish, W. (2010, June). *Single-case designs technical documentation.* What Works Clearninghouse. Retrieved from https://files.eric.ed.gov/fulltext/ED510743.pdf

Ledford, J., & Gast, D. (Eds.). (2018). *Single case research methodology: Applications in special education and behavioral sciences.* Routledge.

Ledford, J., Lane, J., & Tate, R. (2018). Evaluating quality and rigor in single case research. In J. Ledford & D. Gast (Eds.), *Single case research methodology: Applications in special education and behavioral sciences* (3rd ed., pp. 365–392). Routledge.

Maggin, D., Cook, B., & Cook, L. (2019). Making sense of single-case design effect sizes. *Learning Disabilities Research & Practice, 34*(3), 124–132. doi:10.1111/ldrp.12204

Meany-Walen, K., Teeling, S., Davis, A., Artley, G., & Vignovich, A. (2016). Effectiveness of a play therapy intervention on children's externalizing and off-task behaviors. *Professional School Counseling, 20*, 89–101. doi:10.5330/1096-2409-20.1.89

Merrell, K. W. (2011). *Social emotional assets and resilience scales (SEARS).* Psychological Assessment Resources.

Parker, R., Vannest, K., & Davis, J. (2011). Effect size in single case research: A review of nine nonoverlap techniques. *Behavior Modification, 35*, 303–322. doi:10.1177/0145445511399147

Ray, D. (2011). *Advanced play therapy: Essential conditions, knowledge, and skills for child practice.* Routledge.

Ray, D. (2015). Single case research design and analysis: Counseling applications. *Journal of Counseling & Development, 93*, 394–402. doi:10.1002/jcad.12037

Ray, D., Barrio Minton, C., Schottelkorb, A., & Brown, A. (2010). Single-case design in child counseling research: Implications for counselor education. *Counselor Education and Supervision, 49*, 193–208. doi:10.1002/j.1556-6978.2010.tb00098.x

Ray, D., & Schottelkorb, A. (2010). Single case design: A primer for play therapists. *International Journal of Play Therapy, 19*, 39–53. doi:10.1037/a0017725

Ray, D., & Stulmaker, H. (2016). Methodologies suited to the study of play therapy. In K. O'Connor, L. Braverman, & C. Schaefer (Eds.), *Handbook of play therapy* (pp. 631–650). Wiley.

Riley-Tillman, T. C., Burns, M., & Kilgus, S. (2020). *Evaluating educational interventions: Single-case design for measuring response to intervention* (2nd ed.). Guilford Press.

Schottelkorb, A., & Ray, D. (2009). ADHD symptom reduction in elementary students: A single- case effectiveness design. *Professional School Counseling, 13*, 11–22. doi:10.5330/PSC.n.2010-13.11

Swan, K., & Ray, D. (2014). Effects of child-centered play therapy on irritability and hyperactivity behaviors of children with intellectual disabilities. *Journal of Humanistic Counseling, 53*, 120–133.

Tate, R., & Perdices, M. (2019). *Single-case experimental design for clinical research and neurorehabilitation settings: Planning, conduct, analysis and reporting.* Routledge.

Taylor, J. C., & Hill, D. (2017). Using daily behavior report cards during extended school year services for young students with intellectual and developmental disabilities. *Education & Treatment of Children, 40*(4), 525–546. doi:10.1353/etc.2017.0023

Vannest, K., Davis, J., & Parker, R. (2013). *Single case research in schools: Practical guidelines for school-based professionals.* Routledge.

Ware Balch, J., & Ray, D. (2015). Emotional assets of children with autism spectrum disorder: A single case therapeutic outcome experiment. *Journal of Counseling & Development, 93*, 429–439. doi:10.1002/jcad.12041

Wolery, M., Lane, K., & Common, E. (2018). Writing tasks: Literature reviews, research proposals, and final reports. In J. Ledford & D. Gast (Eds.), *Single case research methodology: Applications in special education and behavioral sciences* (3rd ed., pp. 43–76). Routledge.

11

Program Evaluation in Professional School Counseling

Michael S. Trevisan and John C. Carey

Collaborative Evaluation of School Counseling Programs

Collaborating with K–12 schools to conduct evaluations of school counseling programs provides unique opportunities for school counseling university faculty to gain understanding of school counseling outcomes and to have a broader impact on professional practice. These opportunities can be obtained by providing professional development about evaluation for school district school counselors as well as conducting direct evaluations of programs and services. There is no blueprint for this type of work, and it can be challenging for a school counselor educator (SCE) as an outsider to the school and district. However, the experience can be professionally rewarding and worth the effort.

There are a few case examples in the school counseling literature and recommendations and insights from the evaluation literature that can be used to begin fleshing out a strategy to work with K–12 schools (see Chapter 2 for additional details on building strong relationships with school districts). In addition, both authors have experience working with schools and school districts concerning program evaluation. Thus, the ideas here provide a solid foundation for school counseling faculty to embark on productive collaborations with school districts concerning program evaluation.

A starting place for university faculty is the extent to which state or school district support exists to promote evaluation of school counseling programs. This includes policies requiring evaluation, incentives for doing so, and ongoing professional development for school counselors and other school district educators to carry out evaluation work in a credible manner (Martin & Carey, 2012; Trevisan, 2000). When these supports exist, the rationale for

Michael S. Trevisan and John C. Carey, *Program Evaluation in Professional School Counseling* In: *School Counseling Research*. Edited by: Brett Zyromski and Carey Dimmitt, Oxford University Press. © Oxford University Press 2023. DOI: 10.1093/oso/9780197650134.003.0011 university faculty involvement is conceptually stronger than it is without this structure. We recommend that faculty seek to integrate their work within the existing structure. This can be done by reviewing existing policies and conferring with school counseling practitioners and perhaps other district educators, to ensure that what is being offered is perceived to have value for the school counseling program.

There are some lessons found in the literature for working with school districts that could prove useful to university faculty seeking to collaborate with K–12 schools on program evaluation. Astramovich et al. (2005) provided program evaluation professional development to school counseling practitioners in a large school district in the southwestern part of the United States. As an initial task, the authors (Astramovich et al., 2005) administered a survey of school counseling practitioners to get a sense of their interest, prior knowledge and skills, and concerns with evaluation of school counseling programs. They found that most school counselors were eager to learn about evaluation but had not received prior training, either in graduate school or from prior professional development activities. The authors were able to capitalize on this interest and fashioned a workshop that met the direct knowledge and skill needs of the school counseling participants. A key recommendation for university faculty interested in doing evaluation-oriented professional development work with school counselors is to administer a survey that will help them gauge interest, prior experience, and the development of a workshop that will best meet the needs of participants. This seems a useful idea whether or not the school district maintains a support structure for evaluation.

Trevisan and Hubert (2001) worked to establish an evaluation system that met the needs and requirements of a comprehensive, developmental guidance and counseling model, which was being implemented in a medium-sized school district at the time. The work spanned 3 years. The two authors (a university faculty member and a lead school counselor) recommended that an individual within the school district who would champion the evaluation effort is important to maintain commitment to the work. In addition, gaining commitments from school principals and the school board, two key stakeholder groups in the school district, was essential. School principals typically supervise school counselors, and school boards approve school district budgets. Thus, their continued support helped in bringing the evaluation system into fruition. The lead school counselor, with solid relationships with school principals and the school board, was able to make the case for the importance of the work.

Evaluation has been an important component of school counseling for at least the past 40 years. The emergence of comprehensive developmental models of school counseling in the 1980s catalyzed a dramatic shift from the understanding of school counseling as a professional position in schools to a comprehensive program with its own goals and services (Trevisan & Carey, 2020a). Evaluation was considered necessary to improve the program's services and to demonstrate its value. All three foundational comprehensive models of school counseling included robust processes for conducting evaluations (Gysbers & Henderson, 1988; Johnson & Johnson, 1991; Myrick, 1987). The American School Counselor Association (ASCA) National Model (2019), the most recent formulation of a comprehensive developmental model, also recognizes evaluation as an essential school counseling activity.

As mentioned, there are no blueprints or frameworks for collaborating with school districts. The ideas presented here, from experiences that occurred some time ago, will help start and perhaps partially sustain university faculty as they embark on the important work of collaborating with schools and school districts for developing and maintaining evaluation of its school counseling programs. We encourage faculty doing this type of work to reflect and write about their school district collaborations and do so in the peer-reviewed literature. In this way, a rigorously developed set of ideas and recommendations would be available to help other faculty to navigate the oftentimes complex organizational environment of school districts productively.

Reconnecting School Counseling and Evaluation

While the evaluation-related components of the foundational comprehensive models were well grounded in program evaluation best practices in existence at the time, the field of evaluation has continued to develop rapidly. The school counseling profession has not been well connected with these developments (Trevisan & Carey, 2020a). School counseling needs to reconnect with the field of evaluation so that counselors are able to employ the most effective methods for evaluating their program and its services. To facilitate this reconnection, Trevisan and Carey (2020a) recently published a book that infuses current evaluation concepts and methods into school counseling practice. Practitioners interested in a step-by-step guide to program evaluation are encouraged to refer to this book. This chapter provides an overview of concepts and methods presented in the book to support school counseling scholars interested in collaborating with school counselors on program evaluation. In addition, there is an appendix attached to this chapter that provides a more complete look at supporting evaluation work for K–12 school counseling programs.

To facilitate the reconnection of school counseling and the field of evaluation, some semantic confusion must be sorted out to facilitate mutual understanding. The school counseling profession emphasizes that school counseling is an organized program within schools that includes a variety of different interventions, services, and activities. The profession maintains that it is important to evaluate both the program as a whole and the various interventions, services, and activities of the program. The ASCA National Model (2019), for example, includes both a *Program Results Analysis* of the entire program and *Results Report* evaluation of the specific interventions of the program. Professional evaluators use the term "program evaluation" to refer to the evaluation of both the overall program and its constituent parts. The field of evaluation recognizes that different evaluation approaches are needed at these two levels and is concerned with the development and use of effective methods at both levels.

The Joint Committee on Standards in Educational Evaluation (JCSEE) provides a useful definition of program evaluation that has utility for the school counseling profession. Program evaluation is defined as:

> The systematic investigation of the quality of programs, projects, subprograms, subprojects, and/or any of their components or elements together or singly for purposes of decision making, judgments, conclusions, findings, new knowledge, organizational development, and capacity building in response to the needs of identified stakeholders leading to improvement and/or accountability in the users' programs and system and ultimately contributing to organizational or social value. (Yarbrough et al., 2010; p. xxv)

This definition emphasizes that program evaluation is a systematic process based on a clearly articulated evaluation plan that includes rigorous methods of data collection and analysis. It also emphasizes that evaluation results are used in a variety of ways: to guide program improvement, to inform decisions about the merit or worth of a program, and to provide accountability information to stakeholders and the general public.

Within the school counseling profession, program evaluation is also considered to have multiple purposes. Gysbers (2004) has indicated that evaluations should yield information that can be used to improve the school counseling program and to demonstrate its worth to stakeholders and decision makers. Within the profession, the use of evaluation for program improvement has been emphasized by the evidence-based movement (Dimmitt et al., 2007). The use of evaluation to demonstrate effectiveness has been emphasized by the accountability movement (Sink, 2009). Evaluation can be used to improve the work of school counseling and demonstrate that the work has value.

The field of evaluation uses different terms for these two purposes. *Formative evaluation* (Trevisan & Walser, 2015) refers to evaluations that are focused on program improvement. Formative evaluations focus on whether the program and its services are implemented as planned and on ways to improve implementation and service delivery. Formative evaluation methods typically include interviews, focus groups, checklists, observations, open-ended surveys, and questionnaires.

Summative evaluation (Trevisan & Walser, 2015) refers to evaluation approaches that demonstrate the impact of the whole program or its constituent parts on the recipients of services. Summative evaluations assess whether the expected benefits of the program are actually delivered. Summative evaluations are often done on a larger scale, more complex, and conducted or supported by evaluation experts external to the program. Statistical techniques are frequently used to compare students who received services with students who did not, in order to determine whether there are better outcomes for participating students.

Program Evaluation and the ASCA National Model

In all four editions of the ASCA National Model, evaluation of the whole program level and evaluation of specific activities have prominent places. Table 11.1 summarizes the components of the newest edition of the model (ASCA, 2019) that involve program evaluation.

The ASCA National Model (ASCA, 2019) includes elements related to both the evaluation of the whole program and the evaluation of specific activities. For example, the ASCA National Model recommends a *School Counseling Program Assessment* that audits the whole program to determine whether the essential elements of the ASCA National Model have been implemented. The School Counseling Program Assessment assesses whether all the putative active ingredients associated with the program are in place.

The National Model also uses *Action Reports* that assess changes in student behavior and performance that are expected to be associated with specific services or activities. These Action Reports are intended to produce summative evaluation information on the outcomes and benefits to enable the documentation of the delivery of benefits to stakeholders in order to demonstrate their value persuasively.

Table 11.1. Elements of the ASCA National Model (2019) Most Closely Connected to Program Evaluation

Model Component	Element	Description
Management	School Counseling Program Assessment	Audit of the extent to which the ASCA National Model components are implemented
	Annual Data Review	Systematic examination of current existing school achievement, attendance, and discipline data to identify potential areas of focus and goals
	School Data Summary	Identify most salient problematic school achievement data and how data can be improved by the school counseling program.
	Annual Student Outcome Goals	Identify measurable impact the school counseling program is intended to have on student achievement, attendance, and/or discipline.
	Action Plans	Select specific interventions to address identified problems and develop an evaluation plan for each intervention.
	Lesson Plans	Design specific guidance lessons to address identified problems and develop an evaluation plan for each lesson.
	Advisory Council	Stakeholders group selected to review evaluation results and advise the school counseling program regarding needed improvements.
Assessment	Program Assessment	Annual summary of progress toward full implementation of the school counseling program, program strengths, and areas for improvement that is used to guide decisions within the school counseling program to achieve better results for students
	Results Reports	Review of the evaluation data from action plans and lesson plans related to specific interventions to guide improvement and demonstrate impact
	Data Over Time	Review changes in school data over time to assess trends, evaluate impact, and set goals.
	Reporting Program Results	Disseminate evaluation results in order to inform stakeholders and decision makers of the program's impact on student achievement, attendance and discipline and demonstrate accountability.

The development of the ASCA National Model was heavily influenced by public education's investment in data-based decision-making (*DBDM*; Poynton & Carey, 2006) to promote school improvement (Trevisan & Carey, 2020a). Consequently, the ASCA National Model's program evaluation approach has strengths and shortcomings that result from this alignment.

First, DBDM typically focuses on documenting impact (summative evaluation) rather than on improving processes (formative evaluation). It is best suited to situations where there is a strong association between a specific program activity and some existing element of student data. DBDM is much less applicable where the goal of the evaluation is to improve the implementation of an intervention. DBDM typically uses descriptive statistics and simple pre–post comparisons (e.g., changes in the percentages of students displaying some aspect of school behavior) rather than statistical methods to make inferences about the validity of a result. It is best suited to situations where large pre–post changes in the data can reasonably be expected and where there is little "noise" and variability in the data. Finally, DBDM relies heavily on the use of existing school data. It is not appropriate in situations where new data need to be collected in order to conduct a robust evaluation. While DBDM is intended to produce convincing summative evaluation information, this frequently is not possible because of its inherent limitations.

While program evaluation activities under the ASCA National Model reflect a significant advancement for the school counseling profession, there are several ways that they fall short of commonly accepted standards of practice in the field of evaluation. These include:

- a restriction of input from stakeholders (including stakeholders from traditionally underrepresented groups) in guiding program development and improvement resulting from an overreliance on the *Advisory Council*
- an underemphasis on formative evaluation necessary to improve implementation
- a lack of use of logic models in program planning and evaluation
- an overreliance on available school data in planning and evaluation
- the use of overly simplistic methods for quantitative data analysis
- the lack of use of powerful and informative qualitative evaluation methods
- an underemphasis on the contextual factors of culture or race
- scarce attention to social justice or initiatives toward antiracism

The ASCA National Model's simplified approach to program evaluation yields some useful information. However, it cannot be expected to yield the highest quality and most useful information. Broad stakeholder input is necessary, particularly in schools situated in culturally and racially diverse communities. Evaluation designs need to use high-quality data with reliability and trustworthiness. Good decisions are more likely to come out of sophisticated analysis of data. The use of formative evaluation increases the likelihood of robust implementation of interventions. Using outcome measures that are well aligned with the intervention in addition to existing institutional data increases the accuracy and utility of an evaluation. When compared with the JCSEE Program Evaluation Standards (Yarbrough et al., 2010), the program evaluation expectations and processes under the ASCA National Model are found to be lacking. School counseling scholars can assist by connecting school counseling program evaluation efforts to standards and best practices in the field of evaluation and by ensuring that practitioners understand the limitations of the ASCA National Model.

Quality Standards for Program Evaluation

The JCSEE used a rigorous standard-setting process to develop a set of quality standards for program evaluation. The third edition of the JSCEE Program Evaluation Standards (Yarbrough et al., 2010) provides a comprehensive exposition of the most up-to-date thinking about quality in the evaluation field. There are 30 standards organized in five categories: Utility, Feasibility, Propriety, Accuracy, and Evaluation Accountability (see Table 11.2).

Table 11.2. JCSEE Program Evaluation Standards

Attribute	Standard Names	Standard Descriptions
Utility	Evaluator Credibility	Evaluations should be conducted by qualified people who establish and maintain credibility in the evaluation context.
	Attention to Stakeholders	Evaluations should devote attention to the full range of individuals and groups invested in the program and affected by its evaluation.
	Negotiated Purposes	Evaluation purposes should be identified and continually negotiated based on the needs of stakeholders.
	Explicit Values	Evaluations should clarify and specify the individual and cultural values underpinning purposes, processes, and judgments.
	Relevant Information	Evaluation information should serve the identified and emergent needs of stakeholders.
	Meaningful Processes and Products	Evaluations should construct activities, descriptions, and judgments in ways that encourage participants to rediscover, reinterpret, or revise their understandings and behaviors.
	Timely and Appropriate Communicating and Reporting	Evaluations should attend to the continuing information needs of their multiple audiences.
	Concern for Consequences and Influence	Evaluations should promote responsible and adaptive use while guarding against unintended negative consequences and misuse.

Table 11.2. Continued

Attribute	Standard Names	Standard Descriptions
Feasibility	Project Management	Evaluations should use effective project management strategies.
	Practical Procedures	Evaluation procedures should be practical and responsive to the way the program operates.
	Contextual Viability	Evaluations should recognize, monitor, and balance the cultural and political interests and needs of individuals and groups.
	Resource Use	Evaluations should use resources effectively and efficiently.
Propriety	Responsive and Inclusive Orientation	Evaluations should be responsive to stakeholders and their communities.
	Formal Agreements	Evaluation agreements should be negotiated to make obligations explicit and take into account the needs, expectations, and cultural contexts of clients and other stakeholders.
	Human Rights and Respect	Evaluations should be designed and conducted to protect human and legal rights and maintain the dignity of participants and other stakeholders.
	Clarity and Fairness	Evaluations should be understandable and fair in addressing stakeholder needs and purposes.
	Transparency and Disclosure	Evaluations should provide complete descriptions of findings, limitations, and conclusions to all stakeholders, unless doing so would violate legal and propriety obligations.
	P6 Conflicts of Interests	Evaluations should openly and honestly identify and address real or perceived conflicts of interests that may compromise the evaluation.
	Fiscal Responsibility	Evaluations should account for all expended resources and comply with sound fiscal procedures and processes.
Accuracy	Justified Conclusions and Decisions	Evaluation conclusions and decisions should be explicitly justified in the cultures and contexts where they have consequences.
	Valid Information	Evaluation information should serve the intended purposes and support valid interpretations.
	Reliable Information	Evaluation procedures should yield sufficiently dependable and consistent information for the intended uses.
	Explicit Program and Context Descriptions	Evaluations should document programs and their contexts with appropriate detail and scope for the evaluation purposes.
	Information Management	Evaluations should employ systematic information collection, review, verification, and storage methods.

(continued)

Table 11.2. Continued

Attribute	Standard Names	Standard Descriptions
	Sound Design and Analyses	Evaluations should employ technically adequate designs and analyses that are appropriate for the evaluation purposes.
	Explicit Evaluation Reasoning	Evaluation reasoning leading from information and analyses to findings, interpretations, conclusions, and judgments should be clearly and completely documented.
	Communication and Reporting	Evaluation communications should have adequate scope and guard against misconceptions, biases, distortions, and errors.
Evaluation Accountability	Evaluation Documentation	Evaluations should fully document their negotiated purposes and implemented designs, procedures, data, and outcomes.
	Internal Metaevaluation	Evaluators should use these and other applicable standards to examine the accountability of the evaluation design, procedures employed, information collected, and outcomes.
	External Metaevaluation	Program evaluation sponsors, clients, evaluators, and other stakeholders should encourage the conduct of external metaevaluations using these and other applicable standards.

Note: From *The Program Evaluation Standards: A Guide for Evaluators and Evaluation Users* (3rd ed.), by D. B. Yarbrough, L. M. Shulha, R. K. Hopson, & F. A. Caruthers, 2010, Corwin Press. Reproduced with permission from the Joint Committee for Standards in Educational Evaluation.

We recommend consulting Yarbrough et al. (2010) and Trevisan and Carey (2020a) for a comprehensive description of the JCSEE Program Evaluation Standards and their application to school counseling program evaluation.

In evaluating a school counseling program, it is not necessary, prudent, or practical to expect the program to meet every standard. Judgments about which standards are most relevant for a given program will be required. Trevisan and Carey's (2020a) evaluation framework is specifically designed to address the JCSEE Program Evaluation Standards. In short, if this evaluation framework is followed, a high-quality evaluation of program and services can be conducted.

Ethical and Culturally Responsive Program Evaluation

Conducting an evaluation of a school counseling program requires collecting information from people, some of whom may be from "protected groups" and particularly vulnerable to abuses associated with inquiry. When gathering data from children, for example, special care must be taken to anticipate and mitigate any harm that could occur from their participation in the evaluation (see Chapter 3 for additional insight into navigating ethical issues when working with schools). In such cases, evaluators are obliged to use safe, minimal-risk procedures for obtaining information in order to protect the human rights of all participants. School districts often maintain policies and procedures for conducting research within schools. These documents typically provide very useful information for planning and conducting an ethically sound evaluation. We recommend consulting these policies and procedures when conducting a school counseling program evaluation. In this way, a measure of transparency for the evaluation itself is provided.

In addition, school counseling programs typically serve school communities composed of diverse racial, ethnic, and immigrant groups. This multicultural context provides unique challenges for evaluators of school counseling programs.

The JCSEE Program Evaluation Standards (Yarbrough et al., 2010) provide guidance for conducting ethical and culturally responsive evaluation. The propriety standards in particular, speak to the protection of human rights and the promotion of fairness in all aspects of an evaluation. In addition, the American Evaluation Association (AEA) has published a *Public Statement on Cultural Competence in Evaluation*, which provides strong expectations for evaluators in the development of their own cultural competencies with respect to evaluation. The AEA (2011) statement, for example, recommends that evaluators acknowledge the complexity of cultural identity, recognize the dynamics of power, recognize and eliminate bias in language, and employ culturally appropriate methods. We strongly recommend that school counseling scholars familiarize themselves with this statement before engaging in evaluation activities.

Relatedly, Trevisan and Carey (2020b) have reviewed and summarized the literature on culturally responsive evaluation. They made four recommendations that program evaluators should incorporate into their work. They suggest that evaluators should: (1) involve evaluation participants in the development of the program's logic model; (2) involve diverse stakeholders in the planning, implementation, and analysis of the evaluation; (3) systematically and continuously reflect on their evaluation work; and (4) expand their understanding of the cultural context in which the school counseling work is conducted.

Toward Social Justice and Antiracism in School Counseling Evaluation

At this point in time, the evaluation enterprise is doing some internal soul searching to determine precisely what socially just and antiracist evaluation practice is and to make recommendations for evaluation professionals. There is not widespread agreement on what this looks like, and the path forward is uncertain, at least one that is embraced broadly within the profession (see Neubauer & Hall, 2020). For evaluation in the context of school counseling, we think the tenets of ethical and culturally responsive evaluation previously discussed provide the building blocks for socially just and anti-racist evaluation. Coupled with the ideas put forth in this volume regarding school counseling research broadly by Dimmitt and Zyromski (accepted for publication), we think we can offer some practical recommendations for school counselors in conducting evaluations that address social justice and that work toward antiracist educational practice.

Perhaps the clearest and most straightforward recommendation is to identify groups that have been unjustly treated (e.g., African Americans, immigrants, Native populations) and purposefully include members from these groups in all aspects of the evaluation process. As the evaluation is being developed and conducted, provide them with explicit opportunities to help ensure fair representation in the evaluation. If findings warrant, this could also provide them the opportunity to voice their concerns for the equitable distribution of school and school counseling resources. In short, give these stakeholder representatives the opportunity to be advocates for their student groups and to base their advocacy in the evaluation findings.

Within the evaluation design, include data collection strategies that will help reveal unfair treatment and or racism. This would include (a) interview or focus group questions that allow individuals from key stakeholder groups to speak about their treatment, (b) sufficient sample size for group representation in the data, (c) disaggregation of data to make group differences visible, and (d) ways to understand and explain group differences, should they exist. This would include collecting data on contextual factors that disadvantage various ethnic or racial groups within the school community. From a social justice perspective, evaluation of how school counseling resources are distributed and the resultant student outcomes should be interpreted in light of the disadvantages found.

A Six-Component Framework for School Counseling Program Evaluation

Trevisan and Carey (2020a) developed a framework to guide school counseling program evaluation based on their own work as external evaluators of school counseling programs, and on their extensive experience providing professional development training in evaluation methods for school counselors and counselor educators. This framework was intentionally designed to complement the program evaluation practices of the ASCA National Model (ASCA, 2019) and to incorporate the best practices from the field of evaluation as articulated in the JCSEE Program Evaluation Standards (Yarbrough et al., 2010). A comprehensive, practical exposition of the framework can be found in Trevisan and Carey (2020a). Below is a brief version of the framework to help school counseling scholars plan and implement quality program evaluations that dovetail with ASCA National Model expectations and that meet the quality standards of the evaluation field. The six components of the evaluation framework include: stakeholder involvement; theory of action; evaluation questions; evaluation design and methods; data analysis and findings; and communication and use of evaluation results.

Component 1: Stakeholder Involvement

Stakeholders are people who have a vested interest in the program and, by implication, the evaluation. The school counseling program serves multiple stakeholders (e.g., students, parents, teachers, and school leaders). Involving these stakeholders in the evaluation is a central feature of high-quality evaluation. Involving stakeholders also allows the evaluator to address the information stakeholders need from the evaluation better. The evaluation is consequently more likely to be used, the ultimate aim of any evaluation. Reaching out to key stakeholders is thus a foundational task in this process.

Involving stakeholders means involving them in all aspects of the evaluation. Their involvement is predicated on the size of the school community, and a host of pragmatic variables or factors (e.g., stakeholder expertise, time, scope of the evaluation) influence the feasibility of including them in the evaluation process. From a social justice point of view, this means intentionally including stakeholders from underrepresented and marginalized groups. Trevisan and Carey (2020a) provide a variety of practical strategies to organize stakeholder groups and involve stakeholders in all facets of a school counseling program evaluation. We recommend consulting this document in developing strategies to include and organize representatives from various stakeholder groups.

Component 2: Theory of Action

The practice of developing a *theory of action* to guide program evaluation comes from program theory (Sharpe, 2011), an approach to program evaluation that maps the logic underlying a program and its activities and tests whether or not the desired results are being attained (Patton, 1978). Developing a theory of action helps ensure that the program evaluation results in useful information. The development of a theory of action guides both formative and summative evaluations by clearly specifying the resources that are needed for the program and identifying the relationship between the activities of the program and the expected short- and long-term benefits for stakeholders. A theory of action can be used in the evaluation of the whole program or components of the program. A *logic model* is a graphic representation of a theory of action that identifies all the important components of the program or intervention and that articulates the expected relationships among these components.

Trevisan and Carey (2020a) have presented guidance for how to develop logic models for school counseling program evaluations. They suggest including four components in logic models: inputs, activities, outputs, and outcomes. They also suggest differentiating between two types of outcomes—proximal outcomes and distal outcomes. Inputs identify the resources needed for delivery of the program or intervention. Activities are the services that are delivered, that are expected to result in learning and change, and that ultimately result in benefits for students. Activities may include both direct services (e.g., one-on-one counseling sessions) and indirect services (e.g., parent consultation). Outputs are the changes in stakeholder knowledge, attitude, and behavior that are expected to occur immediately after the activity. Outcomes are the longer-term changes that are expected to result as a consequence of participation in the activity. Proximal outcomes are the changes that are expected to occur in the weeks after participation in program activities, whereas distal outcomes are the hoped-for, longer-term stakeholder benefits associated with participation.

Figure 11.1 contains a simple logic model for *Eccomi Pronto* (Bertolani & Carey, 2019), a social and emotional learning curriculum. This logic model

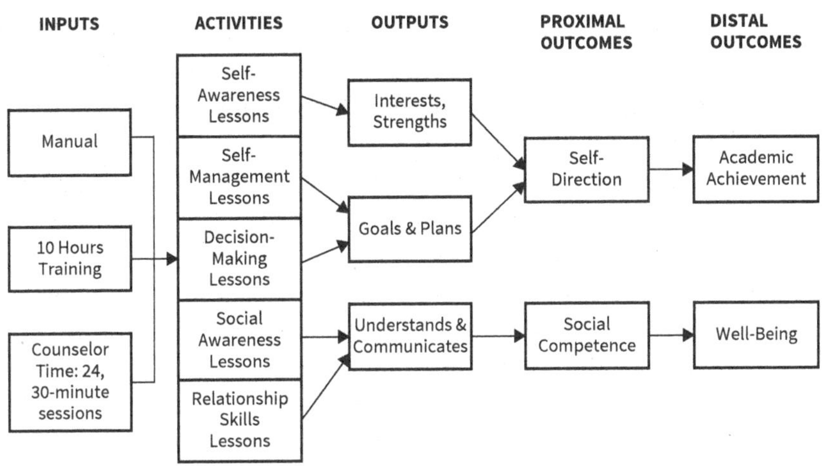

Figure 11.1. Logic Model for Eccomi Pronto

maps the relationships among: the resources required to implement the Eccomi Pronto (inputs), the components of the Eccomi Pronto curriculum (activities), the skills that students are expected to be able to perform after Eccomi Pronto training (outputs), the enhanced competencies that students are expected to show after mastering these skills (proximal outcomes), and the benefits that are expected to result from having these competencies (distal outcomes). The basic theory of action can be expressed as follows: (1) With the noted resources, school counselors will be able to fully implement the five components of the curriculum; (2) after implementation of the curriculum, students will be able to identify their own interests and strengths, construct good goals, make effective plans for themselves, understand others, and communicate effectively with others; (3) this learning will result in their development of increased self-direction and social competence; and (4) the ultimate benefits of having these competencies will be increases in students' academic achievement and well-being.

Logic models also help organize program evaluations by clearly specifying the hypothesized relationships among inputs, activities, outputs, and outcomes that can be tested in formative and summative evaluations. Formative evaluations most frequently involve testing the hypothesized relationships between inputs, activities, and outputs. Formative evaluations can determine if resources are sufficient, activities are being delivered fully and effectively, and students are learning what is intended. Information gleaned from these types of formative evaluation questions is used to improve the program and results in improved implementation and potency.

Summative evaluations most often involve testing the hypothesized relationships among activities and outcomes. Summative evaluations determine if students show the expected immediate positive changes in school-related behavior and if participants receive the intended long-term benefits of participation. Answering these summative evaluation questions guides the assessment of impact and provides evidence for the value and worth of the school counseling program activities.

Logic models can also be used to organize the evaluation of the school counseling program as a whole. Martin and Carey (2014) developed a retrospective logic model to guide the evaluation of ASCA National Model programs (see Figure 11.2) based on an analysis of the model (ASCA, 2012) and its ancillary documents. School counselors can use this logic model to guide the development of logic models for their own programs.

Martin and Carey's (2014) analysis suggests that effective ASCA National Model programs will achieve three major programmatic outcomes: (1) increased student achievement with associated reductions in achievement gaps, (2) systemic change and school improvement, and (3) increased resources for the school counseling program. Summative program evaluations should address these intended outcomes in order to assess the level of success of the program.

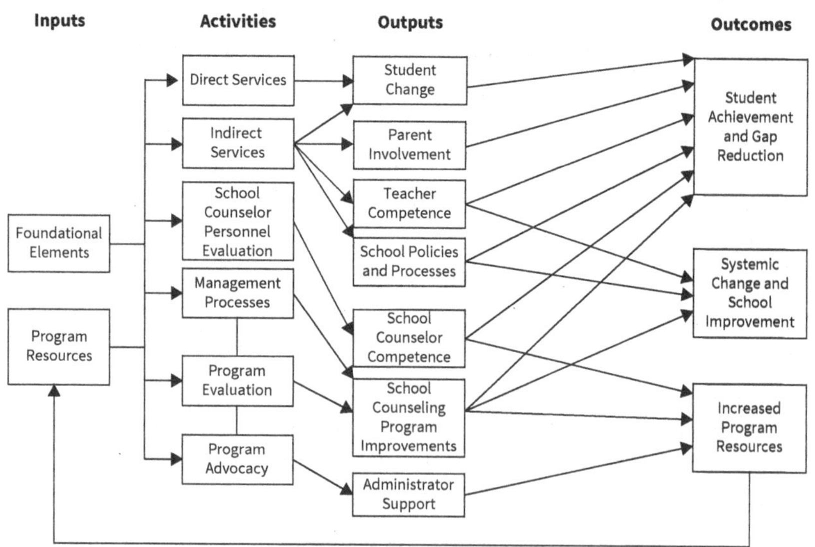

Figure 11.2. Logic Model for an ASCA National Model Program

From "Development of a Logic Model to Guide Evaluations of the ASCA National Model for School Counseling Programs," by I. Martin and J. Carey, 2014, *The Professional Counselor, 4*(5), p. 462, Tracy P. Collins (Ed.), School counselling [Special issue], https://doi.org/10.15241/im.4.5.455. Copyright 2014 by the National Board for Certified Counselors, Inc., and Affiliates. Reprinted with permission.

Martin and Carey's (2014) analysis also identified six categories of program activities: (1) direct services, (2) indirect services, (3) school counselor personnel evaluation, (4) program management processes, (5) program evaluation, and (6) program advocacy. Each activity is expected to result in outputs that in turn are related to one or more outcomes. Formative evaluations should investigate whether the activities are being performed fully and properly and whether the expected changes result from the activities. If the expected outputs do not occur, redesign of the activities is needed.

Finally, Martin and Carey (2014) indicate that full implementation of the program is dependent on foundational elements (e.g., mission statement) and on adequate resources from the school (e.g., appropriate student-to-counselor ratios and appropriate use of counselor time). Formative evaluations need to determine whether the foundational elements are in place and whether adequate levels of resources are provided to support the school counseling program.

Component 3: Evaluation Questions

Evaluation questions provide direction for the development and implementation of the evaluation. They reflect the kinds of things stakeholders are interested in knowing about the program and signal the types of data to be collected. Preskill and Jones (2009) suggest that good evaluation questions provide boundaries for the evaluation work, defining which aspects of the program are part of the evaluation and which parts are not.

Evaluation questions generally focus on either the formative or summative purposes of the evaluation. Formative evaluation questions include "What is working well?" and "What needs improvement?" Summative evaluation questions include "What is the impact of the program?" and "What are unintended consequences of the program?"

The broad spectrum of stakeholders in the school counseling program will differ on what's most important to them about an evaluation of the program. Parents want to know, for example, whether or not the program is working effectively to provide high-quality service. Teachers will want to know if there are aspects of the program that need improvement. School district administrators will likely want to know what the impact of the school counseling program is and whether or not the program is worth the cost. People from historically marginalized groups will want to know if there is a fair distribution of school and school counseling resources and services, and if not, whether students from marginalized groups are being adversely impacted as a result. Incorporating evaluation questions that are of interest to stakeholder groups that have been historically marginalized will move the evaluation toward being socially just and antiracist and result in recommendations that move the program toward more equitable practices in the service of all students.

Component 4: Evaluation Design and Methods

After the evaluation questions are identified, it is time to select the design and the data that will be collected and analyzed in order to answer the questions. There are three choices for design: quantitative, qualitative, and mixed methods (designs involving both qualitative and quantitative elements). Below we will address the fundamental considerations in selecting an evaluation design and illustrate how evaluation methods are effectively applied in a school counseling program evaluation.

Quantitative designs are most applicable when the evaluation questions concern variables that can easily be measured with existing school counselor–constructed surveys. Such questions would include: (1) Are the short-term outcomes of an intervention being achieved? (2) Are the long-term outcomes of an intervention being achieved? (3) Are there individual students or groups of students who are not benefiting from school counseling services? Quantitative designs are typically associated with summative evaluation questions where quantitative measures of outcomes are appropriate. They are also appropriate for formative evaluation questions, when quantitative measures of participation and short-term outcomes are available. These types of evaluation questions typically address whether or not the expected outcomes of the program are being achieved. They may identify places where improvement is needed but cannot inform the types of improvement that are needed.

In contrast, qualitative designs are most useful when the evaluation questions involve variables that are difficult to assess with quantitative surveys, and also when the intent of the evaluation is to gather complex, nuanced data in order guide program improvement. Appropriate questions for qualitative analyses would include: (1) Is the classroom-based curricula being delivered with high fidelity? (2) What changes can be made to ensure that the school counseling program work serves all students? (3) Does the school counseling program have any unanticipated negative consequences? Answering complex and nuanced evaluation questions like these requires the collection and analysis of data based on the perceptions, observations, judgments, and opinions of stakeholders. These evaluation questions require the use of interviews and open-ended surveys in data collection that give stakeholders the freedom to express their views and evaluations and the freedom to probe in order to understand the meaning and significance of the participants' comments. Qualitative questions are essential for the identification of needed program improvements because they focus on how the program is operating rather than on the specific outcomes that the program is producing.

Mixed methods evaluation designs are needed when answering an evaluation question requires the collection and analysis of both quantitative and qualitative data. Evaluations of the whole school counseling program always require a mixed design. For example, it is important to know both if the school counseling program activities are improving students in-school behavior (e.g., attendance or disciplinary referrals) and if stakeholders have ideas for improving the program.

A variety of evaluation designs are available for quantitative, qualitative, and mixed methods approaches. In quantitative evaluations, for example, pre-experimental, quasi-experimental, and experimental designs are possible (Campbell and Stanley, 1963), although it is rare to find a school-based evaluation situation where experimental designs are feasible. Data are typically gathered from one group of students pre- and post-intervention or from two or more groups of students, with a group that did not experience the intervention serving as a "control" or "comparison" group. Surveys, observations, and/or school data are the typical sources of data for quantitative evaluations. Typically, statistical tests (ranging from very simple t-tests to very complex multifactorial analyses of variance) are used to determine the degree of confidence placed in the inference that the observed differences between groups are real.

There are a number of qualitative designs that are useful in evaluation (Patton, 2015; Rallis & Rossman, 2017). In school counseling program evaluations, phonological designs are particularly useful (Trevisan & Carey, 2020a). These designs involve describing and explaining some aspect of a program through the collection and analysis of the beliefs, impressions, and judgments of people who have experienced it (Wertz, 2005). Phenomenological analyses involve the distillation of the meaning inherent in the complex statements of respondents. The actual data can be collected in a variety of ways (e.g., open-ended survey questions, individual interviews, group interviews, and observation). There are many approaches to qualitative analysis—each with particular advantages and limitations (Rallis & Rossman, 2017). Whatever approach is used, it is important to use an established qualitative analysis approach in order to assure the trustworthiness of findings.

Thematic content analysis (Braun & Clarke, 2006) and interpretive phenomenological analysis (Smith et al., 2009) are examples of well-established approaches.

In some evaluations, mixed methods designs may simply involve using quantitative approaches for some evaluation questions and qualitative approaches for other questions. In some instances, however, quantitative and qualitative methods can be used to address the same evaluation question in two phases. Using the explanatory sequential mixed methods design (Subedi, 2016), an evaluation question is first addressed with quantitative methods (using a larger sample and more standardized measures) in order to get a general understanding of the answer to the evaluation question and to determine if differences exist between groups of participants. Subsequently, a more focused qualitative investigation is conducted to understand the issues raised by the quantitative stage of the investigation. The integration of the quantitative and qualitative findings produces a rich answer to the evaluation question. A school counselor scholar addressing an evaluation question regarding how the school counseling program could be improved might first collect quantitative survey data from a large number of students to get a general idea of their level of satisfaction with the different elements of the program. Quantitative analyses would be used to disaggregate these data by subgroup and to identify important differences among student subgroups. Focus groups could then be used to gather qualitative program improvement data from students in these identified groups. In this example, quantitative evaluation provides a general, "broad-brush" answer to the evaluation question and indicates where clarification and further investigation is needed. The follow-up qualitative evaluation zeroes in on these issues and adds detail, nuance, and precision to the answer to the evaluation question.

Before the evaluation is actually conducted, a plan specifying the approach that will be followed for each evaluation question must be generated. It is important to determine what data are needed to answer each question and how these data will be collected and analyzed.

Component 5: Data Analysis and Findings

There are several possible sources of quantitative evaluation data, for example: school data, counselor-constructed surveys, and standardized surveys. Guidance for selecting and developing quantitative measures is widely available (Dimmitt et al., 2007). There are also several possible sources for qualitative evaluation data, including: open-ended surveys, structured individual interviews, and focus group interviews. Guidance for collecting qualitative data is readily accessible (e.g., Rallis & Rossman, 2017; Trevisan & Carey, 2020a). For both types of data, it is important to plan how the data will be analyzed before they are collected.

The ASCA National Model (ASCA, 2019) largely focuses on quantitative data and calls for very simple analyses (e.g., comparing group differences by observation). Because these simple analyses lack power, they may result in inaccurate information. Use of more powerful statistical tests in quantitative evaluation improves the accuracy of the findings and results in better decisions. There are, however, many statistical procedures that are available for use. School counseling scholars can consult as needed with colleagues who are knowledgeable about complex statistical processes to determine which procedure would be advantageous in specific evaluation situations.

The ASCA National Model (ASCA, 2019) does not include the use of qualitative program evaluation approaches. Though understandable, the failure to use qualitative evaluation will result in a lack of information that is most needed to inform program improvement. There are a number of accepted procedures for qualitative analysis that ensure data are analyzed in a systematic fashion and that consequently help ensure that inferences based on the analyses are trustworthy (Patton, 2015; Rallis & Rossman, 2017). Thematic content analysis (Braun & Clarke, 2006) and interpretative phenomenological analysis (Smith et al., 2009) complement each other and are applicable across a wide range of evaluation contexts. School counseling scholars should work to maximize the trustworthiness of findings by explicitly identifying their own beliefs and biases at the beginning of the evaluation, using well-accepted methods for analyzing data, triangulating findings to verify their consistency across different groups and methods, engaging in periodic debriefing with peers during the evaluation, and asking participants and stakeholders to review their analyses and interpretations.

Component 6: Communication and Use of Evaluation Results

The desired outcome of all evaluation is that it be used to make important decisions about the school counseling program. Effective communication about the evaluation (e.g., the evaluation plan, progress of the evaluation, or results) is essential for evaluation use. Stakeholders must know about the evaluation and have an opportunity to react to and be influenced by the evaluation. We recommend that a plan for communication be developed and adjusted as needed. This could include communication through meetings, reports, PowerPoint presentations, and web-based tools.

Evaluation use is more than the development of a final report that stakeholders could use. Professional evaluators have developed a strong and differentiated sense of evaluation use. Mayne (2014) offers a straightforward set of evaluation uses that can be applied to any organization. Three types of use are central to evaluation work. *Instrumental use* refers to acting on the recommendations of an evaluation. *Conceptual use* is the act of being influenced by the evaluation in some way, either immediately or in the future. A school leader coming away from the evaluation with a more refined sense of the school counseling program and its contributions to the school is an example of conceptual use. *Process use* refers to the impact that engaging in the evaluation has for school counselors and stakeholders. Engaging in and discussing the findings of the evaluation creates a deeper understanding of the work and builds capacity to improve it. Engaging in and with the evaluation serves as a means of professional development.

Two Illustrative Program Evaluation Scenarios

The following two scenarios serve as a summary of Trevisan and Carey's six-component evaluation framework and illustrate how it can be used to conduct a formative evaluation of a school counseling classroom curriculum and a summative evaluation of a school counseling program. These scenarios also illustrate how the framework complements the existing program evaluation-related components (see Table 11.1) of the ASCA National Model (ASCA, 2019). As the school counselors partner with local SCEs in each scenario, relevant steps for building positive relationships with schools (see Chapter 2) and navigating the institutional review board (IRB) process (see Chapter 3) need to be followed. For the sake of brevity, we do not detail the steps in each of these processes in the scenarios below but focus solely on the program evaluation components.

Formative Evaluation of a Classroom Curriculum

Tina was one of three school counselors in an urban middle school. She reached out to a local SCE, Dr. Smith, to gauge their interest in conducting a program evaluation of her school counseling program. Tina had primary responsibility for planning, implementing, and evaluating the counseling program's classroom-based curricula. At the time of this scenario, the counselors were beginning to implement an ASCA (2019) program. Dr. Smith worked with Tina to ensure that the school counselors conducted an *annual data review* and developed a *school data summary*. They also had a series of meetings with school administration and outlined a set of *annual student outcome goals* that indicated that the program would contribute to student achievement by helping enhance students' academic motivation, self-direction, and engagement.

Component 1: Stakeholder Involvement

To guide the selection of a classroom curriculum to support this work, Tina discussed the school data summary and annual student outcome goals with the programs' advisory council and also discussed summaries of five potential curricula that included: content, supporting research, implementation requirements, expected benefits, and costs in time and money. The discussion narrowed the field to two feasible curricula. Tina, with Dr. Smith as a consultant, then engaged with groups of teachers and parents to review the two curricula. These discussions identified Eccomi Pronto (Bertolani & Carey, 2019) as the most feasible option.

Component 2: Theory of Action

Dr. Smith and Tina developed a theory of action and logic model (see Figure 11.1) for Eccomi Pronto and shared these with the advisory council, teachers, parents, and school administration.

Component 3: Evaluation Questions

Since this was the first time Eccomi Pronto would be implemented in her school, Dr. Smith encouraged Tina to implement a formative evaluation to make sure that a robust implementation was occurring. They developed three evaluation questions that included:

- Q1: Are all five Eccomi Pronto components being fully implemented?
- Q2: Are the expected, immediate outputs of Eccomi Pronto evident? In other words, are students better able to: describe their interests and strengths, develop smart goals and plans to achieve these goals, and understand others and communicate effectively with them?
- Q3: How can the implementation be improved?

Tina and Dr. Smith included the logic model and evaluation questions in an action plan, and they shared it with the advisory council, teachers, parents, and school leaders.

Component 4: Evaluation Design and Methods

Based on the nature of the evaluation questions and a review of available quantitative measures to address these questions, Dr. Smith decided that a *mixed evaluation design* was needed. To answer Question 1, a simple checklist of content and activities was created to complete after each Eccomi Pronto session to determine the extent to which each of the five components of the curriculum was actually delivered. To answer Question 2, pre–posttest surveys were developed and keyed to each of the three outputs of Eccomi Pronto, and classroom teachers were interviewed about changes they observed in students related to Eccomi Pronto participation. To answer Question 3, the evaluation results for Questions 1 and 2 were presented to a focus group composed of teachers and school leaders, and they were asked to reflect on and identify needed improvements. Methods for data analysis related to these three questions were chosen, and a summary of the evaluation design and methods was included in the Eccomi Pronto action plan.

Component 5: Data Analysis and Findings

Implementation logs were used to determine the extent to which Eccomi Pronto was implemented with fidelity. A dependent t-test was used to analyze students' pre–post changes on the three surveys reflecting Eccomi Pronto outputs. In addition, thematic content analysis (Braun & Clarke, 2006) was used to identify themes in the detailed notes taken during the teacher interviews and the focus group. Findings indicated that full implementation with fidelity was achieved for three of the five components of Eccomi Pronto. The components addressing social awareness and relationship skills were not fully delivered. In these lessons, activities that involved role play and practice were often omitted due to time constraints. Relatedly, students showed significant gains in two of the three output clusters. They failed to show significant pre–posttest gains related to understanding others and communicating effectively with them. Interviews likewise indicated that teachers noticed that students were more engaged in the classroom, more goal oriented, and more able to talk about strengths and areas for improvement. Teachers did not notice changes in students' social behavior. The focus group suggested that Eccomi Pronto be continued with modifications. They suggested that Tina consider either discontinuing the lessons on social awareness and relationship skills or continuing these lessons with more time devoted to them. After consultation with Dr. Young, Tina opted to discontinue these lessons and use another empirically supported curriculum to teach social competencies and planned to formatively evaluate this curriculum the next year. Finally, Dr. Smith and Tina summarized these results, recommendations, and decisions in an Eccomi Pronto results report.

Component 6: Communication and Use of Evaluation Results

The Eccomi Pronto results report was shared with school and district administrators and the program's advisory board. The counselors, with Dr. Smith in the background, presented and discussed the report during meetings with both groups. A summary of the report was created, distributed to all teachers, and posted on the program's section of the school website. In addition, a synopsis of the evaluation in PowerPoint format was presented and discussed at a PTA meeting as part of the school counseling program's annual report. These efforts helped ensure widespread understanding of the results of the evaluation and support for implementing its recommendations.

Summative Evaluation of a School Counseling Program

The counselors at Verona High School were in the process of implementing a comprehensive developmental program following the ASCA National Model (ASCA, 2019). At the time of this scenario, they were beginning their 3rd year of implementation and wanted to complete their first program assessment in the second half of that year in order to document their successes and find ways to improve. They reached out to a Verona University faculty member, Dr. Young, for consultation through the process.

Component 1: Stakeholder Involvement

The counselors met with their advisory council and school leaders to describe the purposes of the program assessment, to gather information to help guide the formulation of the evaluation questions, to identify resources needed for the assessment, and to obtain commitment to provide these resources. The advisory council indicated an interest in learning whether students, teachers, and parents were satisfied with the program's services. School leaders wanted to learn if the program was contributing to students' achievement, discipline, and college placement. The primary resource needed was determined to be permission to reserve sufficient counselor time for program assessment activities.

Component 2: Theory of Action

Dr. Young suggested the Verona High School counselors use Martin and Carey's (2014) Logic Model for ASCA National Programs to plan their evaluation (see Figure 11.2). They discussed this logic model and its associated theory of action with the advisory council and with school leaders and found that it could accommodate the interests and concerns of both groups.

Component 3: Evaluation Questions

Dr. Young and the counselors decided that a summative evaluation was required but that the data and analyses should also pinpoint needed improvements in the program. Based on the logic model and input from the advisory council and school leaders, they developed a set of six evaluation questions. These included:

- Q1: To what extent has the program been successful in implementing the essential components of the ASCA National Model?
- Q2: Are stakeholders (students, parents, teachers, and administrators) satisfied with access, quality, and scope of program services?
- Q3: Has the program been successful in promoting academic achievement and college placement for all students?
- Q4: Has the program been successful in contributing to the school's ability to serve all students?
- Q5: Have the program's successes led to more resources being devoted to support the program's work?
- Q6: Does the program have any unintended negative outcomes for stakeholders?

The logic model and the evaluation questions were included in a program evaluation plan and shared with the advisory council, teachers, parents, and school leaders for input and suggestions.

Component 4: Evaluation Design and Methods

Given the complexity and comprehensiveness of the evaluation, a mixed evaluation design was chosen for the evaluation. To address Question 1, the three yearly school counseling program assessments were reviewed. To answer Question 2, satisfaction survey data were collected from all teachers and administrators and from representative samples of students and parents. Using an explanatory sequential mixed methods design, they first analyzed the disaggregated data and then conducted follow-up focus groups with students and parents selected on the basis of the quantitative survey responses. To address Question 3, they reviewed and summarized the results reports from past years, and action plans related to student achievement and college placement, and they analyzed changes over the last 3 years in the data elements that were targeted in their annual data reviews and school data summaries. To answer Question 4, they conducted focus groups with teachers and interviews with three school leaders regarding contributions of the school counseling program to the school's systemic improvement and ability to educate all students to high standards. To address Question 5, they reviewed the program's budget over the past 3 years and identified the outcomes of their requests for additional support. To answer Question 6, they summarized the findings of Questions 1–4; presented these summaries to focus groups of students, parents, and teachers; and used the groups to explore possible unexpected negative consequences for key stakeholders.

Component 5: Data Analysis and Findings

Inspection of the annual school counseling program assessments determined that all the elements of an ASCA National Model were now in place; however, the current year was the 1st year that all elements were actually implemented. Summaries of the needs assessment items revealed that students, teachers, and administrators were generally very satisfied with program services. While parents were satisfied with most services, services related to career development and college placement were not rated as highly as others. T-test analysis indicated that Hispanic parents were significantly less satisfied than other groups. Thematic content analysis of the follow-up focus groups suggested that this was because Hispanic parents were less informed than other parents about what services were actually being delivered. In the focus group, Hispanic parents suggested that better information distribution was necessary. Quantitative chi-squared and t-test analyses of changes in key school data elements over the past 3 years indicated that significant positive changes were noted for the elements that the program had targeted and addressed. These changes included: reductions in disciplinary referrals, increases in the number of students taking the SAT, and increases in the number of students applying to college. These changes were particularly noteworthy in the data from students from traditionally underserved groups. Thematic content analysis of teacher focus groups and administrator interviews indicated that while both groups valued the school counseling program, neither could identify specific instances where the program had a major role in promoting systemic change and school improvement. An administrator suggested that one of the counselors should join the school leadership council. A focus group suggested that a counselor should attend each academic department's meetings in order to provide input in curricular and instructional decisions. The budgetary analysis indicated that the program's resources had not changed over the past 3 years and that the program's improvements had largely been supported by a redistribution of existing resources rather than by an infusion of new ones. Finally, thematic content analysis of focus groups suggested that only one possible unanticipated negative consequence was noted. The teacher group indicated that due to programmatic changes, less opportunity was now available for them to drop in to consult with counselors regarding problematic student situations. They recommended that the program establish regular weekly times committed to teacher consultation.

Component 6: Communication and Use of Evaluation Results

A synopsis of the program assessment findings was created, and the associated recommendations for improvement were shared with school and district administrators and with the program's advisory council. Dr. Young and the counselors presented and discussed the assessment in meetings with both groups. A summary of the findings and recommendations was distributed to all teachers and posted on the program's section of the school website. Finally, a synopsis of the assessment in PowerPoint format was presented at a PTA meeting as part of the program's annual report and at a meeting of the school board. These activities led to an understanding of the results of the evaluation and support for implementing its recommendations.

Conclusion

Both of these case examples illustrate how Trevisan and Carey's (2020a) framework can be used to develop evaluations for school counseling programs that yield quality information to improve practice and demonstrate impact. The case studies provide concrete examples of both the inherent complexities of conducting a comprehensive assessment that includes both formative and summative evaluation strategies, while including stakeholders in that process. The potential impact on program improvement and the success of our students makes navigating these complexities worthwhile.

References

American Evaluation Association. (2011). *Public statement on cultural competence in evaluation*. Retrieved from www.eval.org

American School Counselor Association. (2012). *The ASCA National Model: A framework for school counseling programs* (3rd ed.).

American School Counselor Association. (2019). *The ASCA National Model: A framework for school counseling programs* (4th ed.).

Astramovich, J., Coker, K., & Hoskins, W. J. (2005). Training school counselors in program evaluation. *Professional School Counseling, 9*(1), 49–54.

Bertolani, J., & Carey, J. C. (2019). Eccomi Pronto: Developing curricula to promote character strength development in primary school students through story telling. In T. Sam George, A. Kumar, N. T. Sudhesh, & R. Sreejari (Eds.), *Handbook on Character Strength Development: Theory, Research and Implications for Practice* (pp. 31–43). Sage.

Braun, V., & Clarke, V. (2006). Using thematic analysis in psychology. *Qualitative Research in Psychology, 3*, 77–101.

Campbell, D. T., & Stanley, J. (1963). *Experimental and quasi-experimental designs for research.* Rand-McNally.

Carey, J., Martin, I., Trevisan, M., & Harrington, K. (2018). Competence in program evaluation and research assessed by state school counselor licensure examinations. *Professional School Counseling, 22*(1), 1–11, doi:10.1177/2156759X18793839

Dimmitt, C., Carey, J., & Hatch, T. (2007). *Evidence- based school counseling: Making a difference with data-driven practices.* Corwin Press.

Dimmitt, C., & Zyromski, B. (2023). Chapter 1: State of the field. In C. Dimmitt & B. Zyromski (Eds.), *School Counseling Research: Advancing the Professional Evidence Base.* Oxford University Press.

Gysbers, N. C. (2004). Comprehensive guidance and counseling programs: The evolution of accountability. *Professional School Counseling, 8*, 1–14.

Gysbers, N., & Henderson, P. (1988). *Developing and managing your school guidance program.* American Association for Counseling and Development.

Johnson, S. K., & Johnson, C. D. (1991). The new guidance: A systems approach to pupil personnel programs. *California Association of Counseling and Development, 11*, 5–14.

Martin, I., & Carey, J. (2012). Evaluation capacity within state-level school counseling programs: A cross-case analysis. *Professional School Counseling, 15*(3), 132–143.

Martin, I., & Carey, J. (2014). Development of a logic model to guide evaluations of the ASCA National Model for school counseling programs. *The Professional Counselor, 4*(5), 455–466. https://doi.org/10.15241/im.4.5.455

Mayne, J. (2014). Issues in enhancing evaluation use. In M. L. Loud & J. Mayne (Eds.), *Enhancing evaluation use: Insights from internal evaluation units* (pp. 1–14). Sage.

Myrick, R. D. (1987). *Developmental guidance and counseling: A practical approach.* Educational Medial Corporation.

Neubauer, L. C., & Hall, M. (2020). Is inciting social change something evaluators can do? Should do? In L. C. Neubauer, D. McBride, A. D. Guajardo, W. D. Casillas, & M. E. Hall (Eds.), *Examining issues facing communities of color today: The role of evaluation to incite change. New Directions for Evaluation, 166*, 129–135.

Patton, M. Q. (1978). *Utilization-focused evaluation.* Sage.

Patton, M. Q. (2015). *Qualitative research and evaluation methods* (4th ed.). Sage.

Poynton, T. A., & Carey, J. C. (2006). An integrative model of data-based decision making for school counseling. *Professional School Counseling, 10*, 121–130.

Preskill, H., & Jones, N. (2009). *A practical guide for engaging stakeholders in developing evaluation questions.* Robert Wood Johnson Foundation Evaluation Series. https://www.rwjf.org/en/library/research/2009/12/a-practical-guide-for-engaging-stakeholders-in-developing-evalua.html

Rallis, S. F., & Rossman, G. B. (2017). *An introduction to qualitative research* (4th ed.). Sage.

Sharpe, G. (2011). A review of program theory and theory-based evaluations. *American International Journal of Contemporary Research, 1*, 72–75.

Sink, C. A. (2009). School counselors as accountability leaders: Another call for action. *Professional School Counseling, 13*, 68–74.

Sink, C. A., & Lemich, G. (2018). Program evaluation in doctoral-level counselor education preparation: Concerns and recommendations. American Journal of Evaluation, 39(4), 496–510. doi:10.1177/1098214018765693

Smith, J. A., Flowers, P., & Larkin, M. (2009). *Interpretative phenomenological analysis: Theory, method and research.* Sage.

Subedi, D. (2016). Explanatory sequential mixed method design as the third research community of knowledge claim. *American Journal of Educational Research, 4*, 570–577.

Trevisan, M. S. (2000). The status of program evaluation expectations in state school counselor certification requirements. *American Journal of Evaluation, 21*, 81–94.

Trevisan, M. S., & Carey, J. C. (2020a). *Program evaluation in school counseling: Improving comprehensive and developmental programs.* Routledge, Taylor & Francis Group.

Trevisan, M. S., & Carey, J. C. (2020b). Evaluating intercultural programs and interventions. In A. Portera, R. Moodley, and M. Milani (Eds.), *Intercultural mediation counseling and psychotherapy in Europe* (pp. 188–210). Cambridge Scholars Publishing.

Trevisan, M. S., Carey, J. C., Martin, I., & Sundararajan, N. K. (2020). US school counselor state licensure requirements for program evaluation. *Journal of School-Based Counseling Policy and Evaluation, 2*(2), 141–152.

Trevisan, M. S., & Hubert, M. (2001). Implementing comprehensive guidance program evaluation support: Lessons learned. *Professional School Counseling, 4*(3), 225–228.

Trevisan, M. S., & Walser, T. M. (2015). *Evaluability assessment: Improving evaluation quality and use.* Sage.

Wertz, F. J. (2005). Phenomenological research methods for counseling psychology. *Journal of Counseling Psychology, 52*, 167–177.

Yarbrough, D. B., Shulha, L. M., Hopson, R. K., & Caruthers, F. A. (2010). *The program evaluation standards: A guide for evaluators and evaluation users* (3rd ed.). Corwin Press.

Appendix A

Counselor Educators as Professional Evaluators

Given the importance of evaluation in school counseling, the need for expert external evaluators to support high-quality evaluations of school counseling programs, the need for quality pre-service training and in-service professional development for school counseling practitioners, the need to train doctor-level evaluation experts in school counseling evaluation, and the need to advance the theory and practice of the evaluation of school counseling programs, prospective school counselor educators should carefully consider how they want to contribute to program evaluation in school counseling and how they can best prepare themselves to make these contributions. The best available evidence suggests that inadequate training in-program evaluation may be the norm at present in doctoral counselor education programs. Sink and Lemich (2018) analyzed the curricula of 81 accredited doctoral programs and found that only 25% of the program offered a moderate level of training while 50% of the programs failed to require or offer specific training in program evaluation. Sink and Lemich (2018) also developed a detailed Program Evaluation Competence Matrix that lists specific doctoral competencies related to different functional evaluation tasks of counselor educators (e.g., "Advance program evaluation model development in school counseling," "Serve as external evaluators of school counsel programs," and "Make curricular decisions regarding program evaluation content"). While this matrix was originally intended as a curriculum review and planning tool for doctoral-level training programs, it can also be very useful for prospective counselor educators as they consider their intended level of involvement with program evaluation and the training they will need. Consistent with Sink and Lemich (2018) we present below some suggestions to help school counselor educators make these decisions related to four levels of involvement with program evaluation.

Participate in Curricular Decisions Regarding Program Evaluation

All school counselor educators need to be able to participate in curricular decisions regarding program evaluation. Current research suggests that both national accreditation standards and state licensure requirements provide inadequate guidance for these decisions at least partially because they confound research competence and program evaluation competence (Carey et al., 2018; Trevisan, 2000; Trevisan et al., 2020). Furthermore, existing approaches to program evaluation in school counseling (e.g., the ASCA National Model) do not reflect best practices (Trevisan & Carey, 2020a). Counselor educators need to make wise decisions based on both an understanding of program evaluation needs in school counseling and best practices in program evaluation. We believe that all school counselor educators need coursework in both the organization and leadership of school counseling programs and in the fundamentals of program evaluation.

Teach Master's Level School Counselors How to Evaluate the School Counseling Program

Many school counselor educators will be involved in teaching master's level school counselors (in preservice or professional development contexts) how to evaluate school counseling programs. This teaching will involve both didactic instruction and the supervision practica involving program evaluation. Since current models for school counseling programs (e.g., the ASCA National Model) do not reflect best practices in program evaluation (Trevisan & Carey, 2020a), school counselor educators will need to supplement model-based training. A high level of practical program evaluation expertise is needed. We believe that school counselor educators need coursework in quantitative and qualitative program evaluation methods and supervised experience conducting school counseling program evaluation in order to be adequately prepared to teach school counseling practitioners how to conduct program evaluations. Grounding in a school counseling program evaluation model based on best practices such as the one presented in this chapter is also essential.

Collaborating With Practitioners on School Counseling Program Evaluations

Some school counselor educators will want to collaborate with practicing school counselors to conduct program evaluations of school counseling programs as part of their service work. Such collaborations may reflect a wide range of types of involvement—ranging, for example, between consulting with school counselors on program evaluation methods and techniques and leading a complex district-wide evaluation of school counseling programs. To function effectively as a program evaluation collaborator, we believe that school counselor educators will need to develop a deeper grounding in modern program evaluation best practices through participation in professional development experiences like those offered by the AEA. Additional practical program evaluation experience including self-reflection, peer consultation, and supervision is also essential.

Contributing to the Knowledge Base of Theory and Practice in School Counseling Program Evaluation

As Trevisan and Carey (2020a) have noted, the discipline of professional evaluation is evolving rapidly due to scholarship on evaluation theory and methods. Scholarship is needed to promote the development of evaluation theory and methods in the context of school counseling. Here, school counselor educators can make important contributions. To be most impactful, these school counselor educators, we believe, will need to be immersed in the discourse of both the profession of school counseling and the discipline of program evaluation and will need to be dedicated to enhancing theory and practice in both areas. They will need to see themselves as both counselor educators and evaluators and will need to participate actively in professional associations related to both areas (e.g., the ASCA and the AEA) and will need to publish their scholarship in journals in both areas. In addition to advanced training and experience in program evaluation, this level of involvement will require the adoption of a more complex identity that encompasses both professions. This level of dedication is necessary for the articulation of the two professions and for the development of more effective school counseling program evaluation models and practices that address the unique evaluation demands of school counseling integrated with best practices in program evaluation.

Summary

Prospective school counselor educators need to consider their level of involvement in program evaluation and seek appropriate training and experiences to prepare themselves to make the type of contributions that are necessary to promote the use of the best evaluation practices in school counseling.

12

Ensuring Treatment Fidelity and Clean Data Collection

Melissa Mariani and Ellen Chance

Ensuring Treatment Fidelity and Clean Data Collection

Implementation fidelity is one of the most critical considerations in any type of sound research; however, it is also a part that is often overlooked. School counseling practitioners, doctoral students, and counselor educators alike are encouraged to put adequate time and consideration into all the various aspects of treatment fidelity, as many times results can be drastically impacted by (how) you do something (*the manner in which you deliver the intervention*) even more so than (what) you do (*the selected intervention itself*). The dearth of highly controlled research studies in the field of school counseling may be one reason why implementation fidelity is often under-considered, or an afterthought (Griffith et al., 2019). Fidelity can be significantly impacted by the environment in which an intervention occurs. Schools can be difficult contexts to control, as practitioner, teacher, administrator, school, parent, student, community, and cultural factors all impact fidelity. Fidelity considerations within school environments are often challenging for the researcher (see Chapters 2 and 5 for additional implications). Partnering with school counseling practitioners, who can serve as facilitators in the implementation process, is a wise choice.

This chapter will highlight implementation fidelity as a critical aspect in any salient action research, outcome research, experimental study, or program evaluation process. We will begin by discussing various components of treatment fidelity, particularly those that should be considered prior to the design stage when you are outlining your study's methodology. We will then move to presenting tips to assist you with organization and fidelity monitoring. The chapter contains reflection questions and ends with a case study scenario

Melissa Mariani and Ellen Chance, *Ensuring Treatment Fidelity and Clean Data Collection* In: *School Counseling Research*. Edited by: Brett Zyromski and Carey Dimmitt, Oxford University Press. © Oxford University Press 2023.
DOI: 10.1093/oso/9780197650134.003.0012

where you can apply your new knowledge. The following are specific goals of this chapter:

1. *To establish implementation fidelity considerations as the cornerstone of sound research practice*
2. *To illustrate aspects of treatment fidelity at various stages of the research process (from literature review, dissertation study, pilot study, to rigorous outcome study) and provide checklists to assist researchers in this process*
3. *To present culturally responsive considerations regarding implementation fidelity from the system (school) and stakeholder perspectives and offer suggestions for addressing these issues*
4. *To offer a case study for readers to apply the concepts, considerations, and checklists provided in order to increase their understanding of treatment fidelity practices*

Benefits of Sound Fidelity Practices

Despite the repeated call from leaders, our field continues to lack outcome research, namely, high-quality studies with strong designs that link school counselor interventions to beneficial results for participating stakeholders (Brigman, 2006; Carey & Dimmitt, 2006; Dimmitt et al., 2005, 2007; Villares & Dimmitt, 2017). In a recent content analysis, Griffith and colleagues (2019) examined the state of school counseling intervention research published in American Counseling Association (ACA)– and American School Counselor Association (ASCA)–affiliated journals over a 10-year time span (2006–2016). They reported that only a small percentage of the 6,656 studies reviewed, less than 1%, even met the criteria for inclusion as intervention research. Specifically related to implementation fidelity, the authors reported that of the studies included, 57% used a standardized curriculum or manual to aid in implementation of the intervention, yet only 40% provided training for the intervention facilitators prior to implementation, and only 21% of studies used both (Griffith et al., 2019). This is concerning as each of these characteristics contributes to increased confidence that the intervention was delivered as intended and the results reported are reliable and valid. Similarly, other researchers suggest that lack of attention to implementation fidelity might result in an approach or program being less effective or efficient (Noell et al., 2002; Wilder et al., 2006). Further, Carroll and colleagues (2007) offer that treatment integrity can greatly impact a study's credibility and be a major contributor to variance in findings. Some even contend that "Diminished fidelity may be why interventions that work well in highly controlled trials may fail to yield the same outcomes when applied in real life contexts" (Breitenstein et al., 2010, p. 164). The case for fidelity becomes even more complicated when one takes into account cultural differences. Castro et al. (2010) referred to a "dynamic tension" that emerges when existing evidence-based interventions (EBIs) are adapted, taking a top-down approach that favors implementation fidelity versus a bottom-up approach that is more case specific and sensitive to an individual's unique needs (p. 2). Both the demand for EBIs and ever-growing diversification in the American population are contributing to the need for culturally adapted approaches (LaRoche & Christopher, 2008; Lau, 2006). "Unfortunately, the infusion of cultural factors into EBIs and tests of their efficacy with subcultural groups have not kept pace with these diversification trends" (Castro et al., p. 2). Racial/ethnic minority groups have rarely been included in samples used for validating the efficacy of EBIs (LaRoche & Christopher, 2008), and this limitation has been slow to change over the past decade. Thus, it is critical that researchers and practitioners understand the impact culture has on all stages of program intervention and evaluation, as well as the research process.

The benefits of employing interventions that have been proven effective in prior, robust outcome studies, as well as tending to implementation fidelity in the interventions we select for our own investigation, cannot be overstated. Furthermore, examining EBIs from a multicultural perspective is vital. Researchers and practitioners must consider how the cultural characteristics of the context, students, school, and community may influence the appropriateness and effectiveness of the EBI. Recall that the purpose of any sound research is to make a clear connection between what was done or delivered to what the outcomes were for participating stakeholders. We want to increase our confidence in the findings by tending to factors that can be controlled or managed, though often this can be quite difficult. If extraneous variables can impact findings in a research lab, how many more factors can be at play in a school setting? Better preparation, including the use of and adherence to manualized interventions (where available), proper training for implementers, tracking activities, and documenting any hiccups, can reduce confusion, stress, and anxiety about doing things "just right" for implementers. Organization and proper planning can also alleviate worry and reduce the time spent for the researcher. Finally, a better product (delivery of the intervention/treatment) increases the likelihood that targeted stakeholders will benefit. Durlak and DuPre (2008) indicated that interventions that follow strict treatment integrity practices yield higher effect sizes, 2–3 times higher, than those that do not. Figure 12.1 denotes the factors associated with high

---

Practice or Program Characteristics

- Addresses students' specific needs and is culturally responsive
- Has been shown to be effective with culturally diverse student populations
- Requires few resources
- Accompanied by a clear and comprehensive instructional manual

Organizational Characteristics

- Adequate funding
- Strong leadership
- Administrative support
- Clear roles and responsibilities
- Shared decision-making

Counselor/Teacher Characteristics

- Perceived need for the practice or program
- Acceptance and belief in the practice or program
- High motivation
- Having or acquiring necessary skills to implement the practice or program

Training

- High-quality professional development
- Ongoing support
- Available technical assistance

Figure 12.1. Factors Associated With High Implementation Fidelity

Adapted from *Promoting Fidelity of Implementation*, by IRIS Center, Peabody College, Vanderbilt University, 2020, https://iris.peabody.vanderbilt.edu/module/fid/cresource/q2/p04/#content

implementation fidelity, as outlined by the IRIS Center at Peabody College, Vanderbilt University (IRIS Center, 2022).

Implementation Fidelity Components

Breitenstein and colleagues (2010) define implementation fidelity as "the degree to which an intervention is delivered as intended and is critical to successful translation of evidence-based interventions into practice" (p. 164). Other common terms used to describe implementation fidelity include *fidelity of implementation, treatment fidelity, treatment integrity, procedural fidelity, intervention integrity, procedural reliability,* and *procedural adherence* (Breitenstein et al., 2010; IRIS Center, 2022). According to Mihalic (2004), implementation fidelity is a necessary component in the successful translation of evidence-based interventions into practice. Think of implementation

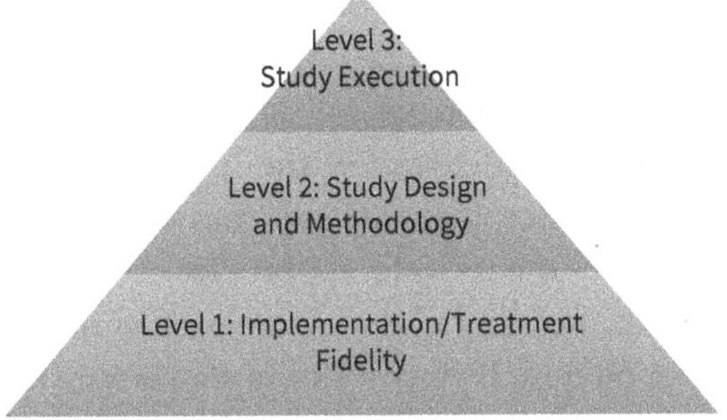

Figure 12.2. Levels of Consideration for a Sound Research Study

fidelity as the foundation or basis for any good study or evaluation practice; it's where all sound investigation should start. As depicted in Figure 12.2, we view implementation fidelity as a critical consideration in both research design and execution.

What Scholars Need to Know About Fidelity of Implementation

Components of Fidelity

The literature regarding fidelity of implementation refers to six components, all of which can impact program integrity and reliability of the findings: (a) adherence, (b) duration, (c) quality of delivery, (d) participant responsiveness, (e) program differentiation, and (f) adaptation (Carroll et al., 2007; Castro & Yasui, 2017; Mowbray et al., 2003). The first aspect, **adherence**, describes the degree to which the implementer conformed to the instructional procedures of the practice or program. Adherence speaks primarily to the delivery of the intervention as it was intended or designed. Following the script and implementing the program among groups of the correct size, age, grade all speak to adherence. The use of manualized interventions makes the adherence process easier, though there's still room for error depending upon how the information is interpreted, and can be influenced by cultural factors. Proper training practices can help alleviate this, removing the likelihood of individual interpretations of the content.

The next component, **duration**, concerns the number, length, or frequency of sessions or lessons, again adhering to these as laid out in the protocol. Modifications to timing, for example, delivering lessons biweekly versus weekly or cutting out content, such as amending a 45-minute session to fit a 30-minute time frame, can have a great impact on outcomes.

Quality of delivery is another critical aspect in maintaining fidelity and describes the skillfulness in delivery of the intervention. This component encompasses both the interpersonal and communication skills used by the implementer to relay the techniques, processes, or methods prescribed in the program. Again, training plays a large part in impacting "how well" the intervention was offered. Proper training also assists in boosting implementer confidence and increasing buy-in, critical aspects of implementer competence.

Participant responsiveness has to do with participants' engagement in and receptivity to the intervention; it is a determinant of how engaged and involved the participants are with the activities and content presented.

Program differentiation describes whether critical features that distinguish the program from the comparison condition are present or absent during implementation. For instance, a key skill presented, fostered, and monitored during delivery of the Student Success Skills small-group program (Brigman et al., 2016) concerns weekly goal setting and reporting on health and wellness as well as academics. Students are taught how to write a specific goal and action plan, share this verbally with a partner, as well as with the larger group, and then work on that goal over the course of the week, returning back to group the following week to report on how that went. If students were successful, they may choose to continue with that area, or reassess, selecting and setting a new goal for the coming week. This skill is intentionally and deliberately taught to those receiving the program, which would distinguish them from others who are not included (comparison/control group).

Lastly, **adaptations**, or the modifications of interventions to meet the specific and unique needs or preferences of the participant(s), can impact implementation fidelity and intervention effectiveness. Carefully considered, and strategic, adaptations that still adhere to the intervention's core goals, have the potential to address implementation problems, increase engagement among participants, and increase the cultural appropriateness of an intervention (Barrera et al., 2017; Castro & Yasui, 2017). Cultural adaptations can be made to address the unique and specific needs of the participant population better and should consider factors such as ethnicity, race, spoken language, cultural values, and risk/protective factors (Barrera et al., 2017). Ultimately, culturally adapting interventions can potentially increase intervention effectiveness and promote high-quality implementation.

Table 12.1. Suggested Checklist for Measuring Fidelity of Implementation

Consideration	Yes/No
An independent external evaluator was used to measure fidelity of implementation periodically throughout the study.	
Fidelity was measured separately for every intervention component.	
Evaluators considered adherence to the treatment/intervention protocol.	
Evaluators considered dosage of the treatment/intervention protocol.	
Evaluators considered quality of delivery of the treatment/intervention protocol.	
Fidelity was reported for the entire sample or a randomly selected subsample.	
An independent evaluator specified thresholds and assessed and reported the extent to which key intervention components were implemented with fidelity.	

Note: The above considerations were modified from *Identifying a Fidelity Measure*, by IRIS Center, 2022. https://iris.peabody.vanderbilt.edu/module/ebp_03/cresource/q3/p05/

Measuring Implementation Fidelity

Measuring implementation fidelity assists the researcher in gathering important information about why, when, and how interventions, programs, and curricula work. Keeping a recorded account regarding adherence to the treatment protocol is considered a smart research practice. Table 12.1 contains a list of recommendations one can use and check off to ensure they are collecting data on various fidelity considerations. Monitoring these areas, researchers can then hone in on items that may result in variations in the outcomes of interest or assist the researcher in course correction, perhaps saving the study from unforeseen errors.

The use of fidelity checklists is strongly recommended, keeping implementers on track and increasing the researcher's confidence in the results. In the next section, we will go into more detail about system and stakeholder considerations and how they can impact implementation and results.

School System and Building Characteristics Required for Implementation Fidelity

Implementation fidelity can be greatly supported or, conversely, greatly impeded by factors at both the school system and school-building levels. In order to promote implementation fidelity, many characteristics must exist, including strong alignment between the school system/district, school leadership, educators, and researchers. In addition, structural supports, clear and detailed logistical planning, adequate resources, and school culture and climate can all significantly impact the fidelity of implementation.

Alignment

When thinking of the word "alignment" one of the first things that comes to mind might be a spine. When the spine is in perfect alignment, the body is strong and mobile. However, when a spine is out of alignment, even simple day-to-day tasks become difficult. The same is true when collaborating researchers and school(s)/district(s) missions and visions are misaligned. A significant contributing factor to implementation fidelity in schools is a strong alignment between stakeholders, more specifically, researchers and district leadership, school leadership, and educators (Roman, 2016). Both district and principal support and policies have an effect on program implementation (Boerm et al., 2007; Payne et al., 2006), making shared decision-making a factor associated with higher implementation fidelity. When a collaborative process is present between researchers, the school system, and the school building, and shared goals are established, as discussed in Steen's Chapter 2, implementation fidelity can be positively impacted (Ruffini et al., 2016; McDougall et al., 2007). Exploratory factor analyses of program, school, and community factors (i.e., school community demographics) revealed that organization capacity is one of the five most significant factors that impact intensity of implementation (i.e., level of use by school personnel, frequency of operation, number of lessons/sessions, duration of implementation, and frequency of student participation; Payne et al., 2006). Overall, organizational capacity for program implementation is impacted by the level of collaboration and shared focus between the aforementioned stakeholders. Lower levels of implementation fidelity are likely when organization capacity is low and support from administration and school principals is lacking (Payne & Eckert, 2010). Additionally, implementation fidelity is positively impacted by incorporating district-level support at the school level, for example, in the role of "coach", and also with a school-level coordinator for leadership on site (Jowers et al., 2007). Therefore, just as alignment is a critical factor in implementation fidelity, so are structural supports.

Structural Supports

In order for fidelity of implementation to occur, various structural supports must be present and in alignment with the school system and school's mission and vision for intervention execution. One of the most important structural factors is the clear and defined implementation plan that considers the logistics necessary for implementation as intended. The plan for implementation should be built into the district and/or school calendar, allocate adequate time for intervention, and clearly define and communicate roles and responsibilities of various stakeholders. In addition, the plan should incorporate resource allocations and outline methods for ongoing support, training, and professional learning. This requires close collaboration between researchers and school decision makers.

Time

One of the key logistical factors is adequate time for implementation and fidelity procedures, including data collection. The critical question to ask is: Does the school schedule allow for enough time to be spent on fidelity of implementation procedures? Inadequate allocation of time due to various competing demands can threaten implementation fidelity (Botvin et al., 2018). Ringwalt et al. (2010) assert that some interventions may serve as a burden on educators' time. Thus, a clear schedule and timeline for implementation—especially when built into the approved school calendar—can allow for sufficient time for planning, implementation, and evaluation of interventions. Additionally, Payne et al. (2006) assert that integration of interventions into normal school operations is related to high-quality program implementation. For example, if a school were to choose to implement a new evidence-based social-emotional learning program adopted by the school district, the school would first develop a plan for when and where the program would be implemented during the school year and what stakeholders would be involved in the delivery and facilitation. In the Institute of Education Sciences (IES) grant-funded project, Randomized Controlled Trial of the Student Success Skills Program on Grade 5 Students' Academic and Behavioral Outcomes (Webb et al., 2019), researchers worked to limit the study's disruption to normal day-to-day school functioning and academic time by building the program delivery into the comprehensive school counseling program delivery (i.e., classroom guidance). This allowed for the curriculum to be implemented without a loss to academic time. Additionally, time was then factored into the appropriate stakeholders' schedules. Furthermore, the plan provided adequate time for data collection and program evaluation by providing necessary support. For example, coverage or additional planning time may need to be allocated for accurate and appropriate planning, implementation, data collection, and collaboration. In order for time to be allocated accurately, defined roles and responsibilities are essential.

Roles and Responsibilities

Defining stakeholder roles and responsibilities is necessary for effective implementation of interventions, as is a process for evaluating accountability. Key individuals should have clearly defined roles, with adequate time to fulfill responsibilities. As previously discussed, it is beneficial to establish alignment between researchers, district-level leadership, school-level leadership, and the educators. Equally as important are the delineation of research roles and acceptance of role differentiation (Pierangelo & Giuliani, 2008). Research has shown it is beneficial to have a district-level support person, or coach, and a school-level coordinator, when possible and applicable (Jowers et al., 2007). The two levels of leadership can create the necessary "checks and balances," promote accountability, and evaluate whether interventions are being implemented as intended. It also provides the structural support to anticipate and address implementation setbacks that may occur.

Webb et al. (2019) conducted a randomized controlled trial in two major Florida school districts, across a total of 60 schools. In each district they appointed district-level project coordinators and identified school counselors as the school-level coordinators and implementers. The district coordinators oversaw the implementation fidelity across participating schools within the district, while the school counselors delivered the Student Success Skills curriculum and documented fidelity of implementation at the school level. Organizing implementation teams of this sort can be a real benefit to researchers. The Institute of Educational Sciences (IES, 2020) details a few examples of roles and responsibilities of implementation team members at the district, school, and educator level, as shown in Table 12.2.

Resources

Another significant factor that contributes to implementation fidelity is the district's and school's access to resources and budgetary items. Having the resources required for implementation readily available impacts fidelity of implementation (Johnson et al., 2006). For example, schools may not have the resources or budget necessary to provide the ongoing training and technical assistance, which can impact the fidelity of implementation (Ringwalt et al., 2010). Researchers can positively impact fidelity of implementation by creating a budget that supports training and ongoing support, sufficient time for implementation, and other associated costs such as substitutes and coverage, as needed (Dusenbery et al., 2003). Securing adequate funding for research projects can be a *make-or-break* factor in ensuring that the necessary resources are made available and, in all reality, whether a research project even makes it off the ground. Thus, research grants can help significantly in

Table 12.2. Summary of IES Roles and Responsibilities for Implementation Team Members

Team Members	Roles and Responsibilities
District-Level Leadership	• Develop district shared vision for intervention implementation. • Provide support for schools to identify (if applicable) specific interventions and implement them. • Provide a list of recommended interventions (if applicable). • Create a stakeholder group to develop tools to support implementation.
School-Level Leadership	• Establish a school implementation team. • Reach out to the district to advocate for the school/obtain necessary resources and support for successful implementation. • Support school-level intervention. • Assess key aspects of the overall organizational performance (e.g., school performance) and provide data to support decision-making to assure continuing implementation of the core intervention components over time.
Educator (i.e., school counselor, classroom teacher, facilitator, etc.)	• Implement and support school-level intervention. • Assess key aspects of the overall organizational performance (e.g., school performance) and provide data to support decision-making to assure continuing implementation of the core intervention components over time.

efforts toward successful project implementation and the fidelity of study outcomes.

Professional Learning and Training

Initial training, ongoing support, and continued professional learning to support implementation protocols are related to greater implementation fidelity (Dusenbury et al., 2003; McIntosh & Goodman, 2016). Botvin et al. (2018) found that increased focus on improving and providing high-quality training is associated with enhanced fidelity. Additionally, when training is comprehensive in nature and provides ongoing coaching, support, and assistance, the implementation fidelity of evidence-based practices (EBPs) is improved (Ringwalt et al., 2007; Rohrbach et al., 2010). School districts that provide initial training of program implementation, access to a coach, and ongoing assistance see greater implementation fidelity for district-wide initiatives (Jowers et al., 2007). In order for the appropriate level of support and training to be provided, resources must be available and appropriately allocated, as previously discussed. The level of researcher commitment to training protocols will likely depend on funding and resources. However, researchers are wise to make training and professional learning a priority in their implementation protocols.

There are various approaches that can be utilized to make training feasible, including a train-the-trainer option that can be both time and cost effective. The researcher can collaborate with the school district coordinator to provide an initial program training to school counselors participating in the research project. As part of this training, school counselors would then be able to go back to their schools and offer training to participating educators. In addition to the cost effectiveness of this approach, there may also be greater educator buy-in and acceptance, as they are being trained by a colleague rather than an external source.

School Culture and Climate

Even when district–school alignment, structural supports, and resources are prioritized, the school culture can either enhance or limit implementation (Williams et al., 2019). When a culture of innovation exists and change is embraced, implementation can be positively impacted (Sheninger & Murray, 2017). Sheninger and Murray (2017) assert that change in any organization is often onerous, particularly during the implementation stage. By focusing on creating a school culture that embraces change, rather than just seeking "buy-in", greater support for program implementation can be gained (Sheninger, 2014). Additionally, a school climate of support predicts higher levels of implementation (Gregory et al., 2007). In fact, teachers and staff in schools with a positive school climate and a high-proficiency culture demonstrate higher fidelity in delivery of EBPs (Williams et al., 2019).

Jowers et al. (2007) noted that program sustainability and fidelity of implementation are impacted by level of enthusiasm among various stakeholders (i.e., district- and school-level administrators, educators, students, and families). School culture also has an impact on teacher absenteeism (Owen, 2010) and retention (Dahlkamp et al., 2017), which can significantly impact implementation fidelity. Ruffini et al. (2016) measured the implementation fidelity of the Response to Intervention (RTI) framework in Milwaukee Public Schools and found that schools with higher rates of teacher retention demonstrated higher average implementation ratings. Conversely, schools with high teacher turnover see lower ratings of implementation fidelity and are less likely to engage in program selection, training, and implementation (Payne & Eckert, 2010). It is important to note that high-poverty schools experience higher rates of teacher turnover and absenteeism (Garcia & Weiss, 2019). Thus, it is necessary to examine how school culture is impacted by such community and societal factors. In high-poverty, high-needs schools, higher rates of trauma and disruptive behaviors are present and can contribute to increased teacher turnover and burnout, while also negatively impacting school culture and climate. Overall, implementation fidelity and responsiveness to EBIs is impacted by the cultural contexts of the students, families, schools, and communities. School leaders, practitioners, and researchers should closely examine the cultural factors and contexts of their student population and the families they serve. Emphasis on culturally responsive practices and multicultural competence can positively impact school culture and the ability of educators to implement interventions with fidelity.

While it is evident that school culture and climate can significantly impact factors associated with implementation fidelity, researchers may have very little impact over school climate and culture. Therefore, it is wise to have a baseline understanding of school climate and culture prior to implementation to check for the viability of their study. Researchers can utilize reliable and valid measures of climate in the form of school and classroom climate surveys (for example, My Class Inventory—Short Form Revised; MCCI-SFR, Sink & Spencer, 2005; and Teacher My Class Inventory—Short Form Revised; TMCI-SFR, Sink & Spencer, 2007), from various stakeholders (i.e., students, parents, and faculty), behavioral measures and data (i.e., suspension and expulsion data), attendance data of both students and faculty, and school- and classroom-level observations. Selecting instruments that have been normed with underrepresented groups and marginalized populations and also offering instruments in the native language of stakeholders are two very important cultural considerations.

School Counselor Roles in Implementation Fidelity

Ideally, school counselors have extensive, graduate-level training in delivering and monitoring data-driven interventions and are influential in promoting school-level change, making them key players in promoting fidelity program implementation and equity in program delivery (Betters-Bubon et al., 2016). As previously discussed, clearly defined roles and responsibilities can positively impact fidelity of implementation. Often school counselors may be the most appropriate professionals for school-level coordination. Many school counselors have advanced, specialized training in data-driven and EBP delivery, often positioning them as leaders of implementation teams for many school-wide interventions. For example, Betters-Bubon et al. (2016) found that school counselors played a key leadership role in the delivery of school-wide Positive Behavior Interventions and Supports (PBIS) and were critical to the implementation fidelity.

School counselors can be influential in the planning, implementation, and evaluation of interventions in schools and so may have a direct impact on fidelity of implementation as program implementers. Ensuring that school counselors have received training in program implementation, have the support of administrators and staff, have sufficient time to dedicate to program implementation and evaluation, and have access to resources and ongoing training can promote fidelity of implementation. Additionally, as previously discussed, it is beneficial to identify a school-level research coordinator. Given what we know about school counselor qualifications and expertise, they are well positioned to be involved in research projects as school-level coordinators.

Ensuring a Clean Data Collection Process

Data collection, or the systematic process of gathering information about an object of study (Lawal, 2013), plays an integral part in ensuring research integrity. Across research disciplines, data collection approaches can have a significant influence on research results and findings and also impact the overall integrity of the research. When formalized, systematic data collection methods and protocols are used, the likelihood of errors resulting in inaccurate conclusions and biased results can be minimized (Mathes et al., 2017). For these reasons, accurate and appropriate data collection procedures must be carefully considered in educational research methods. Critical steps toward a clean data collection process will be reviewed below, including (a) developing a formal data collection procedure, (b) implementing measures for quality assurance and control, (c) developing clear training protocols, and (d) planning for data storage and security.

Developing a Formal Data Collection Protocol

One of the first steps in the data collection process is developing a formalized protocol that delineates the methods for collecting the data and incorporates plans for promoting the reliability and validity of the data collection. First, it is important to formalize *what* will be collected, and then *how* it will be collected—what data collection methods will be utilized. The methods of data collection will vary depending on research design (i.e., quantitative, qualitative, or mixed methods). Instrumentation is an important element, and the protocol should describe the measuring instruments and rationale for using selected measures and report the reliability and validity of each measure. According to Fitzpatrick et al. (2011), utilizing multiple methods of data collection can increase validity of the data and lead to more accurate conclusions. Thus, it is advisable to consider a triangulation strategy when determining data collection methods. Heath (2001) indicates, "at its simplest level, triangulation refers to the use of multiple measures to capture a construct" (p. 15901).

Next, a thoroughly articulated data collection system can provide formalized procedures for *how* the data will be collected and recorded. Developing and closely following a formal protocol that outlines systematic procedures can help ensure high-quality data that are valid and reliable, while also minimizing errors. Furthermore, the protocol should detail specific procedures for administering the data collection instruments and the handling of data. When developing a data collection protocol many *hows* should be considered, including:

1. How will the setting be prepared for data collection in order to protect participant privacy, personal information, and promote comfort (i.e., space, room temperature, lighting, etc.)?
2. How will the instruments be administered, and if needed, has a standardized script for data collectors been developed?
3. How will irregularities, or unanticipated circumstances, be reported?
4. How will cultural factors be addressed (i.e., translation of instruments, cultural adaptation, and relevance, etc.)?
5. How will participant questions be addressed?
6. How will data be handled securely and confidentially once completed?
7. How will data be transported and stored?

Just as plans for implementation should be incorporated into the school's annual calendar and plans, so should a data collection protocol and timeline. A detailed plan for *when* and *where* data will be collected at various points of implementation can ensure that time is proactively built into the schedule and space for collection is secured, resulting in the least disruption to normal school operations. The timeline should be created with both the research design and methods in mind (e.g., will pre/post-data be collected?) and should be relevant to the specific program implementation. Additionally, this timeline should account for when the necessary consent and/or assent for data collection will be sought, if applicable. It is important not to forget that one should account for competing demands within the school building when crafting this timeline. A data collection timeline can easily be derailed if not formally planned and scheduled due to other school priorities and testing schedules.

Equally as important to the ***what-how-when-where*** of data collection protocol is the ***who***. An important consideration in any data collection plan is: Who is qualified and trained to collect the data, and is any special knowledge, experience, training, or certification required? Additionally, has data collection training been developed to ensure data collectors are knowledgeable of the instrumentation and the data collection protocols? The training of data collectors is advisable as it can minimize the risk of errors in the data collection process such as interobserver variability and bias, among other human errors. Villares (2022) captures the various steps that were taken to promote fidelity in the IES-grant-funded project Randomized Controlled Trial of the Student Success Skills Program on Grade 5 Students' Academic and Behavioral Outcomes (Webb et al., 2019). Among the many fidelity protocols implemented in this research project was the formalized training of data collectors. Data collectors received a full-day training on study interventions, logistics of the data collection process (i.e., scope, timeline, data sources, data collection procedures, data transportation, and security), administration of study measures (i.e., data collection scripts), and anticipating and reporting irregularities, participant absenteeism, and/or missing data. Data collectors were trained to utilize a structured data collector manual during each data collection point. Data collectors also completed the Collaborative Institutional Training Initiative (CITI) Human Research Curriculum Social-Behavioral-Educational (SBE) training.

In addition to prioritizing data collector training, the researchers established further methods for promoting clean data collection. During each

Table 12.3. Suggested Checklist for Developing a Formal Data Collection Protocol

Consideration	Yes/No
Data collection methods have been determined (i.e., quantitative, qualitative, or mixed-method).	
Instrumentation has been selected, and a rationale that includes the psychometric properties and cultural relevance/sensitivity of selected measures has been detailed.	
A timeline for implementation and data collection has been developed in collaboration with stakeholders.	
Protocols for obtaining proper consents are in place.	
A data collection protocol has been developed that addresses how data will be collected, recorded, handled, and stored.	
Data collectors have been identified and adequately trained.	

collection window, data collectors followed the data collection procedural manual, completed a data collection checklist to document that procedures were followed, and followed procedures for removing student identifiers and ensuring the confidentiality and security of data collection materials. Finally, data collectors securely transported data to district project coordinators, who maintained formalized procedures for documenting the pickup and return of study materials. Thus, these procedures and training were a pointed effort to promote the fidelity of the project and a clean data collection process, while maintaining the confidentiality and security of the data.

Avoiding Errors in Data Collection

At this point, hopefully it is evident that when a formal data collection procedure is developed and maintained, errors in data collection can be minimized. Some additional steps can also be taken to avoid pitfalls in data collection, such as the loss of data, errors in recording information, and data manipulation.

Can you think back to a time when you made significant progress on a piece of written work and suddenly the application crashes, losing all the headway you just made? While this loss is painful, it pales in comparison to the partial or complete loss of data in a research project. Therefore, steps should be taken to avoid the loss of data, including having duplicate and back-up files and keeping records secure, password protected, and under lock and key.

How Implementation Fidelity Impacts Data Collection—Application

Adhering to sound implementation protocols with fidelity can help ensure reliable data collection. Failing to tend to treatment delivery factors can result in errors in data collection, which, again, impacts confidence in the results. The case study example below provides an example of the steps one school counseling scholar took to ensure implementation fidelity when conducting a school counseling outcome study. After reading the case, work through the discussion questions and determine your new level of knowledge regarding implementation fidelity.

Case Study

A counselor educator (CE) at a large public university is interested in researching the impact of an evidence-based violence prevention curriculum, the Olweus Bullying Prevention program (https://olweus.sites.clemson.edu/index.php), on students' social-emotional health. After reviewing the literature in this area, the CE decides to collect data on students' social-emotional skills by having students complete the Student Engagement Inventory (SEI), to collect data on behavior by analyzing school-level attendance and conduct incident reports, and to collect data on academics by gathering students' grades in core subject areas and standardized test scores. All three types of data have been linked to areas impacted by bullying. The CE thought it important to examine how culture and racial and ethnic disparities may influence this data, and they decide to build this into the research study. The CE is granted permission by a large urban school district to reach out to the principals of the 15 elementary schools to gauge their interest in participating in the study, and five agree to participate. The CE reviews data related to the five schools, including enrollment data, demographic data, and behavioral and achievement data and determines that one of the five is an outlier, not matching up with the other four, but, as they are worried about attrition, they keep that school in the study.

The researcher determines that school counselors will be the program implementers, but in order to participate, the school counselors must be licensed/certified and have had at least 2 years of experience. This eliminates one of the schools, but again the counselor educator decides to keep that school in the study, worried about the numbers. The Olweus program offers and provides 2-day training, which the CE gives the counselors information about but leaves up to them to schedule and complete on their own. Some do; some don't.

When it comes time for the program to be implemented, the school counselors approach their fifth-grade teachers and ask which classes want to participate, and some classes choose to participate and some don't. Next, the CE tells counselors that they should administer/collect any pre-study data and share it via a password-protected Excel spreadsheet, in line with the study's approved Internal Review Board (IRB) protocol. Parental consents are also obtained for all participating students; however, it is important to note that the consent forms that were distributed were written in English. Two of the schools had a low rate of parent consent for student participation. During the pretest period, the counselor has the teachers administer the SEI. Some teachers read the directions in English and each question aloud for the students, making sure that students are following along and understanding each item that is read. Other teachers pass out the survey, provide students the allotted amount of time to complete it, and then collect them.

Pop-Out 12.1. Case Study Reflection Questions

Use the checklists provided in the chapter to assess how this counselor educator did in tending to implementation fidelity. What study factors and implementation fidelity considerations might have cleared things up? Refer to the items outlined in Figure 12.1, "Factors Associated with High Implementation Fidelity"; Table 12.1, "Suggested Checklist for Measuring Fidelity of Implementation"; Table 12.2, "Summary of IES Roles and Responsibilities for Implementation Team Members"; and the "hows" for developing a data collection protocol.

When it comes time for the Olweus program to be implemented, again there are variations. Two of the school counselors deliver the lessons weekly, while the other three have a more difficult time with scheduling and do the lessons when they can; sometimes it's difficult for them to get through the lesson content, so they modify and cut out parts when necessary. After three months, the CE contacts the participating schools and asks for the post-study data to be collected. Again, there are variations in the administration. Upon analysis, the CE determines that the program had little to no impact on the variables of interest.

Summary

This chapter highlighted the importance of implementation fidelity across various forms of research and illustrated fidelity-of-implementation considerations throughout the research process. Particularly in the school setting, collaboration between stakeholders and researchers and clean data collection protocols are essential for sound research practice. The above case study offered the opportunity to apply the concepts, considerations, and checklists provided in order to increase understanding of treatment fidelity practices.

References

Barrera, M., Berkel, C., & Castro, F. G. (2017). Directions for the advancement of culturally adapted preventive interventions: Local adaptations, engagement, and sustainability. *Prevention Science, 18*(6), 640–648. https://doi.org/10.1007/s11121-016-0705-9

Betters-Bubon, J., Brunner, T., & Kansteiner, A. (2016). Success for all? The role of the school counselor in creating and sustaining culturally responsive positive behavior interventions and supports programs. *Professional Counselor, 6*(3), 263–277. doi:10.15241/jbb.6.3.263

Boerm, M., Gingiss, P., & Roberts-Gray, C. (2007). Association of the presence of state and district health education policies with school tobacco prevention program practices. *The Journal of School Health, 77*, 207–214. doi:10.1111/j.1746-1561.2007.00192.x

Botvin, G. J., Griffin, K. W., Botvin, C., Murphy, M., & Acevedo, B. (2018). Increasing implementation fidelity for school-based drug abuse prevention: Effectiveness of enhanced training and technical assistance. *Journal of the Society for Social Work & Research, 9*(4), 599–613. https://doi-org.ezproxy.fau.edu/10.1086/700972

Breitenstein, S. M., Gross, D., Garvey, C. A., Hill, C., Fogg, L., & Resnick, B. (2010). Implementation fidelity in community-based interventions. *Research in Nursing and Health, 33*, 164–173. doi:10.1002/nur.20373

Brigman, G. (2006). Research methods in school counseling: A summary for the practitioner. *Professional School Counseling, 9*, 421–425. https://doi.org/10.1177/2156759X0500900412

Brigman, G., Campbell, C., & Webb, L. (2016). *Student Success Skills: Group manual.* Atlantic Education Consultants. www.studentsuccessskills.com

Carey, J. C., & Dimmitt, C. (2006). Resources for school counselors and counselor educators: The center for school counseling outcome research. *Professional School Counseling, 9*, 416–420. https://doi.org/10.1177/2156759X0500900408

Carroll, C., Patterson, M., Wood, S., Booth, A., Rick, J., & Balain, S. (2007). A conceptual framework for implementation fidelity. *Implementation Science, 2*(1), 40. doi:10.1186/1748-5908-2-40

Castro, F. G., Barrera, Jr., M., & Steiker, H. (2010). Issues and challenges in the design of culturally adapted evidence-based interventions. *Annual Review of Clinical Psychology, 6*, 213–239. doi:10.1146/annurev-clinpsy-033109-132032

Castro, F. G., & Yasui, M. (2017). Advances in EBI development for diverse populations: Towards a science of intervention adaption. *Prevention Science, 18*, 623–629. doi:10.1007/s11121-017-0809-x

Dahlkamp, S., Peters, M. L., & Schumacher, G. (2017). Principal self-efficacy, school climate, and teacher retention: A multi-level analysis. *Alberta Journal of Educational Research, 63*(4), 357–376. doi:https://doi.org/10.11575/ajer.v63i4.56351

Dimmitt, C., Carey, J. C., & Hatch, P. A. (2007). *Evidence-based school counseling: Making a difference with data-driven practices.* Corwin.

Dimmitt, C., Carey, J. C., McGannon, W., and Henningson, I. (2005). Identifying a school counseling research agenda: A Delphi study. *Counselor Education and Supervision, 44*, 214–228. doi:10.1002/j.1556-6978.2005.tb01748.x

Durlak, J. A., & DuPre, E. P. (2008). Implementation matters: A review of research on the influence of implementation on program outcomes and the factors affecting implementation. *American Journal of Community Psychology, 41*, 327–350. doi:10.1007/s10464-008-9165-0

Dusenbury, L., Brannigan, R., Falco, M., and Hansen, W. B. (2003). A review of research on fidelity of implementation: Implications for drug abuse prevention in school settings. *Health Education Research, 18*(2), 237–256. http://dx.doi.org/10.1093/her/18.2.237

Fitzpatrick, J. L., Sanders, J. R., & Worthen, B. R. (2011). *Program evaluation: Alternative approaches and practical guidelines* (4th ed.). Pearson Education, Inc.

Garcia, E., & Weiss, E. (2019, May 30). Challenging working environments ("school climates"), especially in high-poverty schools, play a role in the teacher shortage: The fourth report in "The Perfect Storm in the Teacher Labor Market" series. Economic Policy Institute.

Gregory, A., Henry, D. B., & Schoeny, M. E. (2007). School climate and implementation of a preventive intervention. *American Journal of Community Psychology, 40*(3/4), 250–260. https://doi-org.ezproxy.fau.edu/10.1007/s10464-007-9142-z

Griffith, C., Mariani, M., McMahon, H. G., Zyromski, B., & Greenspan, S. B. (2019). School counseling intervention research: A 10-year content analysis of ASCA- and ACA-affiliated journals. *Professional School Counseling, 23*, 1–12. https://doi.org/10.1177/2156759X19878700

Heath, L. (2001). Triangulation: Methodology. In Neil J. Smelder & Paul B. Baltes (Eds.), *International Encyclopedia of the Social & Behavioral Sciences*, v12 15901–15906, Elsevier.

Institute of Education Sciences. (IES; 2020). *Roles and responsibilities of implementation team members.* https://ies.ed.gov/ncee/edlabs/infographics/pdf/REL_SE_Roles_and_Responsibilities_of_Implementation_Team_Members.pdf

IRIS Center. (2022). *Identifying a Fidelity Measure.* Peabody College, Vanderbilt University. https://iris.peabody.vanderbilt.edu/module/ebp_03/cresource/q3/p05/

IRIS Center. (2022). *How can school personnel effectively implement evidence-based practices or programs?* Peabody College, Vanderbilt University. https://iris.peabody.vanderbilt.edu/module/fid/cresource/q2/p04/

Johnson, E., Mellard, D. F., Fuchs, D., & McKnight, M. A. (2006). *Responsiveness to intervention (RTI): How to do it.* National Research Center on Learning Disabilities.

Jowers, K. L., Bradshaw, C. P., & Gately, S. (2007). Taking school-based substance abuse prevention to scale: District-wide implementation of Keep a Clear Mind. *Journal of Alcohol & Drug Education, 51*(3), 73–91.

La Roche, M., & Christopher, M. S. (2008). Culture and empirically supported treatments: On the road to a collision? *Cultural Psychology, 14*, 333–356. https://doi.org/10.1177/1354067X08092637

Lau, A. S. (2006). Making a case for selective and directed cultural adaptations of evidence-based treatments: Examples from parent training. *Clinical Psychology Science & Practice, 13*, 295–310. https://doi.org/10.1111/j.1468-2850.2006.00042.x

Lawal, I. S. C. (2013). Data collection techniques a guide for researchers in humanities and education. *International Research Journal of Computer Science and Information Systems, 2*(3):40–44. http://www.interesjournals.org/IRJ

Mathes. T., Klaßen, P., & Pieper, D. (2017). Frequency of data extraction errors and methods to increase data extraction quality: Amethodological review. *BMC Medical Research Methodology, 17*(1), 1–8. https://doi.org/10.1186/s12874-017-0431-4

McDougall, D., Saunders, W. M., & Goldenberg, C. (2007). Inside the black box of school reform: Explaining the how and why of change at getting results schools. *International Journal of Disability Development and Education, 54*, 51–89. https://doi.org/10.1080/10349120601149755

McIntosh, K., & Goodman, S. (2016). *The Guilford practical intervention in the schools series. Integrated multi-tiered systems of support: Blending RTI and PBIS.* Guilford Press.

Mihalic, S. (2004). The importance of implementation fidelity. *Emotional and Behavioral Disorders in Youth, 4*(4):83–105.

Mowbray, C. T., Holter, M. C., Teague, G. B., & Bybee, D. (2003). Fidelity criteria: Development, measurement, and validation. *American Journal of Evaluation, 24*, 315–340. https://doi.org/10.1177/109821400302400303

Noell, G. H., Gresham, F. M., & Gansle, K. A. (2002). Does treatment integrity matter? A preliminary investigation of instructional implementation and mathematics performance. *Journal of Behavioral Education, 11*, 51–67. https://doi.org/10.1023/A:1014385321849

Owen, A. T. (2010). *Leadership practices that influence teacher attendance in a low and high teacher absentee school* (Electronic Theses and Dissertations 326) [Doctoral dissertation, Georgia Southern University]. Georgia Southern University Digital Commons. https://digitalcommons.georgiasouthern.edu/etd/326?utm_source=digitalcommons.georgiasouthern.edu%2Fetd%2F326&utm_medium=PDF&utm_campaign=PDFCoverPages

Payne, A. A., & Eckert, R. (2010). The relative importance of provider, program, school, and community predictors of the implementation quality of school-based prevention programs. *Prevention Science, 11*(2), 126–141. https://doi-org.ezproxy.fau.edu/10.1007/s11 121-009-0157-6

Payne, A. A., Gottfredson, D. C., & Gottfredson, G. D. (2006). School predictors of the intensity of implementation of school-based prevention programs: Results from a national study. *Prevention Science, 7*, 225–237. doi:10.1007/s11121-006-0029-2

Pierangelo, R., & Giuliani, G. (2008). *Frequently asked questions about response to intervention.* Corwin Press.

Ringwalt, C. L., Pankratz, M. M., Hansen, W. B., Dusenbury, L., Jackson-Newsom, J., Giles, S. M., & Brodish, P. H. (2007). The potential of coaching as a strategy to improve the effectiveness of school-based substance use prevention curricula. *Health Education and Behavior, 36*(4), 696–710.

Ringwalt, C. L., Pankratz, M. M., Jackson-Newsom, J., Gottfredson, N. C., Hansen, W., Giles, S. M., & Dusenbury, L. (2010). Three-year trajectory of teachers' fidelity to a drug prevention curriculum. *Prevention Science, 11*, 67–76. doi:10.1007/s11121-009-0150-0

Rohrbach, L. A., Gunning, M., Sun, P., & Sussman, S. (2010). The project towards no drug abuse (TND) dissemination trial: Implementation fidelity and immediate outcomes. *Prevention Science, 11*(1), 1–14. https://doi.org/10.1007/s11121009-0151-z

Roman, V. R. (2016). *The importance of fidelity of implementation and factors that impede it for teachers: An interpretative phenomenological analysis* [Unpublished doctoral dissertation or master's thesis]. Northeastern University, Boston, MA.

Ruffini, S. J., Lindsay, J., McInerney, M., Waite, W., & Miskell, R. (2016). *Measuring the implementation fidelity of the Response to Intervention framework in Milwaukee Public Schools* (REL 2017–192). U.S. Department of Education, Institute of Education Sciences, National Center for Education Evaluation and Regional Assistance, Regional Educational Laboratory Midwest. http://ies.ed.gov/ncee/edlabs

Sheninger, E. (2014). *Digital leadership: Changing paradigms for changing times.* Corwin Press.

Sheninger, E. C., & Murray, T. C. (2017). *Learning transformed: 8 keys to designing tomorrow's schools, today.* ASCD.

Sink, C., & Spencer, L. (2005). My Class Inventory-Short Form as an accountability tool for elementary school counselors to measure classroom climate. *Professional School Counseling, 9*(1), 37–48. www.jstor.org/stable/42732642

Sink, C. A., & Spencer, L. R. (2007). Teacher version of the My Class Inventory-Short Form: An accountability tool for elementary school counselors. *Professional School Counseling, 11*, 129–139. doi:10.1177/2156759X0701100208

Villares, E. (2022). Fidelity matters. *Manuscript in Preparation.*

Villares, E., & Dimmitt, C. (2017). Updating the school counseling research agenda: A Delphi study. *Counselor Education and Supervision, 56*, 177–192. doi:10.1002/ceas.12071

Webb, L., Brigman, G., Carey, J., Villares, E., Wells, C., Sayer, A., Harrington, K., & Chance, E. (2019). Results of a randomized controlled trial of the Student Success Skills program on grade 5 students' academic and behavioral outcomes. *Journal of Counseling and Development, 97*(4), 398–408. https://doi.org/10.1002/jcad.12288

Wilder, D. A., Atwell, J., & Wine, B. (2006). The effects of varying levels of treatment integrity on child compliance during treatment with a three-step prompting procedure. *Journal of Applied Behavior Analysis, 39*(3), 369–373. https://doi.org/10.1901/jaba.2006.144-05

Williams, N. J., Frank, H. E., Frederick, L., Beidas, R. S., Mandell, D. S., Aarons, G. A., Green, P., & Locke, J. (2019). Organizational culture and climate profiles: Relationships with fidelity to three evidence-based practices for autism in elementary schools. *Implementation Science: IS, 14*(1), 15. https://doi.org/10.1186/s13012-019-0863-9

13

Data Analysis Procedures in School Counseling Research

Patrick R. Mullen and Dodie Limberg

Data Analysis Procedures in School Counseling Research

Research is akin to a lighthouse as it provides a guiding light for both practitioners and counselor educators navigating their way through the ups and downs of the school counseling profession, the same way a lighthouse helps weary seafarers find their way. The researcher is the lighthouse keeper, the person tasked with ensuring that modern societal and social-justice-based issues in school counseling and education are addressed through the application of empirical studies or use of theory. **Research provides the opportunity to understand better and enhance students' educational outcomes and improve school counseling practice.** Research can also serve as a mechanism to address socially just causes and fuel policy that addresses the needs of all students. In the lighthouse metaphor, data analysis may be best represented by the tools the lighthouse keeper uses to keep the light lit. These tools vary in size and difficulty of use and require special knowledge to employ. If engaged correctly, these tools can help disseminate important findings. If the wrong tool is selected or a tool is not used correctly, the lighthouse may not be sustained, and the light will dim. In any situation, understanding the problem being addressed is the first step to selecting the correct tool. Imagine a lighthouse keeper who tries to use a hammer to fix every problem; it just would not work. Thus, as a researcher, it is vital to know the problem you wish to address and the research question you wish to answer and then select the most effective tool. In Chapter 4 of this book, Lemberger-Truelove and Molina discuss creating research questions and matching research designs, which provides a more detailed description of this process.

Patrick R. Mullen and Dodie Limberg, *Data Analysis Procedures in School Counseling Research* In: *School Counseling Research*. Edited by: Brett Zyromski and Carey Dimmitt, Oxford University Press. © Oxford University Press 2023. DOI: 10.1093/oso/9780197650134.003.0013

In this chapter, we will discuss the use of data analysis for both quantitative and qualitative approaches. The aims here include shining light on some common and important approaches to analyzing school counseling research data. As you work your way through this chapter, we encourage you to continue to ask yourself, "How could I apply this approach to research questions I have?" In addition, we hope you will take advantage of the resources provided and the references we note, as these are practical ways you can further explore and understand the data analysis techniques highlighted in these readings.

An Overview of Data Analysis

Data analysis represents the isolated process by which researchers examine the data they have acquired through their methods of collection. It involves the application of unique procedures to answer specific research questions or test research hypotheses. The type of data analysis a person employs is based on their research questions in combination with the type of data they have collected. As we will discuss later in this chapter, the researcher must take steps to identify which analysis technique is most appropriate for their data. This process can be easy or difficult depending upon the researcher's training and experience with statistical analysis. Additionally, researchers need to consider their own biases and acknowledge how they may impact the way they approach data analysis. It would be beneficial for school counseling researchers to utilize the toolkit offered by Actionable Intelligence for Social Policy (Nelson et al., 2020), which offers positive and problematic practices of data analysis to ensure racial equity in data analysis. One could argue that applying statistical methods is one of the more intimidating aspects of research, because it requires an advanced knowledge of the statistical analyses being applied. The type of analysis applied, and the results of that analysis, can be, simply stated, incorrect. It is this combination of required knowledge and public display of results (via presentations and publications) that likely makes even the knowledgeable researcher timid.

Table 13.1 includes an overview of the main research branches in school counseling research. While much more can be said about the different methods of research represented in Table 13.1 (see Chapters 7 and 8 of this text), our focus in this chapter is on the specific applications of data analysis within them.

Pop-Out 13.1. Salami Sliced Results

Researchers should consider a variety of ethical concerns when conducting research. An article in the *Journal of Counseling and Development* by Wester (2011) outlined some important considerations for all school counseling researchers to review. One unique and often underlooked potential ethical concern that Wester noted involving data was the "salami sliced" publication. Salami slicing data refers to using a single set of data to publish findings in multiple manuscripts in a way that creates papers with overlapping hypotheses or redundant and irrelevant findings.

The demand to publish on one's path to earn tenure can be daunting, and researchers may strategically use a single data set for multiple manuscripts. However, when the findings seem to be very thin, like a salami slice, it may result in findings that have deteriorated value. It is an author's responsibility to avoid salami slicing, and it is the responsibility of an editorial board to evaluate for this concern during the review process.

Table 13.1. Main Branches of School Counseling Research

Branch	Description	Common Software
Quantitative research	Method of evaluating objective theories through the examination of variables either by describing them (descriptive statistics), testing the relationship among variables (correlational research), or examining differences between variables (causal comparative and experimental research)	Variables in quantitative research often involve scores on measures or scales that are analyzed using statistical procedures. Common software packages used are SPSS, AMOS, SAS, R, Liserel, and Mplus.
Qualitative research	Employs strategies to explore and understand the meaning individual participants or groups make regarding a particular problem or experience.	Common software used for qualitative research includes Excel, NVivo, ATLAS.ti, MAXQDA, and Dedoose.
Mixed methods	Include collecting both qualitative and quantitative data in a strategic process to gain a unique insight that would not be available without the use of both approaches in the same study design.	Combination of software from both qualitative and quantitative research

Note: Mills & Gay (2019); Gall et al. (2014).

Data Analysis for Quantitative Approaches

In Chapter 7, Griffith and Villares discussed quantitative research design and its application in school counseling research. The focus of the current chapter is, in part, to discuss different statistical tests used in quantitative research. To start this discussion, we should identify some basic elements in data analysis. The practice or set of processes employed by a school counseling researcher to summarize, investigate, and interpret quantitative data is called statistics (Gall et al., 2014; Mills & Gay, 2019). Data within quantitative research contain numbers that represent a variety of characteristics observed or gathered through collection procedures. The number of available statistical tests to analyze data in quantitative research approaches is vast and continues to grow as new methods are developed and technology makes computing complex statistical analysis easy and fast.

Pop-Out 13.2. QuantCrit in School Counseling Research

Quantitative critical (QuantCrit) is an approach to applying quantitative methods of research consistent with the theoretical tenets of critical race theory (CRT). Gillborn et al. (2018) describe QuantCrit as a set of principles they view "as a kind of toolkit that embodies the need to apply CRT understandings and insights *whenever* quantitative data is used in research and/or encountered in policy and practice" (p. 169). School counseling researchers should recognize that "all counseling research is multicultural research, whether overtly acknowledged or not" (O'Hara et al., 2021, p. 201) and as such should "engage in critical self-reflexivity as a necessary first step for the long journey of deracializing statistics (Garcia et al., 2018, p. 155). With this in mind, school counseling researchers should consider the impact systematic racism has on the facilitation of research and the interpretation of findings and their use in practice.

Principles of QuantCrit from Gillborn et al. (2018, p. 169) are listed below.

- The centrality of racism
- Numbers are not neutral.
- Categories are neither "natural" nor given: for "race," read "racism."
- Voice and insight: data cannot "speak for itself."
- Using numbers for social justice

School counselor educators can learn about QuantCrit and apply this theory into their planning, facilitation, and dissemination of their quantitative research. For a more in-depth understanding of QuantCrit and the principles noted above, researchers should review the sources noted.

Descriptive Analysis

Descriptive analysis is an approach to examining data that involves summarizing characteristics of a sample acquired in a study (Mills & Gay, 2019). In short, descriptive statistics *describe* the sample. Researchers use this approach in two main ways. First, researchers utilize descriptive statistics to describe the qualities of a sample, which is included in the Participants portion of the Methods section in a research article. The second way this form of analysis is used is during survey research whereby the authors' main aim of a study is to describe a phenomenon. Many nonprofit data-based groups, such as the Pew Research Center, utilize descriptive statistics to show national trends in politics, religion, and other important areas. In either case, the use of **descriptive statistics allows for authors to summarize aspects of a sample in meaningful ways.**

The major types of descriptive statistics include frequencies, measures of central tendency, and measures of variability. **The use of frequencies allows a researcher to describe how often a particular construct or nominal variable occurs.** For example, if a school counselor educator (SCE) wanted to demonstrate how many participants in a study work in a Recognized American School Counselor Association Model Program (RAMP), they would capture data on this information and express them in the form of count and percentage data. Frequency count data represent how many occurrences of a particular data point exist, such as saying that in a sample of 1,000 school counselors, 400 worked in a RAMP program. When reporting count data, authors may use a lowercase italicized "n" to represent a subsample or group in a larger sample, whereas the capital "N" represents the total sample. Frequency data can also be presented as a percentage of the sample. Using a percentage helps to give context to the results because it compares it with the entire sample. Read the following sentences and note the different ways the data are reported: (a) "400 school counselors work in a RAMP program" and (b) "40% of the sample works in a RAMP program." Both of these descriptions seem to only tell a portion of the story. A more comprehensive way to present this frequency data is to include both count and percentage frequency data, such as "400 (40%) school counselors work in a RAMP program" or "40% ($n = 400$) of the sample work in a RAMP program."

The measures of central tendency represent a description of values within the relative middle of a data set (Gall et al., 2014; Mills & Gay, 2019). In other words, they present a single value that shows a typical score for the variable under examination. Commonly used and reported measures of central tendency include the mean, median, and mode. The mean (or M) is the most commonly reported value and is the average value of the sample. It is calculated by totaling the values and dividing by the total number of cases. While the mean is a preferable statistic for central tendency, it is susceptible to influence from *outliers*, or variables greatly distant from the mean.

The *median* (or *Mdn*) is the middle value after a person lines up all the values in order from smallest to greatest, with 50% of the scores above and below this value. When there is an odd number of values, the exact middle value is the median, and when there is an even number of values, the two middle numbers are averaged. It is useful to report the median when data are not normally distributed or when outlier cases are present, as it is less influenced by these factors.

The *mode* is the most frequently occurring number in a data set. For example, imagine that a sample of school counselors is surveyed and their ages include the following: 28, 43, 35, 38, 34, 33, 44, 35, 59, and 36. The resulting mean would be 38.5 (average age), the median would be 35.5 (middle score), and the mode would be 35 (most frequent age). Table 13.2 highlights the concepts related to measures of central tendency and variability.

The final descriptive statistic is measures of variability. While measures of central tendency describe the typical score, **measures of variability summarize the spread of scores** (Gall et al., 2014; Mills & Gay, 2019). Some frequently reported measures of variability include the standard deviation, quartile deviation, and range. Standard deviations (*SD*s) are the most widely reported

Table 13.2. Measures of Central Tendency and Variability

Measure	Description
Central tendency	
Mean (*M*)	The sum of all the values for a variable divided by the number of cases
Median (*Mdn*)	The middle values after lining all the values in order
Mode	The most frequently occurring values. Bimodal and trimodal mean there are two or three variables occurring more often than the other variables. Multimodal indicates there are more than three variables occurring more often than the other variables in a set.
Variability	
Standard deviation (*SD*)	Square root of the variance for a particular set of scores
Variance	Amount of spread within a set of scores
Range	The difference between the largest value in a set of data and the lowest
Quartile deviation	Half of the difference between the lower and upper quartile for a distribution of scores

measure of variability and represent the square root of variance for a set of scores. Simply stated, the standard deviation quantifies the amount of variation for a set of data. The standard deviation is the square root of the variance for a particular set of scores, whereas the *variance* is described as the amount of spread within a set of scores. A large variance indicates a wide spread of scores, and a small variance indicates a narrow spread.

In some situations, researchers may also report the range or quartile deviation. Range represents the distance between the lowest and highest value in that spread. The quartile deviation, a less common measure of variability, is half of the difference between the lower quartile (bottom 25% of scores) and upper quartile (top 25% of scores) for a distribution of scores (Mills & Gay, 2019). To help draw these types of descriptive statistics out a bit further, let's look at the data we previously used to demonstrate measure of central tendency. That data set had a standard deviation of 8.57 and a range of 31. The following new data, 29, 33, 35, 32, 28, 31, 35, 32, 34, and 40 have a standard deviation of 3.41 with a range of 12. An inspection of these data makes it clear that the values in the first set have a greater spread of data. If a researcher reports a measure of central tendency, then it is also important to note the variability.

Inferential Statistics

Inferential statistics include the **analysis procedures that evaluate data from a sample obtained in a research study that is intended to represent the population being examined by the study** (Gall et al., 2014; Mills & Gay, 2019). A population represents the entirety of a particular group being studied (i.e., all practicing school counselors) whereas a sample is a subsection of the population that is acquired through data collection procedures (i.e., 200 school counselors who completed a survey). In inferential statistics, researchers make *inferences* about a population based on the analyses applied to the sample they acquired. One form of inferential statistics is hypothesis testing. In hypothesis testing, researchers examine the results of a study to see if their expectations for a study were correct or not. **A *research hypothesis* (or alternative hypothesis) is the researchers' expected outcome of the study, whereas a *null hypothesis* is a prediction that there is no statistical significance** (i.e., no difference or relationship). Researchers seek to either *reject* the null hypothesis or *fail to reject* the null hypothesis based on a test of significance.

An array of statistical tests exists in quantitative research methods, but selecting the tests depends on a number of different study design features and characteristics of the data. *Statistical significance* is "a designation that an observed difference between two sample means is large enough to reject the null hypothesis" (Gall et al., 2014, p. 173). Researchers should determine the standard p-value for statistical significance prior to the study, with .05 being a conventional value for this cutoff. Many researchers, and the findings they get, use significance levels at more conservative p-values, such a .01 or .001. Another way to express a p-value, say $p < .01$, is to say that the researcher is 99% confident that the findings did not occur due to chance.

Along with testing for statistical significance, **researchers should also consider the *effect size* of analysis and the confidence intervals**. One could argue that effect size, or practical significance, which expresses the magnitude of the relationship or difference between groups, is a more important metric to evaluate the results of a study because it looks beyond mere statistical significance. A number of effect size measures exist, such as Cohen's d, eta-squared, and Glass's delta. One useful resource for understanding and evaluating effect sizes is the article by Sink and Stroh (2006), an imperative reading for all school counselor educators (SCEs) conducting quantitative research. The *confidence interval* informs the reader about the range for which the true value of a score would likely fall within for a population being studied based on an a priori percent confidence (i.e., 95% confidence).

One important consideration is whether to use a **parametric or nonparametric statistical test**. Parametric statistics require that the data from a study meet the following assumptions: (a) the data constitute a normal distribution, (b) the data represent interval or ratio scales of measure, (c) determination of

---

Pop-Out 13.3. Effect Sizes in School Counseling Research

In a 2017 study, Mullen et al. conducted a cross-sectional study that looked at the constructs of job satisfaction, stress, and burnout. In the results, they found that the combination of stress and burnout predicted participants' job satisfaction. In their results, the authors reported an R^2 of .40.

In a different study, Ohrt et al. (2015) tested the impact of a wellness intervention on counseling trainees' burnout. The authors employed a repeated-measures analysis of covariance and values for eta squared (η^2), which ranged from 18 to .24.

For both of these examples, readers are encouraged to review the Sink and Stroh (2006) article and look up the guidelines for effect sizes. In reviewing these studies, identify what the effect sizes were for these studies and what they mean for the findings.

the study participants is independent, and (d) there is equal variance within comparison groups (Mills & Gay, 2019). If these assumptions are violated, the scale of measurement is nominal or ordinal, or the type of distribution is unknown, researchers should consider the use of nonparametric statistics. Most parametric statistics have parallel nonparametric statistics. It is also important to note that parametric tests are preferable over nonparametric. The following sections will highlight different tests of significance that are commonly used in school counseling research.

Correlational Statistics

Procedures that utilize correlational statistics seek to determine if a relationship exists between two or more variables and to what degree variables are related (Gall et al., 2014; Mills & Gay, 2019). Bivariate correlation and regression analyses are some common examples of correlational analyses. The strength of relationship is expressed as a correlation coefficient. School counseling researchers can use correlational statistics either to (a) examine the relationship between two variables (i.e., bivariate correlation) or (b) examine these relationships in an attempt to make a prediction (i.e., regression). See Figure 13.1. For example, a researcher may want to see if school counselor self-efficacy is related to their delivery of school counseling services. In this case, a single score for each variable could be used in a bivariate analysis where the correlation coefficient would indicate a strength and direction of the relationship. If the researcher found a strong correlation coefficient between these variables, it would indicate a strong relationship, but it would not indicate causality, or that one variable caused the occurrence of the other variable.

Pop-Out 13.4. Correlations in School Counseling Research

Harris et al. (2019) conducted a study examining factors that influence school counselors' involvement in partnerships with families of color. In this study, 155 school counselors completed a series of measures and the researchers examined bivariate correlations. The Pearson's r values for these analyses ranged from .45 to .27. Consider how you would interpret these ranges: Are these small, medium, or large effects? What does this say about the relationship between the variables being studied?

The correlation coefficient is interpreted as a value that ranges from −1 to 1. A value of 0 indicates no relationship exists; therefore, the closer the value gets to 1 or −1, the stronger the relationship. Positive values suggest positive relationships (as one variable goes up, so does the other), and negative values indicate inverse relationships (as one variable goes up, the other goes down). Along with testing for statistical significance, researchers should examine the effect size of a study. As already noted, Sink and Stroh (2006) provide a detailed description of effect size along with common metrics of effect size in school counseling research. For Pearson r, a common bivariate correlation coefficient, the effect size range includes the absolute values of. 1 (small), .3 (medium), and .5 (large) whereby larger effects indicate greater magnitude in the relationship between variables (Sink & Stroh, 2006).

The degree by which variables differ in a systemic way is called the *common variance* or shared variance. Common variance is a way to understand correlation values, and it represents the extent by which a score varies in connection with another variable (Mills & Gay, 2019). To identify the common variance, a researcher should square the correlation coefficient. For example, if school counselor self-efficacy correlated with delivery of school counseling services at a Pearson's r of .67, the shared variance between the variables would be 45%. As noted, Pearson's r is a common correlation coefficient and should be used if the two variables under consideration are continuous. Other correlation coefficients include Spearman rho, which is a nonparametric form of correlation coefficient used with rank data. Also, the phi coefficient is a common nonparametric correlation coefficient used when variables are dichotomous.

Prediction Studies

If a researcher seeks to examine the ability of **predictor variable(s) (independent variable[s])** to forecast an **outcome or criterion variable (dependent variable)**, they utilize a **prediction study** (Gall et al., 2014; Mills & Gay, 2019). These studies are aimed at identifying which independent variables are most related to some dependent variables. **Multiple regression** is one of the most common forms of prediction studies, as it allows researchers to examine the ability of two or more independent variables (e.g., student anxiety and academic self-efficacy) to predict a dependent variable (e.g., scores on the SAT). With multiple regression, a researcher can examine how each variable and how variables in combination with each other predict an outcome (Gall et al., 2014). It also provides information about how much any two variables vary

Table 13.3. Recommended Readings on Prediction Studies

Regression Analysis:
Cohen, J., Cohen, P., West, S. G., & Aiken, L. S. (2013). *Applied multiple regression/correlation analysis for the behavioral sciences*. Routledge.
Osborne, J. W. (2016). *Regression & linear modeling: Best practices and modern methods*. Sage Publications.
Osborne, J. W., & Waters, E. (2002). Four assumptions of multiple regression that researchers should always test. *Practical Assessment, Research, and Evaluation, 8*(1), Article 2. https://doi.org/10.7275/r222-hv23

Path Analysis and Structural Equation Models:
Byrne, B. (2010). *Structural equation modeling with AMOS: Basic concepts, applications, and programming* (3rd ed.). Taylor and Francis Group.
Schumacker, R. E., & Lomax, R. G. (2014). *A beginner's guide to structural equation modeling* (4th ed.). Routledge.
Weston, R., & Gore, P. A., Jr. (2006). A brief guide to structural equation modeling. *The Counseling Psychologist, 34*, 719–751. https://doi.org/10.1177/0011000006286345

together—co-variance, or shared variance. Shared variance is shown as the square of the correlation coefficient, or r^2. Results from a multiple regression analysis indicate the composite scores that have statistical significance, a test statistic F, and a multiple correlation coefficient R. In addition, the analysis reports individual scores of a b weight, beta weight, and standard errors along with individual predictors' level of statistical significance. Detailed descriptions of these outputs are beyond the depth of this chapter. However, there are further readings in Table 13.3 to consider if looking to apply a regression analysis. Other common forms of regression not discussed here include logistic regression (used with a dichotomous outcome variable) and hierarchical linear regression (used to control for certain variables in a sequential process).

Other common correlation-based analyses include path analysis and structural equation modeling. **Path analysis** is a form of correlational analysis that allows a researcher to develop a sequential causal framework based on theory by which they test a series of relationships between variables, including the testing of mediating and moderating variables. The relationships between variables are explained by a path diagram of the variables under consideration. **Structural equation modeling** (or latent variable modeling) is similar to path analysis with the added attention to examining the measurement models for the scales (i.e., use of factor analysis) and an examination of the relationships between measured and latent variables (i.e., variables that can't be directly measured). Table 13.3 identifies readings that provide more information to start learning these approaches in a comprehensive and practical way.

Pop-Out 13.5. A Learning Tip

As you encounter different forms of data analysis you find interesting and useful, take extra steps to learn more about it. These extra steps may include reading articles that describe the technique, obtaining books related to the approach, or reaching out to authors of an article in which the approach was employed. Undertaking any or all of these steps may help advance your own self-efficacy in that particular data analysis approach while leading to additional learning opportunities.

Example of Use

To draw out this approach to statistical analysis further, next we highlight an example publication. Authors Camp et al. (2019) examined the degree to which school counselors' knowledge and skills supporting homeless students are predicted by their empathy. In this study, they applied hierarchical multiple regression whereby three multiple regression analyses were conducted with a gradual increase in the number of predictor variables (e.g., more predictor variables were added) to account for changes in the scores based on the added variables. In the final multiple regression analysis, they found that the combination or composite of the predictor variables accounted for 32% of the variance of the outcome variable of knowledge and skills regarding homeless students. Additionally, the authors presented a correlation table that reports the bivariate correlations (relationships between two separate variables) between all the variables in the study. It is common for authors using any form of correlational statistic (i.e., regression, path analysis, or structural equation modeling) to include a correlation table of studied variables also. Readers can review this study to see a more detailed description of the study method and results. Table 13.4 lists the different analyses for correlational and prediction studies including a brief description and sample research question.

Hierarchical Linear Modeling

Hierarchical linear modeling (HLM) is a form of ordinary least squares regression analysis that is applied to examine variance in dependent or outcome variables in instances where there are multiple and hierarchical levels that the researcher needs to consider (Arnold, 1992). It is an approach that accounts for individuals who are embedded (or nested) in multiple layers. Think of this approach as similar to a Russian doll that has multiple versions that encapsulate

Table 13.4. Example Analyses for Correlational and Prediction Design Groups

Analysis	Description	Sample Research Question
Bivariate correlation	Examines the relationships between two variables	Is there a relationship between school counselors' perfectionism scores and their school counselor self-efficacy scores?
Multiple regression	Examines the ability of two or more independent variables to predict a dependent variable	Do high school students' GPA and academic self-efficacy predict their life satisfaction?
Hierarchical linear modeling	Examines differences in outcome variables with predictor variables that are at varying hierarchical levels	What is the relationship between school counselor self-efficacy and implementation of the ASCA National Model in a sample of school counselors, adjusting for professional demographic variables (i.e., counseling experience, grade level, and location)?
Path analysis	Form of multiple regression that evaluate a causal framework developed based on theoretical relationships between dependent and independent variables	Do higher levels of multicultural competency and contact with diverse people contribute to a higher degree of cultural humility?
Exploratory factor analysis	Identifies underlying structure of a relatively large set of variables	What is the factor structure of the school counselor self-efficacy scale?
Confirmatory factor analysis	Verifies the underlying structure of a set of variables	Will the confirmatory factor analysis support the factor structure of the school counselor self-efficacy scale?
Structural equation modeling	Combination of mathematical techniques (i.e., confirmatory factor analysis and multiple regression) used to analyze a structural relationship between variables that is based on preexisting theory	Do practicing school counselors' experiences of ethical issues and access to supervision predict their degree of burnout and stress?

Source: Mills and Gay (2019); Pallant (2020).

one another. To truly know its value, one must account for variance across the levels. HLM is particularly relevant for school counselor educators because students operate on multiple levels within schools that include, for example, their individual level, classroom level, grade level, and school level. Now imagine you wish to examine factors that predict high school students' pursuit and attendance in college. If you only acquire data from one of these levels, individual, school, or classroom, you may be missing out on significant factors impacting their college-going chances. Thus, HLM uses statistical methods to account for the levels and understanding of how individuals are nested within these different contexts. The description provided here does not do justice to the complexity of this data analysis approach. For those readers interested in learning this method, which is arguably beneficial for all school counseling researchers, they can start with the articles by Arnold (1992) and Lynch (2012). For a more detailed review of this approach, researchers could review the works of Osborne and Neupert (2013), Garson (2019), Raudenbush and Bryk (2001), and Snijders and Bosker (2011).

Comparison of Means

School counseling researchers employ research designs that commonly use statistical tests to compare mean differences between two or more groups. In these analyses, the aim is to understand if there is a difference in the average scores on a test between two or more groups. For example, if a researcher is studying whether elementary school counselors deliver group counseling services at a different rate than high school or elementary school counselors, they can employ a design to compare means across these three groups. The research designs most closely associated with these statistical tests include causal-comparative designs along with experimental designs. In causal-comparative, researchers identify two groups that differ in some key trait—the independent variable or grouping variable (e.g., grade levels served)—and compare these groups based on a construct of interest, which is the dependent variable (e.g., delivery of group counseling; Gall et al., 2014; Mills & Gay, 2019). In experimental designs, researchers examine the effects of some form of intervention (or variable manipulation) on a construct of interest. A number of experimental models exist across the continuum of pre-experimental, quasi-experimental, and experimental designs. Across these models, common features include the comparison of scores between a control group and/or a pre- and posttest data collection. True experimental designs also include randomized assignment to control/comparison groups and treatment groups. For both causal-comparative and experimental research, the type of analysis a researcher employs is largely dependent on the design of the study. In the following section we will highlight a few common tests of statistical significance that are used in school counseling research.

Comparing Means Between Two Groups

A common statistical test is the independent samples t-test. In this analysis, researchers compare mean scores on a measure of interests (dependent variable) based on assignment to one of two groups (independent variable). The analysis evaluates whether the groups differ significantly based on a selected probability level (i.e., .05). The groups are independent of, or not connected to, one another. As an example, a researcher may want to compare 11th- and 12th-grade high school students' college-going intentions. The researcher can use assigned grade level as the grouping variable whereby the scores on a measure of college-going intentions would be the dependent variable.

The paired samples t-test is a similar analysis with the exception that the two groups being compared are the same, meaning a researcher can compare scores on the same measure (dependent variable) whereby the grouping variable is time of test administration. The analysis evaluates whether the scores from different points in time differ significantly based on a selected probability level (i.e., .05). For example, imagine a researcher is conducting a mental health literacy training. They use a measure to assess participants' levels of mental health literacy at the start of the training (T1) and again at the end of the training (T2). Using a paired samples t-test, the researcher can determine if there is a statistical difference between T1 and T2. Both independent samples t-tests and dependent samples t-tests use parallel nonparametric analyses, which are the Mann-Whitney U test and Wilcoxon matched pairs test, respectively.

Example of Use

To help illustrate the use of mean comparison between two groups, we highlight an article by Zyromski et al. (2019). In this article, the authors were evaluating a school counseling curriculum called *True Goals* with a sample of fourth- and fifth-grade students ($N = 25$). In this study, the authors employed a one-group pretest–posttest design with the aim of evaluating teachers' observations of learning gains that resulted from the program. The authors employed a paired samples t-test using the scores on their measure as the dependent variable and the pretest and posttest administrations of the scale as the grouping variable. Their results returned significant findings ($t[24] = -4.63, p = .001,$) and a large effect size (Cohen's d of .83).

Comparing Means Between Three or More Groups

An analysis of variance (ANOVA) is similar to the t-test with the addition of more than two grouping variables. An ANOVA examines mean differences in a dependent variable based on assignment of three or more grouping variables using a prior probability level. Looking back at our prior example, if we wanted to compare college-going intentions across all four levels of high school–aged students (i.e., grades 9–12), we could apply an ANOVA with grade levels (four groups) as the grouping variable and scores on the college intention measure as the dependent variable. The results would indicate whether there is a difference between these test groups and would be used to identify which combination of groups differ from one another. A repeated measures ANOVA, an approach that is based on comparing means from repeated observations, can be applied to the mental health literacy example in cases where the researcher captured data at three points in time. The three collection points—pretest (Time 1 or T1), posttest (Time 2 or T2), and 1 month follow up (Time 3 or T3)—would represent the three grouping variables, and the assessment of mental health literacy would be the dependent variable. The ANOVA and repeated measures ANOVA also have nonparametric counterparts that include the Kruskal Wallis test and Friedman test. Figure 13.2 provides a decision tree for identifying which mean comparison would be appropriate based on different qualities of the study.

In situations where school counselor researchers have control groups, an analysis of covariance (ANCOVA) can be applied. ANCOVA is an approach that adjusts the dependent variable's scores based on other variables (covariates) that are likely to be impacting the outcomes of the study. For researchers using interventions, ANCOVAs can be used to examine differences between treatment and comparison groups (independent variable) on a construct of interest (dependent variable) after controlling for participants' pretest scores (covariate). In the mental health literacy example, the researcher may include a comparison and control group whereby the control group doesn't undergo a training. Then, an ANCOVA is applied to evaluate posttest score mean differences between groups while also using baseline pretest scores as a covariate.

The final analyses we will mention here are the multivariate analysis of variance (MANOVA) and multivariate analysis of covariance (MANCOVA). These two approaches are similar to ANOVA and ANCOVA with the difference being that MANOVA and MANCOVA include more than one dependent variable as a part of the analysis. Table 13.5 highlights the different tests noted here that can be used for making mean comparisons.

A Nod to Other Approaches and Lifelong Learning

A main purpose of this chapter is to provide information regarding some common quantitative data analysis approaches. An exciting and beautiful aspect of research is that there are a number of statistical methods for examining data in quantitative research. Several approaches were not described in this chapter that could be vital for school counseling researchers. Some examples include growth curve analysis, latent profile analysis, or time series analysis,

Table 13.5. Example Analyses for Comparing Means

Analysis	Description	Sample Research Question
Paired samples t-test	Employs one categorical independent variable (time between interventions) and one continuous dependent variable. Researchers use one group of people and collect data from multiple time points.	Is there a change in students' academic development scores from pretest (Time 1) and posttest (Time 2) scores?
Independent samples t-test	Employs one categorical variable (participant characteristics) with two groups and one continuous dependent variable. Researchers use one group of people and compare differences based on a characteristic with two groups.	Is there a difference in college-going intentions scores for ninth- and 10th-grade students?
One-way between-group analysis of variance (ANOVA)	Employs one categorical variable independent variable with three or more groups and one continuous dependent variable. Researchers use one group of people and compare differences based on a characteristic with three or more groups.	Is there a difference in students' career decision-making self-efficacy scores for 9th-, 10th-, 11th-, and 12th-grade students?
Analysis of covariance (ANCOVA)	Employs one or more categorical independent variables with two or more groups, one continuous dependent variable, and one continuous covariate. Researchers use the covariate to control for a variable that may be influencing the relationship between the independent and dependent variables.	Is there a difference in school engagement scores for students in the Student Success Skills group (Group 1) and the mentoring group (Group 2) while controlling for their school engagement pretest scores?
Multivariate ANOVA (MANOVA)	Employs one or more categorical independent variables with two or more groups and two or more related continuous dependent variables. Researchers use this approach when there are multiple related dependent variables.	Does school counselors' school level (elementary, middle/junior high, and high school) cause any significant differences in their job satisfaction and turnover intentions?

Source: Gall et al. (2014); Mills & Gay (2019); Pallant (2020).

to name a few. School counseling researchers should strive to learn about a variety of statistical methods and to stay attuned to current trends in the profession while also looking for ways to challenge their understanding of statistical methods.

Another approach to learning how other researchers have applied statistical approaches is to read their work (Table 13.6 provides some examples). Learning about statistical analyses may also include working across disciplines (e.g., psychology, public health, or public policy departments) and attending research-focused conferences. Pop-Out 13.6, titled *A Focus on Organizations*, highlights two organizations that may help school counseling researchers learn different and advanced approaches to conducting educational research.

Table 13.6. Example Articles Utilizing Different Approaches to Quantitative Research

Correlational and Prediction Studies:

Camp, A., Foxx, S. P., & Flowers, C. (2019). Examining the relationship between the multicultural self-efficacy, empathy, and training of school counselors and their knowledge and skills supporting students experiencing homelessness. *Professional School Counseling, 22*(1), 1–10. https://doi.org/10.1177/2156759X19867332.

Limberg, D., Lambie, G. W., & Robinson, E. H. (2017). The contribution of school counselors' altruism to their degree of burnout. *Professional School Counseling, 20,* 127–138. https://doi.org/10.5330/1096-2409-20.1.127

Warren, J. M., Locklear, L., & Watson, N. (2018). The role of parenting in predicting student achievement: Considerations for school counseling practice and research. *The Professional Counselor, 8,* 328–340.

Watson, J. C. (2017). Examining the relationship between self-esteem, mattering, school connectedness, and wellness among middle school students. *Professional School Counseling, 21,* 108–118. https://doi.org/10.5330/1096-2409-21.1.108

Hierarchical Linear Modeling:

Allen, A. H., Jones, G. D., Baker, S. B., & Martinez, R. R. (2019). Effect of a curriculum unit to enhance career and college readiness self-efficacy of fourth-grade students. *Professional School Counseling, 23*(1), 1–9. https://doi.org/10.1177/2156759X19886815

Lapan, R. T., Wells, R., Petersen, J., & McCann, L. A. (2014). Stand tall to protect students: School counselors strengthening school connectedness. *Journal of Counseling & Development, 92*(3), 304–315. https://doi.org/10.1002/j.1556-6676.2014.00158.x

Webb, L., Brigman, G., Carey, J., Villares, E., Wells, C., Sayer, A., Harrington, K., & Chance, E. (2019). Results of a randomized controlled trial of the Student Success Skills program on grade 5 students' academic and behavioral outcomes. *Journal of Counseling and Development, 97,* 398–408. https://doi.org/10.1002/jcad.12288

Comparing Means:

Bardhoshi, G., Duncan, K., & Erford, B. T. (2018). Effect of a specialized classroom counseling intervention on increasing self-efficacy among first-grade rural students. *Professional School Counseling, 21,* 12–25. https://doi.org/10.5330/1096-2409-21.1.12

Schietz, R., & Villares, E. (2017). Effects of the Girl Squad Curriculum on grade 5 females' transition to middle school. *Counseling Outcome Research and Evaluation, 8*(1), 2–14. https://doi.org/10.1080/21501378.2017.1327747

Urbina, I., Villares, E., & Mariani, M. (2017). Examining the efficacy of the Spanish cultural translation of the Student Success Skills program to improve academic achievement. *The Journal of Humanistic Counseling, 56*(2), 127–143. https://doi.org/10.1002/johc.12048

Zyromski, B., Hudson, T. D., Baker, E., & Granello, D. H. (2018). Guidance counselors or school counselors: How the name of the profession influences perceptions of competence. *Professional School Counseling, 22*(1), 1–9. https://doi.org/10.1177/2156759X19855654

An innate curiosity for quantitative statistical methods combined with a willingness to try new approaches to data analysis will fuel the lifelong learning of how to answer research questions with various statistical approaches. As school counselor researchers grow in their understanding of research designs that involve complex statistical analysis methods, such as HLM, structural equation modeling, or latent growth curve modeling, the identification of statistical methods will become more intuitive. Table 13.6 highlights some different school counseling research approaches using the different forms of studies discussed in this chapter.

Pop-Out 13.6. A Focus on Organizations

Below are two examples of research association organizations for which school counselor educators could seek professional development in advanced statistical analyses. Check out their websites for more information:

- American Educational Research Association: www.aera.net
- Association for Assessment and Research in Counseling: www.aarc-counseling.org

---

Pop-Out 13.7. Advanced Quantitative Statistical Approaches Sample Articles

---

Growth Curve Analysis:

Gutierrez, D., Conley, A. H., & Young, M. (2016). Examining the effects of Jyoti meditation on stress and the moderating role of emotional intelligence. *Counselor Education and Supervision, 55*, 109–122. https://doi.org/10.1002/ceas.12036

Latent Profile Analysis:

Moate, R. M., Gnilka, P. B., West, E. M., & Bruns, K. L. (2016). Stress and burnout among counselor educators: Differences between adaptive perfectionists, maladaptive perfectionists, and nonperfectionists. *Journal of Counseling & Development, 94*(2), 161–171. https://doi-org.proxy.wm.edu/10.1002/jcad.12073

Time Series Analysis:

Balkin, R. S., & Russo, G. M. (2020). Evaluating perceptions of working alliance and crisis stabilization for adolescent males in residential treatment for substance abuse: A time-series analysis. *Counseling Outcome Research and Evaluation, 12*(1), 4–15. https://doi.org/10.1080/21501378.2020.1776598

Selecting the Right Statistical Test in Quantitative Research

The research process starts with identifying a research question that addresses a gap or need in the field (see Chapter 4). This question helps to determine the method for a study, and in particular, the type of data and data analysis needed to address the question effectively. In quantitative research, most questions focus on examining the relationship between two or more variables or the differences between variables. An easy way to start the process of identifying the relevant analysis procedure is to identify the types of questions you are evaluating, which most often will include a relationship study or mean difference study. Figures 13.1 and 13.2 demonstrate one method to make decisions about relationship and mean difference studies. It is important to know that this process does not include all quantitative analyses, but it should provide some guidance when considering the right statistical test to select. Many SCE researchers consult with colleagues who teach statistics or research methods when needing guidance with identifying the correct statistical test; thus, when in doubt, be sure to consult.

When the question concerns the relationship between two or more variables, we first determine the type of measurement being used, be it ratio/interval, ratio, or nominal. Selecting measures is an important aspect of the research process (see Chapter 6), and the type of measure selected will impact the type of measurement being used. Then, we can identify what number of variables we will be comparing. Based on this final round of information, we can decide between correlation, multiple regression, or nonparametric counterpart. To help illustrate this process, let us start with the following question: "Is there a relationship between school counselors' caseload and their level of job satisfaction?" In this question, we know we are looking at the relationship between variables, the data is ratio/interval, and there are two variables. Looking at Figure 13.1, it is clear that a bivariate correlation is the best answer.

For mean difference, a similar process can be followed. The authors can first identify the number of grouping variables and then the group variable relationship. In the last step, they can determine if a parametric or nonparametric approach should be used. To draw this process out, let's look at the following question: "What is the difference in students' school engagement based on whether they participate in a school club or not?" In this sample, we see the focus is clearly on mean difference and there are two grouping variables (i.e., participation in a school club or not), and the dependent variable is level of school engagement. We can also tell that the grouping variables are independent, and let's assume the data meet the requirements for parametric statistics. This process results in identifying an independent t-test. Figure 13.2 provides a graphical visualization of this process.

As noted earlier, a number of other statistical approaches exist beyond the ones shared in this chapter. The more familiar you become with these methods, the more intuitive it will be to make decisions about which approach to select. Consequently, an effective way to increase the skill of picking a statistical test is to learn more about and try implementing potential approaches.

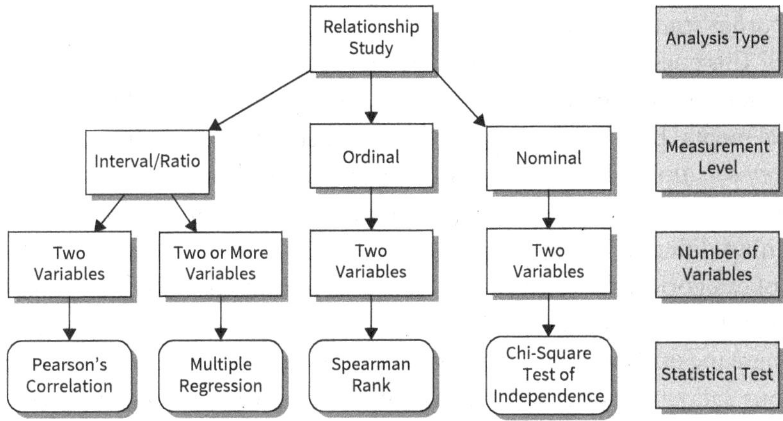

Figure 13.1. Decision-Making Tree for Relationship Studies

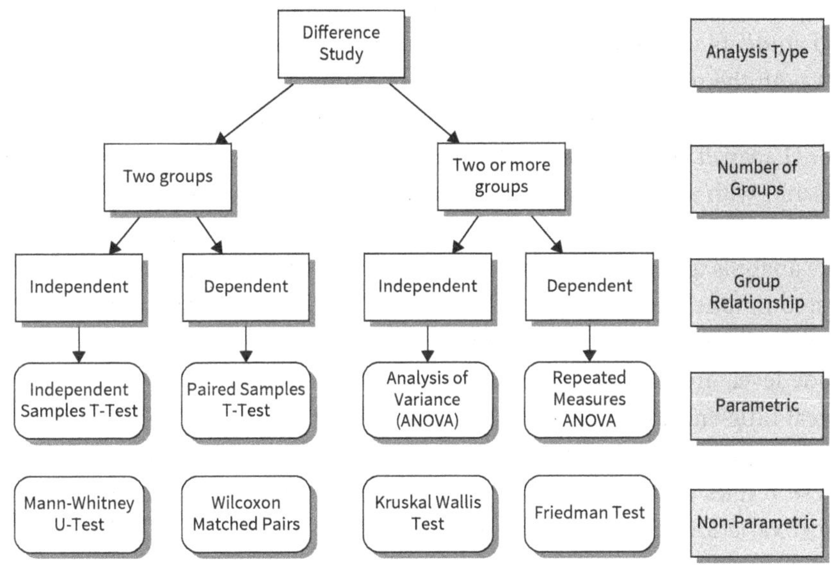

Figure 13.2. Decision-Making Tree for Mean Comparison Studies

Table 13.6 provides a variety of examples of school counseling research that use the different quantitative approaches described in this chapter.

Case Study: Quantitative

A new doctoral student, Aubrey Johns, has a research question that she would like to study. Her question is: *Is there a difference in diagnosable anxiety when comparing students with and without an Individualized Education Program (IEP)?* This question is personally relevant to Aubrey, because she worked as an exceptional education coordinator as a school counselor and felt that the potential mental health concerns faced by these students were often overlooked. Aubrey sets up a causal comparative study that utilizes a sample of 15 high schools in the district she used to work in. The sample includes 350 students spanning different grade ranges. Aubrey has compiled the data, which is a mix of categorical and continuous data, and is ready to analyze it using SPSS. To identify the correct analysis, she first recognizes that the study is going to compare mean differences on three measures—one about anxiety level (continuous data), one about whether or not IEP supports are needed (categorical data), and one about school and student context factors and demographics (categorical data), for which she collected the data. Next, she examines the data qualities and notices they are continuous and normally distributed. Then, she identifies two grouping variables that included students with an IEP and students without an IEP. Thus, she conducts an independent samples t-test with the data and finds insignificant results. Feeling distraught that this work would return non-significant findings, she remembers reading an article (Lapan et al., 2014) that used HLM. Aubrey then reads more about HLM, consults with a faculty member about the approach, and attends a training on the topic. Based on learning more about it, Aubrey uses this approach with her data analysis using the three-level model whereby 350 students (Level 1) were nested in four grade levels (Level 2) nested in 15 schools (Level 3). This approach allows her to examine the contributions of student characteristics, grade level, and school to the reported anxiety among students. The results reveal little variation across students (based on having an IEP), but there is a moderate variation across grade level and a large variation across schools. These results go on to indicate that grade level and school contribute to a larger variation in student anxiety than whether they had an IEP alone.

Data Analysis for Qualitative Approaches

In Chapter 8, Goodman-Scott and Cholewa presented an overview of qualitative research, focusing on grounded theory, phenomenology, and thematic analysis. The purpose of this section is to expand upon methods of analysis of qualitative data. Additionally, we discuss how school counselor researchers can get started and organized to conduct qualitative data analysis and describe the action items needed to conduct various qualitative data analyses. We also go into greater detail about how to establish trustworthiness. Overall, we hope to provide an overview of *how* to analyze qualitative data and recommend that you utilize the resources provided in this chapter, specifically *The Coding Manual for Qualitative Researchers* (Saldaña, 2015) and *Qualitative Data Analysis: An Introduction* (Grbich, 2012). However, qualitative data analysis is influenced by researchers' decisions; therefore, there are multiple ways to engage in this work.

Getting Started

After collecting data during a qualitative study, knowing what to do with all of them can be overwhelming, so having a plan and organization system before gathering data is important. First, it is important to ensure that the data are secure (i.e., following ethical guidelines of data storage) and ideally de-identified, and organizing the data may be as simple as a collection of password-protected Microsoft Word documents, or using Google Docs, or DropBox. Next, selecting a program to help analyze the data may be useful, such as Excel, Nvivo, MAXQDA, ATLAS.ti, Dedoose, or something as simple as a researcher-created coding table aligned with your data analysis process (see Figure 13.3). For example, Ohrt et al. (2016) used a coding table created in Microsoft Word to organize and analyze data as part of their thematic analysis of adolescents' perceptions of their school counselor's impact. Their table consisted of the following columns: (1) data source number, (2) significant statement (i.e., a verbatim statement within the data selected by the researcher), (3) a code name determined by the researcher, and (4) theme.

Once the data are secure and organized, the primary researcher should predetermine if a research team will be utilized. Research teams are recommended for qualitative research (Fernald & Duclos, 2005). If a research team is used, it is important that the members understand and have access to the organization systems being utilized and are provided with training, specifically related to the data analysis, in whatever approach is being used.

Data Source Number	Significant Statement	Code	Theme

Figure 13.3. Example of a Coding Table

The data analysis process for each qualitative approach may vary, but the overall goal is to identify themes, patterns, and relationships among the data. It is important for researchers not only to account for ways to decolonize their data analysis process by acknowledging how their biases may influence their approach, but more importantly to empower the participants to have more influence in the data analysis process by involving them during each step. Additionally, it is important to revisit the research question and the literature to guide and focus your data analysis. Prior to data analysis it is important to follow the steps in Figure 13.4.

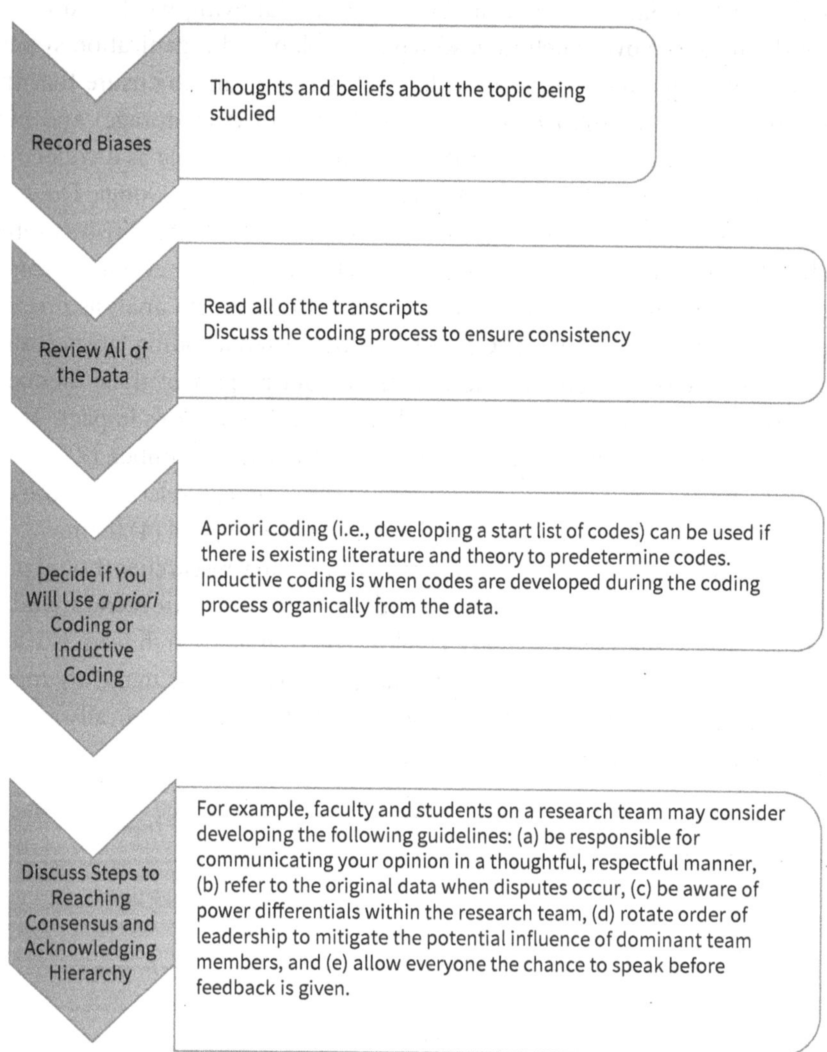

Figure 13.4. General Qualitative Data Analysis Process

Specific Steps of Data Analysis

As noted by Goodman-Scott and Cholewa, the steps to data analysis are different for each approach (e.g., grounded theory, phenomenological, and thematic analysis). We expand upon the data analysis steps for each of these approaches and consensual qualitative research (CQR).

Grounded Theory

There are three coding strategies in grounded theory: (1) open coding, (2) axial coding, and (3) selective coding (Charmaz, 2014; Corbin & Strauss, 2008). See Table 13.7. These three strategies should be done cyclically and are nonlinear. An example of all of these strategies being executed is Finnerty and colleagues' (2019) work focused on experiential group training of school counselors to engage in psychoeducational group lessons with first-generation college students.

Table 13.7. Coding Strategies

Grounded Theory Coding Strategies	How to Conduct the Strategy:
Open Coding	• Read through the data several times and then start to create tentative labels (i.e., inductive coding) for chunks of data that summarize what you are reading. • It is important to record examples of participants' words and establish properties of each code. • Code one transcript line by line together in order to have opportunities to check in and share and compare their open codes. • The remainder of the coding can be divided among the team once everyone has a strong understanding of the process. • Once all the data are coded using open coding, the research team should come back together as a group to develop a master list of the open codes. • It is common to record and report the number of open codes that were developed during this process.
Axial Coding	• The process moves from inductive to deductive analysis using axial coding to identify relationships among the open codes. • The research team works together to identify relationships among the open codes and groups them into categories (i.e., axial codes). • This process includes discussions about the groupings, which may lead to expanding or collapsing the list of axial codes.
Selective Coding	• The research team conducts selective coding to identify core codes/themes that represent all of the data.
Theory Development	• The research team develops a theory using the codes to make meaning of the data. • It is common for a theory to have a visual representation.

Phenomenological

Phenomenological data analysis is a process that results in a thorough description of the meaning of participants' lived experiences of a specific phenomenon (Polkinghorne, 1989), and a collective description that includes the "what" and "how" they experience it (Grbich, 2012; Hays & Singh, 2012). The most common approach is utilizing Moustakas' (1994) seven steps, which are an analytic iteration ranging from developing positionality through self-reflection, to providing support for theme development by citing transcript evidence, to developing a narrative description of the phenomenon. Another common approach is Creswell's (2009) hierarchical analysis. Common steps in phenomenological data analysis include those shown in Figure 13.5.

There are multiple examples of school counselor researchers applying these steps or modified versions of them: (a) Rodriguez et al. (2018) examined school counselors' experiences of implementing a comprehensive model, (b) González (2016) identified factors that facilitate and impede school counselor advocacy for and with LGBT students, and (c) Taylor et al. (2019) studied how school counselors integrated yoga into a comprehensive model.

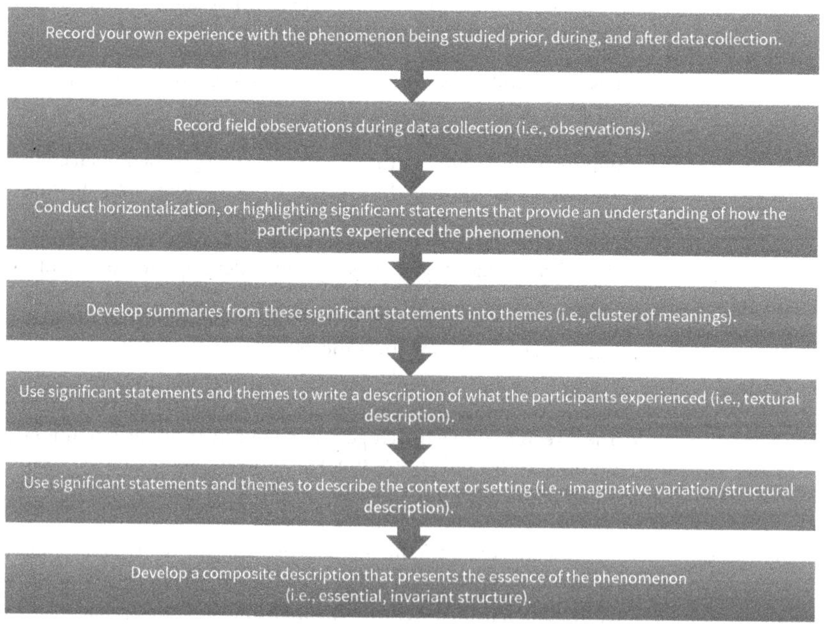

Figure 13.5. Steps in Phenomenological Data Analysis

Thematic Analysis

Thematic analysis is a systematic method for answering a research question by identifying, examining, and describing themes within data (Boyatzis, 1998). Clarke et al. (2015) describe six phases of thematic analysis: (1) familiarize yourself with the data, (2) generate initial codes, (3) search for themes, (4) review themes, (5) define and name themes, and (6) produce a report. Clarke et al. (2015) emphasize the importance of immersing yourself into the data by reading all of the data as a first phase and to make note of initial thoughts during this process. The next phase is generating the initial codes that are a one-word or a short-phrase description of a segment of the data (2012). Research team members should code at least one data source (e.g., transcript, essay) together to ensure that all understand the process. Additionally, this process provides the team members with time to discuss how they developed the codes and an opportunity to have discourse about any disagreements and coming to consensus. The coding process can continue as a team, or once everyone feels confident in the process, team members may do it in pairs, small groups, or individually. Once all data are reviewed for initial codes, a final code list should be created and agreed upon by the research team. During Phase 3, the research team members develop themes by grouping similar codes together to create a possible theme name. During this phase, Clarke et al. (2015) suggest that all codes be included into a theme, and if they do not fit, they can be placed in a miscellaneous theme as a holding place. When reviewing the themes (i.e., Phase 4), the codes should be revisited to ensure that they fit within each theme in a meaningful way. All the themes should also be reviewed to ensure that each theme was distinct from the others but also represented the data as a whole. If themes are not distinct, they may need to be collapsed, or if they represent too much of the data, they may need to be separated. During Phase 5, final theme names are agreed upon by the research team, and clear operational definitions of each theme are developed. The final phase of thematic analysis is producing a report of the findings of the study as they relate to the research question and literature review.

Consensual Qualitative Research

CQR is a combination of phenomenological, thematic analysis, and grounded theory approaches, and it allows researchers to focus on the subjective experiences of humans in their sociological context (Heppner et al., 2008). CQR is becoming more common in school counseling research (Springer et al., 2018). Hill et al. (2005) describe four primary components of CQR: (a) the use of open-ended questions, (b) consensual agreement within the research team regarding the data analysis, (c) the participation of an internal and external auditor throughout data analysis, and (d) identifying domains, core ideas, and categories to utilize a cross-analysis. There are three steps to the CQR data analysis process (see Figure 13.6): (1) identifying domains, (2) summarizing core ideas from the domains, and (3) developing categories and conducting cross-analysis that organizes the core ideas that exist across the cases (Hill et al., 2005).

Springer et al. (2020) provide an example of how they used these three steps to analyze data focused on an intervention to support elementary school faculty in meeting the needs of transgender and gender-nonconforming students.

How to Establish Trustworthiness

Establishing trustworthiness is critical to qualitative analysis because it provides validity, reliability, and overall quality of the findings. We suggest using Tracy's (2010) eight "big-tent" criteria to ensure quality in qualitative research: (a) worthy topic, (b) rich rigor, (c) sincerity, (d) credibility,

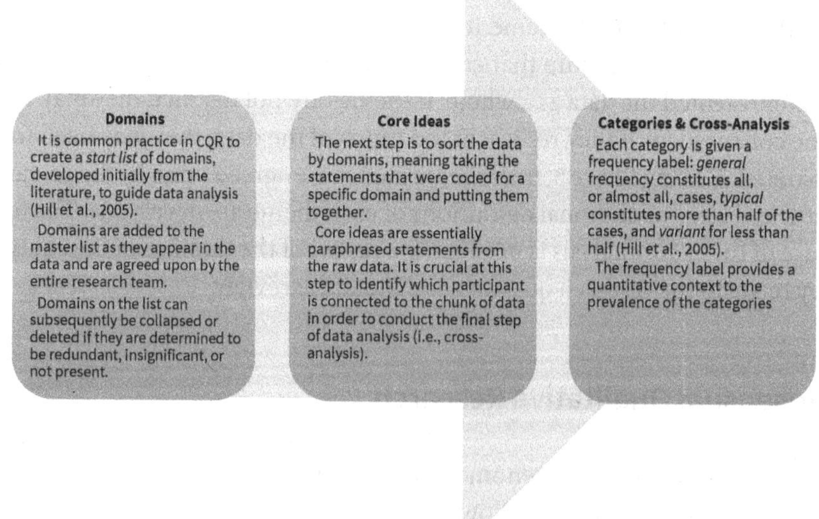

Figure 13.6. Steps in Consensual Qualitative Research (CQR) Data Analysis

Table 13.8. Types of Trustworthiness

Type of Trustworthiness	How To
Positionality	The researcher writes a positionality statement that describes who they are as a person and researcher and including anything specific to the topic.
Memoing	The researcher(s) keeps reflective notes during data collection and data analysis.
Bracketing	The researcher(s) acknowledges and sets aside their biases and personal experiences related to the topic.
Member Checking	The researcher(s) ask participants to review transcripts, preliminary findings, and nearly finished writing throughout the research process and asks them for their feedback and adjusts if needed.
Use of an Auditor	There are two types of auditors: internal and external. The internal auditor is normally a member of the research team and provides live feedback during the data analysis process. An external auditor is not normally a member of the research team but offers feedback at different stages during the data analysis process.
Triangulation	The researcher(s) uses multiple forms of data collection (e.g., demographic survey, review of documents).

(e) resonance, (f) significant contribution, (g) ethics, and (h) meaningful coherence. Goodman-Scott and Cholewa (see Chapter 8) provided an overview of different types of trustworthiness, and we expand on the *how* to conduct them. First, it is important that researchers are aware of and transparent about their own positionality regarding what is being studied. A common way to do this is to write a positionality statement describing who you are as a person and researcher, including anything specific to the topic. To reduce the effects of bias when analyzing data, researchers can apply many measures to support trustworthiness including those listed in Table 13.8.

Presenting Results

The presentation of results from quantitative and qualitative studies varies depending on the type of data analytic procedures employed by the researcher. Luckily, a number of resources are available to aid researchers in adhering to the appropriate standards. In Table 13.9, we list some example articles that will aid readers in describing the results from their studies. Many of these articles focus on publication standards for reporting results based on the individual methods. One important aspect of reporting to consider is the

Table 13.9. Resources for Presenting Results

Research Method	Reference
General Writing	• Hunt, B., & Milsom, A. (2011). Academic writing: Reflections from successful counselor educators. *The Journal of Humanistic Counseling, 50*(1), 56–69. https://doi.org/10.1002/j.2161-1939.2011.tb00106.x • Lambie, G. W., Sias, S. M., Davis, K. M., Lawson, G., & Akos, P. (2008). A scholarly writing resource for counselor educators and their students. *Journal of Counseling & Development, 86*(1), 18–25. https://doi.org/10.1002/j.1556-6678.2008.tb00621.x • Wester, K. L. (2011). Publishing ethical research: A step-by-step overview. *Journal of Counseling & Development, 89*(3), 301–307. https://doi.org/10.1002/j.1556-6678.2011.tb00093.x
Quantitative	• Appelbaum, M., Cooper, H., Kline, R. B., Mayo-Wilson, E., Nezu, A. M., & Rao, S. M. (2018). Journal article reporting standards for quantitative research in psychology: The APA Publications and Communications Board task force report. *American Psychologist, 73*(1), 3. http://dx.doi.org/10.1037/amp0000191 • Balkin, R. S., & Sheperis, C. J. (2011). Evaluating and reporting statistical power in counseling research. *Journal of Counseling & Development, 89*(3), 268–272. https://doi.org/10.1002/j.1556-6678.2011.tb00088.x • Bauman, S. (2006). Using comparison groups in school counseling research: A primer. *Professional School Counseling, 9*, 357–366. • Jackson, D. L. (2010). Reporting results of latent growth modeling and multilevel modeling analyses: Some recommendations for rehabilitation psychology. *Rehabilitation Psychology, 55*(3), 272. • Schreiber, J. B., Nora, A., Stage, F. K., Barlow, E. A., & King, J. (2006). Reporting structural equation modeling and confirmatory factor analysis results: A review. *The Journal of Educational Research, 99*(6), 323–338. https://doi.org/10.3200/JOER.99.6.323-338 • Trusty, J. (2011). Quantitative articles: Developing studies for publication in counseling journals. *Journal of Counseling & Development, 89*(3), 261–267. https://doi.org/10.1002/j.1556-6678.2011.tb00087.x • Ware, W. B., & Galassi, J. P. (2006). Using correlational and prediction data to enhance student achievement in K–12 schools: A practical application for school counselors. *Professional School Counseling, 9*(5), 344–356.
Qualitative	• Choudhuri, D., Glauser, A., & Peregoy, J. (2004). Guidelines for writing a qualitative manuscript for the *Journal of Counseling & Development. Journal of Counseling & Development, 82*(4), 443–446. • Hunt, B. (2011). Publishing qualitative research in counseling journals. *Journal of Counseling & Development, 89*(3), 296–300. https://doi.org/10.1002/j.1556-6678.2011.tb00092.x • Kline, W. B. (2008). Developing and submitting credible qualitative manuscripts. *Counselor Education and Supervision, 47*(4), 210–217. https://doi.org/10.1002/j.1556-6978.2008.tb00052.x • Levitt, H. M., Bamberg, M., Creswell, J. W., Frost, D. M., Josselson, R., & Suárez-Orozco, C. (2018). Journal article reporting standards for qualitative primary, qualitative meta-analytic, and mixed methods research in psychology: The APA Publications and Communications Board task force report. *American Psychologist, 73*(1), 26. http://dx.doi.org/10.1037/amp0000151 • Paris, D., & Winn, M. T. (Eds.). (2013). Humanizing research: Decolonizing qualitative inquiry with youth and communities. Sage. • Ponterotto, J. G., & Grieger, I. (2007). Effectively communicating qualitative research. *The Counseling Psychologist, 35*(3), 404–430. http://dx.doi.org/10.1177/0011000006287443

correct usage of Greek letters throughout reporting processes. A second important consideration is the correct usage of tables. Both of these reporting topics are discussed in detail within the American Psychological Association's publication manual (2020), a book that should be owned by all school counseling researchers, as it contains the reporting standards for research in our discipline.

Case Study: Qualitative

A 3rd-year doctoral student, Edison Gonzalez, is in the process of completing his dissertation using the multi-article dissertation format (Limberg & Ohrt, 2019). This format requires that he complete and submit a collection (i.e., two to four) of manuscripts based on two to three studies on the same topic. Edison's topic is school counseling and using multi-tiered support systems (MTSSs) with children with emotional behavioral disorders (EBD). Edison was awarded a dissertation grant from the American Educational Research Association (AERA) to support his research. He decides to complete a qualitative study first to understand the experiences of elementary school counselors with MTSSs. He will use the results from this study to inform his next study, which will use single-case design to examine a preventative school counseling intervention to reduce disruptive behaviors of first-grade students who are diagnosed with EBD.

Edison decides to use a phenomenological approach to explore the lived experiences of school counselors using MTSSs. He recruits and provides a stipend, from his grant, for his research team that consists of one faculty member, two doctoral students, a master's-level student, and a practicing school counselor. Edison and his team conduct two semi-structured interviews with 15 elementary school counselors and also ask them to complete a survey that asks about characteristics of their school and their training. Multiple points of data collection are used to triangulate the data. Prior to data analysis, Edison's research team decides they will use the statistical software MAXQDA to help organize and analyze their data. Additionally, Edison trains his team on phenomenological research, specifically the steps of data analysis. First, they discuss and record their own biases about school counselors and MTSSs and agree to memo and record their observations throughout the data analysis. Next, all members of the team read all of the transcripts and send them out to participants for review and feedback as part of member checking. They use the first transcript to complete horizontalization coding (i.e., highlighting significant statements that provide an understanding of how the participants experienced the phenomenon) together and then divide into pairs to continue analyzing the rest of the transcripts. They come back together to develop summaries from these significant statements into themes. The team use the significant statements and themes to write a description of what the participants experienced related to MTSSs (i.e., textural description) and how participants experienced MTSSs (i.e., structural description). During this process, they acknowledge the hierarchy that exists on the team and follow their agreed-upon data analysis discussion process, which includes rotating leaders and allowing time to speak. Next, they review the data from the survey the participants completed and compare and contrast them with the themes they have developed to triangulate the data. Finally, they develop a composite description that presents the essence of the phenomenon (i.e., essential, invariant structure) that connects with their research question.

Conclusion

In summary, this chapter highlighted elements of statistical analysis for quantitative and qualitative research. We focused on descriptive statistics, correlational and prediction studies, and comparison of mean differences. For qualitative research, we highlighted common practices for data analysis in grounded theory, phenomenology, and thematic analysis approaches. Throughout this chapter we highlighted different recommended readings and provided examples of published works. Data analysis is a critical aspect of the overall research process. Learning different approaches and applying them correctly is vital to presenting the most robust result and accurate results and findings. The information in this chapter should be a starting point in this journey.

Thought to Application

Take some time and talk with a classmate or another scholar about your research questions. Share with them some general ideas or questions you have regarding the field of school counseling. Then, try to write out the research question in detail—Chapter 4 by Lemberger-Truelove and Molina may be a useful resource for accomplishing this task. After crafting the question, work with your classmate to identify the statistical approach needed to answer this question. Ask and discuss the following questions:

a. What type of research design is being employed?
b. What do I need to know about the data?
c. What software options are available?
d. What book or article can I use as a guide for this method?
e. What are some example articles that use this approach?
f. What challenges do I foresee and how can I overcome them?

References

Allen, A. H., Jones, G. D., Baker, S. B., & Martinez, R. R. (2019). Effect of a curriculum unit to enhance career and college readiness self-efficacy of fourth-grade students. *Professional School Counseling, 23*(1), 1–9. https://doi.org/10.1177/2156759X19886815

American Psychological Association. (2020). *Publication manual of the American psychological association* (7th ed.). Author.

Appelbaum, M., Cooper, H., Kline, R. B., Mayo-Wilson, E., Nezu, A. M., & Rao, S. M. (2018). Journal article reporting standards for quantitative research in psychology: The APA Publications and Communications Board task force report. *American Psychologist, 73*(1), 3. http://dx.doi.org/10.1037/amp0000191

Arnold, C. L. (1992). An introduction to hierarchical linear modeling. *Measurement and Evaluation in Counseling and Development, 25,* 58–90.

Balkin, R. S., & Russo, G. M. (2020). Evaluating perceptions of working alliance and crisis stabilization for adolescent males in residential treatment for substance abuse: A time-series analysis. *Counseling Outcome Research and Evaluation, 12*(1), 4–15. https://doi.org/10.1080/21501378.2020.1776598

Balkin, R. S., & Sheperis, C. J. (2011). Evaluating and reporting statistical power in counseling research. *Journal of Counseling & Development, 89*(3), 268–272. https://doi.org/10.1002/j.1556-6678.2011.tb00088.x

Bardhoshi, G., Duncan, K., & Erford, B. T. (2018). Effect of a specialized classroom counseling intervention on increasing self-efficacy among first-grade rural students. *Professional School Counseling, 21,* 12–25. https://doi.org/10.5330/1096-2409-21.1.12

Bauman, S. (2006). Using comparison groups in school counseling research: A primer. *Professional School Counseling, 9,* 357–366.

Boyatzis, R. E. (1998). *Transforming qualitative information: Thematic analysis and code development.* Sage.

Byrne, B. (2010). *Structural equation modeling with AMOS: Basic concepts, applications, and programming* (3rd ed.). Taylor and Francis Group.

Camp, A., Foxx, S. P., & Flowers, C. (2019). Examining the relationship between the multicultural self-efficacy, empathy, and training of school counselors and their knowledge and skills supporting students experiencing homelessness. *Professional School Counseling, 22*(1), 1–10. https://doi.org/10.1177/2156759X19867332

Charmaz, K. (2014). *Constructing grounded theory.* Sage.

Choudhuri, D., Glauser, A., & Peregoy, J. (2004). Guidelines for writing a qualitative manuscript for the *Journal of Counseling & Development*. *Journal of Counseling & Development*, 82(4), 443–446.

Clarke, V., Braun, V., and Hayfield, N. (2015). Thematic analysis. In J. A. Smith (Ed.), *Qualitative psychology: A practical guide to research methods* (3rd ed., pp. 222–248). Sage Publications.

Corbin, J., & Strauss, A. (2008). *Basics of qualitative research: Techniques and procedures for developing grounded theory* (3rd ed.). Sage.

Creswell, J. W. (2009). *Research design: Qualitative, quantitative, and mixed methods approaches* (3rd ed.). Sage.

Fernald, D. H., & Duclos, C. W. (2005). Enhance your team-based qualitative research. *The Annals of Family Medicine*, 3(4), 360–364. https://doi.org/10.1370/afm.290

Finnerty, S., Luke, M., & Duffy, J. T. (2019). A grounded theory of experiential group training of school counselors to engage in psychoeducational group lessons with first-in-family students. *The Journal for Specialists in Group Work*, 44(2), 99–117. https://doi.org/10.1080/01933922.2019.1599476

Gall, M. D., Gall, J. P., & Borg, W. R. (2014). *Applying educational research: How to read, do, and use research to solve problems of practice* (7th ed). Prentice Hall.

Garcia, N. M., López, N., & Vélez, V. N. (2018). QuantCrit: Rectifying quantitative methods through critical race theory. *Race Ethnicity and Education*, 21(2), 149–157. https://doi.org/10.1080/13613324.2017.1377675

Garson, G. D. (2019). *Multilevel modeling: Applications in Stata, IBM SPSS, SAS, R, & HLM*. Sage.

Gillborn, D., Warmington, P., & Demack, S. (2018). QuantCrit: Education policy, "Big Data," and principles for a critical race theory of statistics. *Race Ethnicity and Education*, 21(2), 158–179. https://doi.org/10.1080/13613324.2017.1377417

González, M. (2016). Factors that facilitate and impede school counselor advocacy for and with LGBT students. *Journal of Counselor Leadership and Advocacy*, 3(2), 158–172. https://doi.org/10.1080/2326716X.2016.114739

Gutierrez, D., Conley, A. H., & Young, M. (2016). Examining the effects of Jyoti meditation on stress and the moderating role of emotional intelligence. *Counselor Education and Supervision*, 55, 109–122. https://doi.org/10.1002/ceas.12036

Grbich, C. (2012). *Qualitative data analysis: An introduction*. Sage.

Harris, P. N., Shillingford, M. A., & Bryan, J. (2019). Factors influencing school counselor involvement in partnerships with families of color: A social cognitive exploration. *Professional School Counseling*, 22, 1–10. https://doi.org/10.1177/2156759X18814712

Hays, D. G., & Singh, A. A. (2012). *Qualitative inquiry in counseling and education*. Guilford Press.

Heppner, P. P., Wampold, B. E., & Kivlighan, Jr., D. M. (2008). *Research design in counseling* (3rd ed.). Wadsworth.

Hill, C. E., Knox, S., Thompson, B. J., Williams, E. N., Hess, S. A., & Ladany, N. (2005). Consensual qualitative research: An update. *Journal of Counseling Psychology*, 52(2), 196. https://doi.org/10.1037/0022-0167.52.2.196

Hunt, B. (2011). Publishing qualitative research in counseling journals. *Journal of Counseling & Development*, 89(3), 296–300. https://doi.org/10.1002/j.1556-6678.2011.tb00092.x

Hunt, B., & Milsom, A. (2011). Academic writing: Reflections from successful counselor educators. *The Journal of Humanistic Counseling*, 50(1), 56–69. https://doi.org/10.1002/j.2161-1939.2011.tb00106.x

Jackson, D. L. (2010). Reporting results of latent growth modeling and multilevel modeling analyses: Some recommendations for rehabilitation psychology. *Rehabilitation Psychology*, 55(3), 272.

Kline, W. B. (2008). Developing and submitting credible qualitative manuscripts. *Counselor Education and Supervision*, *47*(4), 210–217. https://doi.org/10.1002/j.1556-6978.2008.tb00052.x

Lapan, R. T., Wells, R., Petersen, J., & McCann, L. A. (2014). Stand tall to protect students: School counselors strengthening school connectedness. *Journal of Counseling & Development*, *92*(3), 304–315. https://doi.org/10.1002/j.1556-6676.2014.00158.x

Lambie, G. W., Sias, S. M., Davis, K. M., Lawson, G., & Akos, P. (2008). A scholarly writing resource for counselor educators and their students. *Journal of Counseling & Development*, *86*(1), 18–25. https://doi.org/10.1002/j.1556-6678.2008.tb00621.x

Levitt, H. M., Bamberg, M., Creswell, J. W., Frost, D. M., Josselson, R., & Suárez-Orozco, C. (2018). Journal article reporting standards for qualitative primary, qualitative meta-analytic, and mixed methods research in psychology: The APA Publications and Communications Board task force report. *American Psychologist*, *73*(1), 26. http://dx.doi.org/10.1037/amp0000151

Limberg, D., Lambie, G. W., & Robinson, E. H. (2017). The contribution of school counselors' altruism to their degree of burnout. *Professional School Counseling*, *20*, 127–138. https://doi.org/10.5330/1096-2409-20.1.127

Limberg, D., & Ohrt, J. H. (2019, September). *Implementing a multiple article dissertation format to increase counselor education doctoral students' research identity development [Conference presentation]*. AARC 2019 Conference, San Antonio, TX.

Lynch, M. F. (2012). Using multilevel modeling in counseling research. *Measurement and Evaluation in Counseling and Development*, *45*, 211–224. https://doi.org/10.1177/0748175612437045

Mills, G., & Gay, L. (2019). *Educational research: Competencies for analysis and application* (12th ed.). Pearson Merrill Prentice Hall.

Moate, R. M., Gnilka, P. B., West, E. M., & Bruns, K. L. (2016). Stress and burnout among counselor educators: Differences between adaptive perfectionists, maladaptive perfectionists, and nonperfectionists. *Journal of Counseling & Development*, *94*(2), 161–171. https://doi.org.proxy.wm.edu/10.1002/jcad.12073

Moustakas, C. (1994). *Phenomenological research methods*. Sage.

Mullen, P. R., Blount, A. J., Lambie, G. W., & Chae, N. (2017). School counselors' perceived stress, burnout, and job satisfaction. *Professional School Counseling*, *21*(1). https://doi.org/10.1177/2156759x18782468

Nelson, A. H., Jenkins, D., Zanti, S., Katz, M. F., Berkowitz, E., Burnett, T. C., & Culhane, D. P., et al. (2020). *A toolkit for centering racial equity throughout data integration*. Actionable Intelligence for Social Policy, University of Pennsylvania. Available from: https://www.aisp.upenn.edu/aisp-Toolkit_5-27-20/

O'Hara, C., Chang, C. Y., & Giordano, A. L. (2021). Multicultural competence in counseling research: The cornerstone of scholarship. *Journal of Counseling and Development*, *99*(2), 200–209. https://doi.org/10.1002/jcad.12367

Ohrt, J. H., Limberg, D., Griffith, C., Sherrell, R., & Bordonada, T. (2016). Adolescents' perceptions of their school counselors' impact. *Journal of Children and Adolescent Counseling*, *2*, 1–15. https://doi.org/10.1080/23727810.2015.1133996

Ohrt, J. H., Prosek, E. A., Ener, E., & Lindo, N. (2015). The effects of a group supervision intervention to promote wellness and prevent burnout. *The Journal of Humanistic Counseling*, *54*, 41–58. https://doi.org/10.1002/j.2161-1939.2015.00063.x

Osborne, J. W., & Neupert, S. D. (2013). A brief introduction to hierarchical linear modeling. In T. Teo (Ed.), *Handbook of Quantitative Methods for Educational Research*. Sense Publishers.

Osborne, J. W., & Waters, E. (2002). Four assumptions of multiple regression that researchers should always test. *Practical Assessment, Research, and Evaluation*, *8*(1), Article 2. https://doi.org/10.7275/r222-hv23

Pallant, J. (2020). *SPSS survival manual: A step-by-step guide to data analysis using IBM SPSS.* (7th ed). McGraw Hill.

Paris, D., & Winn, M. T. (Eds.). (2013). Humanizing research: Decolonizing qualitative inquiry with youth and communities. Sage.

Polkinghorne, D. E. (1989). Phenomenological research methods. In R. S. Valle & S. Halling (Eds.) *Existential-phenomenological perspectives in psychology* (pp. 41–60). Springer.

Ponterotto, J. G., & Grieger, I. (2007). Effectively communicating qualitative research. *The Counseling Psychologist, 35*(3), 404–430. http://dx.doi.org/10.1177/0011000006287443

Raudenbush, S. W., & Bryk, A. S. (2001). *Hierarchical linear models: Applications and data analysis methods* (2nd ed.). Sage.

Rodriguez, A. J., Watson, J. C., & Gerlach, J. (2018). Comprehensive school counseling programs. *Journal of Professional Counseling: Practice, Theory & Research, 45*(2), 95–110. https://doi.org/10.1080/15566382.2019.1646082

Saldaña, J. (2015). *The coding manual for qualitative researchers.* Sage.

Schietz, R., & Villares, E. (2017). Effects of the Girl Squad Curriculum on grade 5 females' transition to middle school. *Counseling Outcome Research and Evaluation, 8*(1), 2–14. https://doi.org/10.1080/21501378.2017.1327747

Schreiber, J. B., Nora, A., Stage, F. K., Barlow, E. A., & King, J. (2006). Reporting structural equation modeling and confirmatory factor analysis results: A review. *The Journal of Educational Research, 99*(6), 323–338. https://doi.org/10.3200/JOER.99.6.323-338

Schumacker, R. E., & Lomax, R. G. (2014). *A beginner's guide to structural equation modeling* (4th ed.). Routledge.

Sink, C. A., & Stroh, H. R. (2006). Practical significance: The use of effect sizes in school counseling. *Professional School Counseling, 9,* 401–411.

Snijders, T. A. B., & Bosker, R. J. (2011). *Multilevel analysis. An introduction to basic and advanced multilevel modeling.* Sage.

Springer, S. I., Land, C. W., Moss, L. J., & Cinotti, D. (2018). Collecting school counseling group work data: Initiating consensual qualitative research through practitioner– researcher partnerships. *The Journal for Specialists in Group Work, 43*(2), 128–143. https://doi.org/10.1080/01933922.2018.1431346

Springer, S. I., Mason, E. C., Moss, L. J., Pugliese, A., & Colucci, J. (2020). An intervention to support elementary school faculty in meeting the needs of transgender and gender nonconforming Students. *Journal of Child and Adolescent Counseling, 6*(3), 181–199. https://doi.org/10.1080/23727810.2019.1689765

Taylor, J. V., Gibson, D. M., & Conley, A. H. (2019). Integrating yoga into a comprehensive school counseling program: A qualitative approach. *Professional School Counseling, 22*(1). https://doi.org/10.1177/2156759X19857921

Tracy, S. J. (2010). Qualitative quality: Eight "big-tent" criteria for excellent qualitative research. *Qualitative inquiry, 16*(10), 837–851. https://doi.org/10.1177/1077800410383121

Trusty, J. (2011). Quantitative articles: Developing studies for publication in counseling journals. *Journal of Counseling & Development, 89*(3), 261–267. https://doi.org/10.1002/j.1556-6678.2011.tb00087.x

Urbina, I., Villares, E., & Mariani, M. (2017). Examining the efficacy of the Spanish cultural translation of the Student Success Skills program to improve academic achievement. *The Journal of Humanistic Counseling, 56*(2), 127–143. https://doi.org/10.1002/johc.12048

Ware, W. B., & Galassi, J. P. (2006). Using correlational and prediction data to enhance student achievement in K–12 schools: A practical application for school counselors. *Professional School Counseling, 9*(5), 344–356.

Warren, J. M., Locklear, L., & Watson, N. (2018). The role of parenting in predicting student achievement: Considerations for school counseling practice and research. *The Professional Counselor, 8,* 328–340. https://doi.org/10.15241/jmw.8.4.328

Watson, J. C. (2017). Examining the relationship between self-esteem, mattering, school connectedness, and wellness among middle school students. *Professional School Counseling, 21,* 108–118. https://doi.org/10.5330/1096-2409-21.1.108

Webb, L., Brigman, G., Carey, J., Villares, E., Wells, C., Sayer, A., Harrington, K., & Chance, E. (2019). Results of a randomized controlled trial of the Student Success Skills program on grade 5 students' academic and behavioral outcomes. *Journal of Counseling and Development, 97,* 398–408. https://doi.org/10.1002/jcad.12288

Wester, K. L. (2011). Publishing ethical research: A step-by-step overview. *Journal of Counseling & Development, 89,* 301–307. https://doi.org/10.1002/j.1556-6678.2011.tb00093.x

Weston, R., & Gore, P. A., Jr. (2006). A brief guide to structural equation modeling. *The Counseling Psychologist, 34,* 719–751. https://doi.org/10.1177/0011000006286345

Zyromski, B., Hudson, T. D., Baker, E., & Granello, D. H. (2018). Guidance counselors or school counselors: How the name of the profession influences perceptions of competence. *Professional School Counseling, 22*(1), 1–9. https://doi.org/10.1177/2156759X19855654

Zyromski, B., Martin, I., & Mariani, M. (2019). Evaluation of the true goals school counseling curriculum: A pilot study. *The Journal for Specialists in Group Work, 44,* 170–183. https://doi.org/10.1080/01933922.2019.1634781

14

Bridging the Research-to-Practice Gap

Mandy Savitz-Romer and Amy L. Cook

Bridging the Research-to-Practice Gap

Most school counseling scholars enter doctoral programs with an interest in improving some aspect of the field. Whether you wanted to discover improved practices and approaches for supporting students or wished to explore school counselor competencies and skills, the path to the doctoral program began with an end in mind. It is with that same "end in mind" that we conclude this book with a chapter on bridging the gap between research and practice. The process of sharing your results with the aim of improving the field of school counseling requires a thoughtful plan. However, the field of education has long grappled with a persistent gap between what scholars produce and what educators use. Whereas there is no shortage of educational research, research may not be *usable*, or applicable or relevant, to the school community members whom researchers intend to impact. It is imperative that research production is relevant to individuals at the ground level who support positive development and address challenges, inequities, and experiences of marginalization. This final chapter is dedicated to discussing this critical final act of research—disseminating your findings for a meaningful, tangible impact.

Take a moment, before continuing on, to see if you can identify what inspired your research. Chances are, most of you identified some aspect of your work or the field of education you hoped to change or improve, or at the least, better understand. Indeed, many counselor educators can trace their research interests back to their direct practice as a counselor. That was certainly the case for us. I (Mandy) chose a career path in academia that would allow me to better understand the conditions that influence school counselors' everyday practice. I began my career as a high school counselor in a large, urban high school in Boston. The majority of my students were Black, Latinx, or Southeast Asian, and all of them were first-generation college-bound students. Despite the joy I found in my role, I confronted too many obstacles in my work. I chose to pursue a Ph.D. to explore questions I had about the field. For example, I often

Mandy Savitz-Romer and Amy L. Cook, *Bridging the Research-to-Practice Gap* In: *School Counseling Research*. Edited by: Brett Zyromski and Carey Dimmitt, Oxford University Press. © Oxford University Press 2023. DOI: 10.1093/oso/9780197650134.003.0014 felt ill prepared to support my students' college aspirations and goals and thus chose a graduate program in higher education to understand my students' experiences better as they transitioned to college. My goal was to engage in research and then communicate findings to my counseling colleagues so that counselors could be more effective. Today, much of my research continues to examine counselor preparation and the working conditions that enable counselors to be effective. As a senior lecturer at the Harvard Graduate School of Education, I find myself in the unique position as a non-tenured faculty, teaching preservice school counselors as well as other educators who share an interest in postsecondary readiness. And, importantly, I have continued to research the experiences of counselors and identify changes that are needed for them to support young people and their communities. While there are certainly drawbacks to a non-tenure-track faculty position (i.e., no tenure), it enables me to focus my energy engaging in research that is driven by the field and communicate my work directly to practitioners and policymakers. Over time, I have come to see my role as researcher and translator, ensuring that my work and that of my colleagues is accessible and usable to educators.

I (Amy) strive to engage in research that can make a meaningful impact on the communities I partner with. As an associate professor of counseling and school psychology at the University of Massachusetts Boston, I came to academia after working as a counselor for over 6 years in urban schools and communities. I worked as a school mental health counselor in Boston, serving primarily Spanish-speaking Latinx clients and families. Through this work, I learned the key importance of community supports, extended family networks, and equitable access to resources in supporting student needs. Framing my work in this way, I began to employ an ecological systems perspective in counseling, which appreciates the impact of sociocultural and contextual factors beyond individual, biological, and personal markers. This interest in larger systems led me to pursue doctoral studies and eventually work in academia as a counselor educator where my research and teaching efforts are focused. Bronfenbrenner's (1994) ecological model suggests there are multiple factors, both internal and external, that interconnect to impact an individual's development. Through this framework, in my previous practice as a counselor and currently as a counselor educator and researcher, I have sought to understand the various external influences that may facilitate and impede a child's development, including the immediate environment, a child's family, school, peers, etc. (microsystem), as well as the local community, media, local politics (exosystem), and broader systems and cultures (macrosystem). Today, my research draws upon ecological systems theory by challenging the assumption that evidence-based practices (EBPs) can be studied and implemented with an exclusive one-size-fits-all approach. To accomplish this, I approach research by building community-engaged participatory relationships with partner schools and organizations. In doing so, I conduct research that directly serves local schools and communities by integrating local knowledge contributions to address issues and advance the needs of communities.

For both of us, **staying closely connected to the users of our research** to ensure active use of our findings is a priority. Likewise, our respective relationships to the field contribute to the co-production of knowledge and our thoughts about how to bridge our work in the academy with those working in schools and directly with students. That is, we see the field as not just consumers of our work, but as contributors.

Purpose of This Chapter

Considering how and where to communicate your research is an important part of the research process. The purpose of this chapter is **to provide ideas for counselor educators to disseminate their research findings in ways that are usable and meaningful to the school communities and students served by the field.** As the preceding chapters suggest, there is great diversity within school counseling research, including how it is conceived, how it is carried out, and, as we will describe in this chapter, how it is communicated. We aim to cover the following key issues that school counseling scholars should consider regarding dissemination:

- designing research projects that matter to the field of school counseling
- understanding the range of options for disseminating your results
- learning the tensions and choice points in the decision-making process
- gaining resources for future dissemination of results

The Gap Between Research and Practice

The gap between educational research and applied practice has been a topic of great interest for over two decades (Cook et al., 2013; Kempe, 2019; Silver & Lunsford, 2017). Most of what has been written about the barriers impeding utilization of academic research considers shortcomings on the part of scholars. **Many argue that scholars have done little to ensure the active**

and usable dissemination of research findings, charging a range of reasons (Broekkamp & van Hout-Wolters, 2007; Silver & Lunsford, 2017). Some have asserted that researchers lack the background in the field to identify practical suggestions (Cook et al., 2013), while others question whether scholars see themselves as responsible for drawing real-world implications from their research or wonder if they assume educators will know how to apply the results of their work (Broekkamp & van Hout-Wolters, 2007). On the other hand, it is likely that the individuals affected within the school communities, particularly individuals from marginalized backgrounds whose voices may go unheard, need to be consulted to understand how best to apply research findings (Cammarota & Fine, 2008). Additional reasons for this gap include limited access to scholarly journals, overuse of jargon and academic language making research hard to understand, and the failure of researchers to articulate the implications of their research (Cook et al., 2013).

A common critique of scholars is that their research questions and methodology are too often not influenced by the field but, rather, conceived of in the academy with little input from those whom they are intended to support. In the words of Gordon and Conaway (2020, p. 4), research is "designed by and for researchers, rather than practitioners." Thus, it may not be surprising when educators then fail to seek it out or apply it to their work. Likewise, when scholars fail to incorporate the perspectives of those who are being researched, particularly when the sample includes minoritized youth or practitioners, research questions and methodologies are more likely to reinforce deficit-based narratives (Compton-Lilly et al., 2022).

While these arguments have merit, educational researchers counter that the organizational constraints of working in the academe are largely to blame. The pressure academics feel to publish, especially during the pre-tenure period, leads them to focus their dissemination efforts on publications in journals that may not be easily accessed or understood by practitioners. Likewise, some academic journals emphasize methodological rigor in their submission guidelines, thereby pressuring scholars to choose methodologies that will garner acceptance in a publication. In this way, researchers may choose a research approach that favors potential publication over a method that values the users of the research. This also leads to diminished accessibility of research findings and restricts their availability to predominantly white, middle-class, highly educated individuals—often other researchers. Anderson (2007) suggests that any of these barriers, combined with the usual time constraints, can lead to low levels of motivation and interest in making sure their work is accessible, usable, or looking for new ways to reach stakeholders.

Yet, scholars alone are not responsible for a lack of uptake of empirical research. Educators may not have the time or see the value in consulting educational research to inform their work (Broekkamp & van Hout-Wolters, 2007; Gordon & Conaway, 2020; Behrstock-Sherratt et al., 2011). Given the competing demands for their time, teachers report that using research is low on their list of priorities (Behrstock-Sherratt et al., 2011). Besides time, a lack of relevance is the most cited barrier to seeking out and using educational research. When educators do not see a connection between research and their everyday experience, they are unlikely to find it useful. Moreover, heavy use of research jargon and advanced methodological approaches can make it difficult for them to understand or apply the research findings. Gordon and Conaway (2020) suggest that educators may become overwhelmed by the statistical elements of research and miss out on key findings that common sense might otherwise help explain. Instead, research on teachers finds that they are more likely to consult other sources, such as colleagues, trade journals, or the Internet to address pressing concerns (Behrstock-Sherratt et al., 2011).

Research finds that educators are more likely to seek out and consult educational research when there is strong support for them to do so (Behrstock-Sherratt et al., 2011; See et al., 2016). Brown and colleagues (2016) found that when school climates value constant improvement, learning new approaches, and drawing on EBPs, teachers and other educators report more use of empirical research. Such climates consist of school leaders who create expectations and support for using research, dedicated time to read and discuss research, and even screen research to identify that which is of greatest value to educators (See et al., 2016).

Similar concerns emerge regarding a gap between research and policymakers. Those in the policy arena claim that educational research fails to align with the needs policymakers find most pressing (Hess, 2008; Ion et al., 2019). Plank (2014) suggests that the persistent gap between policymakers and those who engage in policy-related research can be traced to how each group conceives of questions, noting that the questions researchers most wish to explore are out of sync with what policymakers need answered. Thus, like the research–practice gap, the utilization of research for public policy purposes is similarly fraught with questions about the utility of research and its relevance to users outside of the academy.

The barriers described here contribute to a persistent **disconnect between research and practice.** Breaking down barriers between these multiple parties is necessary to ensure that your work has its intended impact and positions counselors to address pressing issues of inequality in their schools. Employing a diverse strategy for sharing your research results is one way to accomplish this.

Promising Examples

Research in the field of school counseling is constantly improving and evolving, and thus, while there are barriers to the use of empirical findings, there are fine examples of researchers who have successfully bridged the gap between research and practice to suggest a way forward for new and experienced scholars. As the school counseling profession is still relatively young, our scholarly community is still learning how our work can be carried out and disseminated to be most useful to students, families, and schools. Nonetheless, essential and impactful research in school counseling has already begun to positively influence our profession.

Student Success Skills (SSS) is a notable example of how empirical research has contributed to improvements in the field of school counseling broadly. This skills-oriented curriculum draws from a large research base on cognitive, behavioral, and social skills and distills the science behind these concepts into a practice-based intervention. The K–12 curriculum, which was designed to be led by counselors in classrooms and group counseling settings, has been empirically supported by multiple studies showing a positive influence on a range of outcomes, including student engagement, academic achievement, math and reading scores, and feelings of connectedness (Bowers et al., 2015; Renda & Villares, 2015; Villares et al., 2012; Webb et al., 2005). The curriculum's widespread use speaks to the potential for researchers to use evidence to shape practice through intentional dissemination strategies and the creation of evidence-based curricula and tools.

Research on **comprehensive school counseling models** and the **American School Counselor Association (ASCA) National Model** has also gone a long way to shape the field, both in research and in practice. Research has found improvements in student outcomes when counselors are able to implement comprehensive school counseling models (Borders & Drury, 1992; Gysbers & Henderson, 2005; Lapan, 2005). As a result, some school districts and even states have mandated this model to organize counselors' practices. However, even without mandates in place, some states recommend this model as a best practice guideline to organize school counselors' practices. For example, the Massachusetts *Model 3.0: A Framework for Comprehensive School Counseling Programs* (Massachusetts School Counselor Association, 2020) has been a driving force to guide school counseling practice, promoting equitable access to school counseling programs across the state. Furthermore, there has been a burgeoning global impact of the National Model with the development of the International Model for School Counseling Programs (Fezler & Brown, 2011).

Dissemination of Research Findings

A common feature among these successful and influential research programs leading to action is strategic and thoughtful **dissemination**. In this chapter, we define **dissemination as the intentional process of communicating research results with a range of audiences for the purpose of improving educational practices and policy.** More recently, some scholars have embraced a similar term, **knowledge mobilization**, to describe the process of making evidence usable and accessible across multiple stakeholders (Campbell et al., 2017). This term reflects a shift away from dissemination, which may connote a passive approach, to highlight the responsibility of scholars to ensure research has value and impact. Irrespective of the specific terminology, how you engage in this final step in the research process will influence whether your findings will lead to action in the field. It is not enough simply to "put out results," but, rather, as a scholar, it is your **responsibility to ensure your results are understandable, usable, relevant, and practical.** We recommend three strategies to ensure your work is usable and impactful:

1. Begin with the end in mind.
2. Target different avenues for dissemination.
3. Translate your results into actionable steps.

Begin With the End in Mind

School counselor researchers largely aim to disseminate research findings in ways that advance the field and support EBPs (Carey & Dimmitt, 2008; Zyromski et al., 2018). To bridge the gaps between research and practice, focusing on research methods that start with consideration of dissemination needs can shift the traditional ways that research unfolds. Scholars are increasingly urging the use of action-oriented research practices to counter problematic power dynamics as described in Chapter 9 (e.g., Manfra, 2019; Rowell, 2006). In this way, family–school–community stakeholders guide and shape the research questions and implementation strategies with key dissemination outcomes in mind.

Collaborative Research Approaches

Types of research that lead with the needs of school communities commonly include **collaborative research** approaches that actively engage communities throughout the research process. The reasons for implementing collaborative community-engaged research may vary, from the desire to make research more relevant and meaningful to the communities where research is conducted, to striving for research that supports equity-oriented outcomes (Warren et al., 2018). The term "collaborative research" refers broadly to collaborations between researchers and community stakeholders who are simultaneously participants in the research process. As explored in Chapter 2, and expounded upon in Chapter 9, this domain of research includes but is not limited to **action research, participatory action research, youth participatory action research, community-based research, community-engaged scholarship,** and others.

Research Practice Partnerships

Research practice partnerships develop in myriad ways, often guided by mutual needs and interests shared among researchers and schools. We recommend developing partnerships with **mutuality** as the organizing framework. School counseling scholars can first use the concepts offered in Chapter 2 by Steen and authors and then expand those concepts using the Bryan and Henry (2012) model for building family–school–community partnerships, which emphasizes key principles of shared collaboration, empowerment, and social justice. Following those principles will produce a groundwork for research practice partnerships. Many organizations and nonprofits provide resources for community-based scholars, organization leaders, and educators, while bringing together researchers and school community members to focus research efforts on mutual areas of interest. Some examples of organizations that provide a valuable platform from which to disseminate results from research practice partnerships include:

- SERP (Strategic Education Research Partnership) Institute[1]
- URBAN Research Network[2]
- The Wallace Foundation[3]

Sustainability is also essential to developing research practice partnerships. Well-established research practice partnerships allow for transformative change to occur where research outcomes can inform future practices and lead to continued improvements within the school community. For example, Cook et al. (2019) described fieldwork conducted with a long-standing school partner where training outcomes of the research collaboration resulted in advancing multicultural and social justice counseling skills for school counselor trainees and, in turn, improved youth development in the areas of academic perseverance and self-direction. This work builds upon previous collaborative research within the schools employing a Professional Development Schools Model (Cook et al., 2016; Cuccaro & Casey, 2007), where practicum fieldwork is completed as a group cohort at the same school, year after year. In this way, school counselor educators (SCEs) provide a mechanism to offer school counseling training that builds specific counseling skills (such as social justice competencies) and simultaneously supports a school's needs so that the administration and counseling department can rely on a long-standing research/practice partner. Outcomes of the research practice partnership have allowed for the graduate students in collaboration with the school-based partners to build on the previous year's work, such as creating and adding to a legacy project, that directly supported school counseling programming.

In addition to sustainability, these collaborations should be guided by forming **trusting relationships** with all school community stakeholders (not only with those in leadership positions, but also parent councils, students, and other faculty and staff). Moreover, it behooves researchers to recognize the ways in which the research process itself can be harmful by its inherent focus on revealing the knowledge and lived experiences of disadvantaged populations, those who may have high levels of distrust of researchers due to the history of exploitative, deficit-based, problem-oriented, and other unethical legacies of research (Datta, 2017). Collaborative research practice partnerships can enable inclusive practices that actively seek full engagement to develop research-based proposals that improve the quality of life for marginalized communities by offering ways for relevant participation. Doing so ensures that the cumulative findings are relevant and of interest to stakeholders.

Many scholars of color, feminist scholars, youth scholars, and white scholar allies who have explicitly positioned themselves as interested members of the communities where they form research practice partnerships may encounter **resistance when communicating findings** (Cook & Krueger-Henney, 2017). That is, they begin by seeking ways for their scholarship to promote transformative change, yet the findings may

---

Pop-Out 14.1. Case Vignette

You are an assistant professor and white scholar ally who works at a research-intensive university that values community-engaged research. As you enter your 4th year as a school counselor educator, you are excited to report that you have established a strong research collaboration and trusting relationship with several members of the leadership team from a local public school. As your partnership unfolds, you learn about the school's efforts to improve school climate and desire to strengthen academic outcomes, especially for students of color, English learners, and students who receive special education services. Because your research agenda focuses on promoting racial equity in education, you are thrilled about the opportunity to support these educational goals.

You mutually agree upon evaluating outcomes of antiracism dialogues that a community-based organization has been leading within the school community among parents and teachers. To conduct the evaluation, you get approval from the school and university institutional review boards, which includes recruiting participants to engage in post-interviews to inform your understanding of the impact of antiracism dialogues on school climate. The study procedures unfold without any challenges, and it is now time to communicate your findings. However, you are dismayed to discover that the school would prefer you to not disseminate widely. Although the leadership team expressed appreciation for your efforts (you provided an executive summary, shared findings in a presentation, and offered several tangible recommendations for next steps), you sense there is some discomfort with the qualitative findings pointing toward systemic barriers and persistent racist policies. You assure the school leadership team that the participant names and school name will not be disclosed. You are starting to ask yourself whether the work you have done will make a difference, especially considering that within the findings you identified specific needs for improvement to overcome the systemic barriers noted.

---

not be readily welcomed and put into action due to institutional and political constraints inherent within the organizational environment (Ozer, 2016). Take, for example, the following case scenario that displays this tension.

To ensure that your research findings will be welcomed by your partners, some groundwork is necessary. At the outset of the study, it is important to agree upon the different ways that the findings will be disseminated. For example, findings may be disseminated to the larger research community via scholarly publications and presentations. In these instances, confidentiality is of utmost importance where identifying information related to the location of the school and participants is not disclosed. Community-engaged researchers will often provide an executive summary and deliver a PowerPoint presentation to the partner organization but leave it up to the partner to identify action steps. As a result, change and improvements may be slow, which in turn can lead to a sense of mistrust by the very community participants who are at the forefront of a community-engaged researcher's work. How can you as the researcher promote transformational change and create a positive impact on the local community without inadvertently sustaining the status quo of institutionalized racism you and your partner set out to dismantle?

Helpful to answering this question is turning our attention to decolonizing, critical, and liberatory research methodologies that aim to reclaim participant rights and empower researchers. Included among these research methods are participatory action research and other collaborative methodologies, many of which were described in Chapter 9. Table 14.1 presents a list of sources describing decolonizing research practices and ways to overcome barriers to implementation.

Table 14.1. Liberatory Methodologies

Authors	Summary
Cammarota & Fine (2008)	This chapter within the text *Revolutionizing Education* describes how youth learn the skills of critical inquiry to examine social issues impacting their lives and then identify actions to redress the issues leading to systematic change and social justice. By connecting case studies with theory, research, and reflection, the authors provide the reader with a solid foundation of how adults partner with youth in overcoming obstacles to transformative change.
Ozer et al. (2013)	This article documents Youth Participatory Action Research (YPAR) findings with 77 youth across four high schools with a focus on the promotion of youth power despite constraints they encountered with different aspects of the research process, including limited power to define the problem to be researched and teacher buy-in.
Datta (2017)	In this article, the researcher describes a personal account of how engaging in decolonizing research transforms Western research practices into more empathic and meaningful outcomes for participants and communities.
Kohfeldt et al. (2011)	These researchers describe the importance of attending to a multiplicity of sociocultural factors when engaging youth in YPAR such that structural challenges and systemic constraints can be understood to influence possibilities for youth empowerment.

Some examples of organizations that provide a valuable platform for disseminating results from research practice partnerships include:

- YPAR Hub[4]
- International Lab for Liberatory Research[5]
- Public Science Project[6]
- Research for Organizing[7]

In sum, research practice partnerships that develop and support joint partner goals and produce meaningful outcomes at the outset are likely to weather changes in leadership over time and are most valuable to practitioners. This often means identifying the relevant action items and deliverables that each organization needs and can implement. It also means making sure you think creatively about how and where you share your results, which is what we describe next.

Target Different Avenues for Disseminating Your Results

Irrespective of your methodological approach, planning how to disseminate your research results takes careful thought and consideration of your audience and purpose. A diverse approach that carefully considers traditional barriers is warranted. **It is essential to consider *who* you want to reach, *how* you want to reach them, and *where* they can find your work.** Previously, we described the various ways that community-engaged scholars strive to make a meaningful impact on the local school or community. This may be achieved through the delivery and sharing of a program evaluation and/or presentation to the partner school or organization. Often SCEs may simultaneously strive to make larger impacts and thereby decide to disseminate their research findings more broadly. In this way, similar types of schools and communities can benefit from the research findings and recommendations. Ways to share research more broadly include the publication of works in scholarly peer-reviewed journals, state and national newsletters or trade journals, and books, and at academic and professional conferences. Depending on your topic, it might also warrant writing a book for a popular audience or placing an opinion piece in a local or national newspaper. If your goal is to reduce the gap between research and practice, while also reaching the broadest audience and influencing local, state, national, and global contexts, chances are you will need a **diverse approach** to sharing your results.

Who Would Benefit From Knowing About My Research?

One line of inquiry in school counseling research focuses on student outcomes and how specific counseling practices can improve student development and outcomes across the three professional domains: academic, social emotional, and postsecondary. Another area of school counseling inquiry examines the profession and how school counselors engage in their work and how they work with their colleagues, such as school and district leaders and role partners like teachers, social workers, and school psychologists. Thus, our sphere of influence is quite broad, and articulating your **target audience** is the first step in creating your dissemination plan. In Figure 14.1, we suggest a set of questions to help you determine the best audience for your research.

Understanding your audience is central to how you communicate and disseminate research findings. Do you aim to influence other practitioners, scholars, counselor educators, educators in general, students, families, and/or policymakers? Journal and conference outlets differ by their audience, and that should impact your choice of research outlet. Likewise, if your research has implications for school or district leaders or for students, families, or communities, sharing results with those stakeholders is just as important as communicating with counselors.

Where Can I Reach My Audience?

Once you have determined who your audience is, your next step is to **assess the best way to reach them.** Finding the right outlet for communicating your work will depend on your audience, professional expectations (i.e., tenure requirements), and even your budget. We have organized this next section into written and oral communication of findings. They both have their merits and differential impacts, and, thus, it is up to the researcher to decide which is best. When deciding which medium (written or oral) is best and where to

---

- Who stands to benefit from this research (i.e., students, school counselors, parents)?
- Who would benefit from learning about my research?
- Who bears responsibility for the implications of my research?
- What decision makers might need to learn about my work in order to support the implications of my findings?
- What professions or disciplines might be interested in my findings?

Figure 14.1. Questions for Determining Audience

> - Where does my audience go for professional learning?
> - What conferences do they attend?
> - What sources do they read?
> - Where else does my audience seek knowledge to inform their work?

Figure 14.2. Questions for Determining Appropriate Venues for Communicating Your Research

share your work, educational researchers consider a range of possibilities. In Figure 14.2, we suggest a set of questions to help you determine how best to reach your audience.

Disseminating Your Findings: Writing

Once scholars complete their research, their first step is to decide **where to communicate and/or publish research findings**. This decision-making process is often informed by guidelines and pressures within the academy that may reward certain publication and dissemination outlets over others, and which may take time away from being able to communicate results in areas that are most impactful to community stakeholders. More specifically, scholars who work in the academy at a research-intensive college or university will often feel bound by tenure guidelines that stress the importance of scholarly outputs in **peer-reviewed outlets**, including journals and conferences, or in scholarly books. The peer-review process, depending on the publication or sponsoring organization, is demanding and time consuming. This process typically includes extensive research, planning, writing, and revision processes. As a result, this pressure and time commitment needed to publish in peer-reviewed journals can reduce the researcher's ability to disseminate in ways that positively impact the communities they partner with. Despite these pressures, it is important to keep audience and purpose of your research in mind.

Academic Audiences

The most common outlet for educational research is the **academic journal**. Writing results for potential publication in a peer-reviewed journal involves a rigorous review of a manuscript typically by two to three "blind" reviewers. Peer-reviewed journals provide potential authors with guidelines that should be closely followed and are typically published on a journal's website. When submitting a manuscript for potential publication, the author(s) should not include identifying information so that the reviewers can provide a review that is not influenced by collegial relationships within the field.

When communicating results to scholars and colleagues in the field in peer-reviewed journals, the researcher will need to determine the best-fitting academic journal to submit to as a first step. Identifying the journal at which to target one's submission will depend on the focus of the manuscript, including research goals, type of research conducted, research study rigor, and audience being targeted. **Peer-reviewed journal** outlets may organize their journal by topic or type of research and seek manuscripts accordingly. For example, the *Professional School Counseling* journal includes featured research (encompassing empirical research and meta-analyses), conceptual articles (research presenting novel perspectives on timely topics), and practitioner-focused research (brief studies that document evidence of school counseling practice). Journals may also publish special issues on a specific topic and seek submissions accordingly. In addition, within the school counseling field, there are related discipline-specific journals that may be of interest to the researcher depending on the focus of the research completed. For example, within the American Counseling Association (ACA), school counseling research can be published in a variety of academic journals, including the *Journal of Child and Adolescent Counseling* and the *Journal of Multicultural Counseling and Development.*

Determining which journal to publish research in not only depends on the focus of the research and targeted audience but also may be guided by a researcher's institutional recommendations that are often connected to tenure and promotion. For researchers who teach at intensive research institutions and must conduct research to achieve tenure and promotion, they will be guided by best practices within the academy and typically seek publication outlets with high rigor. Determining level of rigor involves the identification of a journal's impact factor. The **impact factor is a measure that refers to the frequency that an article in a specific journal has been cited each year,** which then results in an overall rank and importance of that journal in its field (Sharma et al., 2014). Although counseling journals tend to have lower impact factors (or none at all) compared with journals from other fields such as medicine and health sciences, the metric may serve as one of many ways to inform the tenure review process. For professions that traditionally possess high demands for empirical inquiry, such as medicine, science, and technology, the impact factor of related journals tends to be high, whereas for the counseling profession, which has a relatively low readership and level of empirical research in comparison with other fields, the impact factors tend to be low or not calculated at all. For example, *Nature,* which is an interdisciplinary peer-reviewed journal that publishes empirical research in science, technology, and the natural sciences, has an impact factor of 42.778. On the other hand, the *Journal of Counseling & Development* has an impact factor of 1.381, and *Professional School Counseling* does not have an impact factor published. Table 14.2 provides a sample of journals that publish school counseling research, along with their reported impact factor.

Table 14.2. Sample Peer-Reviewed Journals with Impact Factor

Discipline/ Focus	Journal Name	Impact Factor
Education General	*American Educational Research Journal*	2.462
	American Journal of Education	1.316
	Educational Researcher	3.483
	Teachers College Record	1.072
	Theory Into Practice	1.432
	Educational Policy	1.765
Counseling	*Professional School Counseling*	Not published
	Journal of Counseling Psychology	3.697
	Journal of Multicultural Counseling and Development	1.594
	Counselor Education and Supervision	1.28
	Journal of Counseling & Development	1.381
	Counseling Outcome Research and Evaluation	1.05
	Journal of School-Based Counseling Policy and Evaluation	Not published

These traditional scholarly demands within the academy inevitably result in a knowledge production that is typically led and communicated by the academy, while the voices of the very individuals affected by the research (e.g., partners and participants) are excluded. However, community-engaged researchers, those who seek participatory approaches to research, aim to shift this traditional stance to widen knowledge contributions (Fox, 2015). They do so in a variety of ways throughout the research process involving participant feedback in the analyses, seeking input from community partners, and occasionally involving research collaborators to join in the writing process (Christopher et al., 2008). Relatedly, youth participatory action research (YPAR) is designed to build the capacity of young people to undertake research and action to address immediate needs in their lives or in their schools (Cammarota and Fine, 2008). YPAR builds on the emancipatory pedagogy of Paulo Freire (1970) and elevates youth with experiences of their own power to produce knowledge of use to themselves and their communities, a practice that marginalized youth typically do not experience in schools. Outcomes of YPAR studies have been documented in peer-reviewed journals and thereby provide opportunities to meet the publishing requirements within the academy while simultaneously promoting community capacity (see, for example, Smith & Hope, 2020).

Practitioner Audiences

Seeking tenure in the academy will govern, to some extent, where you choose to publicize your work. However, ensuring your findings fall into the hands of practitioners or policymakers will require you to write for non-academic publications as well. Writing for a non-academic audience is not an easy task. Thoughtfully preparing written pieces for practitioners requires careful consideration of your audience and an intentional effort to avoid the academic style and format you may have learned in graduate school. The goal here is to write clearly, concisely, and with a focus on application of your findings. Similar to the academic community, writing for practitioners includes many possible venues for your work. **Professional trade journals** are an ideal avenue for reaching practitioners, both school counselors and related stakeholders such as school leaders or social workers. Professional organizations typically publish their own journals, and scholars can share their research findings without enduring the more comprehensive peer review process of academic journals. Table 14.3 offers examples of popular magazines and trade journals that are good outlets for school counseling–related research.

When presenting work in these types of publications, scholars should establish clear goals for content and keep their audience in focus. We recommend

Table 14.3. Examples of Professional Trade Journals by Audience

School counselors	*The School Counselor*[a]; *Counseling Today*[b]
School leaders	*The School Administrator*[c]; *Educational Leadership*[d]
All educators	*American Educator*[e]; *Phi Delta Kappan*[f]; *Middle Ground*[g]
Role partners	*Social Work Today*[h]

[a] https://www.schoolcounselor.org/magazine

[b] https://ct.counseling.org/

[c] https://www.aasa.org/schooladministrator.aspx

[d] http://www.ascd.org/publications/educational-leadership.aspx

[e] https://www.aft.org/ae

[f] https://kappanonline.org/

[g] http://www.amle.org/servicesevents/middleground/tabid/174/default.aspx

[h] https://www.socialworktoday.com/

> - <u>Begin with an opening hook:</u> Use a scenario or other story that sets the context for your research. This should set up the reader to understand the real-world application of your findings.
> - <u>Provide background context:</u> Provide a brief snapshot of the literature that grounds your research to situate the significance of your work.
> - <u>Describe your findings:</u> Choose two to four key themes that are most relevant to your audience.
> - <u>Offer concrete recommendations for practice or policy:</u> Offer three to five concrete recommendations that answer the question "How should I adapt my role/work?"

Figure 14.3. Sample Template for Trade Journal Articles

submissions that are engaging and offer educators clear recommendations for their work. Many of these outlets publish specific guidelines for submissions. I (Mandy) use a particular format to structure trade journal articles, shown here in Figure 14.3.

If you are unsure of whether or not a particular source is appropriate, sending the editor a brief query is acceptable. Doing so will not only save you time but also let you know if there is a special topic issue to which you can contribute. For a good example of special issues outside of the school counseling field, see the *College, Careers, Citizenship* issue of *Educational Leadership*.[8]

Some scholars prefer to communicate their findings in a **research brief**, which rarely requires a formal review process and is an ideal choice when a concise summary of the research is sufficient, and the researcher hopes to communicate their work to a wide audience within a short time frame. A research brief typically includes an executive summary and brief description of your data, methodology, and findings. One challenge to using research briefs is that you need a way to deliver the brief to your audience. One solution is to partner with a research center or other organization to share the brief with their members or networks. The Ronald H. Fredrickson Center for School Counseling Outcome Research and Evaluation (CSCORE)[9] has published a number of school counseling research briefs. Additional organizations that produce counseling-related research briefs include: the American School Counselor Association,[10] The Education Trust,[11] and the Forum for Youth Investment.[12]

An important audience we have not yet discussed are **policymakers**. Many researchers hope their findings will influence public policy so that they can promote structural, institutional, and societal change; however, they lack familiarity with how to communicate or reach these constituents. Although policymakers may read empirical research or professional trade publications, and thus many of the previously suggested outlets should be explored, policy-focused journals and policy briefs are additional avenues for publication.

A policy-focused school counseling journal such as the *Journal of School-Based Counseling Policy and Evaluation* (*JSCPE*)[13] may be a great fit for policy-related research. Alternatively, counselor educators may choose to share their work in general policy journals such as *Educational Policy.*[14] Professional organizations with a commitment to professional advocacy may produce policy briefs, and, thus, researchers might consider partnering with those organizations to share relevant findings. Like research briefs, **policy briefs** offer scholars a dissemination option that includes a brief synopsis of one's research with an emphasis on policy implications. The National Association of College Admissions Counselors[15] and The Education Trust[16] produce excellent examples of policy briefs related to school counseling and are available on their websites.

Many educational researchers also use **published books** to disseminate their research, including **academic press books**, **trade books**, **textbooks**, and **curricular books**. Whereas **academic press books** are defined as a long-form publication detailing in-depth academic study, **textbooks** are comprehensive in nature and focus on a specific area of study. Although textbooks are most often used by educators, some instructors will also use **trade books** in their teaching. Trade books, a term used to describe a wide array of book types, are often used in education to reach a broader, or more practice-oriented, audience. For example, ASCA publishes a resource series for scholars to share practice-oriented scholarship. Some books provide useful templates and tools, known as **curricular books**. These practical texts are often organized around specific learning objectives and guide the reader to adopt new strategies. You may elect to use books to share your results if:

- You have a lot of data from multi-year projects or longitudinal research.
- You wish to share accompanying resources developed to be put into use based on the research.
- Your work has value to a broad audience.
- Your findings have value to those who teach in academia.

You may be wondering, "How do I know if someone is willing to publish my book?" The short answer is that you will never know if you don't ask! Very rarely do publishers *ask* scholars to publish books. It is more often the case that authors submit proposals, for which guidelines are accessible on publishers' websites. However, you can always request a short meeting or send a query to a book editor to explore the possibility. Table 14.4 illustrates the range of book types that have been used by counselor educators or related scholars to share their work.

Table 14.4. Range of Book Types With Examples and Publisher

Academic Press Books	Trade Books	Textbooks	Curricular Books
The Privileged Poor (Jack, 2019), Harvard University Press.	*Interrupting Racism: Equity and Social-Justice in School Counseling* (Atkins & Oglesby, 2019), Routledge.	*Multicultural Issues in Counseling: New Approaches to Diversity* (Lee, 2014), John Wiley & Sons.	*Leading for Change Through Whole-School Social-Emotional Learning: Strategies to Build a Positive School Culture* (Rogers, 2019), Corwin.

As we have shown, scholars have many choices about where they can write about their research. Importantly, researchers may **publish in more than one source**, often highlighting different findings or aspects of their data. However, it is important to avoid duplicating your writing, as publishing sources have strict rules about this. In addition, time constraints may hinder scholars' ability to publish in both academic and trade or popular publications. As noted above, where you are in your career ladder may also play a role in this choice. For some scholars, their scope of work in the academy involves an emphasis on teaching and service efforts over research, which tends to be the case for clinical faculty or lecturers at research-intensive institutions, or for faculty at institutions with low research demands. In these instances, scholars use a variety of the formats described above to reach their desired audience. Regardless of your rank, we recommend thinking critically about your intended audience and how your written work can reach them.

With any publication type, *how* you communicate your research matters. How you tell the story of your research, including what you share and how you share it, will determine its value to the field. When preparing findings for translational activities, remember that the stakeholders we present to are, for the most part, untrained in research methods. What is potentially confusing to them about the analyses? What do they need to understand? Have we included graphs or visuals that might be confusing, misleading, or difficult to interpret? What are common misconceptions that might arise? These are important questions to ask yourself as you prepare your written work. The following resources provide tips and strategies for communicating your research:

- *Going Public: Writing About Research in Everyday Language*[17]
- *Writing Well About Research in Education*[18]
- *Communicating Research: Readings, Tips, and Strategies*[19]
- *Public Communication for Researchers*[20]
- *How to Put Educational Research to Work*[21]

Disseminating Your Findings: Presentations

In addition to written communication of results, counselor educators may elect to disseminate findings at **academic and professional conferences** that bring together researchers and practitioners as an opportunity to share findings, network, and build knowledge on trending topics and new perspectives. Academic and professional conferences serve audiences locally, at the state level, nationally, and internationally. The following section provides greater detail about academic and professional conferences, including examples and key recommendations for presenting your research.

The Academic Conference

Perhaps the most common place for scholars to share the results from empirical research is the academic or research conference, including national and regional options. These conferences, sometimes referred to as **scholarly** or **scientific conferences**, offer a valuable venue for researchers to share their work and learn about scholarship in their field. The avenues through which findings are presented include posters, round-table discussions, paper presentations, and symposium presentations. They will also typically include an invited guest speaker who presents on a particular topic that is relevant to the theme of the conference. Given the different options for sharing findings, presenters will need to choose the modality through which they disseminate research in this context. Typically, when it is a first-time presentation or attendance at a conference, presenters may choose to submit a poster presentation. This allows the presenter to share findings while also learning more about the conference. The modality of presentation is also guided by the extent of research completed. If the research is in its beginning phase of data collection or only preliminary results are known, a poster presentation may be the best approach for sharing information. Once findings are complete, the presenter may opt for disseminating results via a paper presentation. Conducting a round-table discussion is another option for researchers when the research is in its exploration phase as a means to share and learn from others who are interested in the same topic. Round-table discussion can also facilitate sharing on timely topics or ideas but may not intend to share study findings. For an overview of these different types of submissions to academic conferences, see Calarco (2020).

School counseling researchers have many choices about where they can present their work, considering **international**, **national**, **regional**, or **local** school counseling–specific conferences, or those that focus on related disciplines (i.e., school psychology, educational research). I (Mandy) sometimes present at the Association for the Study of Higher Education (ASHE) conference because my work on college access aligns well with higher education. I (Amy) sometimes present at the Association for Assessment and Research in Counseling (AARC) because I can learn and share best practices related to research methodologies within the counseling profession. Because much of my research is about how we conduct research, I find method-oriented conferences particularly of value. Identifying conferences will likely be determined by your research topic, method, and the relevance of the findings. Examples of additional school counseling–related academic conferences include:

- ACES (Association for Counselor Education and Supervision)[22]
- AERA (American Educational Research Association)[23]
- ACA (American Counseling Association)[24]
- ACAC (Association for Child and Adolescent Counseling)[25]
- EBSCC (Evidence-Based School Counselor Conference)[26]
- NCDA (National Career Development Association)[27]
- SRCD (Society for Research in Child Development)[28]
- SREE (Society for Research on Educational Effectiveness)[29]

Preparing for your first academic conference can be daunting, especially when you are new to the field; however, it is important to remember that these are ideal places not only to share your findings but also to receive **feedback** prior to submitting your work for publication. Academic conferences enable you to network with others in your field, stay abreast of new scholarship, and learn new types of methodologies. One of the best ways to prepare for disseminating your results at academic conferences is to attend as a graduate student or early career researcher. Doing so will help you understand how they operate and learn about expectations for presenting through observation. Ultimately, these professional gatherings are important spaces for our field and a valuable way to become part of a larger professional community.

Professional Conferences

Whereas the audience at an academic conference is likely made up of academics, **professional conferences** offer researchers the chance to communicate their work to practitioners in the field. These conferences create opportunities for networking, while learning new ways to solve challenges encountered in the field. Presentations typically include **posters, roundtable discussions, paper presentations**, and **symposium presentations** similar to academic conferences. However, typically the content communicated will be focused on professional practice, whereas academic conferences will often include research-focused presentations in addition to practice-based presentations. Below, we have listed some of the most common professional conferences where school counseling research and best practices are shared.

- ASCA (American School Counselor Association)[30]
- AMCD (Association for Multicultural Counseling and Development)[31]
- NACAC (National Association of College Admission Counseling)[32]
- NCDA (National Career Development Association)[33]
- NCAN (National College Attainment Network)[34]
- EBSCC (Evidence-Based School Counseling Conference)[35]
- SXSWEdu (South by Southwest EDU)[36]

Like the written dissemination process, selecting venues for presenting your work will depend on your audience. For example, if your research examines the relationship between school counselors and school administrators, you may want to present at the National Principals Conference,[37] hosted by the National Association of Secondary School Principals (NASSP) or at the Association for Supervision and Curriculum Development (ASCD)[38] annual conference. Certainly, all research related to school counseling will have relevance at the professional counseling conferences; however, taking the time to consider additional **stakeholders** will increase the likelihood that your work will be utilized. Examples of conferences attended by counselors' role partners include:

- NASSP Conference[39]
- The Boost Conference[40]
- School Mental Health Conference
- National Family Engagement Summit[41]
- National Center for School Mental Health Conference[42]

An important consideration when presenting your research is whether to include others in your presentation. Whether at a professional or academic conference, there may be times when **co-presenting** your work is appropriate. Being part of a research team or collaborating on a research project certainly lends itself to co-presenting. However, as a researcher, you may also consider partnering with a practitioner when sharing your results. SCEs who are no longer practicing as school counselors will have less knowledge related to the most recent changes in the field. Thus, joining with a practitioner to present helps counselor educator researchers to build connections between research and practice. Moreover, audiences will appreciate the chance to hear a practitioner present how they make meaning of your findings. Finally, including high school or graduate students in your presentations is an important part of mentoring new leaders in the field.

Conferences are not the only places to present your work; however, given their scope and size, they arguably offer the best pathway for reaching a wide or cross-sectional group of professionals. Additional opportunities for sharing your work via presentations include guest lectures in classes, campus events, professional development workshops in schools and districts, and university colloquia. While these presentations offer valuable opportunities for getting your work into the hands and minds of educators, an important secondary benefit is the feedback you will gain for use on future scholarly pursuits.

Beyond the Basics

Thus far, this chapter has reviewed traditional formats for sharing your research findings. In addition, many educational researchers utilize other venues for reaching a wider audience such as newspaper op-ed's, social media channels, podcasts, webinars, or blogs. Some of these media do require invitations; however, in most cases, researchers may choose to solicit invitations to submit something.

Op-Eds or Opinion Pieces

There may be instances in which sharing findings through **newspaper op-eds** is a good option. Often, these are best used when your research is related to a timely issue and your recommendations carry a sense of urgency. Generally, turnaround time for opinion pieces is very short. For example, I (Mandy) wrote about how school counselors perceived the high-profile Varsity Blues scandal in which wealthy families were paying large sums of money to ensure college admission for their children. Because my research was focused on calling attention to the key role school counselors play in widening access to college, and this case called into question inequitable admissions practices, the scandal and widespread attention to it offered a good platform to reinforce my recommendations that we better support counselors' college readiness work. Some good options for opinion pieces related to counselor educators' research include:

- *The Hechinger Report*[43]
- *Education Week*[44]

- *The Chronicle of Higher Education*[45]
- *NEA Today*[46]
- *Phi Delta Kappan*[47]
- Local/State newspapers

Social Media

Another way that academics have recently begun to share their research findings is through **social media channels** (Cooper, 2014). According to some research, "as of 2010, just four years after Twitter launched, as many as 40 percent of academics were creating accounts, and since then, scholars have harnessed the site as a way to disseminate ideas beyond the 'Ivory Tower'" (Dickinson, 2019, para. 9). In recent years, these tools have been used not just to share findings, but also to raise stature and representation in a given field. These platforms provide incredible access to a wide range of stakeholders and a way to connect with practitioners to move the field forward. One of the benefits to using social media to share results includes the rapid manner in which researchers can get their work out and the breadth of people who can be reached in a single space. For a valuable resource on using social media to disseminate research, see "Communicating Your Research with Social Media" by Mollet and colleagues (2017).

Webinars and Podcasts

In addition to the digital platforms we have discussed so far, **webinars** and **podcasts** are another medium used by researchers to communicate their findings. Webinars enable scholars to reach a wide target audience and promote greater research access to practitioners. For example, the ASCA posts webinars on various topics that are available to ASCA members free of charge. State school counseling associations likewise regularly provide their members with opportunities to access webinars. In order to lead or coauthor a webinar, often a leader of the association will reach out to the researcher after publication of an article or book. However, it is possible to reach out to the ASCA or your local state school counseling association to share your research and pitch a webinar idea.

Similar to webinars, **podcasts** provide researchers an outlet for disseminating findings; however, they do so in a manner that is less restricted to the sponsoring organization's charge. Podcasts provide a venue free of the guidelines and structures common to academic journals and conferences and instead invites researchers to talk about their research in their own voice and with emphasis on whatever may be of interest to a **lay audience**. In this way, it is more of a "conversation with a curious layperson" (Raman, 2018, para. 4). Like social media, podcasts offer the benefit of making research accessible to a broad audience, reaching new audiences that might not otherwise know about your work (Mollet et al., 2017). One potential challenge is that oftentimes researchers wait to be invited to join an episode of an existing podcast. However, scholars can certainly reach out and request opportunities to participate, or as counselor educator Trish Hatch has done, start your own! At the time of publication, some good examples include *Hatching Results Podcast*, ASCA *Podcast, Research in Action, School Psyched, Leading Equity,* and *How to Talk to Kids About Anything.*

University and Related Resources

Many universities have in-house **marketing and communication departments** that are willing, and often eager, to promote faculty research. At a minimum, these departments can include your work in regular materials (magazines, websites); however, some have specific initiatives intentionally aimed at sharing findings with the field using faculty research newsletters. A relatively new trend in some professional schools is the adoption of usable knowledge centers. These centers act as a mediator between faculty research and related constituents (typically alumni). Usable Knowledge[48] hosted by the Harvard Graduate School of Education, is one example of this format for sharing new ideas generated by empirical research with educators. Another good example, the Consortium for Policy Research in Education (CPRE) Knowledge Hub,[49] is an online portal designed to increase practitioners' and policymakers' use of educational research. Both of these online platforms offer podcasts, research and policy briefs, and other kernels of data from educational research. Relatedly, research and social networking sites exist for researchers to disseminate and find collaborators on research projects, including ResearchGate, Google Scholar, and Scholarworks. These sites allow users to upload and share research, data, proposals, and presentations.

Throughout this section, we have discussed various approaches to closing the persistent gap that traditionally prevents scholars' research from reaching and being used by practitioners. Ultimately, educational researchers have to choose a dissemination strategy that takes into account their audience, professional expectations, skill set, and research goals. In Table 14.5, we outline a hypothetical dissemination plan that could be used to communicate results from a research study that tested out a suicide prevention intervention in a large urban district.

Table 14.5. Sample Research Project Dissemination Plan

Who Needs to Hear This?	Where Can I Reach Them Through Written Work?	Where Might I Present Findings?	Other Possible Communication Strategies
Participants	Research brief or summary	Staff professional development	Family–School–Community events
School District Community	Research brief; infographic of findings	Staff professional development	Union newsletter, school board meeting
School Counselors	Trade journal (*The School Counselor*)	Conference (*American School Counselor Association; State School Counselor Association*)	Twitter, state professional organization newsletters
School Leaders	Trade journal (*The School Principal*)	Conference (*Council of Great City Schools*)	University newsletter
Philanthropists	Open access publication (*The Chronicle of Philanthropy*)	Conference (*Grantmakers in Education*)	Opinion editorial
Developmental Psychologists/ Counselors	Peer-reviewed journal (*Journal of Adolescent Development; Journal of Child and Adolescent Counseling*)	Conference (*Association for Child and Adolescent Counseling*)	Twitter
Counselor Educators	Peer-reviewed journal (*Counselor Education and Supervision; Journal for Social Action in Counseling and Psychology*)	Conference (*Association for Counselor Education and Supervision*)	Blog (e.g., *Counseling Today*)
Academics in Related Fields	Peer-reviewed journal (*Journal of Counseling and Development*)	Conference (*American Association of Suicidology*)	

Translate Your Results Into Actionable Steps

We have described dissemination of your findings as the final step in the research project. Regardless of whether you are sharing your results with participants from your study, or a broader audience, it is essential that your results clearly outline **implications** for their work, both in future research and practice.

When writing for academic audiences, educational researchers typically highlight **future areas for research**. As a newly minted expert on your topic, you are well positioned to suggest to your readers how your findings might shape scholars' work in the field. This can be an opportunity to highlight avenues for inquiry you chose not to pursue in your study, or new questions that emerge through your analysis. In some cases, researchers will suggest further research that addresses limitations to their study. For example, if a limitation to your research on school counselors' experiences broaching topics of racial identity was the limited number of counselors of color in your study, you might call for future scholarly work to understand the experiences of school counselors of color better.

As we discussed with collaborative research approaches, an important context for sharing your results is with the participants themselves. It is considered courteous to offer your participants a research summary as a "thank you" for taking part in a study. And, as was discussed in several chapters in this book, this step is a valuable way to check your findings with participants or, even, gather information to inform subsequent projects. However, it is also critical to make sure your results are **translated into actionable steps**. Consider the case example in Pop-Out 14.2 as illustrative of how to translate your work into concrete steps for practitioners.

Pop-Out 14.2. Case Vignette

Two associate professors were conducting research on student engagement and belonging at a nearby high school. The faculty collaborated closely with the school principal and school counselors to ensure that the research questions reflected areas of concern and interest to the school staff and community. When the analyses were complete, the research team created a **Translation Team** consisting of faculty, graduate students, and several staff members from the school. The purposes of the Translation Team included:

- Receiving feedback for the research team, both in terms of reactions to past/current analyses and directions for future analyses
- Answering questions from the stakeholders about the research process
- Prompting reflection and informing stakeholders' practice
- Building trust and furthering the collaborative relationship between research team and school site

The team met biweekly to interpret findings and create weekly **data snapshots** to be shared with the full school staff. Each snapshot consisted of a "Did you know [insert data point]?" and "Something you might consider [insert recommendation for practice]." The data snapshots were shared with teachers via weekly staff bulletins and presented on bulletin boards around the school. The Translation Team also met with students from the school to hear how they made meaning of the results and to solicit their ideas for promoting improved student engagement and belonging.

This case vignette reflects how translating your results into action steps for your participants is a valuable step in ensuring that your work is understood and applied. However, the same rules apply when writing or presenting to practitioner audiences. This translation process calls for researchers to think creatively about their findings and offer clear guidance for what this means for the reader's work. This can be achieved by asking the question "What do the results mean for what I do on Monday morning?"

Conclusion

Whether you pursue publications, presentations, data snapshots, or tweets, sharing and communicating results with the intent to make change is an important final act in the research process. This will require sustained interactions between researchers and practitioners and policymakers. These connections will inform your research agenda, while also giving you valuable insight into possible avenues for dissemination. In short, conceiving of dissemination as an integral path toward ensuring that your research leads to action is as important as the research process itself.

Notes

1. https://www.serpinstitute.org/
2. https://urbanresearchnetwork.org/
3. https://www.wallacefoundation.org
4. http://yparhub.berkeley.edu/
5. https://www.liberatoryresearch.org/
6. http://publicscienceproject.org/
7. https://www.researchfororganizing.org
8. http://www.ascd.org/publications/educational-leadership/apr12/vol69/num07/Ready,-Willing,-and-Able.aspx
9. https://www.umass.edu/education/center/school-counseling/research
10. https://www.schoolcounselor.org/
11. https://edtrust.org/our-resources/publications/
12. https://forumfyi.org/knowledge-center/
13. https://scholarworks.wm.edu/jscpe/
14. https://journals.sagepub.com/home/epx
15. https://www.nacacnet.org/advocacy--ethics/policy-briefs/
16. https://edtrust.org/our-resources/publications/?q=
17. https://files.eric.ed.gov/fulltext/ED545224.pdf
18. https://www.phledresearch.org/post/writing-well-about-research-in-education
19. https://www.gse.harvard.edu/news/uk/communicating-research

20. https://www.cmu.edu/student-org/pcr/
21. https://digitalpromise.org/2014/09/09/how-we-can-put-educational-research-to-work/
22. https://acesonline.net/aces-conference-information/
23. https://www.aera.net/Events-Meetings/Annual-Meeting
24. https://www.counseling.org/conference/conference-2021
25. http://acachild.org/news-and-events/join-us-at-aca-in-san-francisco/
26. https://www.ebscc.org/
27. https://www.ncda.org/aws/NCDA/pt/sp/conference_home
28. https://www.srcd.org/event/srcd-2021-biennial-meeting
29. https://www.sree.org/conferences
30. https://www.schoolcounselor.org/
31. https://www.multiculturalcounselingdevelopment.org/
32. https://www.nacacnet.org/
33. https://www.ncda.org/
34. https://www.ncan.org
35. https://www.ebscc.org/
36. https://www.sxswedu.com/
37. https://www.principalsconference.org/
38. http://www.ascd.org/Default.aspx
39. https://www.principalsconference.org/
40. http://www.boostconference.org/
41. https://nfesummit.com/
42. http://www.schoolmentalhealth.org/Conferences/Annual-Conference-on-Advancing-School-Mental-Health/
43. https://hechingerreport.org/?
44. https://www.edweek.org/
45. https://www.chronicle.com/
46. https://www.nea.org/publications
47. https://kappanonline.org/
48. https://www.gse.harvard.edu/uk
49. https://cprehub.org/

References

Anderson, T. R. (2007). Bridging the educational research-teaching practice gap: The importance of bridging the gap between science education research and its application in biochemistry teaching and learning: Barriers and strategies. *Biochemistry and Molecular Biology Education*, 35(6), 465–470. https://doi.org/10.1002/bmb.20136

Atkins, R., & Oglesby, A. (2019). *Interrupting racism: Equity and social justice in school counseling*. Routledge.

Behrstock-Sherratt, E., Drill, K., & Miller, S. (2011). *Is the supply in demand? Exploring how, when, and why teachers use research*. American Institutes for Research.

Borders, L. D., & Drury, S. M. (1992). Comprehensive school counseling programs: A review for policymakers and practitioners. *Journal of Counseling & Development*, 70(4), 487–498. https://doi.org/10.1002/j.1556-6676.1992.tb01643.x

Bowers, H., Lemberger, M. E., Jones, M. H., & Rogers, J. E. (2015). The influence of repeated exposure to the Student Success Skills program on middle school students' feelings of connectedness, behavioral and metacognitive skills, and reading achievement. *The Journal for Specialists in Group Work*, *40*(4), 344–364. https://doi.org/10.1080/01933922.2015.1090511

Broekkamp, H., & van Hout-Wolters, B. (2007). The gap between educational research and practice: A literature review, symposium, and questionnaire. *Educational Research and Evaluation*, *13*(3), 203–220. https://doi.org/10.1080/13803610701626127

Bronfenbrenner, U. (1994). Ecological models of human development. In *International Encyclopedia of Education* (Vol. 3, 2nd ed.). Elsevier. (Reprinted from *Readings on the development of children*, 2nd ed., pp. 37–43, by M. Gauvain & M. Cole, Eds., 1997, Freeman.)

Brown, C., Daly, A., & Liou, Y.-H. (2016). Improving trust, improving schools: Findings from a social network analysis of 43 primary schools in England. *Journal of Professional Capital & Community*, *1*(1), 69–91. https://doi.org/10.1108/JPCC-09-2015-0004

Bryan, J., & Henry, L. (2012). A model for building school-family-community partnerships: Principles and process. *Journal of Counseling & Development*, *90*(4), 408–420. https://doi.org/10.1002/j.1556-6676.2012.00052.x

Calarco, J. (2020). *A field guide to grad school: Uncovering the hidden curriculum*. Princeton University Press.

Cammarota, J., & Fine, M. (2008). Youth participatory action research. In J. Cammarota, & M. Fine (Eds.), *Revolutionizing education* (pp. 89–124). Routledge.

Campbell, C., Pollock, K., Briscoe, P., Carr-Harris, S., & Tuters, S. (2017). Developing a knowledge network for applied education research to mobilise evidence in and for educational practice. *Educational Research*, *59*(2), 209–227. https://doi.org/10.1080/00131881.2017.1310364

Carey, J., & Dimmitt, C. (2008). A model for evidence-based elementary school counseling: Using school data, research, and evaluation to enhance practice. *The Elementary School Journal*, *108*(5), 422–430. https://doi.org/10.1086/589471

Christopher, S., Watts, V., McCormick, A. K. H. G., & Young, S. (2008). Building and maintaining trust in a community participatory research partnership. *American Journal of Public Health*, *98*(8), 1398–1406. https://10.2105/AJPH.2007.125757

Compton-Lilly, C., Ellison, T. L., Perry, K. H., & Smagorinsky, P. (2022). *Whitewashed critical perspectives: Restoring the edge to edgy ideas*. Taylor and Francis. https://doi.org/10.4324/9781003087632

Cook, A. L., Brodsky, L., Gracia, R., & Morizio, L. J. (2019). Exploring multicultural and social justice counseling training outcomes on school counselor and youth development. *Counseling Outcome Research and Evaluation*, *10*(2), 78–93. https://doi.org/10.1080/21501378.2017.1422681

Cook, A. L., Krell, M., Hayden, L. A., Gracia, R., & Denitzio, K. (2016). Fieldwork using professional development schools model: Developing social justice advocacy. *Journal of Multicultural Counseling and Development*, *44*(3), 176–188. https://doi.org/10.1002/jmcd.12045

Cook, A. L., & Krueger-Henney, P. (2017). Group work that examines systems of power with young people: Youth participatory action research. *Journal for Specialists in Group Work*, *42*(2), 176–193. http://dx.doi.org/10.1080/01933922.2017.1282570

Cook, B. G., Cook, L., & Landrum, T. J. (2013). Moving research into practice: Can we make dissemination stick? *Exceptional Children*, *79*(3), 163–180. https://doi.org/10.1177/001440291307900203

Cooper, A. (2014). The use of online strategies and social media for research dissemination in education. *Education Policy Analysis Archives*, *22*(88), 1–24. https://doi.org/10.14507/epaa.v22n88.2014

Cuccaro, C., & Casey, J. M. (2007). Practicum in counseling: A new training model. *Journal of School Counseling, 5*(26), 1–21. https://eric.ed.gov/?id=EJ901187

Datta, R. (2017). Decolonizing both researcher and research and its effectiveness in Indigenous research. *Research Ethics, 14*(2), 1–24. https://doi.org/10.1177/1747016117733296

Dickinson, E. E. (2019, Spring). The promise and peril of academia wading into Twitter. *John Hopkins Magazine.* https://hub.jhu.edu/magazine/2019/spring/more-academics-turn-to-twitter/

Fezler, B., & Brown, C. (2011). *The international model for school counseling programs.* Association of American Schools in South America (AASSA) / U.S. State Department Office of Overseas Schools.

Fox, M. (2015). Embodied methodologies, participation, and the art of research. *Social and Personality Psychology Compass, 9*(7), 321–332. https://doi.org/10.1111/spc3.12182

Freire, P. (1970). *Pedagogy of the oppressed.* Herder and Herder.

Gordon, N., & Conaway, C. (2020). *Common-sense evidence: The education leader's guide to using data and research.* Harvard Education Press.

Gysbers, N. C., & Henderson, P. (2005). Designing, implementing, and managing a comprehensive school guidance and counseling program. In C. A. Sink (Ed.), *Contemporary school counseling: Theory, research, and practice* (pp. 151–183). Houghton Mifflin.

Hess, Frederick M. (Ed.). (2008). *When research matters: How scholarship influences education policy.* Harvard Education Press.

Ion, G., Iftimescu, S., Proteasa, C., & Marin, E. (2019). Understanding the role, expectations, and challenges that policy-makers face in using educational research. *Education Sciences, 9*(2), 81. https://doi.org/10.3390/educsci9020081

Jack, A. (2019). *The privileged poor: How elite colleges are failing disadvantaged students.* Harvard University Press.

Kempe, U. R. (2019). Teachers and researchers in collaboration. A possibility to overcome the research-practice gap? *European Journal of Education, 54*(2), 250–260. https://doi.org/10.1111/ejed.12336

Kohfeldt, D., Chhun, L., Grace, S., & Langhout, R. D. (2011). Youth empowerment in context: Exploring tensions in school-based yPAR. *American Journal of Community Psychology, 47*(1–2), 28–45. https://doi.org/10.1007/s10464-010-9376-z

Lee, C. C. (Ed.). (2014). *Multicultural issues in counseling: New approaches to diversity.* John Wiley & Sons.

Lapan, R. (2005). Evaluating school counseling programs. In C. A. Sink (Ed.), *Contemporary school counseling: Theory, research, and practice* (pp. 257–293). Houghton Mifflin.

Manfra, M. (2019). *Action research for classrooms, schools, and communities.* SAGE Publications.

Massachusetts School Counselors Association. (2020). *Massachusetts model 3.0: A framework for comprehensive school counseling programs.* Massachusetts School Counselors Association.

Mollet, A., Brumley, C., Gilson, C., & Williams, S. (2017). *Communicating your research with social media: A practical guide to using blogs, podcasts, data visualizations and video.* SAGE Publishing.

Ozer, E. J. (2016). Youth-led participatory action research. In L. A. Jason, & D. S. Glenwick (Eds.), *Handbook of methodological approaches to community-based research: Qualitative, quantitative, and mixed methods* (pp. 263–272). Oxford University Press.

Ozer, E. J., Newlan, S., Douglas, L., & Hubbard, E. (2013). "Bounded empowerment": Analyzing the tensions in the practice of youth-led participatory research in urban public schools. *American Journal of Community Psychology, 52*(1–2), 13–26. https://doi.org/10.1007/s10464-013-9573-7

Plank, D. N. (2014). Minding the gap between research and policy making. In C. F. Conrad & R. C. Serlin (Eds.), *The SAGE handbook for research in education: Pursuing ideas as the keystone of exemplary inquiry* (pp. 43–58). SAGE Publications.

Raman, U. (2018, November). Why researchers are using podcasts to share their findings. *The Hindu.* https://www.thehindu.com/education/why-researchers-are-using-podcasts-to-share-their-findings/article25576931.ece.

Renda, M. R., & Villares, E. (2015). The effect of a student achievement curriculum on grade 9 completion rate and student engagement. *Counseling Outcome Research and Evaluation, 6*(2), 113–125. https://doi.org/10.1177%2F2150137815598812

Rogers, J. E. (2019). *Leading for change through whole-school social-emotional learning: Strategies to build a positive school culture.* Corwin Press.

Rowell, L. (2006). Action research and school counseling: Closing the gap between research and practice. *Professional School Counseling, 9*(4), 376–384. https://doi.org/10.1177/2156758X0500900409

See, B. H., Gorard, S., & Siddiqui, N. (2016). Teacher's use of research evidence in practice: A pilot study of feedback to enhance learning. *Educational Research, 58*(1), 56–72. https://doi.org/10.1080/00131881.2015.1117798

Sharma, M., Sarin, A., Gupta, P., Sachdeva, S., & Desai, A. V. (2014). Journal impact factor: Its use, significance and limitations. *World Journal of Nuclear Medicine, 13*(2), 146. https://doi.org/10.4103/1450-1147.139151

Silver, E. A., & Lunsford, C. (2017). Linking research and practices in mathematics education: Perspectives and pathways. In J. Cai (Ed.), *Compendium for research in mathematics education* (pp. 135–540). National Council of Mathematics Teachers.

Smith, C. D., & Hope, E. C. (2020). "We just want to break the stereotype": Tensions in Black boys' critical social analysis of their suburban school experiences. *Journal of Educational Psychology, 112*(3), 551–566. https://doi.org/10.1080/10888691.2019.1630277

Villares, E., Frain, M., Brigman, G., Webb, L., & Peluso, P. (2012). The impact of Student Success Skills on math and reading scores: A meta-analysis. *Counseling Outcome Research and Evaluation, 2*(1), 3–16. https://doi.org/10.1177/2150137811434041

Warren, M. R., Calderón, J., Kupscznk, L. A., Squires, G., & Su, C. (2018). Is collaborative, community-engaged scholarship more rigorous than traditional scholarship? On advocacy, bias, and social science research. *Urban Education, 53*(4), 445–472. https://doi.org/10.1177/0042085918763511

Webb, L. D., Brigman, G. A., & Campbell, C. (2005). Linking school counselors and student success: A replication of the Student Success Skills approach targeting the academic and social competence of students. *Professional School Counseling, 8*(5), 407–413.

Zyromski, B., Dimmitt, C., Mariani, M., & Griffith, C. (2018). Evidence-based school counseling: Models for integrated practice and school counselor education. *Professional School Counseling, 22*(1), 1–12. https://doi.org/10.1177/2156759X18801847

About the Authors

Jennifer Betters-Bubon is an associate professor and program coordinator in the counselor education program at the University of Wisconsin-Whitewater, where she teaches future clinical and school counseling students. Prior to her role in academia, Dr. Betters-Bubon spent 11 years working as a school counselor and 1 year as a special education teacher. Her research agenda focuses on the school counselor role within multi-tiered systems of support as well as trauma-informed schools. She is co-editor of *The School Counselor's Guide to Multi-Tiered Systems of Support* and *Making MTSS Work* and has published in numerous peer-reviewed journals.

John C. Carey is emeritus professor of School Counseling at the University of Massachusetts and a visiting researcher in the Center for Intercultural Studies at the University of Verona, Italy. He has recently coauthored (with Dr. Trevisan) the first textbook exclusively devoted to evaluation in school-based counseling, *Program Evaluation in School Counseling*. Carey has published numerous journal articles including a 10-nation study of school-based counseling practice, and statewide evaluations of the effectiveness of school counseling programs in Utah and Nebraska. Carey has worked as a Fulbright specialist in India and Korea and has offered workshops in evaluation on four continents.

Ellen Chance is a core faculty member for Capella University Department of Counselor Education in Minnesota. Her areas of specialization include comprehensive data-driven school counseling, assessment in counseling, SEL, and crisis response and intervention in counseling. Prior to serving as a counselor educator, Dr. Chance was the school counseling/SEL coordinator for FAU Lab Schools in Boca Raton, Florida. She has been an active member of state and national professional counseling organizations for several years and has presented at numerous professional conferences. She works passionately to advocate for the role of the school counselor and comprehensive data-driven school counseling programs.

Blaire Cholewa is an associate professor at the University of Virginia. Her scholarship focuses on addressing the discrepancies in academic opportunity and discipline for low-income and/or students of color by investigating ways in which we can improve the educational experiences of K–16 youth. She has published over 17 national, peer-reviewed publications and has three published book chapters. She is one of three cochairs for the Evidence-Based School Counseling Conference, serves on editorial boards (e.g., Professional School Counseling), is a reviewer for multiple journals, and serves as the secretary of the ACES School Counseling Interest Network.

Demetrius Cofield is a PhD. student in the Counselor Education and Supervision program at University of North Carolina at Charlotte. He is a licensed clinical mental health counselor supervisor and licensed clinical addictions specialist. His research interests focus on anti-Black racism and mental health in the Black community.

Amy L. Cook, Ph.D., is an associate professor in the Counseling and School Psychology Department, College of Education and Human Development at the University of Massachusetts Boston. She received a Ph.D. in Educational Psychology from the University of Connecticut Storrs. She has worked in urban schools and community mental health organizations, providing counseling services to students and families. Her research interests focus on promoting racial justice, youth development, and systems change in schools via community-engaged participatory research with youth and educators in partner schools and organizations.

Carey Dimmitt is Program Coordinator and a Professor in the school counseling program at the University of Massachusetts Amherst, where she also serves as Director of the Ronald H. Fredrickson Center for School Counseling Outcome Research and Evaluation (CSCORE, at https://www.cscoreumass.org/). Dr. Dimmitt's scholarship focuses on evidence-based school counseling, metacognition, and – most recently – implicit bias. From 2007-2014 she served as the counseling content expert for ERIC. In addition to multiple journal articles and book chapters, she has co-authored the books *Evidence-Based School Counseling: Making a Difference with Data-Driven Practices* (Corwin, 2007) and *The School Counseling and Social Work Treatment Planner* (Wiley, 2015). She is co-founder and co-chair of the annual Evidence-Based School Counseling Conference (http://www.ebscc.org).

Ileana Gonzalez is an assistant professor in the School of Education at Johns Hopkins University. Dr. Gonzalez earned her Ph.D from the University of Maryland, College Park, in Counselor Education in 2013. More importantly, she is a first-generation college student and daughter of immigrants, which informs her beliefs in equity and access to a quality education for all students, particularly those from marginalized populations. Her research interests include urban school counselor preparation, school counselor social justice belief systems, and antiracist training and multicultural competence in counselor preparation.

Emily Goodman-Scott is an associate professor at Old Dominion University in Virginia and previously worked as a school counselor, as a special education teacher, and in mental health settings. Dr. Goodman-Scott is passionate about school counseling research: publishing 30 + journal articles and two books (*A School Counselor's Guide to MTSS*, 2019, and *Making MTSS Work*, 2020). She serves on professional boards (e.g., 10 years with Virginia School Counseling Association (VSCA), including chair; president for ACES) and has co-coordinated the ACES School Counseling and Qualitative Interest Networks. She serves on editorial review boards (e.g., *Professional School Counseling*) and facilitates school counseling trainings and consultations throughout the United States. She is a proud recipient of the 2020 ACA Research Award.

Catherine Griffith is an assistant associate professor in the school counseling program at the University of San Diego and a former associate director for the Ronald H. Fredrickson Center for School Counseling Outcome Research and Evaluation (CSCORE). She received her PhD in Counselor Education at the University of Central Florida. A passionate advocate for creating school environments that are responsive to vulnerable students and families, her primary research activities include the development and validation of strengths-based counseling interventions and assessments, with a special focus on queer youth. Dr. Griffith is a member of the American Counseling Association (ACA) Research and Knowledge Committee and is on the Evidence-Based School Counseling Conference (EBSCC) Advisory Board.

Holly Kortemeier is an elementary school counselor in the state of Wisconsin. She received her MS in Counseling from the University of Wisconsin-Whitewater in 2018. Her work titled "Pupils to Peers: Socializing Graduate Students to the Counseling Profession" was published in the academic journal *Sociological Imagination*, and she coauthored the chapter "Culturally Responsive MTSS: Advocating for Equity for Every Student" in *The School Counselor's Guide to Multi-Tiered Systems of Support*. Holly has presented at state, regional, and national conferences.

Matthew E. Lemberger-Truelove is a professor of counseling at the University of North Texas and the current editor of the *Journal of Counseling and Development*. Dr. Lemberger-Truelove's scholarly works generally pertain to school counseling theory, practice, and scholarship. He is especially interested in how culturally responsive social and emotional learning and mindfulness-based interventions can contribute to students' personal, social, and learning development. He is a former elementary and high school counselor.

Dodie Limberg, PhD, is an associate professor in the Department of Educational Studies in the counselor education program at the University of South Carolina. She completed her doctoral studies at the University of Central Florida. Dodie is a certified K–12 school counselor. She has worked as a school counselor and clinical mental health counselor in Florida, Switzerland, and Israel. Dodie has been awarded over $2.5 million grant dollars to support her current projects focused on the school counselor's role in career development, supporting students with emotional behavioral disorders, and counselor education doctoral student's research identity development. She currently serves as the associate qualitative editor for *Counseling and Values Journal* and is on the editorial review board for *Professional School Counseling* and *Counselor Education and Supervision*.

Melissa Mariani, PhD, is an associate professor and doctoral program coordinator in the Department of Counselor Education at Florida Atlantic University (FAU). She has published and presented on student success, school climate, school counseling interventions and outcome research, and higher education and K–12 collaboration. She coauthored the book *Facilitating Evidence-based, Data-Driven School Counseling: A Manual for Practice* with Dr. Brett Zyromski (OSU). In 2016, Dr. Mariani was recognized as both the University and College of Education's Scholar of the Year. She also serves as a national trainer for *Student Success Skills* and is a co-developer of *SSS for SEL Success*.

Shekila Melchior has a decade of school counseling experience, is a Nationally Board-Certified Counselor, licensed professional school counselor, and an assistant professor at George Mason University. She received her Ph.D. from Virginia Tech and holds a master's degree from North Carolina A&T. Dr. Melchior is the Counselors for Social Justice (CSJ) School Counselor representative and the president of the Virginia Alliance for School Counseling, a division of the Virginia Counselors Association (VCA). Dr. Melchior serves on the VCA Racial Justice and Diversity Task Force and is chair of the Equity Task Force at Mason's College of Human Development. Research interests include social justice identity development, activist wellness, issues of race, undocumented students/immigrants, and professional identity development for school counselors.

Jennifer Melfie holds a master's degree in education and specializes in school counseling. Jennifer is currently a full-time professional school counselor in a middle school in Virginia. Prior to her current position, Jennifer worked as a substitute teacher/counselor and graduate research assistant. Her research interests include investigating school-based interventions, the use of data, and integrating technology into school counselor practice. Additionally, Jennifer is coauthoring an article that explores school-based group counseling and therapeutic factors for racially, ethnically, and culturally identified students. Recently, Jennifer presented a session covering interactive and engaging multimedia lessons at the VSCA's annual conference.

Taryne M. Mingo, PhD, is an assistant professor and school counseling program director in the Department of Counseling at the University of North Carolina at Charlotte. Dr. Mingo has a professional background in elementary school counseling, and promoting an intersectional approach to address the academic, social, and emotional needs of diverse children.

Citlali E. Molina is an assistant professor of School Counseling and School Counseling program coordinator at the University of Texas at Tyler. She is a certified school counselor and a licensed professional counselor in Texas. She has published on topics related to school counseling, career counseling, and addictions. Her experiences as a public-school educator and school counselor led her to study teacher–student relationships. Her research interests include culturally responsive evidence-based school counseling interventions to support teacher–student relationships, specifically related to social emotional learning and mindfulness–based approaches, as well as training school counselors to advocate for underserved students and families.

Patrick R. Mullen, PhD, is an associate professor in the Department of School Psychology and Counselor Education at the William & Mary School of Education. He completed his doctoral studies at the University of Central Florida. Dr. Mullen teaches graduate students in the master's and doctoral counselor education programs with a focus on school counseling. Furthermore, he is on the editorial board for the *Journal of Counseling and Development, Counseling Outcome Research and Evaluation*, and *Measurement and Evaluation in Counseling and Development*. He also serves as an associate editor for *Counseling and Values* and editor for the *Journal of School-Based Counseling Policy and Evaluation*. Dr. Mullen's general research areas include school counseling, counselor education and supervision, and counselor well-being.

Timothy Poynton, Ed.D., is an Associate Professor and Counselor Educator at the University of Massachusetts Boston committed to improving the transition from high school into young adulthood through his research and teaching. A former school counselor, he has also published several research articles and chapters related to school counseling, career development, and college readiness, and was recognized in 2011 as the Counselor Educator of the Year by the American School Counselor Association. He is also an instructor for the Facilitating Career Development program with the National Career Development Association and has spoken at conferences across the United States.

Dee C. Ray, PhD, LPC-S, NCC, RPT-S, is Distinguished Teaching Professor and Elaine Millikan Mathes Professor in Early Childhood Education in the counseling program and director of the Center for Play Therapy at the University of North Texas. Dr. Ray has published over 150 articles, chapters, and books, specializing in research specifically examining the process and effects of child-centered play therapy in schools. She served as board member for the Association for Child and Adolescent Counseling and Association for Play Therapy, founding editor of the *Journal of Child and Adolescent Counseling*, and an American Counseling Association Fellow.

Mandy Savitz-Romer, Ph.D. is the Nancy Pforzheimer Aronson Senior Lecturer in Human Development and Education at the Harvard Graduate School of Education (HGSE). Her research examines how schools structure counseling support systems and, specifically, what conditions are critical to effective practice. She writes and speaks extensively on college and career readiness and school-based counseling, specifically as they relate to students of color and first-generation college students. Dr. Savitz-Romer is the author of *Fulfilling the Promise: Reimagining School Counseling to Advance Student Success* and coauthor of *Ready, Willing, and Able: A Developmental Approach to College Access and Success*.

Sam Steen, an associate professor at George Mason University, and licensed professional school counselor, specializes in group work and cultivating Black students' academic identity development. Dr. Steen was a school counselor for 10 years, and these practitioner experiences shape his research agenda, approach to teaching, and service. Dr. Steen is a Fellow for the Association for Specialists in Group Work, a division of the ACA. Recently, Dr. Steen received the Professional Advancement Award from the Association for Specialists in Group Work recognizing his outstanding efforts advancing the field of group work through research and development of new and innovative strategies for schools, families, and marginalized communities.

Tori Stone, PhD, LPC, has more than twenty years of experience as a school counselor, counselor educator, and national presenter. As an Assistant Professor of Counseling at George Mason University, in Fairfax, Virginia. Dr. Stone trains School Counseling and Clinical Mental Health Counseling students in counseling skills and theories, creative counseling interventions, and theory-based, practical approaches to work with children and teens. Dr. Stone also works in consultation with several school divisions to provide training on teen brain development, school climate, and mental health.

Michael S. Trevisan is dean of the College of Education at Washington State University and professor of Educational Psychology. He has coauthored three books on evaluation, published numerous evaluation journal articles and chapters, and presents regularly at national and international meetings. Trevisan is chair-elect of the International Society for Policy Research and Evaluation in School-Based Counseling, an international group of university researchers, administrators, and policy advocates who seek to promote school-based counseling worldwide through rigorous policy research and evaluation. Trevisan has provided evaluation workshops, seminars, and consultations internationally, in such countries as Canada, Greece, India, Italy, Korea, and Thailand.

Chia Vang is currently a high school counselor in the Milwaukee Public Schools district. Before becoming a school counselor she worked as a graduate assistant for the University of Wisconsin-Whitewater's counselor education program. As a graduate student, she cofounded the Association for Graduate Students of Color student organization. In her work, Chia creates relationships to enhance the self-worth of youth and strives to ensure that school environments are equitable and accepting for all.

Elizabeth Villares, PhD, is a professor in the Department of Counselor Education at Florida Atlantic University. Since 1997, Dr. Villares has served in various education roles (e.g., secondary teacher, school counselor, counseling program director, and counselor educator). Her research foci include developing and evaluating school counselor-led interventions' effectiveness to improve the academic, career, social/emotional development, and college and career readiness of K–16 students. She is a leader in several counselor associations, received numerous awards for her scholarship, and coauthored the book *Evidence-Based School Counseling - A Student Success Approach* (Routledge, 2018) and Student Success Skills curricula.

Anita Young is an associate professor in the School of Education at Johns Hopkins University. She earned her PhD from The Ohio State University (OSU). Her research agenda has a twofold strand: school counselor leadership preparation and examining data and accountability strategies that promote equitable college access for all K–12 students, especially in urban settings. Dr. Young has coauthored two books, published research in scholarly journals, and served on editorial boards. She has presented at numerous local, state, regional, and national conferences specific to her research interests. Combined, her scholarly publications and presentations have contributed to the school counseling profession.

Brett Zyromski, Ph.D., is an Associate Professor at The Ohio State University. His scholarship focuses on how school-based counselors can enhance protective factors and positive childhood experiences for students that have experienced adverse childhood experiences. His research also explores the impact of evidence-based interventions in school counseling, evidence-based school counselor education, and evaluation in school counseling. He currently serves as an Associate Editor for the Professional School Counseling journal. Dr. Zyromski has published dozens of peer-reviewed articles and book chapters related to school counseling issues, delivered over 150 international, national, regional, and local presentations and has served as numerous international and state conference keynote. A research Fellow at the University of Massachusetts Ronald H. Fredrikson Center for School Counseling Outcome Research and Evaluation and a Faculty Affiliate at The Ohio State University Center on Education and training for Employment, Dr. Zyromski is also co-author of *Facilitating Evidence-Based, Data-Driven School Counseling: A Manual for Practice* (Corwin, 2016). He co-founded and is co-chair of the annual Evidence-Based School Counseling Conference (http://www.ebscc.org) and has served as project manager or Co-Primary Investigator for over $9,000,000 worth of federal and state grants.

Index

For the benefit of digital users, indexed terms that span two pages (e.g., 52–53) may, on occasion, appear on only one of those pages.